Ecclesiastical Megalomania

Books by John W. Robbins

Answer to Ayn Rand 1974
The Case Against Indexation 1976
God's Hammer: The Bible and Its Critics (editor) 1982
Cornelius Van Til: The Man and the Myth 1986
Education, Christianity and the State (editor) 1987
Pat Robertson: A Warning to America 1988
Gordon H. Clark: Personal Recollections (editor) 1989
Essays on Ethics and Politics (editor) 1992
A Man of Principle: Essays in Honor of Hans F. Sennholz (editor) 1992
Against the World: The Trinity Review 1978-1988 (editor) 1996
Without a Prayer: Ayn Rand and the Close of Her System 1997
Ecclesiastical Megalomania:
The Economic and Political Thought of the Roman Catholic Church 1999

Forthcoming

The Church Effeminate and Other Essays (editor)
A Different Gospel: The Theology of the Roman Catholic Church (editor)

Ecclesiastical Megalomania

*The Economic and Political Thought
of the Roman Catholic Church*

John W. Robbins

The Trinity Foundation

COVER PHOTO:
Pope John Paul II Visits United Nations

UN 190488 • UNITED NATIONS NEW YORK • 5 October 1995

John Paul II visited the United Nations today, at the invitation of Secretary-General Boutros Boutros-Ghali, and addressed the General Assembly at 11 a.m. During his stay at the U.N., the Pope met high government leaders attending the General Assembly session. He was greeted by a group of children from the U.N. International School, dressed in national costumes, who sang, "Let There Be Peace on Earth." He gave a separate address to the staff of the U.N. Secretariat and spoke briefly to representatives of the press and to non-governmental organizations, as well as to U.N. delegates and dignitaries. The visit of the pope is the third papal visit to the U.N. John Paul II previously visited the U.N. on 2 October 1979, at the invitation of then Secretary-General Kurt Waldheim. The late Paul VI visited the U.N. on 4 October 1965, at the invitation of then Secretary-General U Thant.

UN/DPI PHOTO/E. SCHNEIDER

Ecclesiastical Megalomania:
The Economic and Political Thought of the Roman Catholic Church
Copyright 1999 John W. Robbins
Published in the United States of America
ISBN: 0-940931-78-8 (hardback)
ISBN: 0-940931-52-4 (paperback)

Contents

Preface *9*
Introduction *12*

PART 1
ENVY EXALTED
THE ECONOMIC THOUGHT OF THE ROMAN CATHOLIC CHURCH
27

One ∽ Private Property *29*
Two ∽ The Universal Destination of Goods *38*
Three ∽ *Rerum Novarum:* On the Condition of the Working Classes *43*
Four ∽ Subsequent Encyclicals *60*
Five ∽ Feudalism and Corporativism *72*
Six ∽ Liberation Theology *77*
Seven ∽ The Redistributive State and Interventionism *81*
Eight ∽ Has the Pope Beatified Ayn Rand? *95*

PART 2
AUTOCRACY ADORED
THE POLITICAL THOUGHT OF THE ROMAN CATHOLIC CHURCH *109*

Nine ∽ Lord Acton on Roman Catholic Political Thought *111*
Ten ∽ Roman Catholic Political Theory *114*
Eleven ∽ The Political Thought of Thomas Aquinas *127*
Twelve ∽ Persecution, Inquisition, and Slavery *133*
Thirteen ∽ The Nineteenth Century *142*

Fourteen ~ The Magisterium *147*
Fifteen ~ Solidarity, Subsidiarity, and the Common Good *151*
Sixteen ~ Fascism and Nazism *161*
Seventeen ~ Totalitarianism *174*
Eighteen ~ Strategy for Subverting a Republic *183*
Nineteen ~ World Government *187*
Twenty ~ 2000: Jubilee, Punctuated by Apologies *196*

APPENDICES *201*

The Donation of Constantine *203*
The Vatican Decree of 1870 *285*

Bibliography *288*
Index *300*
Scripture Index *325*
The Crisis of Our Time *327*
Intellectual Ammunition *334*

To Zachary and Connor

*May God grant
that the boys live forever
in freedom as Christian men.*

Preface

ONE HUNDRED fifty years ago, the English historian Thomas Babington Macaulay (1800-1859) wrote: "There is not, and never was on this earth, a work of human policy so well deserving of examination as the Roman Catholic Church." The Roman Church-State is the oldest institution continually in existence, tracing its roots at least to the sixth century, and if one believes the Church's own claims, to the time of Christ himself. For much of that time, it has been the most powerful institution in Europe, and though its fortunes fell after the Reformation in the sixteenth century, it has made a remarkable resurgence in the past century. In addition to being the world's oldest institution, the Roman Church-State is also the world's largest, numbering over one billion subjects, one-sixth of the planet's population. One Roman Catholic priest in America, comparing his Church to a corporation, wrote: "The Catholic Church must be the biggest corporation in the United States. We have a branch office in every neighborhood. Our assets and real estate holdings must exceed those of Standard Oil, AT&T, and U.S. Steel combined. And our roster of dues-paying members must be second only to the tax rolls of the United States Government."[1] Worldwide, of course, the Roman Church-State's roster of members ranks behind the entire populations of only two nations: China and India.

In addition to being the world's oldest, largest, most powerful and most influential politico-ecclesiastical institution, the Roman Church-State may also be the world's wealthiest. Certainly, considered merely as a church, it is the world's wealthiest institution; only the assets of a handful of civil governments might surpass its massive wealth. It is very difficult to ascertain the assets of the Roman Church-State; the organization does not report its holdings to anyone, including its members,

---

1. Richard Ginder, as quoted in Nino Lo Bello, *Vatican, U.S.A.*, New York: Trident Press, 1972, 23.

9

ECCLESIASTICAL MEGALOMANIA

and researchers who have endeavored to discover its riches have found no limits to them, only to their ability to see the horizon. According to Canon Law, the control of all property of the Roman Church-State belongs to the pope, its supreme emperor.[2] That property includes tens of thousands of buildings; millions of acres of land; tons of gold, silver, and precious stones; art collections; rare documents; and millions of shares in business corporations throughout the globe. Since the Roman Church-State is an even more formidable organization than it was at the time Macaulay wrote, this study of her economic and political thought needs no further explanation or justification.

What does require some explanation, however, is the relative lack of attention to the Roman Church-State by serious non-Catholic scholars. Most of the works quoted in this book were written by Roman Catholics. The world of American scholarship seems to have partitioned itself, at least with regard to the study of the Roman Church-State, so that the study of the Roman Church-State has been reserved for Roman Catholics. Perhaps it is the fear of being labeled "anti-Catholic" that has dissuaded non-Catholic scholars from writing about the Church-State – a fear that undermines all scholarship.[3] Scholars, apparently more solicitous of their academic reputations than of learning itself, have shied away from studies such as this. Perhaps there are other, more legitimate, reasons, such as the excessive secrecy of the

---

2. Canon 1273 provides that "By virtue of his primacy in governance the Roman Pontiff is the supreme administrator and steward of all ecclesiastical goods." Canon 332 provides that "The Roman Pontiff obtains full and supreme power in the Church by means of legitimate election [by the college of cardinals] accepted by him together with episcopal consecration…." The pope is not even bound by any promises he made to the college of cardinals in order to be elected pope: "…the current rules [of a conclave] state that the pope is not bound by any promises he made to get votes, even if he promised under oath" (Thomas J. Reese, S. J., *Inside the Vatican: The Politics and Organization of the Catholic Church,* Harvard University Press, 1996, 69). And "Once a pope is elected, his election cannot be invalidated even if he bought the election" (*Inside the Vatican,* 100). His power is absolute.

3. The same sort of fear of losing their academic reputations and respectability dissuaded some scholars, for much of the twentieth century, from writing critically about Communism, both in America and in other nations. To do so would have cost them at least their reputations, if not their jobs. The only permissible critics of Communism were Communists and socialists. Academe, like Hollywood, far from being "neutral," "disinterested," and "unbiased," is ruled by intellectual goon squads. The phenomenon of political correctness originated and flourished in the universities, long before the phenomenon had been named.

PREFACE

papacy. But whatever the reason, the Roman institution has not received the attention and scrutiny it deserves from American scholars.[4]

It should also be needless to say, although it probably is not, that this analysis and criticism of Roman Catholic social thought does not imply any endorsement of the social thought of non-Catholic ecclesiastical organizations such as the World Council of Churches and the National Council of Churches. In fact, the economic thought of these organizations is in many ways similar to that of the Roman Church-State. Their theologies, from which their economics and politics flow, while nominally Protestant, are actually non-Protestant, for they have formally or practically abandoned the two fundamental principles of the Protestant Reformation: The Bible alone is the Word of God, and justification is by belief alone. If the words *Protestant* and *Evangelical* are used as they were in the sixteenth and seventeenth centuries, there are few Protestant and Evangelical organizations in the United States at the end of the second millennium after Christ. American churches and churchmen have realized this, and they have sought to have some sort of alliance, if not full communion, with Rome.

It is the author's hope that this study of the social thought of one of the most powerful institutions in the world today will not only contribute to our fund of knowledge about the Roman Church-State, but also stimulate others to undertake the task of examining its role in United States domestic and foreign policy, as well as in world affairs.

---

4. Thomas J. Reese, a Jesuit who recently published *Inside the Vatican*, commented repeatedly that "Despite the importance of the papacy for the Catholic church and its prominent role in international affairs, its internal workings are little known to Catholics, to world leaders, or to the world at large. This is partly a result of the secretive nature of the Vatican…" (*Inside the Vatican*, 4).

Introduction

IN 1904 and 1905 a non-Catholic German sociologist, Max Weber, published an essay that sociologists, economists, and theologians have been arguing about ever since: *The Protestant Ethic and the Spirit of Capitalism*. Weber argued that the obvious disparities in the economic development of European and American countries were due in part to their differing theologies. Those countries whose economies had grown most rapidly were Protestant, and those whose economies had lagged behind were Roman Catholic. Now the disparities that Weber noted were a commonplace of the eighteenth and nineteenth centuries; Jacob Viner told us that no observer in the nineteenth century disputed that fact.[1] In the body of this book I shall quote the English historian Macaulay, Charles Dickens, and several other writers who commented on a fact of life that was as obvious to them as the assertion that there are economic disparities between first world and third world countries is to us.[2] Indeed, this contrast between Roman Catholic and Protestant communities has continued into the twentieth century. Emilio Willems, for example, reported that

> Our field data indicate that in many communities [in Brazil and Chile] Protestants have gained the reputation among non-Protestants of being especially reliable, conscientious, and industrious. Numerous in-

---

1. "I have found, I repeat, no writer, Catholic or non-Catholic, who seriously disputed the claim that Protestant countries were generally more prosperous than Catholic ones." "There was almost universal agreement before Weber, however, that there was a close historical association between Protestantism and the development of capitalism in its modern forms" (Viner, *Religious Thought and Economic Society*, Melitz and Wick, editors. Durham: Duke University Press, 1978, 182, 185).

2. "Thus, even if we allow for the influence of other factors, the data unambiguously suggest that Protestantism is more conducive to business activity than Catholicism" (Stanislav Andreski, "Method and Substantive Theory in Max Weber," in Eisenstadt, *The Protestant Ethic and Modernization: A Comparative View*, New York: Basic Books, 1968, 55).

terviews with employers left no doubt that Protestant workers are especially sought after and even given advantages.... Numerous Protestants assured us that their conversions, regularly described as "rebirth," had led to economic improvement. The reason given was that prior to conversion they had spent a great deal of money on alcohol, lottery tickets, gambling, tobacco, cosmetics, movies, and prostitution. Once they gave up these "sins," substantial amounts of money were available for permissible and necessary things. Industriousness, pride, and thrift were often mentioned subjectively to explain improved economic conditions.... It is hardly surprising that Protestant families living by the code of a puritanic ethic have better housing, clothes, more sewing machines, bicycles, radios, and so on than do non-Protestants of comparable social status.[3]

For the past century, Weber has frequently been criticized as overstating his case for the linkage between Protestantism and capitalism; my criticism of Weber is quite different: Weber understated the linkage by narrowly limiting his discussion to the "Protestant ethic" and the "spirit" of capitalism.[4] He did so apparently because of an inadequate understanding of Protestantism, specifically Calvinist theology. Weber rested the bulk of his argument on the Protestant doctrines of predestination and calling, and, it is true, those doctrines are important in the theologies of both Martin Luther and John Calvin and their followers. But the radical nature of Protestantism and its import for economic development go much deeper and further. One of Weber's early critics, Felix Rachfahl, pointed out six ways in which Protestantism had fostered the economic growth of Europe:

(1) Protestantism permitted the intellect to be devoted to secular pursuits, not just religious;

(2) Protestantism brought education to the masses;

(3) Protestantism did not encourage indolence and distaste and disdain for labor as Roman Catholicism did;

---

3. Willems, "Culture Change and the Rise of Protestantism in Brazil and Chile," in Eisenstadt, *The Protestant Ethic and Modernization: A Comparative View*, 197. See also David Martin, *Tongues of Fire: The Explosion of Protestantism in Latin America*. Basil Blackwell, 1990.

4. "The contention that Protestantism stimulated the growth of capitalism in indirect ways which cannot be subsumed under Weber's concept of economic ethics, far from disproving Weber's thesis, merely amplifies it" (Andreski, "Method and Substantive Theory in Max Weber," in Eisenstadt, *The Protestant Ethic and Modernization: A Comparative View*, 58).

(4) Protestantism championed independence and individual responsibility;

(5) Protestantism created a higher type of morality;

(6) Protestantism fostered the separation of church and state.

"In all these respects," Rachfal wrote, "Protestantism produced a liberating and stimulating effect upon economic life, but Catholicism a constricting and obstructive one."[5]

Weber's view of the economic and social impact of Protestantism on Europe and the United States was narrowed by his truncated understanding of the theology of the Reformers and their heirs. It was not only the spirit of capitalism that was born with the Protestant Reformation, but also the spirit of constitutionalism, the necessary political corollary of laissez-faire capitalism. Constitutional capitalism is a social consequence of the theology of the Reformers. How the theology of the Reformers achieved this is a story that secular historians have only begun to appreciate, 500 years after the fact.[6] Out of the religious liberty that is implicit in the idea of the Reformation – the end of an ecclesiastical monopoly enforced, as all genuine monopolies must be, by a system of command, coercion, and control; the liberty not to belong to or attend the Roman Church-State; the liberty not to contribute to its maintenance; the liberty not to believe whatever the Roman Church-State required – flow all the liberties with which this nation, and to a lesser extent Europe, Canada, and the Pacific Rim, have been blessed: constitutional government, civil rights (by which I mean the freedoms protected by the Bill of Rights), and economic liberties. Religious liberty is the mother of all liberties; it is deliberately listed first in the First Amendment in the Bill of Rights; and historically it is the fountainhead from which all other liberties have flowed.

Luther's theological revolution – relocating the source of theological, ecclesiastical, social, and political authority to a book and away from men; to a stable, written, permanent, infallible document and away from a changing, unwritten, oral tradition dispensed from Rome as if

---

5. "Kapitalismus und Kalvinismus" in the *Internationale Wochenschrift für Wissenschaft, Kunst und Technik*, 1909; as quoted in Kurt Samuelsson, *Religion and Economic Action: A Critique of Max Weber*. New York: Harper Torchbooks, [1957] 1961, 9-10.

6. See, for example, *The Origins of Modern Freedom in the West*, R. W. Davis, editor. Stanford University Press, 1995.

INTRODUCTION

the Delphic Oracle had been moved there along with Mary's house – changed the world forever. Luther's re-discovery of the nature of salvation – that it is a divine gift, not a human or synthetic accomplishment – revolutionized not only the churches, but also the world. But Luther's efforts to reform the Roman Church failed, and that institution has continued on its own course for the past 500 years.

For a thousand years and more, because of the Roman Church-State's doctrines that salvation was the result of cooperation between the sinner and God, and the saving grace of God was infused into the souls of men, men had been preoccupied – obsessed in many cases – with doing the good works prescribed by the sole dispensers of their salvation, the bishops and priests of the Roman Church-State hierarchy. Their gifts to the Church-State made it the largest property owner in Europe in the Middle Ages; they also gave gifts to the poor, including mendicant friars and other "religious"; the devout made pilgrimages to shrines; venerated relics; performed penance; and so forth.[7] The enormous wealth that had been wasted on such activities was, after the Reformation in Protestant countries, available for and invested in all sorts of improvements in education, homes, farms, shops, manufactures, transportation, and schools. Roman Catholic good works were accompanied by a religious introspection that became more and more obsessive as the believer's devotion to the Church-State increased. The more devout and intelligent were enjoined to become religious – monks, priests, and nuns – to devote themselves entirely to religious callings, so that they could earn their salvation more quickly in the service of the Church-State, free of the worldly cares of family, friends, and earning a living. The religious were in the state of grace; the secular were in the state of nature. The religious belonged to a higher church; the secular to a lower. Those with secular occupations would get to Heaven only after great struggle and millions of years in Purgatory; those who were religious avoided a lot of difficulty both in this world and the next. Since God's saving grace in Roman Catholic theology was actually infused into the heart of the Catholic by means of the sacraments, devout Catholics searched their hearts for evidence of this *gratia infusa*, and

---

7. For a description of religious life in the fifteenth and early sixteenth centuries in Europe, see Carlos M. N. Eire, *War Against the Idols: The Reformation of Worship from Erasmus to Calvin*. Cambridge University Press, 1986.

Europe was drowned in a flood of internal religious subjectivism on the one hand, and external religious idolatry on the other, both of which effectively precluded economic initiative and social improvement for a millennium.

Then in the sixteenth century a German monk, one of the most devout sons of Mother Church, not being able to discover a sufficient quantity of God's saving grace in his life to assure him of salvation, despite his rigorous daily regimen of religious good works, discovered in the Bible the doctrine of justification by faith alone, in the imputed righteousness of Christ alone, through the grace of God alone. Reading the Apostle Paul's letters to the Christians in Rome and Galatia, Luther understood and believed the Biblical idea that salvation is not earned by sinners, nor by cooperation with God, nor dispensed by the Church, but received as a free gift directly from God, who sovereignly causes his people to believe the Gospel. Luther concluded that all the "good works" he had done as a monk and Roman Catholic were worse than useless, and not only his works, but all the works inculcated and enforced by the Church-State for a millennium on millions of souls. Not only is salvation received as a free gift of God, granted directly to the sinner without the mediation or intervention of popes, bishops, and priests; but every Christian man has an honorable calling, and a good work is any work undertaken for the purpose, not of earning salvation, but of expressing our gratitude to God for a redemption already accomplished by Christ and applied to the believer by the Holy Spirit. Such good works were neither primarily those of service to church nor to charity, but the competent and faithful daily performance of one's calling. The importance of this change in the definition of "good works" for economic development was suggested by Stanislav Andreski:

> An economic system whose propelling force is private accumulation of capital will not develop very fast if people are inclined to stop working as soon as they reach a certain level of affluence. Progress of such a system requires that those who have already enough for their needs should go on working and accumulating. The connection with Protestantism, particularly in its Calvinist variety, is that it taught people to regard work as a form of prayer.... Another important influence of Protestantism was its insistence on work as the only legitimate road to riches. Other religions, of course, also prohibit robbery and theft, but Protestant Puritanism is unique in condemning gambling. The religious

INTRODUCTION

ideals of work, thrift, and enrichment without enjoyment and by means of work only constitute what Weber calls "worldly asceticism."[8]

The abject fear of God and loathing of life that characterized the Middle Ages was swept away by the good news of the Gospel of Jesus Christ: God in Christ had done what no mere man could do; he had placated the wrath of God against sinners; he had himself provided the perfect righteousness demanded by the justice and holiness of God for entry into Heaven; and salvation, far from being uncertain or unattainable, is guaranteed to those who believe the Gospel. This grace of God was not received by rites, ceremonies, or sacraments; not obtained by confession or penance; but received by belief in the finished work of Christ alone. The Church, far from being indispensable to salvation, was at most instrumental – but only if it preached the Gospel; and its rites were entirely dispensable. Christians did not need ecclesiastical intermediaries, for there was only one mediator between God and man, the man Jesus Christ. All Christians are priests, and Jesus Christ is their only high priest. The entire social, ecclesiastical, economic, and political hierocracy of the Middle Ages was razed by the Biblical doctrine of the priesthood of all believers, and the parallel ideas that all men are equal before God, and that God is no respecter of persons. The notion of republican and democratic government received its impetus in the modern world from the doctrine of the priesthood of all believers, which overturned the class structure of the medieval Church-State. The Protestants of Europe were religiously, politically, economically, and psychologically liberated from a totalitarian Church-State that had browbeaten and beaten their fathers for generations.

The source of this revolutionary good news was not the Roman Church-State, which had suppressed the Gospel for a thousand years; the source was the Bible, which the Roman Church had also suppressed. The liberating effect of the Gospel had been taught by Christ himself: "If you abide in my Word, you are my disciples indeed. And you shall know the truth, and the truth shall make you free."[9] Luther's *Schriftprinzip* was the axiom of Protestantism, just as the Roman Church-

---

8. Stanislav Andreski, "Method and Substantive Theory in Max Weber," in Eisenstadt, *The Protestant Ethic and Modernization: A Comparative View*, 53-54. It should be pointed out that Protestantism, unlike Catholicism, also prohibited mendicancy.

9. John 8:31-32.

17

State's *Führerprinzip* was the axiom of Catholicism. Luther never tired of repeating his first principle, which was sufficient to transform an entire culture and to create a new civilization. A typical expression of the *Schriftprinzip* is the following:

> [P]utting aside all human writings, we should spend all the more and all the more persistent labor on Holy Scriptures alone.... Or tell me, if you can, who is the final judge when statements of the fathers contradict themselves? In this event the judgment of Scripture must decide the issue, which cannot be done if we do not give Scripture the first place...so that it is in itself the most certain, most easily understood, most plain, is its own interpreter, approving, judging, and illuminating all the statements of all men....Therefore nothing except the divine words are to be the first principles for Christians; all human words are conclusions drawn from them and must be brought back to them and approved by them.[10]

The complete and infallible Bible, not the fallible Church; a permanent, public, written document, not fallible, living men, is the sole authority in doctrine; the decrees of councils and popes must conform to Scripture; Scripture is not to be reinterpreted to conform to papal decrees or some mystical or gnostic oral tradition. This book, Luther argued from the Bible itself, was addressed to all men; and therefore all men had the right to read it and to interpret it. The Church had no monopoly on Scripture, either its reading or its interpretation. Every man was a priest charged with the duty of reading and rightly understanding the revelation that God had graciously given to men. The Bible itself was addressed to men of all classes and callings. It was not addressed only to popes – they are not even mentioned in Scripture – nor only to bishops or deacons, but to all men without distinction. Each man would answer directly to God at the last Judgment – no priest or pope would be there to intercede for him; each man was responsible for the salvation or perdition of his own soul; each man would be required to give an account of the deeds he had done on Earth; and therefore each man had the right to read the Bible for himself. So was born the individualism that transformed the communal ancient and medieval worlds. The importance of the individual soul, a soul that is immortal, is far greater than any earthly institution, including the institutional church.

---

10. *What Luther Says*, Ewald M. Plass, editor. St. Louis: Concordia Publishing House, 1959, 87-88.

INTRODUCTION

The nineteenth and early twentieth century historian Ernst Troeltsch argued that the Calvinist wing of the Reformation carried this individualism even further than the Lutheran wing, with even more spectacular social consequences:

> Thus from all sides the individualism of the "Reformed" [that is, Calvinist] Church was impelled toward activity; the individual was drawn irresistibly into a whole-hearted absorption in the tasks of service to the world and to society, to a life of unceasing, penetrating, and formative labor…. Above all, however, this specifically Calvinistic individualism possesses this peculiar characteristic that in its refusal to expand on the emotional side, and in its habit of placing confidence in God in the foreground and all human relations in the background, in going out of itself it always directs its attention toward concrete aims and purposes.[11]

Out of the theology of the Reformers came not only the idea of the calling and the Protestant work ethic,[12] but far more: the emphasis on

---

11. Ernst Troeltsch, *The Social Teaching of the Christian Churches*. Olive Wyon, translator. Two volumes. London: George Allen and Unwin. New York: Macmillan [1931] 1949, II, 589. Eisenstadt wrote: "Following the preceding analysis of Protestantism, we propose that the transformative potential of a given religion is greater the stronger is the emphasis in it on transcendentalism, on individual responsibility and activism, on an 'open' unmediated relationship between the individual and the sacred tradition…and on a high degree of social openness among the religiously active groups…. In Catholicism and even more in Eastern Christianity, the situation was different. Many of the sects were ritualistic and/or more withdrawn from active participation in the secular world; and even when they did participate in secular life their aim was the conservative one of accommodation to the existing order, not change or transformation" (S. N. Eisenstadt, "The Protestant Ethic Thesis in an Analytical and Comparative Framework" in *The Protestant Ethic and Modernization: A Comparative View*, New York: Basic Books, 1968, 20).

12. The Protestant work ethic was not something concocted by the Reformers, but merely a discovery of what the Bible itself taught about work. Here are a few relevant statements: "God rested from all his work" (*Genesis* 2); "Six days you shall labor and do all your work" (*Exodus* 20); "…the people had a mind to work" (*Nehemiah* 4); "Do you see a man who excels in his work? He will stand before kings" (*Proverbs* 22). "My Father works hitherto, and I work" (*John* 5); "…if any would not work, neither should he eat" (*2 Thessalonians* 3); "Whatever you do, do it heartily, as to the Lord and not to men" (*Colossians* 2). There are scores of relevant passages about the necessity, dignity, even the divinity, of work in the Scriptures. The God of Abraham, Isaac, Jacob, and Jesus, unlike the gods of the Greeks and Romans, worked. Troeltsch pointed out that "The Calvinistic ethic shared the Lutheran view about work, to which it assigned a high value, regarding it as the practical exercise of a calling appointed by God, and therefore as Divine worship; it also regarded it as a method of self-discipline and of diverting evil desires" (Troeltsch, *The Social Teaching of the Christian Churches*, II, 641).

19

universal education and literacy, since each soul has the right and the duty to read the Bible for himself; democracies and republics, as opposed to monarchies and aristocracies, since all believers are priests, and all men are equal before God and the law; economic initiative and creativity, since men are made in the image of God, saved by the grace of God, and do not need to ask permission to pursue their callings; the free exercise of religion, the right to assemble, to speak, and to publish, and much more. Luther wrote:

> The spiritual power is to reign only over the soul, seeing to it that it comes to Baptism and the Sacrament of the Altar, to the Gospel and true faith, over which matters emperors and kings have no jurisdiction.... Just so we clergymen have no command to take people by the neck if they will not listen to us.... We should learn to separate spiritual and temporal power from each other as far as Heaven and Earth, for the pope has greatly obscured this matter and has mixed the two powers....[13]

The twentieth century American historian Harold Berman pointed out that

> the key to renewal of law in the West from the sixteenth century on was the Protestant concept of the power of the individual, by God's grace, to change nature and to create new social relations through the exercise of his will. The Protestant concept of the individual became central to the development of the modern law of property and contract. Nature became property. Economic relations became contract.... The property and contract rights so created were held to be sacred and inviolable, so long as they did not contravene conscience [informed by Scripture].... And so the secularization of the state, in the restricted sense of the removal of ecclesiastical controls from it, was accompanied by a spiritualization, and even a sanctification, of property and contract.[14]

Not only did Protestant theology revolutionize law in Europe, it revolutionized economics as well. Luthy wrote:

> The evangelical injunction to charity, *mutuum date nihil inde sperantes* – give and hope not for a return – was interpreted [by the Roman Church-State] as a law of economic behavior which condemned not only usury

---

13. *What Luther Says*, Plass, 294.
14. Harold Berman, *The Interaction of Law and Religion*, London: SCM Press, 1974, 64-65.

but every form of profitable activity, and it was unflinchingly applied in doctrine to market and bargaining, prices and wages, overseas trade and capital investment. In practical terms this meant, quite simply, that the whole of economic life as lived in nonagrarian societies was a life of sin, and as the injunction to charity could not be enforced as a market regulation, the market economy was thus abandoned to wallow in its sinfulness. This act of abandonment had in fact taken place long ago. For centuries before the Reformation, the treatises of the Schoolmen on such subjects as trade, the laws of exchange, or value and payment, had become mere casuistry, a doctrine consisting solely of exceptions without a rule. And the result of this was a state of intellectual, moral, and legal chaos, in which everything was permitted precisely because all was sinful, and in which all the blasphemies of the Banco dello Spirito Santo and of the Fuggers' inflation of bills of indulgence drawn on the Saints' Treasury of Merit could flourish unchecked....

Calvin's breach with the body of ecclesiastical doctrine was in the first instance a painful act of intellectual honesty and clarity, in accord with the deep impulse of the Reformation age to establish a more truthful conformity between doctrine and life, between word and deed.... The full importance, not only economic but also and perhaps primarily intellectual, of the breach with the scholastic tradition would be a subject not for one essay, but for a full-length study. Only when a rational legitimation of capital and interest accounts permitted the introduction of the time coefficient into economic calculations did rational economic thought first become possible at all. But to say that more simply in Calvinist terms: Only the clear...distinction between the realm of private voluntary charity toward other human beings in want..., and on the other hand the realm of acquisitive economic activity, where the worldly precepts, anchored in positive rights and laws, of probity, legality, and fairness apply – *la loi d'équité* in Calvin's phrase – only the drawing of this distinction permitted the redemption of the human condition, the material, existential needs and worries of mankind, from the general and indiscriminate curse of sinfulness which simply abandoned everything this side of the grave to sin. In place of this cure it substituted, in this world in which men have to live and act, the simple demand that law and human honesty, so far as this is obtainable, be realized here on Earth.

In the Protestant work ethic the breach with the Schoolmen's image of the world and of society was even wider. The Schoolmen had seen misery and pauperism as an eternal evil, willed by God upon a sinful world. Against humanity's mass misery, the Middle Ages knew no gesture save that of the beggar resignedly holding out his hand and that of the rich man with equal resignation dropping his alms into it. [15]

Before Weber wrote on the economic consequences of the Reformation, the nineteenth century German historian Leopold von Ranke had called John Calvin the "virtual founder of America." Berman put it in these words:

> Calvinism has also had profound effects upon the development of Western law, and especially upon American law. The Puritans carried forward the Lutheran concept of the sanctity of individual conscience and also, in law, the sanctity of individual will as reflected in property and contract rights.... [S]eventeenth century Puritans, including men like [John] Hampden, [John] Lilburne, [Walter] Udall, William Penn and others, by their disobedience to English law, laid the foundations for the English and American law of civil rights and civil liberties as expressed in our respective constitutions: freedom of speech and press, free exercise of religion, the privilege against self-incrimination, the independence of the jury from judicial dictation, the right not to be imprisoned without cause, and many other such rights and freedoms. We also owe to

---

15. Herbert Luthy, "Once Again: Calvinism and Capitalism," in Eisenstadt, *The Protestant Ethic and Modernization: A Comparative View*, 105-107. William Perkins, one of the greatest Protestant theologians of the seventeenth century, clearly distinguished the Biblical and Protestant view from the Roman Catholic by posing and answering this question: "...if every man...must shewe himself to be a pilgrime and stranger in this world....is it not a good state of life for a man to contemne the world, and all things in it, and to betake himself to perpetuall beggarie and voluntarie poverty?" He answered in this fashion: "The [word] world in Scripture is taken divers ways; first, for the corruptions and sinnes of the world: and these must be contemned by all means possible.... Secondly, for temporal blessings, as, money, lands, wealth, sustenance, and such like outward things, as concerne the necessarie or convenient maintenance of this naturall life. And in this sense the world is not to be contemned, for in themselves, the earthly things are the good gifts of God, which no man can simply contemne, without injurie to God's disposing hand and providence, who both ordained them for natural life" (William Perkins, *The Works*, London, 1612-1613, III, 102-103). Perkins also explained, following Luther's commentary on the Apostle Paul's *Epistle to the Galatians*, what good works are: "Now the works of every calling, when they are performed in an holy manner, are done in faith and obedience and serve notably for Gods glory, be the calling never so base.... The meannesse of the calling doth not abase the goodnesse of the worke: for God looketh not at the excellence of the worke, but at the heart of the worker. And the action of a sheepheard in keeping sheep, performed as I have said, in his kind, is as good a worke before God, as is the action of a Judge, in giving a sentence, or of a Magistrate in ruling, or a Minister in preaching" and much better, we might add, than the actions of priests, nuns, and monks in their parishes, convents, and monasteries (Perkins, *The Works*, I, 758).

INTRODUCTION

Calvinist congregationalism the religious basis of our concepts of social contract and government by consent of the governed.[16]

Perhaps the most ironic thing about the Reformation is that the Reformers did not and could not have foreseen the long-term effects their preaching would have on Europe and its Protestant colonies. The development of our political and economic freedoms was partially an unintended consequence of their preaching of the Gospel. But those consequences were not unintended by God, and he had already told us so, in one of the most misunderstood passages from Christ's Sermon on the Mount:

> Therefore I say to you, do not worry about your life, what you will eat or what you will drink; nor about your body, what you will put on. Is not life more than food and the body more than clothing?
>
> Look at the birds of the air, for they neither sow nor reap nor gather into barns; yet your heavenly Father feeds them. Are you not of more value than they?…
>
> Consider the lilies of the field, how they grow: They neither toil nor spin. And yet I say to you that even Solomon in all his glory was not arrayed like one of these.
>
> Now if God so clothes the grass of the field, which today is, and tomorrow is thrown into the oven, will he not much more clothe you, O you of little faith? For after all these things the Gentiles seek. For your heavenly Father knows that you need all these things.
>
> But seek first the kingdom of God and his righteousness, and all these things shall be added to you.[17]

At the time of the Reformation the Roman Church-State had neither sought nor taught the kingdom of God and his righteousness for a millennium, but had sought to establish its own righteousness, wealth, and power. As soon as the Gospel was preached and believed, the economic system of Europe began to change, just as Jesus had promised.

Constitutional capitalism – *laissez faire* capitalism – in which government has only two functions, the punishment of evildoers and the praise of the good, as Paul wrote in *Romans* 13,[18] is the economic and

---

16. Berman, *The Interaction of Law and Religion*, 66-67.
17. *Matthew* 6.
18. Some will object to limiting the legitimate powers of government on the ground that Paul did not forbid government to perform other functions, such as operate schools,

23

political consequent and counterpart of Christian theology; it is the practice of which Christian theology is the theory. It might be expected that an institution such as the Roman Church-State, ruled by an absolute emperor,[19] structured in a rigid hierarchy, supranational in scope, aristocratic in character, and none of whose officials is elected – an institution that in more than one way is an anachronism, an intrusion of the ancient world into the modern – would not favor constitutional capitalism. But how deep-seated its hostility to freedom and free enterprise is was a surprise even to this author. The popes have expressed their hatred, not only for Protestantism (a hatred perhaps muted recently, not by a change of mind, but by the relativism of the Church-State influenced by a postmodern culture), but also for the political and economic expression of Christianity: capitalism. In the pages that follow, the reader will find scores of such statements from the Magisterium of the Roman Church-State. They are part of a system of thought that is one of the most impressive systems yet devised by men. They are not disjointed statements, but the logical conclusions of premises accepted in Roman theology. They are offered to the world by the Roman Magisterium as part of a package deal, and we are not at liberty, as some American Catholics would prefer to do, to accept the Church-State's theology and reject its economic and political philosophy. That flies in the face, not only of the claims of the Church-State itself, but of reason as well. The author hopes that those who read this book will come away with a better understanding of *what* Rome has said in the fields of political and economic theory, and *why* it has said it.

---

provide health care, old age pensions, and national parks, but such an objection misses the point. Government is authorized to do only what Scripture authorizes it to do. To argue that Paul's silence is actually an authorization for government to do anything it chooses is to reject the view that government has only enumerated powers and to adopt the notion that the powers of government are in fact totalitarian. This argument would force us to the conclusion that since Paul did not forbid government any function or activity, government is authorized to do everything. If a similar argument were applied to the Great Commission, for example, in which Christ commands his disciples to preach the Gospel, we would have to conclude that Christ was actually authorizing them to teach everything, not just the Gospel, since he did not forbid them to teach materialism and polytheism.

19. "As ruler of Vatican City the pope is the last absolute monarch in Europe, with supreme legislative, judicial, and executive authority. He also controls all the assets of the Vatican, since this is a state economy without private property other than personal possessions of the employees and residents" (Reese, *Inside the Vatican*, 16).

INTRODUCTION

And if there be any Roman Catholic readers who are inclined to favor freedom and free enterprise, may they understand that their Church does not, and therefore they must choose to be either good Catholics, or good Christians.

PART I
ENVY EXALTED

∞

THE ECONOMIC THOUGHT
OF THE
ROMAN CATHOLIC CHURCH

Ecclesiastical economics is envy exalted.
Peter T. Bauer

One
❧
Private Property

HISTORIANS of economic thought know of only a few scattered and, with the possible exception of the pseudo-Aristotelian *Economics, ad hoc* statements on economic matters during the millennium surrounding the earthly life of Jesus Christ. Most such discussions of economic matters occur in the context of political and moral questions, not as independent matters to be pondered and analyzed at length.[1] In the thirteenth century the Italian who became the official philosopher of the Roman Church-State, Thomas Aquinas, wrote no treatise on economics, but his thinking, based on that of Aristotle, is foundational for understanding the economic thought of the Roman Church-State.[2] Essays and treatises on economics did not appear until the sixteenth, seventeenth, and eighteenth centuries, when, following the Reformation and the emergence of capitalism, economies developed to the point that it occurred to some observers that there was something worth writing about. When continuous market order appeared on a large scale after the Reformation, rather than merely the localized scale that had until then characterized the West, some astute observers noticed that this order, a human order not achieved by human design, was a phenomenon that required an explanation. The discipline of economics was born. Most of these writers, however, were not Roman Catholic, and they wrote outside the control of the Roman Church-State.

---

1. See Joseph Schumpeter, *History of Economic Analysis*, New York: Oxford University Press, 1954.
2. "A complete and authoritative statement of medieval economic thought may be found in the writings of Saint Thomas Aquinas (1225-1274), a great figure in medieval scholasticism whose system of thought was to become, and has remained to the present time, the official Catholic philosophy" (Henry William Spiegel, *The Growth of Economic Thought*. Revised edition. Durham: Duke University Press, 1983, 57).

Moreover, it was not Roman Catholic countries whose economies developed most rapidly, but the economies of Protestant countries. The economic thought of the Roman Church-State has been remarkably consistent for centuries, adhering to the primitive and erroneous dogmas of Aristotle and Thomas Aquinas. Its fundamental principles have remained the same, even while their development and application have differed over the centuries.

Roman Catholic economic thought, as developed by the popes in their encyclicals and by Roman Church-State councils, has been a contributor to, if not the only source of, several forms of anti-capitalist political and economic organization during the long hegemony of the Roman Church-State. Among these forms are

(1) feudalism and guild socialism in Europe during the Middle Ages;

(2) fascism in Italy, Spain, Portugal, Croatia, and Latin America in the twentieth century;

(3) Nazism in Germany in the twentieth century;

(4) interventionism and the redistributive state in the West, including the United States in the twentieth century; and

(5) liberation theology in Latin America and Africa in the twentieth century.

To understand how the economic thought of the Roman Church-State spawned these anti-capitalist systems, we begin with Thomas Aquinas' discussion of private property. Private property is the central economic institution of civilized societies, and it is the Roman Church-State's rejection of private property that contributed to the establishment of several varieties of destructive anti-capitalism throughout the world.

To understand Thomas' doctrine of private property, we must first understand his view of law. According to Thomas, there are four kinds of law. First, there is *eternal law*, which is God's plan for the universe and all its inhabitants. Thus it is part of the eternal law that rocks, for example, fall to the ground when dropped; and plants, for example, grow toward the light. Second, there is *natural law*, which is the participation of rational creatures in the eternal law. Thus man is by nature a social animal. When men speak to each other and live in societies, they are doing what is natural to them, just as rocks and plants do. Third, there is *positive law*, which is customs, laws, and regulations made by rulers attempting to apply the natural law to individuals and societies. Finally, there is *divine law*, such as the Ten Commandments.

Private property, according to Thomas, is neither part of the natural law nor an absolute right, but an invention of human reason. It is a creation of and regulated by positive law. Rather than private property being part of the natural law, the possession of all things in common is the natural law. Thomas wrote: "...'the possession of all things in common and universal freedom' are said to be of the natural law because, to wit, the distinction of possessions and slavery were not brought in by nature, but devised by human reason for the benefit of human life."[3] The institution of private property, like slavery, is a positive, not a natural, institution, and therefore rightfully subject to human regulation. The "community of goods," wrote Thomas,

> is ascribed to the natural law, not that the natural law dictates that all things should be possessed in common and that nothing should be possessed as one's own, but because the division of possessions is not according to the natural law, but rather arose from human agreement, which belongs to positive law.... Hence the ownership of possessions is not contrary to the natural law, but an addition thereto devised by human reason.[4]

It is important to keep in mind that according to Roman Catholic economic thought, here represented by its greatest and only official philosopher, Thomas Aquinas, that communism (with a small "c") – what Thomas called the community of goods – is part of the natural law; and that private property is part of the positive law. Private property is an "addition to" the natural law. Though private property is not contrary to the natural law, it is not itself natural, and it does not enjoy the same metaphysical or ethical status as the community of goods. While men cannot change the natural law – rather, they are required to conform to it, according to Roman Church-State thought – they can change positive law, and they may do so in whatever manner is expedient and moral.

Now several things might make such a community of goods expedient, but one makes the community of goods morally imperative: need. Thomas wrote:

---

3. *Summa Theologiae*, ii-ii, 5th article.
4. *Summa Theologiae*, ii-ii, 2nd article.

Things which are of human right cannot derogate from natural right or divine right.... The division and appropriation of things which are based on human law do not preclude the fact that man's needs have to be remedied by means of these very things. Hence, whatever certain people have in superabundance is due, by natural law, to the purpose of succoring the poor.[5]

Because the goods of some are due to others by the natural law, there is no sin if the poor take the goods of their neighbors. Thomas wrote: "In cases of need, all things are common property, so that there would seem to be no sin in taking another's property, for need has made it common."[6] Not only is such taking of another's property not a sin, it is not even a crime, according to Thomas:

> ...it is lawful for a man to succor his own need by means of another's property by taking it either openly or secretly; nor is this, properly speaking, theft and robbery.... It is not theft, properly speaking, to take secretly and use another's property in a case of extreme need; because that which he takes for the support of his life becomes his own property by reason of that need.... In a case of a like need a man may also take secretly another's property in order to succor his neighbor in need.[7]

In Thomas' philosophy, need is the moral criterion for the rightful and lawful possession of property: Whoever needs property ought to possess it. Need makes another's goods one's own. Need is the ultimate and only *moral* title to property. Neither possession, nor creation, nor production, nor gift, nor inheritance, nor divine commandment (with the exception of Roman Church-State property[8]) grants title to property that is immune to the prior claim of need.

Thomas' view was, of course, not original. He received it from the theologians of the early church, who in turn received it from Greek and Roman philosophy. In the *Pseudo-Clementines* we read that "For all men, possessions are sins." John Chrysostom (354-407) wrote in his homily on *1 Timothy* 4:

---

5. *Summa Theologiae*, ii–ii, 7th article.
6. *Summa Theologiae*, ii–ii, 7th article.
7. *Summa Theologiae*, ii–ii, 7th article.
8. Canon 1254: "The Catholic Church has an innate right to acquire, retain, administer and alienate temporal goods in pursuit of its proper ends independently of civil power." Canon 1260: "The Church has an innate right to require from the Christian faithful whatever is necessary for the ends proper to it."

PRIVATE PROPERTY

> Mark the wise dispensation of God! That he might put mankind to shame, he has made certain things common, as the sun, air, earth, and water...whose benefits are dispensed equally to all as brethren...observe, that concerning things that are common there is no contention, but all is peaceable. But when one attempts to possess himself of anything, to make it his own, then contention is introduced, as if nature herself were indignant, that when God brings us together in every way, we are eager to divide and separate ourselves by appropriating things, and by using those cold words "mine and thine." Then there is contention and uneasiness. But where this [private property] is not, no strife or contention is bred. This [communal] state therefore is rather our inheritance, and more agreeable to nature.[9]

Basil, bishop of Caesarea in Cappadocia (329-379) asked:

> Tell me, what is yours? Where did you get it and bring it into the world? It is as if one has taken a seat in the theater and then drives out all who come later, thinking that what is for everyone is only for him. Rich people are like that. For having pre-empted what is common to all, they make it their own by virtue of this prior possession. If only each one would take as much as he requires to satisfy his immediate needs, and leave the rest to others who equally needed it, no one would be rich and no one would be poor.[10]

Ambrose, bishop of Milan (339-397), even though he argued against the Stoicism of Cicero, agreed with Stoic teaching on property:

> Nature has poured forth all things for men for common use. God has ordered all things to be produced, so that there should be food in common to all, and that the earth should be a common possession for all. Nature, therefore, has produced a common right for all, but greed (*usurpatio*) had made it a right for a few.

In the fifth century before Christ, the Greek playwright Aristophanes (445-388 B.C.), in *Ecclesiazusae*, put these words into the mouth of Praxagora, a leading character:

> All shall be equal, and equally share all wealth and enjoyment, nor longer endure that one should be rich and another be poor, that one

---

9. As quoted in Martin Hengel, *Property and Riches in the Early Church: Aspects of a Social History of Early Christianity*. Philadelphia: Fortress Press [1973] 1974, 1-2.

10. As quoted in Hengel, *Property and Riches in the Early Church*, 2.

should have acres, far stretching and wide, and another not even enough to provide himself with a grave: that this at his call should have hundreds of servants and that none at all. All this I intend to correct and amend, now all of all blessings shall freely partake, one life and one system for all men I'll make.

It was a common opinion in Greek and Roman thought (as well as the thought of other ancient cultures) that there had been a golden age in which all men lived in innocence and all things were common. Virgil (70-19 B.C.) wrote that "Even to mark the field or divide it with bounds was unlawful. Men made gain from the common store, and Earth yielded all, of herself, more freely, when none begged for her gifts."[11]

Hengel commented on the views of the early church theologians:

> This thesis that private property came into being as a result of the Fall had great influence in the history of the church. We find it later among the Franciscan theologians and then again in Zwingli and Melanchthon.... Of course, "theories of property" like this, which are to be found in the early church, are not specifically based on the New Testament. Appeal could be made equally well to philosophy and natural law for the thesis of Gregory Nazianzen that private property, riches and poverty are a consequence of the Fall.[12]

One could hardly tell the Stoic Seneca's views on property from those of Gregory Nazianzen:

> [Philosophy] has taught us to worship that which is divine, to love that which is human; she has told us that with the gods lies dominion, and among men, fellowship – This fellowship remained unspoiled for a long time, until avarice tore the community asunder and became the cause of poverty.... But avarice broke in upon a condition so happily ordained, and by its eagerness to lay something away and to turn it to its own private use, made all things the property of others and reduced itself from boundless wealth to straitened need.[13]

---

11. *Georgics*, 1, 126ff.
12. Hengel, *Property and Riches in the Early Church*, 3.
13. *Epist.* 90. 3, 38; as quoted in Hengel, *Property and Riches in the Early Church*, 6-7. Hengel commented: "The connections between the ancient theories of a lofty moral 'primal communism' or of a 'primal catastrophe,' allegedly introduced by the division of labor and private possessions, and the modern 'historical myths' of popular Marxism are evident. Rousseau's 'back to nature,' like Proudhon's theory 'property is theft,' are not original ideas, but go back to ancient sources" (*Property and Riches in the Early Church*, 7).

Neither the early church theologians nor Thomas, unfortunately, informed us what *need* is or how it might be ascertained. Furthermore, the needy person and the public authorities seem to be the proper judges of whether someone needs his neighbor's goods or not. No one can know how hungry another is, nor how much he requires medical care or needs information. Each person must be the sole judge of his own need simply because no one else can be. But the public authorities must get involved because such a situation would leave each person judge of his own need, as the later encyclicals make clear. The only person who is not a judge and has no moral authority in the matter seems to be the actual owner of the property that is being taken.

From these doctrines of the natural community of goods and the moral primacy of need developed all the forms of anti-capitalist social organizations that the Roman Church-State has supported for the past thousand years. The Roman Catholic doctrine of private property is echoed in the nineteenth century Communist slogan, "From each according to his ability; to each according to his need." The Roman Catholic doctrine reverberates in the slogan of twentieth century American liberals: "Human rights are more important than property rights." It was the creed of Lyndon Johnson's Great Society: "We shall take from the haves and give to the have-nots, who need it so much." It appears in the literature of fascism, Nazism, liberation theology, interventionism, and socialism. Collectivists of all sorts agree with Thomas that those who own property are morally and legally obligated to surrender their goods to those in need. Collectivists agree with Thomas that those in need are morally and legally justified in taking the goods of their neighbors. Perhaps, if they are inconsistent or hesitant, they might not defend looting or direct expropriation of property owners, but they do endorse indirect action through government expropriation, taxation, and regulation. These Thomistic notions – that private property is merely a construct of human reason and government, and that need gives the needy title to the goods of others – are the reason the Roman Catholic bishops in Brazil in 1998 pronounced that looting is neither a sin nor a crime.[14] The needs of the looters give the looters

---

14. *The San Diego Union-Tribune* carried an Associated Press story by Stan Lehman from Arcoverde, Brazil, on May 8, 1998: "Souza, one of an estimated 10 million Brazilians facing starvation from a devastating drought, says he will do anything to save his family. 'I'll loot to survive,' he said defiantly. He won't be alone. The [Roman] Catholic

title to the goods they are taking. According to Roman Catholic doctrine, the looters are, by natural and divine law, the rightful owners of those goods.

Cardinal Tommaso Cajetan (1469-1534) explained some of the implications of the Thomistic view of property:

> Now what a ruler can do in virtue of his office, so that justice may be served in the matter of riches, is to take from someone who is unwilling to dispense from what is superfluous for life or state, and to distribute it to the poor. In this way he [the ruler] just takes away the dispensation power of the rich man to whom wealth has been entrusted because he is not worthy. For according to the teaching of the saints, the riches that are superfluous do not belong to the rich man as his own, but rather to the one appointed by God as dispenser, so that he can have the merit of a good dispensation. The legal obligation in this case is founded on the justice obligations of riches themselves. These [riches] belong in the classification of useful goods. And superfluity that is not given away is kept in a way that goes counter to the good of both parties. It is counter to the good of the one who hoards it, because it is his only so that he can preside at the giving away. And it is counter to the good of the indigent because someone else continues to possess what has been given for their [the indigents'] use.... And therefore an injury is done to the poor in not dispensing the superfluous. And this injury is something that the prince,

---

Church says looting to stave off hunger is neither a crime nor a sin." In an earlier story (May 2), Lehman had reported: "The Landless Rural Workers Movement has endorsed looting as a tactic to pressure the government for aid, and the [Roman] Catholic Church was quick to defend the action. 'It is not a crime to resort to this kind of action when in extreme need,' [Roman Catholic Bishop Francisco de] Mesquita [Filho of Afogados da Ingazeira] told a meeting of the National Conference of Brazilian Bishops in Campinas." In a story datelined April 27, 1998, Inter Press Service reported that "Roman Catholic Bishop Orlando Dotti said the military should be sent in 'to distribute food to the people,' rather than to defend property. A well-known member of the progressive branch of Brazil's clergy, Dotti defended the right to loot 'in extreme cases of hunger.' Speaking at the General Assembly of the Brazilian Episcopal Conference, which opened last Wednesday in Indaiatiba, 100 kms from Sao Paulo, the bishop argued that the [Roman] Catholic Church's social doctrine admitted stealing as a last resort, when survival was at stake. He pointed out that over 15 [sic] centuries ago, St. Thomas of Aquinas argued that the right to life took priority over the right to property.... Conservative and moderate bishops like Amaury Castanho, whose diocese is located on the outskirts of Sao Paulo, said 'Stealing to eat, in cases of hunger' was admitted by Christian doctrine, according to which goods become commonly owned in the case of extreme necessity."

who is the guardian of the right, should set to rights by the power of his office.[15]

The dispensing of riches to the needy is not merely a private moral obligation in Thomistic thought, as fundamentally important as that is, but a public legal obligation that is properly enforced by the public authorities. That this is the position officially adopted by the Roman Church-State shall become abundantly clear.

---

15. Tommaso de Vio Cajetan, *Summa Theologica cum commentariis Thomae de Vio Cajetan*, t. 6 (Rome 1778), II-II, 118, 3, page 188; as quoted in John C. Cort, *Christian Socialism*. Maryknoll, New York: Orbis Books, 1988.

Two

The Universal Destination of Goods

THE THOMISTIC notion of original communism — the denial that private property is part of the natural law, but that common property is both natural and divine — is foundational to all the Roman Catholic arguments for various forms of collectivism, from medieval feudalism and guild socialism to twentieth century fascism and liberation theology. The popes refer to this original communism as the "universal destination of all goods." Take, for example, John Paul II's expression of it in his 1987 encyclical *On Social Concern*:

> It is necessary to state once more the characteristic principle of Christian social doctrine: the goods of this world are originally meant for all. The right of private property is valid and necessary, but it does not nullify the value of this principle. Private property, in fact, is under a "social mortgage," which means that it has an intrinsically social function, based upon and justified precisely by the principle of the universal destination of goods.[1]

This principle — the universal destination of goods — is so important in Catholic social thought that all rights are to be subordinated to it. Paul VI made the point quite clear in his 1967 encyclical *On the Progress of Peoples*:

> ...each man has therefore the right to find in the world what is necessary for himself. The recent Council [Vatican II] reminded us of this: "God intended the earth and all that it contains for the use of every human being and people. Thus, as all men follow justice and unite in charity, created goods should abound for them on a reasonable basis." All other rights whatsoever, including those of property and of free commerce, are to be subordinated to this principle.[2]

1. John Paul II, *Sollicitudo Rei Socialis, On Social Concern* (1987), 42.
2. Paul VI, *Populorum Progressio, On the Progress of Peoples* (1967), 22.

THE UNIVERSAL DESTINATION OF GOODS

Please note the words: "All other rights whatsoever, including those of property and of free commerce, are to be subordinated to this principle." "All other rights whatsoever," of course, includes not only the right to private property and the right to free enterprise, but the rights to worship, speak, teach, write, think, and publish freely – indeed, the right to life itself. In Roman Catholic economic thought, there is a hierarchy of principles, and the most important of these principles, to which all others are subordinate, is the principle of the universal destination of goods.[3] This is the economic corollary of the principle of solidarity, which we shall discuss in Part 2 on Roman Catholic political thought.

The popes have not been hesitant to apply this fundamental Roman Catholic principle. In 1990, speaking on the so-called ecological crisis, John Paul II wrote that

> ...the earth is ultimately a common heritage, the fruits of which are for the benefit of all. In the words of the Second Vatican Council, "God destined the earth and all it contains for the use of every individual and all peoples" (*Gaudium et Spes*, 69). This has direct consequences for the problem at hand. It is manifestly unjust that a privileged few should continue to accumulate excess goods, squandering available resources, while masses of people are living in conditions of misery at the very lowest level of subsistence.[4]

According to John Paul II, not only is it unjust that Americans have cars and houses while Chinese walk and live in huts, but it is "manifestly unjust," that is, so obviously unjust that one need not even bother to argue the point. It is manifestly unjust because the Earth and everything in it belong to all people in common – because of the fundamental principle of the universal destination of goods.

---

3. In *Laborem Exercens, On Human Labor* (1981), John Paul II referred to this principle as "the first principle of the whole ethical and social order, namely, the principle of the common use of goods" (46). In *Mater et Magistra, On Christianity and Social Progress* (1961), John XXIII wrote: "Concerning the use of material goods, our predecessor [Pius XII, 1941] declared that the right of every man to use them for his own sustenance is prior to all other rights in economic life, and hence is prior even to the right of private ownership" (43). Please notice the papal distinction between ownership and use. This distinction between legal ownership of property and the right to use that property is characteristic of feudalism, and the basis for modern fascism.

4. John Paul II, *The Ecological Crisis: A Common Responsibility* (January 1, 1990), 8.

Gaudium et Spes, the Vatican II *Constitution* that John Paul II quoted, explained at greater length:

> God intended the earth with everything contained in it for the use of all human beings and peoples.... The right of having a share of earthly goods sufficient for oneself and one's family belongs to everyone.... If one is in extreme necessity he has the right to procure for himself what he needs out of the riches of others. Since there are so many people prostrate with hunger in the world, this Sacred Council urges all, both individuals and governments, to remember the aphorism of the Fathers, "Feed the man dying of hunger, because if you have not fed him, you have killed him."[5]

One must always keep the primacy of need, the original community of goods, the universal destination of goods, and their privileged and superior status in natural law in mind when one reads statements from the Roman Church-State that seem to defend private property. The Church-State does not defend private property on moral grounds – of course, it claims supernatural, divine rights to its own property – but only as a human institution that may or may not be expedient at any given time. Furthermore, not only is private property at some times inexpedient, it is at all times of inequality (which is apparently indistinguishable from need) manifestly unjust; that is, private property is obviously immoral at all times, since there are no times of equality. Economic equality is an illusion, an impossible state of affairs. Therefore, because private property is immoral, all men – individuals and governments – have the moral obligation to redistribute goods held unjustly by property owners.

Now this position is similar to that of Communists and socialists, but the Roman Church-State has attempted to distinguish its position on property from both the Communist and the capitalist view. John Paul II, writing in *Laborem Exercens*, said:

> The above principle [the right to private property], as it was then stated and as it is still taught by the Church, diverges radically from the program of collectivism as proclaimed by Marxism and put into practice in various countries in the decades following the time of Leo XIII's encyclical [*Rerum Novarum*, 1891]. At the same time it differs from the

---

5. The Second Vatican Council, *Gaudium et Spes, Pastoral Constitution on the Church in the Modern World* (1965), 69.

program of capitalism practiced by liberalism and by the political systems inspired by it. In the latter case, the difference consists in the way the right to ownership to property is understood. Christian tradition has never upheld this right as absolute and untouchable. On the contrary, it has always understood this right within the broader context of the right common to all to use the goods of the whole of creation; the right to private property is subordinated to the right to common use, to the fact that goods are meant for everyone.[6]

Please note that while John Paul II asserted that the Church-State doctrine of property differs from that of the Marxists, he did not explain how it does so. He simply asserted that it "diverges radically." He explained only how the Church-State doctrine of property differs from the capitalist idea of private property. Marx also taught an original communism – that goods at one time in early human history belonged to all, and that all ought to have the use of such goods today. Like Marx, the Roman Church-State teaches that the phrase "all goods" includes not just the goods found in nature but manufactured goods as well. John Paul II declared that all men must have "...access to those goods which are intended for common use: both the goods of nature and manufactured goods."[7]

Because private property is a creation of human reason and government, governments may regulate and control it as they see fit: Pius XI explained in *On Social Reconstruction*:

> Provided that the natural and divine law be observed, the public authority, in view of the common good, may specify more accurately what is licit and what is illicit for property owners in the use of their possessions.... History proves that the right of ownership, like other elements of social life, is not absolutely rigid....[8]

Pius XI added a logical blunder to the false premise of the universal destination and common use of goods: History may in fact illustrate that private property has been regulated by governments in various ways, but history cannot show that this regulation is right, or that the right of ownership is not absolute. Perhaps – just perhaps – governments, when they have regulated private property in various ways, were

---

6. John Paul II, *Laborem Exercens* (1981), 34-35.
7. John Paul II, *Laborem Exercens* (1981), 46.
8. Pius XI, *Quadragesimo Anno, On Social Reconstruction* (1931), 25.

violating that right and interfering with the principle of private property. To appeal to history – even a long history – of regulation of private property by government as proof that the principle itself is not absolute is to confuse history with ethics, the "is" with the "ought," or in this case, to confuse "what has been" with "what ought to be."[9]

The Second Vatican Council reiterated the doctrine: "...it is the right of public authority to prevent anyone from misusing his private property to the detriment of the common good."[10] The common good, as we shall see in our discussion of the political thought of the Roman Church-State, is the fiction by which the public authorities justify whatever they please to do.

---

9. Of course, theories of natural law and tradition, to which the Roman Church-State is committed, make the same logical blunder.
10. The Second Vatican Council, *Gaudium et Spes* (1965), 71.

Three

Rerum Novarum
On the Condition
of the Working Classes

ONE OF the Roman Church-State's most influential statements on economic matters is the 1891 encyclical *Rerum Novarum, On the Condition of the Working Classes*. In this encyclical the Roman Church-State allied herself with the proletariat, which in Marxism is the great and final enemy of the capitalist order. The encyclical's Marxism is so blatant that one Roman Catholic writer declared that "much of the encyclical [*Rerum Novarum*] appeared only to repeat in more orthodox language what Marx had said ten years before."[1] (Marx's *Das Kapital* had been published in 1881.) More recently, the Marxist turned Roman Catholic, Eugene Genovese, wrote:

> The Marxists were right: the twentieth century has been a century of the "general crisis of capitalism," even if they erred badly on the nature of that crisis, which has been primarily a crisis of the spirit engendered by the loss of faith in God and a transcendent law. Still, the Marxist critique of capitalism had much in common with the critique offered in *Rerum Novarum*, much as did the critique offered by the organic conservatives of nineteenth-century Europe and by the southern slaveholders in our own country.[2]

---

1. Anthony Rhodes, *The Power of Rome in the Twentieth Century*. New York: Franklin Watts, 1983, 104.

2. Eugene D. Genovese, "Secularism in the General Crisis of Capitalism," *The American Journal of Jurisprudence*, Volume 32, 1997, 196. Published by Notre Dame Law School, Natural Law Institute. Genovese's essay is the annual Natural Law lecture delivered at Notre Dame Law School, April 17, 1997.

For centuries the Roman Church-State had resisted the advance of the Reformation and its economic system, capitalism. In opposing capitalism it had allied itself with the medieval aristocracy. Now when that aristocracy was disappearing, a new ally had to be found.[3] The Austrian economist Mises wrote in his book on socialism in 1922:

> Historically it is easy to understand the dislike which the [Roman] Church has shown for economic liberty and political Liberalism in any form.... It was Liberalism that undermined the power of the classes that has for centuries been closely bound up with the [Roman] Church.... The [Roman] Church stubbornly resented modernity and the modern spirit. What wonder, then, that it allied itself with those whom resentment had driven to wish for the break-up of this wonderful new world...?[4]

Indeed, there are paragraphs, if not pages, in *The Communist Manifesto* that might have been written by the pope or any other reactionary rather than by Marx and Engels. Here is an example:

> The bourgeoisie, wherever it has got the upper hand, has put an end to all feudal, patriarchal, idyllic relations. It has pitilessly torn asunder the motley feudal ties that bound man to his natural superiors, and has left remaining no other bond between man and man than naked self-inter-

---

3. Aaron I. Abell, Professor of History at the University of Notre Dame, writing in *The Review of Politics* in 1945, remarked, "Taken as a whole, the Encyclical marked the emergence of three new trends...first: the decision of the [Roman State] Church in a democratic age to seek popular in place of princely support..." ("The Reception of Leo XIII's Labor Encyclical in America, 1891-1919," *The Review of Politics*, October 1945, 467). Later in his essay Abell remarked that there were a few "progressive Catholics" in the United States who discerned that "the Church's true interests were best served through cooperation with the growing social movement..." and they ultimately prevailed at the Vatican (472). Notice that Abell characterized the Church-State's decision as a pursuit of interest rather than a pursuit of truth.

4. Ludwig von Mises, *Socialism: An Economic and Sociological Analysis*. Indianapolis: Liberty Fund, no date [1922], 382. Amintore Fanfani, the influential Roman Catholic Italian philosopher and politician whose 1934 book *Catholicism, Protestantism, and Capitalism* summarized Roman Catholic social thought, agreed with Mises (though Fanfani may not have read Mises' book): "...the Church, in the persons of her most authoritative exponents and her most devoted sons, fought against dawning capitalism, basing herself on the medieval corporative order, and opposed triumphant capitalism.... In the Middle Ages, by supporting the intervention of public bodies in economic life as a check to individual activity and to defend the interests of society as a whole; in our own time, by calling for State intervention for the same reasons, the Church has remained faithful to her anti-capitalistic ethics..." (*Catholicism, Protestantism, and Capitalism*, University of Notre Dame Press [1934] 1984, 158-159).

est and callous cash payment. It has drowned the most heavenly ecstasies of religious fervor, of chivalrous enthusiasm, of philistine sentimentalism, in the icy water of egotistical calculation. It has resolved personal worth into exchange value, and in place of the numberless indefeasible chartered freedoms, has set up that single, unconscionable freedom – free trade....

The bourgeoisie has stripped of its halo every occupation hitherto honored and looked up to with reverent awe. It has converted the physician, the lawyer, the priest, the poet, the man of science, into its paid wage laborers.

The bourgeoisie has torn away from the family its sentimental veil, and has reduced the family relation to a mere money relation.[5]

Despite, or rather because of *Rerum Novarum's* reactionary character, Pius XI, writing in 1931, declared that "*Rerum Novarum*, however, stood out in this, that it laid down for all mankind unerring rules for the right solution of the difficult problem of human solidarity, called the Social Question...."[6] Subsequent popes have been equally effusive in their praise for *Rerum Novarum*. John XXIII in *Mater et Magistra*, wrote:

By far the most notable evidence of this social teaching and action, which the Church has set forth through the centuries, undoubtedly is the very distinguished Encyclical Letter *Rerum Novarum*, issued seventy years ago....The norms and recommendations contained therein were so momentous that their memory will never fall into oblivion.[7]

Pius XI, in his encyclical celebrating the fortieth anniversary of *Rerum Novarum*, wrote:

With regard to the civil power, Leo XIII boldly passed beyond the restrictions imposed by Liberalism, and fearlessly proclaimed the doctrine that the civil power is more than the mere guardian of law and order.... It is true, indeed, that a just freedom of action should be left to individual citizens and families: but this principle is only valid as long as the common good is secure and no injustice is entailed.[8]

---

5. Karl Marx and Friedrich Engels, *The Communist Manifesto*, New York: Washington Square Press [1848] 1964, 61-62. Medievalists, agrarians, and reactionaries of many stripes, of course, not just the Roman Church-State, have raised similar objections to individualism and capitalism.
6. Pius XI, *Quadragesimo Anno* (1931), 4.
7. John XXIII, *Mater et Magistra* (1961), 7-8.
8. Pius XI, *Quadragesimo Anno* (1931), 13.

In this statement, Pius XI said that Leo XIII fearlessly and boldly passed beyond the restrictions on state power imposed by liberalism. Those restrictions, as Pius XI explained, were that civil power is merely the guardian of law of order. It was that view of government – the Apostle Paul's view in *Romans* 13 – that Leo XIII "boldly" and "fearlessly" attacked. Of course, there was little to be feared, since Pius XI himself, in the same encyclical, described the principles of liberalism as "tottering" in 1891:

> In fact, the Encyclical *Rerum Novarum* completely overthrew those tottering tenets of Liberalism which had long hampered effective interference by the government. It prevailed upon the peoples to develop their social policy more intensely and on truer lines, and encouraged the elite among Catholics to give such efficacious help and assistance to rulers of the State, that in legislative assemblies they were not infrequently the foremost advocates of the new policy. Furthermore, not a few recent laws dealing with social questions were originally proposed to the suffrages of the people's representatives by ecclesiastics thoroughly imbued with Leo's teaching, who afterwards with watchful care promoted and fostered their execution.[9]

Pius XI told us that the encyclical *Rerum Novarum* was instrumental in ending *laissez-faire* capitalism in the twentieth century by ushering in the era of "effective interference by the government." Leo XIII had encouraged Roman Catholics to influence their various civil governments, and Pius XI told us that they have done so. In fact, they have been the "foremost advocates of the new policy" of interference. Indeed, Pius XI disclosed that in many cases ("not a few") new laws were originally proposed by ecclesiastics – that is, by bishops and priests – themselves, who afterwards promoted and fostered their execution.

Pius XI's claims, though they need no confirmation, are corroborated by a column Joe Klein wrote for *Newsweek*, February 19, 1996, titled "A Lurch Toward Love." Telling us that Pat Buchanan, who at that time was running for President, "has got religion," Klein explained:

> The religion is Roman Catholicism, the most significant in American politics, the ultimate swing vote. Catholics were the heart of the New Deal coalition. They were the Daley machine in Chicago, the Curley machine in Boston, Tammany Hall in New York. Jimmy Carter was the

---

9. Pius XI, *Quadragesimo Anno* (1931), 14.

last Democrat to win a Catholic majority. Clinton got 43 percent of their support in 1992 (Perot had 20) [that leaves 37 percent for Bush], but Catholics voted overwhelmingly, 57 percent, for Democratic Congressional candidates.

Much of the interference by federal, state, and local governments in the affairs of citizens, both Joe Klein and the papacy have told us, is due to Roman Catholic influence in American politics. Corrupt municipal political machines were constructed and operated by Roman Catholics, following the Church-State's support for a policy of effective interference: Tammany Hall, the Daley machine, the Curley machine, and so on. Klein could have mentioned much more.[10] Following Vatican directives, Roman Catholic politicians, legislators, and intellectuals brought us the Progressive movement, the labor union movement, the graduated income tax, the New Deal, and the growth of government in the United States. The growth of government was not only in the United States, of course; perhaps the United States, because it is the nation in which Biblical Christianity had the most impact, is also the country where the least growth of government has occurred. In other nations in which Roman Catholic influence was greater, governments became even more socialist than they did in the United States. In Italy, for example, an overwhelmingly Roman Catholic country, the Communist Party was once the largest Communist Party in the world outside the Soviet Union and China. The nationalization, taxation, and regulation of private enterprise and life have progressed much further in other countries than they have in the United States. One of the reasons is that Roman Catholicism theoretically justifies and has historically fostered authoritarian, interventionist – not to say totalitarian – governments.[11]

---

10. See Aaron I. Abell, "The Reception of Leo XIII's Labor Encyclical in America, 1891-1919," *The Review of Politics*, October 1945. As early as the 1841, bishop John Hughes of New York organized a slate of candidates for the state assembly elections. "Seven of his ten nominees repudiated his support, but all ten were elected, with the twenty-two hundred votes on the Catholic ticket holding the balance. Hughes had demonstrated that the Democrats could not carry the city [New York] without Catholic support" (David J. O'Brien, *Public Catholicism*, second edition. Maryknoll, New York: Orbis Books, 1996, 46).

11. "Although Jesuit control [in Paraguay] came to an end, in theory, a half century before independence, nevertheless their lessons in complete and abject submission to the clerical will continued to be taught by their successors, the Franciscans. Thus,

Pius XI, not wanting to boast, of course, wrote in his encyclical, *Quadragesimo Anno* (1931):

> We do not, of course, deny that even before the Encyclical of Leo, some rulers had provided for the more urgent needs of the working classes and had checked the more flagrant acts of injustice perpetrated against them. But after the Apostolic Voice had sounded from the Chair of Peter throughout the world, the leaders of the nations became at last more fully conscious of their obligations, and set to work seriously to promote a broader social policy.[12]

Rerum Novarum, by clearly aligning the Roman Church-State with the working classes and against capitalism, thus fostering class warfare, was the voice of moral authority needed to ensure the development of effective interference by all governments in the twentieth century. Pius XI wrote:

> It is not surprising, therefore, that under the teaching and guidance of the Church, many learned priests and laymen earnestly devoted themselves to the problem of elaborating social and economic science in accordance with the conditions of our age.... Under the guidance and in light of Leo's Encyclical [*Rerum Novarum*, 1891] was thus evolved a truly Christian social science, which continues to be fostered and enriched daily by the tireless labors of those picked men whom we have named the auxiliaries of the Church.... Nor were these the only blessings, which followed from the Encyclical. The doctrine of *Rerum Novarum* began little by little to penetrate among those who, being outside Catholic unity, do not recognize the authority of the Church; and these Catholic principles of sociology gradually became part of the intellectual heritage of the whole human race. Thus too, we rejoice that the Catholic truths proclaimed so vigorously by our illustrious Predecessor [Leo XIII], are advanced and advocated not merely in non-Catholic books and journals, but frequently also in legislative assemblies and in courts of justice.[13]

---

when the time came for the Paraguayans to assume control of their own political destinies, they were the least fit for the task of all the peoples of Spanish America. How natural was it then, that they should bow submissively to the absolute will of a domineering personality" (J. Lloyd Mecham, *Church and State in Latin America: A History of Politico-Ecclesiastical Relations*. Chapel Hill: University of North Carolina Press, 1934, 235-236). As we shall discuss in Part 2, the Roman Church-State not only has a moral and constitutional affinity for authoritarian and totalitarian regimes, its political theory justifies and engenders such regimes.

12. Pius XI, *Quadragesimo Anno* (1931), 14.
13. Pius XI, *Quadragesimo Anno* (1931), 11.

Pius XI here discloses the enormous influence *Rerum Novarum* had not only within the Church-State, but also in non-Catholic intellectual circles worldwide, and in political and judicial activity worldwide.[14] He refers darkly to "those picked men whom we have named the auxiliaries of the Church" who have been so instrumental in ending the free enterprise system of the nineteenth century and substituting a system of effective interference by government in the twentieth century. Who those "picked men" are, I do not know.[15]

Before we continue our discussion of *Rerum Novarum* and the economic thought of the Roman Church-State, we ought to define *capitalism*. Capitalism, which is sometimes called the free enterprise system, the private property order, or *laissez-faire*, is the economic system in which individuals and groups are free to own property of all sorts and to dispose of it as they see fit. It is the economic counterpart to the political system of limited government in which the only functions of government are the punishment of evildoers, that is, criminals, and the praise of the good.[16] In a purely capitalist system, government does not interfere with private property, free association, freedom of contract, or the other freedoms protected in the Bill of Rights. Its only function is the apprehension and punishment of criminals, and the protection of life and property from criminal action. In a capitalist system, government does not own or control the means of production, subsidize churches or other institutions, provide or pay for education, retirement benefits, health insurance, recreation, or any of the other innumerable goods and services provided by governments at the end of the twentieth century.

Capitalism is not a system of greed, as its myriad detractors, including the Roman Church-State, have alleged. The German sociologist

14. John XXIII wrote in *Mater et Magistra* (1961): "…the State should see to it that labor agreements are entered into according to the norms of justice and equity…. On this point Leo XIII's letter delineated the broad principles regarding just and proper human existence. These principles modern States have adopted in one way or another in their social legislation, and they have…contributed much to the establishment and promotion of that new section of legal science known as labor law" (21).

15. Michael Novak noted that "In the crowd in St. Peter's Square receiving the new Pope's [Pius XI] first blessing [January 1922] was Benito Mussolini, soon to assume dictatorial power in Italy and to become the first exponent of totalitarianism, which he described succinctly as *la feroce volonta* – the ferocious will of a single leader" (*The Catholic Ethic and the Spirit of Capitalism*, New York: The Free Press, 1993, 71).

16. See *Romans* 13.

49

Max Weber established that point a century ago. In his seminal book *The Protestant Ethic and the Spirit of Capitalism*, Weber argued:

> The impulse to acquisition, pursuit of gain, of money, of the greatest possible amount of money, has in itself nothing to do with capitalism. This impulse exists and has existed among waiters, physicians, coachmen, artists, prostitutes, dishonest officials, soldiers, nobles, crusaders, gamblers, and beggars. One may say that it has been common to all sorts and conditions of men at all times and in all countries of the earth, wherever the objective possibility of it is or has been given.... Unlimited greed for gain is not in the least identical with capitalism, and is still less its spirit. Capitalism may even be identical with the restraint, or at least a rational tempering, of this irrational impulse. But capitalism is identical with the pursuit of profit, and forever renewed profit, by means of continuous, rational, capitalistic enterprise.[17]

Weber pointed out that far from encouraging unscrupulousness and sharp practice, capitalism curbs them:

> The universal reign of absolute unscrupulousness in the pursuit of selfish interests by the making of money has been a specific characteristic of precisely those countries whose bourgeois-capitalistic development, measured according to Occidental standards, has remained backward. As every employer knows, the lack of *conscienziosita* [conscience or conscientiousness] of the labourers of such countries, for instance Italy as compared with Germany, has been and to a certain extent still is, one of the principal obstacles to their capitalistic development. Capitalism cannot make use of the labour of those who practice the doctrine of undisciplined *liberum arbitrium* [free will], any more than it can make use of the businessman who seems absolutely unscrupulous in his dealings with others....[18]

The British socialist, R. H. Tawney, writing an introduction to Weber's book, summarized part of Weber's argument:

> The pioneers of the modern economic order were, he [Weber] argues, *parvenus*, who elbowed their way to success in the teeth of the established aristocracy of land and commerce. The tonic that braced them for the conflict was a new conception of religion, which taught them to regard the pursuit of wealth as not merely an advantage, but a

---

17. Max Weber, *The Protestant Ethic and the Spirit of Capitalism*, 17.
18. Weber, *The Protestant Ethic and the Spirit of Capitalism*, 57.

duty. This conception welded into a disciplined force the still feeble bourgeoisie, heightened its energies, and cast a halo of sanctification round its convenient vices. What is significant, in short, is not the strength of the motive of economic self-interest, which is the common-place of all ages and demands no explanation. It is the change of moral standards which converted a natural frailty into an ornament of the spirit, and canonized as the economic virtues habits which in earlier ages had been denounced as vices. The force which produced it was the creed associated with the name Calvin. Capitalism was the social counterpart of Calvinist theology.[19]

"Calvinism," Tawney continued,

> at least in certain phases of its history, was associated with an attitude to questions of social ethics which contemporaries regarded as peculiarly its own. Its critics attacked it as the sanctimonious ally of commercial sharp practice. Its admirers applauded it as the school of economic virtues. By the middle of the seventeenth century the contrast between the social conservatism of Catholic Europe and the strenuous enterprise of Calvinist communities had become a commonplace. "There is a kind of natural inaptness," wrote a pamphleteer in 1671, "in the Popish religion to business, whereas, on the contrary, among the Reformed, the greater their zeal, the greater their inclination to trade and industry, as holding idleness unlawful." The influence of Calvinism was frequently adduced as one explanation of the economic prosperity of Holland.[20]

Thomas Babington Macaulay, in his *History of England*,[21] echoed what a long line of observers had noted since soon after the Reformation:

> Whoever passes in Germany from a Roman Catholic to a Protestant principality; in Switzerland from a Roman Catholic to a Protestant canton; in Ireland from a Roman Catholic to a Protestant county, finds that he has passed from a lower to a higher grade of civilization. On the other side of the Atlantic the same law prevails. The Protestants of the United States have left far behind the Roman Catholics of Mexico, Peru, and Brazil.

---

19. Weber, The *Protestant Ethic and the Spirit of Capitalism*, 2.
20. Weber, *The Protestant Ethic and the Spirit of Capitalism*, 5-6.
21. London, 1889, I, 24.

ECCLESIASTICAL MEGALOMANIA

In an 1845 letter to a Mr. Foster, Charles Dickens wrote:

> In the Simplon, at the bridge of St. Maurice, where the Protestant Canton ends and a Catholic Canton begins, you might separate two perfectly distinct and different conditions of humanity by drawing a line with your stick in the dust on the ground. On the Protestant side, neatness, cheerfulness, industry, education, continued aspiration after better things. On the Catholic side, dirt, disease, ignorance, squalor and misery. I have so constantly observed the like of this since I first came abroad, that I have a sad misgiving that the religion of Ireland lies at the root of all its sorrows.[22]

In 1846 Dickens wrote: "If I were a Swiss with £100,000, I would be as steady against the Catholic canons and the propagation of Jesuitism as any radical among them; believing the dissemination of Catholicity to be the most horrible means of political and social degradation left in the world."[23]

Now it is this economic system of capitalism, the most moral economic system on Earth because it is the only economic system logically compatible with what the Bible requires of government and personal ethics, the economic system that has permitted more people to live and to prosper than ever before in the history of the world – it is this Biblical, moral, and productive system that the Roman Church-State views as one of her greatest enemies. The Roman Church-State rightly understands this system to be the economic counterpart of Protestantism, and it is determined to destroy both Protestantism and capitalism. Thomas Aquinas expressed his hostility to the distinctive activity of capitalism, trading, in the *Summa Theologiae*:

> ...it is the function of traders to devote themselves to exchanging goods. But, as the Philosopher says (*Polit.*, I, 5, 6), there are two kinds of exchange. One may be called natural and necessary...and this kind of trading is not the function of traders, but rather of household managers or of statesmen.... The other kind of exchange is that of money for money or of things for money, not to meet the needs of life, but to acquire gain; and this kind of trading seems to be the function of traders, according to the Philosopher (*Polit.*, I, 6). Now the first kind of ex-

---

22. As quoted in Ernest Phillipps, *Papal Merchandise*. London; Charles J. Thynne, 169-170.
23. As quoted in Ernest Phillipps, *Papal Merchandise*, 169-170.

change is praiseworthy, because it serves natural needs, but the second is justly condemned, because, in itself, it serves the desire for gain, which knows no limit but extends to infinity.[24]

In writing this, Thomas was echoing the consensus of pre-Christian pagan (Greek and Roman) economic thought, and the State-Church has carried that ancient, pagan consensus into the modern era.

Leo XIII's "unerring rules," laid down in *Rerum Novarum*, began with an adoption of the Marxist analysis of capitalism. Discussing the transition from medieval feudalism and guild socialism to capitalism, Leo XIII wrote:

> In fact, new developments in industry, new techniques striking out on new paths, changed relations of employer and employee, abounding wealth among a very small number and destitution among the masses, increased self-reliance on the part of workers as well as a closer bond of union with one another....[25]

Here we see a telltale Marxist reference to changed relations among employers and employees resulting from new techniques and new developments in industry, resulting in the concentration of wealth in the hands of the few and increased poverty among the masses. Leo XIII used Marxist analysis and categories to describe the industrial system of the nineteenth century: "It is hard indeed to fix the boundaries of the

---

24. Question 77, Article 4, in Arthur Eli Monroe, *Early Economic Thought: Selections from Economic Literature Prior to Adam Smith*. Harvard University Press, 1930, 63. Thomas was also opposed to interest-taking as well: "...to receive usury for money lent is, in itself, unjust..." (*Summa Theologiae*, Q.78, Article 1). The twentieth-century economist Jacob Viner wrote: "Among the Greek and Roman philosophers hostile or contemptuous attitudes towards trade and the merchant were common, based in the main on aristocratic and snobbish prejudice, and with no or naïve underpinning of economic argument. Thus Aristotle maintained that trade was an unseemly activity for nobles or gentlemen, a 'blameable' activity. He insisted that wealth was essential for nobility, but it must be inherited wealth. Wealth was also an essential need of the state, but it should be obtained by piracy or brigandage, and by war for the conquest of slaves, and should be maintained by slave workers....The early Christian fathers on the whole took a suspicious if not definitely hostile attitude towards the trade of the merchant or middleman, as being sinful or conducive to sin ("Early Attitudes Towards Trade and the Merchant" in *Essays on the Intellectual History of Economics*, Douglas Irwin, editor. Princeton University Press, 1991, 39-40). Of course, piracy, brigandage, and the conquest of slaves was exactly what happened in Central and South America under the auspices of the Roman Catholic states of Europe.

25. Leo XIII, *Rerum Novarum* (1891), 1.

rights and duties within which the rich and the proletariat – those who furnish material things and those who furnish work – ought to be restricted in relation to each other."[26] Leo concluded, "In any event, We see clearly, and all are agreed that the poor must be speedily and fittingly cared for, since the great majority of them live unreservedly in miserable and wretched conditions."[27] Capitalism was responsible for these miserable and wretched conditions,[28] conditions that were inherently unjust and immoral, conditions that had not existed in medieval times.

During those happier times, according to Leo, the Church-State and her institutions had protected workers from exploitation.[29] Now, when the Church-State has been attacked by so-called reformers, and when the ancient institutions of feudalism have disappeared, the workers are left utterly defenseless:

> After the old trade guilds had been destroyed in the last century [the eighteenth], and no protection was substituted in their place,... it gradually came about that the present age handed over the workers, each alone and defenseless, to the inhumanity of employers and the unbridled greed of competitors. A devouring usury, although often condemned by the Church, but practiced nevertheless under another form by avaricious and grasping men, has increased the evil; and in addition the whole process of production as well, as trade in every kind of goods has been brought almost entirely under the power of a few, so that a very few rich and exceedingly rich men have laid a yoke almost of slavery on the unnumbered masses of non-owning workers.[30]

26. Leo XIII, *Rerum Novarum* (1891), 4.
27. Leo XIII, *Rerum Novarum* (1891), 5.
28. John XXIII agreed that "...the order of economic affairs was, in general, radically disturbed [at the time of *Rerum Novarum*]" (*Mater et Magistra* [1961], 12).
29. In his encyclical *Inscrutabile*, Leo XIII wrote: "The eighteenth century destroyed the old corporations and guilds which had provided protection for the poor and lowly; and it substituted nothing in their place. Henceforth, the workers found themselves defenceless, delivered to the greed of their masters. The concentration of power and resources in the hands of a few is a distinctive feature of the economy today, the result of unbridled competition" (quoted in Rhodes, *The Power of Rome in the Twentieth Century*, 103).
30. Leo XIII, *Rerum Novarum* (1891), 6. James Sadowsky, S.J. of Fordham University commented: "No socialist, no liberation theologian could have brought forth a stronger indictment" ("Classical Social Doctrine in the Roman Catholic Church," *Religion, Economics and Social Thought*, Walter Block and Irving Hexham, editors. Canada: The Fraser Institute, 1986, 4). Ironically, when Leo XIII was writing about "wage slavery," the Roman Church-State endorsed slavery, and had done so for 1,400 years.

Leo XIII lamented the destruction of the medieval guild system, the guild socialism that had rendered the medieval economy virtually stagnant for a thousand years, and the fact that the "present age," which had been roundly denounced by his predecessor in the *Syllabus of Errors*, handed over the solitary and defenseless worker to the inhumanity and greed of the capitalists. Usury – that is, receiving interest on loans – has aggravated the wickedness of capitalism, and the whole process of production and trade has been usurped by a few very rich and powerful men. So much so, Leo XIII wrote, that the capitalist system could be described as a form of virtual slavery. The resemblance between the sentiments of the encyclical and the writings of Marx are not coincidental; Leo XIII is deliberately adopting a Marxist analysis of the capitalist system. Marx also referred to capitalism as a system of wage slavery.[31]

Leo XIII even adopted Marx's theory of value:

> To produce these goods the labors of the workers, whether they expend their skill and strength on farms or in factories, is most efficacious and necessary. Nay, in this respect, their energy and effectiveness are so important that it is incontestable that the wealth of nations originates from no other source than from the labor of workers....[32]

Labor alone – "no other source," Leo wrote – is the source of the wealth of nations.

There is, to be sure, no coincidence between the statements of Marx and Leo XIII on the one hand, and actual history on the other. Capitalism allowed workers and their children to live and flourish as medieval feudalism and socialism had not, so that during the wretched and miserable nineteenth century – so cruel compared to the beatific thirteenth and fourteenth centuries, not to mention the paradisiacal ninth and tenth centuries – the population of those nations that had passed from the long dark night of Roman Catholic economy into the dawn of capitalism multiplied several times. The Protestant United States, not having so much economic and political baggage to jettison as the Old World, and not burdened with the Roman Church-State as the

---

31. Pius XI later wrote:"…it is patent that in our days not alone is wealth accumulated but immense power and despotic economic domination is concentrated in the hands of a few…" (*Quadragesimo Anno* [1931], 50).

32. Leo XIII, *Rerum Novarum* (1891), 51.

unfortunate wretches of Latin America[33] were, led the way.[34] Hundreds of thousands of people – especially children – who had formerly died each year because of Leo XIII's vaunted medieval economic system, now lived in capitalism and freedom.

After his aristocratic-Marxist attack on capitalism, Leo XIII attacked socialism and defended private property.[35] There is sort of a moral equivalence theme that runs through the papal encyclicals: Capitalism is bad, but so is socialism, or at least Communism. Both must be condemned.[36] In many encyclicals, either both are condemned, or capitalism alone. In the major documents that emerged from Vatican II, capitalism is condemned, but Communism is not even mentioned. John

---

33. Keating, the sympathetic translator of Pablo Joseph de Arriaga's *The Extirpation of Idolatry in Peru*, noted: "The Spanish means of controlling the Indian population of their new territory was almost as efficient as the rule of the Inca, and far more ruthless" (xii). Peru, it should be noted, at that time included all of modern Peru, plus Ecuador, Bolivia, and northern Chile.

34. "Perhaps even more striking from the standpoint of our analysis is the comparison between the pioneering activities of Catholic and Protestant settlers in the New World. Moog's perceptive, if impressionistic, analysis shows how the difference between the 'bandeirantes' or 'piratic' settlements in Brazil and the more economically expansive and democratic settlements in the [North] American colonies can be largely attributed to differences in religious outlook among the Catholic and Puritan settlers" (S. N. Eisenstadt, "The Protestant Ethic Thesis in an Analytical and Comparative Framework," in *The Protestant Ethic and Modernization: A Comparative View*, 9).

35. Leo XIII, *Rerum Novarum* (1891), 7-8.

36. Fulton J. Sheen, a Roman bishop, television personality, and popularizer of Roman doctrine in the United States in the mid-twentieth century, wrote: "The Church says both [capitalism and communism] are wrong, for though the right to property is personal, the use is social.... The Christian concept denies there is an absolutely owned private property exclusive of limits set by the common good of the community and responsibility to the community" (*Communism and the Conscience of the West*. New York: Bobbs-Merrill, 1948, 79-80). Bishop Sheen seemed to be countenancing the use of force when he wrote: "Something had to be done to counteract individual selfishness and economic inequalities and the flouting of standards; some way had to be discovered to lift men out of their individual egotism and make them look for the good of all, but how make man realize he is his brother's keeper? Religion could have done it by restoring a sense of morality and justice from the *inside*, but since religion was rejected as a solution, partly because minds had lost the love of truth, there was only one way left, and that was to *force* them to live for the general welfare; that is, seize wealth and use power to equalize inequalities.... If the sheep will not of themselves run together in the unity of the sheepfold, then dogs must be sent barking at their heels. If individuals will not be responsive to their God-given consciences prompting them to recognize their social responsibilities, then dictators will force them to do so." As we shall see in Part 2, Roman Catholic political thought engenders such dictators.

XXIII maintained the usual pattern of moral condemnation in his 1961 encyclical *Mater et Magistra*: "For the unregulated competition which so-called liberals espouse or the class struggle in the Marxist sense, are utterly opposed to Christian teaching and also to the very nature of man" (23). John XXIII condemned unregulated competition without any qualification, but he condemned class struggle only in the "Marxist sense." Capitalism is condemned in unqualified terms, socialism in qualified terms. Furthermore, as we have seen, the Roman Church-State's defense of property is not a defense of private property on moral principle, but a semi-defense of private property as a secondary and subordinate right, a right created by human reason and government, not by natural or divine law, as common property is. This semi-defense of property is found not only in Leo XIII, but also in all the economic thought of the Roman Church-State, and it leads the Church to endorse fascism and reject Communism.

Leo XIII, perhaps innovating a little with Thomas, wrote that to own goods privately is a right "natural to man," but he makes the distinction that while property may be privately owned, it must be publicly used. He wrote:

> To own goods privately, as We saw above, is a right natural to man, and to exercise this right, especially in life in society, is not only lawful; but also clearly necessary.... But if the question be asked: How ought man use his possessions, the Church replies without hesitation: "As to this point, man ought not regard external goods as his own, but as common...."[37]

Leo XIII's distinction between private legal ownership and common use is the economic and legal theory behind twentieth-century fascism. In Communist states, property – that is, the means of production – is both legally owned and controlled by the government. This "complete collectivization" is condemned by the Roman Church-State. But in fascist states, much property is privately owned, while being regulated and controlled by the government for public use and the

---

37. Leo XIII, *Rerum Novarum* (1891), 36. "It has been argued since 1950 that the conception of a natural right to property is an importation into Catholic theology. It is in fact a Protestant innovation, curiously enough, and over the last 90 years it has been successively squeezed out [of Catholic theology] again" (Anthony Waterman in *Religion, Economics and Social Thought*, Block and Hexham, editors, 37).

common good. Under fascism, property owners may keep their property titles and deeds, but the use of their property is, as Leo XIII wrote, "common." Fascism is a form of socialism that retains the forms and trappings of capitalism, but not its substance. Under fascism, property titles and deeds are intact, but the institution of private property has disappeared. Government regulations and mandates have replaced it. For this distinction between legal ownership and actual use, the fascists owe a debt to the Roman Church-State.[38]

The economist Mises explained:

> ...nowadays there are tendencies to abolish the institution of private property by a change in the laws determining the scope of the actions which the proprietor is entitled to undertake with regard to things which are his property. While retaining the term private property, these reforms aim at the substitution of public ownership for private ownership. This tendency is the characteristic mark of the plans of various schools of Christian socialism and of national socialism. But few of the champions of these schools have been so keen as the Nazi philosopher Othmar Spann who explicitly declared that the realization of his plans would bring about a state of affairs in which the institution of private

---

38. "In order to place definite limits on the controversies that have arisen over ownership and its inherent duties there must be first laid down as a foundation a principle established by Leo XIII: The right of property is distinct from its use" (Pius XI, *Quadragesimo Anno* [1931], 47). The Jesuits controlled Paraguay for 150 years and in that time created the sort of theocratic fascist state that results from Thomism. Thompson's comments on the Jesuit regime in Paraguay are apropos: "The Jesuits had a fairer and better field for the display of their peculiar characteristics, and for the successful establishment of the principles of their constitution, during the existence of the Government founded by them in Paraguay, than ever fell to the lot of any other society or select body of men." What was that Jesuit society like? "At each Reduction [village] the natives were allowed to select a secular magistracy, with limited and unimportant powers over such temporal affairs as could be intrusted to them without impairing the theocratic feature of the Government." "The principles of socialism or communism – very much as now understood – governed all the Reductions. Everything necessary to the material comfort and prosperity of the Indians was common." While each family was given a private plot to cultivate, "the earnings of the whole were deposited in common storehouses at each Reduction, and distributed by the Jesuits in such portions to each individual as necessity required.... Everything was conducted in obedience to them, and nothing contrary to their orders was tolerated. Rigid rules of conduct and hours of labor were prescribed, and the violators of them were subject to corporal punishments" (R.W. Thompson, *The Footprints of the Jesuits*, New York: Thomas Y. Crowell Company, 1894, 168-176). Leo XIII was, of course, educated by the Jesuits.

property will be preserved only in a "formal sense, while in fact there will be only public ownership."[39]

When the Roman Church-State sometimes may appear to defend private property, it is defending property only in the formal sense. Private property, which is not part of the natural law, is condemned on moral grounds, because of inequality. So while the Roman Church-State seems to defend private property at times, it uses the term in an equivocal manner.

---

39. Ludwig von Mises, *Human Action: A Treatise on Economics.* Third edition. Chicago: Henry Regnery Company [1949] 1966, 682-683.

Four

Subsequent Encyclicals

AFTER Leo XIII, other popes, including John Paul II, have repeatedly endorsed *Rerum Novarum*. We have already heard from Pius XI; John Paul II wrote in his encyclical *Laborem Exercens* (1981):

> This question [which John Paul II refers to as the "proletariat question"] and the problems connected with it gave rise to a just social reaction and caused the impetuous emergence of a great burst of solidarity between workers, first and foremost industrial workers. The call to solidarity and common action addressed to workers – especially to those engaged in narrowly specialized, monotonous, and depersonalized work in industrial plants when the machine tends to dominate man – was important and eloquent from the point of view of social ethics. It was the reaction against the degradation of man as the subject of work, and against the unheard of accompanying exploitation in the field of wages, working conditions, and social security for the worker.[1]

John Paul II not only accepted a Marxist analysis of industrial work,[2] which degrades and exploits man, but he specifically said that the reaction against capitalism was "just."

> Following the lines laid down by the Encyclical *Rerum Novarum* and many later documents of the Church's Magisterium, it must be frankly recognized that the reaction against the system of injustice and harm that cried to heaven for vengeance and that weighed heavily upon the

---

1. John Paul II, *Laborem Exercens* (1981), 20. "…we must first of all recall a principle that has always been taught by the Church: the principle of the priority of labor over capital" (28).
2. We ought to keep in mind that John Paul II's observation of industrial work did not occur in a capitalist or even a semi-capitalist country; it occurred in Communist Poland.

workers in that period of rapid industrialization was justified from the point of view of social morality. This state of affairs was favored by the liberal sociopolitical system....[3]

In these words John Paul II described capitalism as "the system of injustice and harm that cried to heaven for vengeance." In addition to the falsity of his authoritative and allegedly infallible declarations, we must point out that John Paul II has not used such language in speaking of Communism or socialism. Moreover, he made it clear that he was attacking not only the economic system, but also the entire "liberal sociopolitical system." It is not just capitalism that John Paul II condemned, but its political counterpart, a limited constitutional republic.

In the 1960's Paul VI assailed capitalism whenever he could. His encyclical, *Populorum Progressio, On the Progress of Peoples*, issued in 1967, was a sustained assault on capitalism. He wrote:

> But it is unfortunate that on these new conditions of society a system has been constructed which considers profit as the key motive for economic progress, competition as the supreme law of economics, and private ownership of the means of production as an absolute right that has no limits and carries no corresponding social obligation. This unchecked liberalism leads to dictatorship rightly denounced by Pius XI as producing "the internal imperialism of money." One cannot condemn such abuses too strongly.... But if it is true that a type of capitalism has been the source of excessive suffering, injustices and fratricidal conflicts whose effects still persist, it would also be wrong to attribute to industrialization itself evils that belong to the woeful system which accompanied it.[4]

Paul VI wanted industrialization, but not capitalism; that is also what the Marxists want. He even denounced capitalism as a "woeful system" and a "dictatorship," while rejecting on moral grounds profit-making, competition, and private ownership of the means of production.

---

3. John Paul II, *Laborem Exercens* (1981), 20. John Paul II repeated the historical opposition of the Roman Church-State to capitalism: "From this point of view, the position of 'rigid' capitalism continues to remain unacceptable, namely the position that defends the exclusive right to private ownership of the means of production as an untouchable 'dogma' of economic life. The principle of respect for work demands that this right should undergo a constructive revision, both in theory and in practice" (*Laborem Exercens* [1981], 35-36).

4. Paul VI, *Populorum Progressio* (1967), 26.

Commenting on *Populorum Progressio*, Ayn Rand asked, "If concern for human poverty and suffering were one's primary motive, one would seek to discover their cause. One would not fail to ask: Why did some nations develop, while others did not?"[5] Rand's *modus tollens* is conclusive: Concern for human poverty is not the Vatican's primary motive. The Roman Church-State was in no position to ask any questions about economic development, for its own teachings and hegemony were the cause of economic stagnation, poverty, and suffering. Where those teachings had been abandoned and its hegemony cast off, economies developed rapidly, after more than a millennium of economic stagnation under its rule.

Populorum Progressio was such a strident attack on capitalism that the editorial staff of *The Wall Street Journal* made excuses for it.[6] The *Journal*[7]

> declared, in effect, that the Pope didn't mean it. The encyclical, it alleged, was just a misunderstanding caused by some mysterious conspiracy of Vatican translators who misinterpreted the Pope's ideas in transferring them from the original Latin into English. "His Holiness may not be showering compliments on the free market system, but he is not at all saying what the Vatican's English version appeared to make him say."[8]

Unfortunately for *The Wall Street Journal*, and all others who try to excuse the infallible pope by saying he has incompetent translators, the Vatican has had thirty years to correct the allegedly incorrect translation, but the encyclical reads as it did in 1967. The Vatican means what it says, though it does not always say what it means.

Peter T. Bauer of the London School of Economics clearly saw what the editorial writers at the *Journal* did not want to see:

> According to the opening paragraph of *Populorum Progressio*, the document is to help people "to grasp their serious problems in all its dimensions...at this turning point in human history." The promise is not fulfilled. The papal letters are not theological, doctrinal or philosophical statements reaffirming Christian beliefs or helping people to

---

5. Ayn Rand, "Requiem for Man," *Capitalism: The Unknown Ideal*, New York: Signet/Penguin, 1967, 308.

6. A similar situation arose in 1996 when John Paul II endorsed the theory of evolution. At that time newspaper columnist Cal Thomas, among others, attempted to excuse the pope by claiming that his translators garbled his words.

7. May 10, 1967, as quoted by Rand.

8. Ayn Rand, "Requiem for Man," in *Capitalism: The Unknown Ideal*, 317.

find their bearings. They are political statements supported by bogus arguments, and as such can only confuse believers....The Pope has lost all contact with reality, both in what he says and what he ignores. Amidst large-scale civil conflict (as in Nigeria and Vietnam at the time of *Populorum Progressio*), massacres, mass persecution and expulsions in ldcs [lesser developed countries], the Pope wrote about the solidarity and brotherhood of humanity in the less developed world, and also stated that governments always act for the common good. He ignores the relation between culture and economic achievement and the relevance of mores and beliefs to economic performance and progress.... Even the eternal verities are overlooked. The responsibility of the person for the consequences of his actions and the fundamental distinction between mankind and the rest of creation are basic Christian tenets. They are pertinent to the issues raised by the Pope; but they are ignored throughout these documents....They [the encyclicals] are indeed even un-Christian. Their Utopian chiliastic ideology, combined with an overriding preoccupation with economic differences, is an amalgam of the ideas of millennarian sects, of the extravagant claims of the early American advocates of foreign aid, and of the Messianic component of Marxism-Leninism.... Such a stance has been regularly advanced to justify pervasive coercion and brutal policies.... *Populorum Progressio* and *Octogesima Adveniens* are documents which are immoral on several levels. To begin with they are incompetent, and they are immoral because they are incompetent.... The documents are also immoral in that they give colour to the notion that envy can be legitimate; and they spread confusion about the meaning of charity.⁹

Ayn Rand, who understood the ethical and economic differences between capitalism and collectivism, pointed out that *Populorum Progressio* "was endorsed with enthusiasm by the Communist press the world over. 'The French Communist Party newspaper, *L'Humanité*, said the encyclical was "often moving" and constructive for highlighting the evils of capitalism long emphasized by Marxists,' reports *The New York Times* (March 30, 1967)."¹⁰

∼

Pius XI published his encyclical *Divini Redemptoris* (*On Atheistic Communism*) in 1937. In the course of that encyclical letter he referred

9. "Ecclesiastical Economics: Envy Legitimized," in *Reality and Rhetoric: Studies in the Economics of Development*. Harvard University Press, 1984, 87-89.
10. Ayn Rand, "Requiem for Man," in *Capitalism: The Unknown Ideal*, 316.

to the Roman Catholic employers and industrialists in Europe and North America who "are saddled with the heavy heritage of an unjust economic regime whose ruinous influence has been felt through many generations."[11] Now, one might think that the pope was speaking of socialism or Communism, especially since that was the subject of the encyclical, but the "unjust economic regime" he was actually condemning was capitalism.[12] Apparently those same Roman Catholic businessmen had been so disturbed by his 1931 encyclical *Quadragesimo Anno* that they had succeeded in blocking its dissemination. The pope asked:"What is to be thought of the action of those Catholic employers who in one place succeeded in preventing the reading of Our Encyclical *Quadragesimo Anno* [*On Social Reconstruction*] in their local churches? Of those Catholic industrialists who even to this day have shown themselves hostile to a labor movement that We Ourselves recommended?"[13] One can only praise those Roman Catholic businessmen. If only they had been as enlightened as Luther, they might have heated their factories by burning papal encyclicals in their furnaces.[14]

What had Pius XI said in his 1931 encyclical that so disturbed some Roman Catholic businessmen? Reiterating a fundamental principle of Roman Catholic political thought, Pius taught that "...the state brings private ownership into harmony with the needs of the common good...."[15] In order to do that, the state must reorder the economic

11. Pius XI, *On Atheistic Communism* (1937), 50.

12. John C. Cort, a Catholic socialist, commented,"It is significant that about one-quarter of this encyclical...is devoted to communism and three-quarters is devoted to 'the lamentable ruin into which amoral liberalism has plunged us' and advice about how to scramble out of it. The encyclical might better have been entitled 'On Atheistic Capitalism' " (*Christian Socialism*, 300).

13. Pius XI, *Divini Redemptoris, On Atheistic Communism* (1937), 50. Abell reported that "Catholic employers, with few exceptions, did not take kindly to the three 'Programs' – Rerum Novarum, the Bishops' Program of Social Reconstruction, and the Pastoral Letter" (*American Catholicism and Social Action: A Search for Social Justice, 1865-1950*, 216).

14. Because one must praise these Roman Catholic businessmen, one must condemn those Roman Catholic priests and intellectuals who are now attempting to reinterpret the statist, fascist, and interventionist encyclicals and rewrite history in order to make it appear that the Roman Church-State has historically defended capitalism, private property, and economic freedom.

15. Pius XI, *Quadragesimo Anno* (1931), 49. The liberal Protestant magazine *Christian Century* praised *Quadragesimo Anno* as "a weighty deliverance which may in time become a notable landmark in social history" (as quoted in Abell, *American Catholicism and Social Action: A Search for Social Justice*, 238).

system, for "Property, that is, 'capital,' has undoubtedly long been able to appropriate too much to itself."[16] The ideas of the free market economists, whom Pius XI called "Manchesterian liberals," are "false" and "erroneous."[17] These erroneous ideas have allowed an immoral and manifestly unjust system to exist:

> ...the immense multitude of the non-owning workers on the one hand and the enormous riches of certain very wealthy men on the other establish an unanswerable argument that the riches which are so abundantly produced in our age of "industrialism" as it is called, are not rightly distributed and equitably made available to the various classes of the people.[18]

Therefore, the state must bring private ownership into harmony with the common good by redistributing wealth: Wealth "ought to be so distributed among individual persons and classes that the common advantage of all, which Leo XIII had praised, will be safeguarded; in other words, that the common good of all society will be kept inviolate."[19]

Pius XI endorsed a form of syndicalism,[20] advocated the theory of just wages and prices,[21] and made constant appeals to the "common good," to "nature," and to "social justice." He condemned the evil of individualism and endorsed feudalism:

> When we speak of the reform of institutions, the State comes chiefly to mind, not as if universal well-being were to be expected from its activity, but because things have come to such a pass through the evil of what we have termed "individualism," that, following upon the overthrow and near extinction of that rich social life which was once highly developed through associations of various kinds....[22] The social policy

---

16. Pius XI, *Quadragesimo Anno* (1931), 54. "Capital, however, was long able to appropriate to itself excessive advantages; it claimed all the products and profits, and left to the laborer the barest minimum necessary to repair his strength and to ensure the continuation of his class.... These false opinions and specious axioms [of the "so-called Manchester School"] were vehemently attacked...." (29). Pius XI rejected the "false opinions" of the Manchester School and adopted the false opinions of the Marxists.
17. Pius XI, *Quadragesimo Anno* (1931), 54.
18. Pius XI, *Quadragesimo Anno* (1931), 60.
19. Pius XI, *Quadragesimo Anno*, (1931), 57.
20. Pius XI, *Quadragesimo Anno* (1931), 65-68.
21. Pius XI, *Quadragesimo Anno* (1931), 72, 76.
22. Pius XI, *Quadragesimo Anno* (1931), 78.

of the State, therefore, must devote itself to the re-establishment of the Industries and Professions.[23]

Pius XI's assault on capitalism was sustained and strident:

>...the right ordering of economic life cannot be left to a free competition of forces. For from this source, as from a poisoned spring, have originated and spread all the errors of individualist economic teaching.... Free competition, while justified and certainly useful provided it is kept within certain limits, clearly cannot direct economic life – a truth which the outcome of the application in practice of the tenets of this evil individualistic spirit has more than sufficiently demonstrated. Therefore, it is most necessary that economic life be again subjected to and governed by a true and effective directing principle.[24]

Like collectivists of all stripes, Pius XI decried free competition and individualism. Like statists of all stripes he demanded – it is "most necessary," he declared – that economic life be again – notice the *again* – subjected to and governed by a true and effective governing principle. The experiment with economic freedom, Pius XI wrote, must end, and economic life must again be subjected to planning and government. Writing in the 1930s, Pius XI's ideas were little different from those being put forward by the fascists in Italy or Germany or the United States. Indeed, were the names of the authors deleted, one would be hard-pressed to tell who wrote much of this document: Mussolini, Pius XI, the New Dealers, or the theoreticians of the Nazi movement. It is no wonder some Roman Catholic businessmen had the encyclical suppressed. But the worst was yet to come.

Pius XI not only adopted the Marxist theory of the concentration of wealth but also denounced the "dictatorship" of capitalism. "In the first place, it is obvious that not only is wealth concentrated in our times but an immense power and despotic economic dictatorship is consolidated in the hands of a few...."[25] "This dictatorship," Pius XI declared,

---

23. Pius XI, *Quadragesimo Anno* (1931), 82.
24. Pius XI, *Quadragesimo Anno* (1931), 88. "Free competition, kept within definite and due limits, and still more economic dictatorship, must be effectively brought under public authority" (110).
25. Pius XI, *Quadragesimo Anno* (1931), 105. The Church-State did not decry the concentration of wealth *per se*, but the concentration of wealth in hands other than its own. During the Middle Ages, the Roman Church-State accumulated great wealth and holds enormous wealth today. When it could, the Church-State collected strict

is being most forcibly exercised by those who, since they hold the money and completely control it, control credit also and rule the lending of money. Hence they regulate the flow, so to speak, of the life-blood whereby the entire economic system lives, and have so firmly in their grasp the soul, as it were, of economic life that no one can breathe against their will.[26]

In these words one can hear the echoes of the denunciations of money and usury from the medieval Roman Church-State, denunciations that shaded almost imperceptibly into the anti-Semitism of the Roman Church-State. After all, capitalism, money, and the Jews were closely connected in the minds of the Roman Catholics, for when the Church-State succeeded in preventing Roman Catholics from taking interest on loans,[27] the Jews became the bankers of Europe. To denounce the bankers was virtually to denounce the Jews, and vice versa. "Free competition has destroyed itself," Pius XI wrote, "economic dictatorship has supplanted the free market; unbridled ambition for power has likewise succeeded greed for gain; all economic life has become tragically hard, inexorable, and cruel."[28]

After repeatedly denouncing capitalism in lurid terms, Pius XI had some kind words for socialism: "Socialism inclines toward and in a certain measure approaches the truths which Christian tradition has always held sacred; for it cannot be denied that its demands at times come very near those that Christian reformers of society justly insist upon."[29]

Not only does socialism "incline" toward and "approach" Roman Catholic principles, coming "very near" them, but

---

tithes from even the peasants' gardens. See E. Ray Canterbery, *The Literate Economist*, Harper Collins, 1995.

26. Pius XI, *Quadragesimo Anno* (1931), 106.

27. One of the advances of the Reformation was the rejection of the Aristotelian and Roman Catholic notion that money is sterile and therefore interest-taking is wrong. Troeltsch wrote: "Calvin and the Calvinistic ethic rejected the canonical veto on usury and the scholastic theory of money..." (*The Social Teaching of the Christian Churches*, II, 643).

28. Pius XI, *Quadragesimo Anno* (1931), 109.

29. Pius XI, *Quadragesimo Anno* (1931), 113. "It would seem as if Socialism...were drifting towards the truth which Christian tradition has always held in respect; for it cannot be denied that its programs often strikingly approach the just demands of Christian social reformers" (54).

...it can even come to the point that imperceptibly these ideas of the more moderate socialism will no longer differ from the desires and demand of those who are striving to remold human society on the basis of Christian principles. For certain kinds of property, it is rightly contended, ought to be reserved to the State since they carry with them a dominating power so great that cannot without danger to the general welfare be entrusted to private individuals.[30]

In the same encyclical, Pius XI wrote:

The war declared against private ownership has also abated more and more in such a way that nowadays it is not really the possession of the means of production which is attacked, but that type of social rulership, which, in violation of all justice has been seized and usurped by the owners of wealth. This rulership in fact belongs, not to the individual owners, but to the State. If these changes continue, it may well come about that gradually the tenets of mitigated socialism will no longer be different from the program of those who seek to reform human society according to Christian principles. For it is rightly contended that certain forms of property must be reserved to the State....[31]

John Paul II wrote *Sollicitudo Rei Socialis, On Social Concern* in 1987 because

It is necessary to state once more the characteristic principle of Christian social doctrine: the goods of this world are originally meant for all. The right to private property is valid and necessary, but it does not nullify the value of this principle. Private property, in fact, is under a "social mortgage," which means that it has an intrinsically social function, based upon and justified precisely by the principle of the universal destination of goods.[32]

"The teaching and spreading of her social doctrine are part of the Church's evangelizing mission," said John Paul II.[33] Its social doctrine

---

30. Pius XI, *Quadragesimo Anno* (1931), 114. John Paul II agreed: "From this point of view, therefore, in consideration of human labor and of common access to the goods meant for man, one cannot exclude the socialization, in suitable conditions, of certain means of production" (*Laborem Exercens* [1981], 35).
31. Pius XI, *Quadragesimo Anno* (1931), 55.
32. John Paul II, *Sollicitudo Rei Socialis* (1987), 42.
33. John Paul II, *Sollicitudo Rei Socialis* (1987), 41. The popes have repeated this statement innumerable times in the past century.

is based on the ideas of "...the common fatherhood of God, of the brotherhood of all in Christ...."[34]

What the Roman Church-State advocates is not materialist socialism or Communism, for it has denounced the materialism and classless society of Marx and some other socialists.[35] Nor does it advocate a revolutionary socialism in the Marxist sense. What it does advocate is an evolutionary socialism, a sort of ecclesiastical Fabianism, in order to restructure society along lines that are consistent with its ethical and social doctrine. John Paul II, in his 1987 encyclical *Sollicitudo Rei Socialis*, offered what he called "a faithful echo of the centuries-old tradition of the Church regarding the 'universal purpose of goods'...."[36] In today's world, wrote the pope, "We are...faced with a serious problem of unequal distribution of the means of subsistence originally meant for everybody."[37]

The encyclical included a statement that might be viewed as a justification of armed revolutions and wars of aggression: "Peoples ex-

---

34. John Paul II, *Sollicitudo Rei Socialis* (1987), 40. These theological ideas, which, as we have seen, are foundational to the Roman Church-State's social teaching, may easily be recalled by the acronym FOGBOM – Fatherhood Of God, Brotherhood Of Man.

35. "He [the Christian] cannot adhere to the Marxist ideology, to its atheistic materialism, to its dialectic of violence and to the way it absorbs individual freedom in the collectivity, at the same time denying all transcendence to man and his personal and collective history; nor can he adhere to the liberal ideology which believes it exalts individual freedom by withdrawing it from every limitation, by stimulating it through exclusive seeking of interest and power, and by considering social solidarities as more or less automatic consequences of individual initiatives, not as an aim and a major criterion of the value of the social organization" (Paul VI, *Octogesima Adveniens* [1971], 26). This document, *The Coming Eightieth*, commemorating the eightieth anniversary of *Rerum Novarum*, is replete with references favorable to the proletariat, proletarianism, the common good, solidarity, and so forth. Paul VI even sounds like John Kenneth Galbraith at one point: "Unlimited competition utilizing the modern means of publicity incessantly launches new products and tries to attract the consumer, while earlier industrial installations which are still capable of functioning become useless. While very large areas of the population are unable to satisfy their primary needs, superfluous needs are ingeniously created" (*Octogesima Adveniens*, May 14, 1971). It even refers to woman's "equal rights to participate in cultural, economic, social, and political life," and discusses other alleged rights: the right to work, the right to equitable remuneration, the right to assistance in case of need arising from sickness or age, labor union rights, the right to strike, the inalienable right to marriage and procreation, etc.

36. John Paul II, *Sollicitudo Rei Socialis* (1987), 7.

37. John Paul II, *Sollicitudo Rei Socialis* (1987), 9.

cluded from the fair distribution of the goods originally destined for all could ask themselves: why not respond with violence to those who first treat us with violence?"[38] It would not be the first time a pope had justified aggressive wars or socialist revolutions.[39] Not only does Roman Church-State economic thought justify wars of aggression, it also justifies crime, as we have seen in the pronouncements of Roman Catholic bishops in Brazil, following the teaching of Thomas Aquinas, that looting to satisfy needs is neither a crime nor a sin.

What stands in the way of peace, John Paul II declared, is profit: "On the contrary, in a different world, ruled by concern for the common good of all humanity, or by concern for the 'spiritual and human development of all' instead of by the quest for individual profit, peace would be possible...."[40] Throughout his 1987 encyclical, John Paul II frequently used the argot of the collectivists: *equality, interdependence, exploitation, human rights, common good, the social question*, etc. He frequently engaged in attacks on selfishness, individualism, and profit. What Ayn Rand wrote of *Populorum Progressio*, Paul VI's 1967 encyclical, might accurately be said of John Paul II's 1987 encyclical:

> The encyclical "Populorum Progressio" ("On the Development of Peoples") is an unusual document: it reads as if a long-repressed emotion broke out into the open past the barrier of carefully measured, cautiously calculated sentences, with the hissing pressure of centuries of silence. The sentences are full of contradictions; the emotion is consistent.... The encyclical is the manifesto of an impassioned hatred for capitalism....[41]

38. John Paul II, *Sollicitudo Rei Socialis* (1987), 10.
39. In his book on *Socialism* Mises wrote: "The true aggressors, say these German, Italian and Japanese nationalists, are those nations who by means of trade and migration barriers have arrogated to themselves the lion's share of the natural riches of the earth. Has not the Pope [Christmas Eve Broadcast, *The New York Times*, December 25, 1941] himself declared that the root causes of the World Wars are 'that cold and calculating egoism which tends to hoard the economic resources and materials destined for the use of all to such an extent that the nations less favored by nature are not permitted access to them'? The war that Hitler, Mussolini, and Hirohito kindled was from this point of view a just war, for its only aim was to give to the have-nots what, by virtue of natural and divine right, belongs to them" (507).
40. John Paul II, *Sollicitudo Rei Socialis* (1987), 10.
41. Ayn Rand, "Requiem for Man," in *Capitalism: The Unknown Ideal*, 297. The popes, however, had not been silent. Their hatred for capitalism was clearly expressed in the nineteenth century. Their disdain for merchants, for trading, and for interest taking had been a matter for record for centuries.

Continuing the Marxist analysis of capitalism that had been adopted by Leo XIII at the end of the nineteenth century and repeated by every pope who has written on these issues in the past hundred years,[42] John Paul II wrote in 1987: "Everyone recognizes the reality and growing seriousness of this problem in the industrialized countries.... the sources of work seem to be shrinking, and thus the opportunities for employment are decreasing rather than increasing."[43] This, of course, is Marx's thesis of the immiseration of the proletariat under capitalism, resulting in a growing army of unemployed workers that will finally overthrow their cruel and ruthless masters, the capitalists.

John Paul II reiterated that "...the Church's social doctrine adopts a critical attitude towards both liberal capitalism and Marxist collectivism."[44] Both concepts, he wrote, in keeping with the moral equivalence theme of the Vatican, are "imperfect and in need of radical correction."

---

42. For example, Paul VI: "Unless combated and overcome by social and political action, the influence of the new industrial and technological order favors the concentration of wealth, power and decision-making in the hands of a small public or private controlling group. Economic injustice and lack of social participation keep a man from attaining his basic human and civil rights" (*The Synodal Document on the Justice on the World*, November 1971, approved by Paul VI).
43. John Paul II, *Sollicitudo Rei Socialis* (1987), 18.
44. John Paul II, *Sollicitudo Rei Socialis* (1987), 21.

Five
Feudalism and Corporativism

ONE OF THE most influential laymen responsible for articulating and implementing Roman economic thought was the Italian philosopher and politician, Amintore Fanfani. Fanfani was a leader of the Christian Democratic Party in Italy in the middle of the twentieth century. He was elected to the Constituent Assembly in 1946 and to Parliament in 1948. He served as Minister of Labor in 1947, Minister of Agriculture in 1951, Minister of the Interior in 1954, was Premier in 1954, and again from 1958 to 1963. He was Minister of Foreign Affairs from 1965 to 1968, when he was elected President of the Italian Senate. In 1934 Fanfani published *Catholicism, Protestantism and Capitalism* (*Cattolicesimo e Protestantesimo nella Formazione Storica del Capitalismo*), which was immediately translated into English and published in London in 1935 by the Roman Catholic publishing house Sheed and Ward.

The theme of the book, based on the Roman Church-State social doctrine, was that "the essence of capitalism ... can only meet with the most decided repugnance on the part of Catholicism."[1] Elaborating on the official Roman Church-State denunciations of capitalism, its praise for feudalism[2] and corporativism,[3] and its calls for re-establishing a

---

1. Amintore Fanfani, *Catholicism, Protestantism, and Capitalism*. University of Notre Dame Press, 1984, 149.

2. "At one period there existed a social order which though by no means perfect in every respect, corresponded nevertheless in a certain measure to right reason..." (Pius XI, *Quadragesimo Anno* [1931], 47-48). The Roman Church-State created this social order: "...the Church has given new life to human society. Under its influence arose prodigious charitable organizations, great guilds of artisans and workingmen of every type. These guilds, ridiculed as 'medieval' by the liberalism of the last century, are today claiming the admiration of our contemporaries in many countries who are endeavoring to revive them in some modern form" (Pius XI, *On Atheistic Communism* [1937], 37). The "contemporaries" of whom Pius spoke in the 1930's included the fascist parties of Europe.

3. "We have indicated how a sound prosperity is to be restored according to the

corporativist social order,[4] Fanfani's book remains one of the best summaries of Roman economic thought yet written. Unlike Michael Novak's and Robert Sirico's recent attempts to place a capitalist spin on Roman Catholic social thought,[5] Fanfani's is a fairly accurate statement of Roman economic thought. Fanfani's book is a counterpart to Weber's, for he provided another aspect of the argument, an aspect that Weber had not developed: Catholicism is inimical to capitalism.[6]

Following the popes, Fanfani described feudalism in favorable terms:

---

true principles of a sane corporative system, which respects the proper hierarchic structure of society..." (Pius XI, *On Atheistic Communism* [1937], 32). The proper hierarchic structure of society is based on the idea that "It is not true that all have equal rights in civil society" (*On Atheistic Communism* [1937], 33).

4. "The aim of social legislation must therefore be the re-establishment of vocational groups" (Pius XI, *Quadragesimo Anno* [1931], 41). "When we speak of the reform of the social order it is principally the state we have in mind. Not indeed that all salvation is to be hoped from its intervention, but because on account of the evil of 'individualism', as We called it, things have come to such a pass that the highly developed social life which once flourished in a variety of prosperous institutions organically linked with each other, has been damaged and all but ruined..." (40).

5. See Michael Novak, *The Catholic Ethic and the Spirit of Capitalism*, New York: Basic Books, 1993; and Robert Sirico, "Catholicism's Developing Social Teaching," *The Freeman*, December 1991. Oddly, the exact title of Novak's book was suggested by the translator of Bernard Groethuysen's 1927 study, *The Bourgeoisie: Catholic vs. Capitalism in Eighteenth-Century France*. "The title of this book," Mary Ilford wrote, "might well have been – 'The Catholic Ethic and the Spirit of Capitalism'" (x). Novak did not include a bibliography in his book, nor does the name "Groethuysen" appear in his index. Groethuysen, of course, took the opposite point of view from Novak. That is the only tenable position to take. Fischoff's comments on other Roman Catholic writers apply to Novak and Sirico as well: "Generally speaking, the reaction of Catholic writers to the Weber-Troeltsch thesis regarding the connection of Protestantism and capitalism has been to make propaganda for Catholicism. The Catholic students of this problem approach it with a distinctive bias, seeking on the one hand to find in Catholic ethics the honorific attitudes that might culminate in the industrious innerworldly ascetic conduct attributed by Weber to the Puritan; and on the other hand to defend Catholicism from any blame for capitalism, or more correctly for the spiritually dysgenic effects of capitalistic activity. The general conclusion then drawn is that since modern capitalism is an outgrowth of Protestantism, all the evils of modern capitalism are due to Protestantism, and hence the only cure for the ills of our economic life is to be found in Catholicism" (Ephraim Fischoff, "The Protestant Ethic and the Spirit of Capitalism: The History of a Controversy" in Eisenstadt, *The Protestant Ethic and Modernization: A Comparative View*, 82-83).

6. Andreski wrote: "Some weight must be assigned to the complete lack of arguments in favor of the contrary thesis that Catholicism is or was more propitious than Protestantism to the development of capitalism" ("Method and Substantive Theory in Max Weber," in Eisenstadt, *The Protestant Ethic and Modernization: A Comparative View*, 58).

ECCLESIASTICAL MEGALOMANIA

The pre-capitalist age is the period in which definite social institutions such as, for instance, the Church, the State, the Guild, act as guardians of an economic order that is not based on criteria of individual economic utility. The Corporation or Guild is typical of the period. It is the guardian of a system of economic activity in which the purely economic interests of the individual are sacrificed either to the moral and religious interests of the individual – the attainment of which is under the control of special public institutions – or to the economic and extra-economic interests of the community. Competition was restricted; the distribution of customers, hence a minimum of work, was assured; a certain system of work was compulsory; trade with various groups might be forbidden for political or religious reasons; certain practices were compulsory, and working hours were limited; there were a number of compulsory feasts; prices and rates of increase were fixed; measures were taken to prevent speculation.[7]

Fanfani reports that during the Middle Ages when the Roman Church-State was the dominant institution in Europe, the economic well-being of the individual was "sacrificed" so that the economic well-being of others might be enhanced – that is, the individual's well-being was sacrificed to the "common good." Furthermore, the individual's economic well-being was sacrificed for his own religious and moral good: "Special public institutions," meaning the Roman Church-State and its apparatus of command, coercion, and control, maintained the "moral and religious well-being" of the individual.[8] Of course, neither the individual nor the community as a whole was better off religiously, morally, or economically during the Middle Ages. The Reformation, with its rediscovery of the Bible and Christianity, which had been buried for a thousand years beneath the superstition, pageantry, preserved paganism, and corruption of the Roman Church-State, ended the rampant religious superstition of the Middle Ages[9] and elevated the

---

7. Fanfani, *Catholicism, Protestantism, and Capitalism*, 50-51.

8. That this is the normative order may be understood from these statements of Pius XI: "Such is the positive task, embracing at once theory and practice, which the Church undertakes in virtue of the mission, confided to her by Christ, of constructing a Christian society.... It is the duty of the Christian state to concur actively in this spiritual enterprise of the Church, aiding her with the means at its command..." (*On Atheistic Communism* [1937], 73).

9. See Carlos M. N. Eire, *War Against the Idols*. New York: Cambridge University Press, 1986.

mores of societies and individuals far above those of the Middle Ages. Luthy wrote:

> The Reformation marks a profound spiritual breach between the Middle Ages and the modern world, bringing a ferment into Western history which has changed its course irreversibly, far beyond the domain of the Protestant churches and communities, to imprint its mark on the whole Western world; that without Calvin we could not imagine…the Founding Fathers; that the modern industrial society, as well as creative science, the rule of law, constitutionalism, in brief the free society, first appeared (and have flourished best) in those countries which were molded by Calvinism….[10]

Fanfani continued:

> In an age in which the Catholic conception of life had a real hold over the mind [the Middle Ages], capitalistic action could only have manifested itself as something erroneous, reprehensible, spasmodic, and sinful, to be condemned by the faith and knowledge of the agent himself. Never could such an age have seen the beginning of the century-long development that has brought capitalistic society into being….As a matter of fact, we cannot doubt that in a perfectly Catholic age purely technical progress would not have found such powerful incentives as in a capitalistic civilization.[11]

This view, of course, is a Roman Catholic layman's confirmation of Max Weber's discussion of the Protestant ethic and the spirit of capitalism. Fanfani, consistently and insightfully, went even further than Weber and asserted that Roman Catholicism could never have resulted in capitalism, for the motives and behavior that created capitalism were regarded as erroneous, reprehensible, and sinful. The development of technology, one of the effects of capitalism, would also have stagnated. In fact, we need not say that Roman Catholicism merely would have thwarted the development of society and technology; it did in fact thwart their development. The Roman Catholic Middle Ages saw the development of almost no significant technical innovations.[12]

---

10. Herbert Luthy, "Once Again: Calvinism and Capitalism" in Eisenstadt, *The Protestant Ethic and Modernization: A Comparative View*, 91.

11. Fanfani, *Catholicism, Protestantism, and Capitalism*, 140–141.

12. Some economic historians regard the three-field system of crop rotation, an improvement upon the two-field system, as being the major technical innovation of the Middle Ages.

"Catholic ethics," Fanfani wrote, "in virtue of the ends they set before man and society and of the Catholic conception of human nature and creation, is necessarily in favor of State intervention...."[13] While favoring intervention, which the popes sometimes called "interference," the Roman Church-State disapproves of individualism.

> Moreover, the Catholic conception cannot grant the individualism that is a postulate of capitalism, still less can it agree that society should be organized on an individualistic basis. This is why the Popes of the last two centuries have so definitely condemned liberalism, seeking to circumscribe its effects in the economic and social spheres by indirect and direct encouragement of social legislation, and looking forward to the time when it should give place to a corporative organization of society.

Because it rejects individualism and favors state intervention, "Catholicism cannot recognize certain liberties in the absence of which capitalism becomes transformed and dies."[14] "[T]here is an unbridgeable gulf between the Catholic and the capitalistic conception of life."[15] "The essence of capitalism...can only meet with the most decided repugnance on the part of Catholicism."[16]

---

13. Fanfani, *Catholicism, Protestantism, and Capitalism*, 139.
14. Fanfani, *Catholicism, Protestantism, and Capitalism*, 142.
15. Fanfani, *Catholicism, Protestantism, and Capitalism*, 143.
16. Fanfani, *Catholicism, Protestantism, and Capitalism*, 148-149.

Six

Liberation Theology

ONE OF THE more recent forms the collectivism of the Roman Church-State has taken is liberation theology. The movement began in Latin America in the late 1960s, following Vatican II, whose pronouncements, as well as the entire body of Roman Church-State economic thought, encouraged its development. The tradition of the Church demanded action for social justice. Had not Pius XI, in the encyclical *On Atheistic Communism* referred to "...an age like ours, when unusual misery has resulted from the unequal distribution of the goods of this world"?[1] Had the pope not upheld the justice of demanding a redistribution of worldly goods when he referred to "...the very real abuses chargeable to the liberalistic economic order, and by demanding a more equitable distribution of this world's goods (objectives entirely and undoubtedly legitimate)...."?[2] Had not Thomas Aquinas himself said that need makes all goods common, and when the poor take the goods of the rich, for their own or their neighbor's benefit, it is not a sin?

In 1993 the Pontifical Biblical Commission itself explained the origin of liberation theology:

> The theology of liberation is a complex phenomenon, which ought not be oversimplified. It began to establish itself as a theological movement in the early 1970s. Over and beyond the economic, social, and political circumstances of Latin America, its starting point is to be found in two great events in the recent life of the Church: the second Vatican Council, with its declared intention of *aggiornamento* [renewal or updating] and of orienting the pastoral work of the Church toward the needs

---

1. Pius XI, *On Atheistic Communism*, March 19, 1937.
2. Pius XI, *On Atheistic Communism* (1937), 15.

of the contemporary world; and the Second General Conference of the Episcopate of Latin America [CELAM] held at Medéllin [Colombia] in 1968, which applied the teachings of the Council to the needs of Latin America. The movement has since spread also to other parts of the world (Africa, Asia, the black population of the United States).[3]

The Vatican itself traces the origin of liberation theology to the Roman Church-State, specifically to Vatican II (1962-1965) and the 1968 Conference of Roman Bishops in Medéllin, Colombia, a conference whose statements the pope himself approved. One of the influential figures at the Medéllin conference was Gustavo Gutierrez. Born in Peru in 1928, Gutierrez was ordained a Roman Church-State priest in 1959. His *Theology of Liberation* was published in Spanish in 1971. Despite those wishful thinkers who believe that the Roman Church-State has a fundamental economic disagreement with liberation theology, Gutierrez has never been reprimanded or defrocked for his publications. The only disagreements the Vatican has had with some aspects of liberation theology are its secular elements, the insufficient obsequiousness of some liberation theologians to the pope, and their sometime advocacy of a systematic use of violence to achieve goals that the Roman Church-State has always approved: social justice, the common good, and the universal destination of goods. The Church-State has never criticized the economic views of the liberation theologians.

In 1971 the Second General Assembly of the Synod of Bishops issued another document approved by the Holy See, *Justice in the World*, in which the General Assembly made the following statements:

> The mission of preaching the Gospel dictates at the present time that we should dedicate ourselves to the liberation of man even in his present existence in this world. For unless the Christian message of love and justice shows its effectiveness through action in the cause of justice in the world, it will only with difficulty gain credibility with the men of our times.[4]

---

3. Pontifical Biblical Commission, *The Interpretation of the Bible in the Church*. Washington, D. C.: United States Catholic Conference [1993] 1996, 16.

4. Second General Assembly of the Synod of Bishops, *Synodal Document on Justice in the World*. Approved by the Holy See. Boston: Daughters of St. Paul, no date [November 30, 1971], 12-13.

The evangelizing of the world "dictates" that we should liberate man "in this world" through "action in the cause of justice." In a 1986 letter to the Brazilian bishops, John Paul II wrote:

> The Church does not hesitate to defend fearlessly the just and noble cause of human rights and to support courageous reforms, leading to a better distribution of goods, including earthly goods such as education, health services, housing, and so forth.... We are convinced that the theology of liberation is not only timely but useful and necessary. It should constitute a new stage of the theological reflection initiated with the apostolic tradition and continued by the great Fathers and Doctors, by the Magisterium and by the rich patrimony of the Church's social doctrine, expressed in documents from *Rerum Novarum* to *Laborem Exercens*.[5]

In that same month, the Vatican, through the Sacred Congregation for the Doctrine of the Faith, issued the *Instruction on Christian Freedom and Liberation*. In the course of its *Instruction*, the Congregation discussed freedom: "Freedom is not the liberty to do anything whatsoever. It is the freedom to do good."[6]

The Vatican endorsed the "basic communities" of the liberation movement, making no objection to the economic thought of liberation theology,[7] and reiterated its social doctrine as "a set of principles for reflection and criteria for judgment and also directives for action so that the profound changes demanded by situations of poverty and injustice may be brought about...."[8] The *Instruction* reiterated the principles of

---

5. John Paul II, Letter to Brazilian Bishops, April 9, 1986.

6 Sacred Congregation for the Doctrine of the Faith, Joseph Cardinal Ratzinger, Prefect, *Instruction on Christian Freedom and Liberation*. Boston: Daughters of St. Paul, 1986, 16.

7. "The new basic communities or rather groups of Christians which have arisen to be witnesses to this evangelical love are a source of great hope for the Church. If they really live in unity with the local Church and the universal Church they will be a real expression of communion and a means of constructing a still deeper communion. Their fidelity to their mission will depend on how careful they are to educate their members in the fullness of the Christian Faith through listening to the Word of God, fidelity to the teaching of the Magisterium, to the hierarchical order of the Church and to the sacramental life. If this condition be fulfilled, their experience, rooted in the commitment to the complete liberation of man, becomes a treasure for the whole Church" (69). Notice that the Vatican's concerns are exclusively ecclesiastical: The basic communities must remain in subjection to the papacy. There is no objection to the economics of liberation theology, for it is in fact the economics of the Roman Church-State.

8. Sacred Congregation for the Doctrine of the Faith, *Instruction on Christian Freedom and Liberation* (1986), 72.

solidarity and subsidiarity, and declared that "the Church's doctrine is opposed to all the forms of social or political individualism."[9]

The *Instruction* condemned the "systematic recourse to violence put forward as the necessary path to liberation" as a "destructive illusion." But "One must condemn with equal vigor violence exercised by the powerful against the poor...."[10] In fact, the Church endorsed armed revolution; it merely objected to the "systematic recourse to violence": "whether there is recourse to armed struggle, which the Church's Magisterium admits as a last resort to put an end to an obvious and prolonged tyranny which is gravely damaging the fundamental rights of individuals and the common good."[11] So the Roman Church-State, in the end, has no objection to a socialist revolution. The reader must not be misled by the language of rights in some of the papal documents; the Rights of Man[12] was a theme of the French Revolution, too.

Under the headings "National and international common good," "Priority of work over capital," "In-depth reforms," "A new solidarity," and "Goods are meant for all," the *Instruction* emphasized the centuries' old principles of the Roman Church-State: "Material goods are meant for all," and "The right to private property is inconceivable without responsibilities to the common good. It is subordinated to the higher principle which states that goods are meant for all."[13]

---

9. Sacred Congregation for the Doctrine of the Faith, *Instruction on Christian Freedom and Liberation* (1986), 73. "The obstacles to the progress, which we wish for ourselves and for mankind, are obvious. The method of education very frequently still in use today encourages narrow individualism" (*Justice in the World* [1971], 16).

10. Sacred Congregation for the Doctrine of the Faith, *Instruction on Christian Freedom and Liberation* (1986), 76.

11. Sacred Congregation for the Doctrine of the Faith, *Instruction on Christian Freedom and Liberation* (1986), 79.

12. The English translation of the *Instruction*, in paragraph 32, a translation executed by Vatican translators, uses that very phrase and capitalizes it just as the French Revolutionaries did in 1789.

13. Sacred Congregation for the Doctrine of the Faith, *Instruction on Christian Freedom and Liberation* (1986), 84, 87.

Seven

The Redistributive State and Interventionism

In the United States, the influence of Roman Catholic economic thought has resulted in the creation of a redistributive state, in which the government intervenes in the economy and society in order to protect the "common good" and establish "social justice." Of course, it was not Roman Catholic economic thought exclusively that ushered in interventionist government in the twentieth century, but by the last third of the nineteenth century, the Roman Catholic Church had become the largest religious organization in the United States. By lending its moral authority to interventionist policies, the Roman Church-State played an indispensable role in the centralization, politicization, and socialization of American society and economy in the twentieth century.

The mainline Protestant churches, which, like the Roman Catholic Church, had also abandoned both Christianity and capitalism, were promoting what came to be called the Social Gospel, whose political expressions were the Progressive movement and later the New Deal. One of the prominent figures in the Social Gospel movement was Lyman Abbott, editor of the *Christian Union* and *Outlook*, and successor to Henry Ward Beecher as pastor of Plymouth Church in Brooklyn. Abbott lauded the Roman Catholic Church for its vision for social justice and "joyfully proclaimed the virtues of reforming Catholics as he recorded their deeds in his own community and throughout the country."[1] Abell pointed out that many American Roman Catholics

---

1. Aaron I. Abell, *American Catholicism and Social Action: A Search for Social Justice, 1865-1950*, 90.

were imitating the English Cardinal Henry Edward Manning, "whose success as social reformer stemmed largely from his willingness to work with men of every religious persuasion."[2] They were following, according to the American Roman Catholic Edward McSweeney, the instructions of Leo XIII in *Immortale Dei* (*On the Christian Constitution of States*), to "take part in public affairs," with a "fixed determination to infuse into all the views of the state, as most wholesome sap and blood, the wisdom and virtue of the Catholic religion."[3] This cooperation between Roman Catholics and liberal Protestants was enthusiastically endorsed by Cardinal Gibbons of Baltimore, who in his 1889 book, *Our Christian Heritage*, wrote, "far from despising or rejecting their [Protestants'] support, I would gladly hold out to them the right hand of fellowship, so long as they unite with us in striking the common foe. It is pleasant to be able to stand sometimes on the same platform with our old antagonists."[4] Not only did the Cardinal stand on the same platform with liberal Protestants when it came to social action, he stood on the same platform as religionists of all stripes at the World's Parliament of Religions held in Chicago in 1893. There the Cardinal remarked, while "we differ in faith, thank God there is one platform on which we stand united, and that is the platform of charity and benevolence."[5]

Two of the most influential Roman officials in the United States at the end of the nineteenth and beginning of the twentieth centuries were Cardinal James Gibbons of Baltimore and John A. Ryan of the Catholic University of America in Washington, D. C., both devoted disciples of Leo XIII.[6] Gibbons reversed the Church-State's initial hostility to labor unions in the United States.[7] In 1889 and 1893, two years

---

2. Abell, *American Catholicism and Social Action: A Search for Social Justice, 1865-1950*, 90.

3. As quoted in Abell, *American Catholicism and Social Action: A Search for Social Justice, 1865-1950*, 94.

4. As quoted in Abell, *American Catholicism and Social Action: A Search for Social Justice, 1865-1950*, 95. See "The Ethical Kinship between Protestant Radicalism and Catholic Conservatism," in the *Christian Register* (Unitarian), July 27, 1893.

5. As quoted in Abell, *American Catholicism and Social Action: A Search for Social Justice, 1865-1950*, 118.

6. Other important figures include Dorothy Day, founder of the *Catholic Worker*, May 1, 1933; and John LaFarge, S. J., 1880-1963, who wrote on "interracial justice."

7. See Aaron I. Abell, "The Reception of Leo XIII's Labor Encyclical in America, 1891-1919," in *The Review of Politics*, October 1945, 464-495. Sirico wrote in his essay "Catholicism's Developing Social Teaching," in *The Freeman* (December 1991, 468)

before and two years after Leo XIII issued *Rerum Novarum*, the Roman Church-State hierarchy in America, the leader of which was Cardinal Gibbons, organized two major congresses, the first in Baltimore and the second in Chicago, in order to mobilize clergy and laity for "progressive social action."[8] Speakers at these congresses, in keeping with Leo XIII's program, denounced capitalism, socialism, and Communism, and called for more government interference in the economy, especially heavy progressive taxes on the rich. Both congresses voted to establish study groups and distribute copies of *Rerum Novarum* far and wide.

The Roman Catholic priest John A. Ryan (1869-1945), who has been called "the foremost academician of the American Catholic social movement" and derogatorily nicknamed the "Right Reverend New Dealer,"[9] published his first book in 1906, *A Living Wage: Its Ethical and Economic Aspects*. It was a sustained argument for a legally mandated minimum wage, which we have had nationally since the 1930s.[10] Richard Ely, the founder of the American Economic Association and a member of the Social Gospel movement, praised the book as "the first attempt in the English language to elaborate what may be called a

---

that Cardinal Gibbons believed that the labor movement and state intervention were "the most efficacious means, almost the only means" to combat individual and corporate monopolies and their "heartless avarice which, through greed of gain, pitilessly grinds not only the men, but even the women and children in various employments."

8. Abell, as quoted in Sirico, "Catholicism's Developing Social Teaching," *The Freeman*, December 1991, 473. (Sirico cited the incorrect page in Abell.)

9. The Roman Catholic priest Charles Coughlin, a demagogic radio preacher, gave the nickname to Ryan after the Roosevelt Administration failed to nationalize industries as quickly as Coughlin wanted. Coughlin "publicized Catholic social teaching more widely than any contemporary, not only on radio, but on the public platform and after 1934 through the propaganda of the Union for Social Justice and its weekly journal, *Social Justice*" (Abell, *American Catholicism and Social Action: A Search for Social Justice, 1865-1950*, 240). As a radio preacher, Coughlin attracted a national audience estimated at ten million in 1931, far bigger than Rush Limbaugh's audience in the 1990s. Coughlin was a scathing critic of the Hoover administration and an ardent supporter of Roosevelt and the New Deal; his slogan was "Roosevelt or ruin." It was only when Roosevelt failed to implement a more thorough-going socialism by nationalizing the banks that Coughlin became a critic.

10. State governments enacted minimum wage laws as early as 1912. The first state to do so was heavily Roman Catholic Massachusetts. For a historical study of the effects of minimum wages, see Simon Rottenberg, *The Economics of Legal Minimum Wages*. Washington, D. C.: American Enterprise Institute, 1981. The deleterious effect of legally mandated minimum wages is one of the few ideas on which most economists are agreed.

Roman Catholic system of political economy."[11] Ryan's subsequent books, essays, and articles advocated many other interferences in the market: a legally mandated eight-hour workday; restrictions on the labor of women and children; the legalization of picketing during strikes; compulsory arbitration in labor disputes; state employment bureaus; unemployment insurance; legally mandated accident, sickness, and old age insurance; public housing programs; government ownership of natural monopolies; graduated income taxes; graduated inheritance taxes; prohibition of speculation in the markets; and so forth.[12] Ryan called his program "Essential Economic Socialism" and "Semi-Socialism." Ryan became the leader of a worldwide Roman Catholic movement for social reform in 1908. One of its largest and most influential member groups was the *Central Verein* in Germany.

In 1917, the Roman Church-State hierarchy in the United States formed the National Catholic War Council (later to be named the National Conference of Catholic Bishops). In 1919 its administrative committee issued a plan written by John Ryan, the *Bishops' Program of Social Reconstruction*. The plan advocated government unemployment, sickness, invalidity, and old age insurance; a federal child labor law; legal enforcement of labor's right to organize; public housing; graduated taxation on inheritances, incomes, and excess profits; regulation of public utility rates; worker participation in management, and so on.[13] It is not surprising, then, that when Franklin Roosevelt was elected President in 1932, he invited Professor Ryan to join his administration. Ryan had been a proponent of the New Deal for decades, long before Franklin Roosevelt was elected to office. Abell pointed out that "During the Great Depression of the 1930s the Catholic social movement seemingly flourished. All the immediate measures set forth in the *Bishops' Program* of 1919 were adopted in whole or in part."[14]

Ryan was vociferous in his calls for government action, and the Roman Catholic press in the United States was unanimous. In 1931

---

11. Francis L. Broderick, *Right Reverend New Dealer*. New York: Macmillan, 1963, 46.

12. Abell, "The Reception of Leo XIII's Labor Encyclical in America, 1891-1919," *The Review of Politics*, October 1945.

13 Abell, "The Reception of Leo XIII's Labor Encyclical in America, 1891-1919," *The Review of Politics*, October 1945, 494.

14. Abell, *American Catholicism and Social Action: A Search for Social Justice, 1865-1950*, 234.

THE REDISTRIBUTIVE STATE AND INTERVENTIONISM

Ryan wrote:"The workers have a claim upon industry for all the means of living, from the time they begin to work until they die. When industry does not do it directly...then it is the business of government to enforce it upon industry."[15]

The Roman Church-State's fundamental economic principle of the universal destination of goods resulted in the creation of a plethora of new rights that government must preserve, protect, and defend. Below is a long, though incomplete, list of these rights as they have appeared in various papal encyclicals since 1891. These are some of the new rights that require intervention by government in all aspects of society and economy:

Right of freely founding unions for working people
Right to culture
Right to emigrate
Right to immigrate
Right to food
Right to clothing
Right to rest
Right to medical care
Right to a just wage
Right to life
Right to a safe environment
Right to personal security of workers
Right to family life
Right to private property
Right to common use of all goods
Right to work
Right to a pension
Right to insurance for old age
Right of association
Right to security
Right to bodily integrity
Right to necessary social services
Right to strike
Right to choose a state of life freely
Right to found a family

15. O'Brien, *Public Catholicism*, 171.

85

Right to education
Right to employment
Right to a good reputation
Right to respect
Right to appropriate information
Right to activity in accord with the upright norm of one's own conscience
Right to protection of privacy
Right to rightful freedom
Right to professional training
Right to quality education
Right to adequate health care.

This list is by no means complete. I offer it merely as an illustration of a basic point of political philosophy: An appeal to human rights is not necessarily a basis for limiting the power of government at all. That is one of the lessons of the French Revolution. What the papacy has realized is that by constantly enlarging the Rights of Man, to use the Vatican's own phrase, it can offer ever new moral arguments for enlarging the size, scope, and power of government. *Gaudium et Spes,* one of the major documents issued by the Second Vatican Council, is typical of the many pronouncements of the Church-State in favor of such governmental interference in the economy:

> Therefore, there must be made available to all men everything necessary for leading a life truly human, such as food, clothing, and shelter; the right to choose a state of life freely and to found a family, the right to education, to employment, to a good reputation, to respect, to appropriate information, to activity in accord with the upright norm of one's own conscience, to protection of privacy and to rightful freedom, even in matters religious.[16]

Notice first the moral imperative: There *must* be made available. *What* must be made available? Notice the universals: *Everything* must be made available. To whom? To *all men.* The Vatican then gives us a partial list of what sort of things it has in mind: food, clothing, shelter, education, employment,[17] information, and so on. Later in the same docu-

---

16. The Second Vatican Council, *Gaudium et Spes* (1965), 26.

17. "It must likewise be the special care of the State to create those material conditions of life without which an orderly society cannot exist. The State must take every

THE REDISTRIBUTIVE STATE AND INTERVENTIONISM

ment the Vatican said that the complexity of today's society makes government interference all the more urgent and justified: "The complex circumstances of our day make it necessary for public authority to intervene more often in social, economic and cultural matters...."[18] John XXIII stated the Roman Church-State's position in his encyclical *Pacem in Terris*:

> It is therefore necessary that the [civil] administration give wholehearted and careful attention to the social as well as to the economic progress of the citizens, and to the development, in keeping with the development of the productive system, of such essential services as the building of roads, transportation, communications, water supply, housing, public health, education, facilitation of the practice of religion, and recreational facilities...insurance systems.... The government should make similarly effective efforts to see that those who are able to work can find employment in keeping with their aptitudes, and that each worker receives a wage in keeping with the laws of justice and equity.[19]

Let us examine more closely this Roman Catholic welfare state. The Roman Church-State has taken much of the credit for creating the entire field of labor law through the influence of *Rerum Novarum*. In the United States, that law is a complex and unintelligible body of statues, regulations, and decrees that few can understand, let alone obey. In labor economics, the basic policy of the Roman Church-State is the demand that employers pay employees a "living wage," sometimes called a "just wage," or a "family wage." John Paul II explained:

> Just remuneration for the work of an adult who is responsible for a family means remuneration which will suffice for establishing and properly maintaining a family and for providing security for its future. Such remuneration can be given either through what is called a family wage – that is, a single salary given to the head of the family for his work, sufficient for the needs of the family without the other spouse having to take up gainful employment outside the home – or through other social

---

measure necessary to supply employment, particularly for the heads of families and for the young... measures taken by the State with this end in view ought to be of such a nature that they will really affect those who actually possess more than their share of capital resources, and who continue to accumulate them to the grievous detriment of others" (Pius XI, *On Atheistic Communism* [1937], 75).
18. The Second Vatican Council, *Gaudium et Spes* (1965), 75.
19. John XXIII, *Pacem in Terris, On Peace on Earth* (1963), 64.

87

measures such as family allowances or grants to mothers devoting themselves exclusively to their families. These grants should correspond to the actual needs, that is, to the number of dependents for as long as they are not in a position to assume proper responsibility for their own lives.[20]

This so-called just wage, please note, is not adjusted according to the knowledge, skill, experience, or productivity of the employee, but according to the number of dependents he has. If wages are to be determined by a criterion not related to the productivity of the employee, such as the number of dependents, there is no good reason why they might not be regulated by other irrelevant criteria, such as race. Roman Catholic economic thought requires, on moral grounds, that two workers doing the same job in the same labor market be paid unequally, simply because one has more dependents than the other. Now there may have been some (inadequate) excuse for such statements a thousand years ago, during the long, dark ages before the dawn of capitalism and the Reformation, but making such statements in the twentieth century indicates a complete ignorance of the market and of justice.[21] Were the pope's views enacted into law, they would ensure that employees who had more children would not be hired at all; that is, the pope's economic policies would hurt precisely those people the pope intends to help.[22]

In fact, the pope wanted his family wage enacted into law. He referred to "social measures such as family allowances or grants to mothers devoting themselves exclusively to their families. These grants should correspond to the actual needs...." Every mother should be a welfare mother, and the more children she can produce the larger her welfare check should be.

In addition to paying a family wage, the government must provide unemployment insurance:

> The obligation to provide unemployment benefits, that is to say, the duty to make suitable grants indispensable for the subsistence of unem-

---

20. John Paul II, *Laborem Exercens* (1981), 46.
21. One statement from Pius XI's 1931 encyclical *Quadragesimo Anno* illustrates the ignorance the papacy has of economic matters: "If the business makes a smaller profit on account of bad management, want of enterprise or out-of-date methods, this is not a just reason for reducing the workingmen's wages."
22. Roman Catholic economic directives have partially been enacted into law in the form of minimum wage laws.

ployed workers and their families, is a duty springing from the fundamental principle of the moral order in this sphere, namely, the principle of the common use of goods or, to put it in another and still simpler way, the right to life and subsistence.[23]

John Paul II did not argue that such programs are expedient or prudent; he asserted that they are morally obligatory. He speaks of the "obligation to provide unemployment benefits," the "duty to make suitable grants," and he asserted that these obligations and duties spring from "the fundamental principle of the moral order," the common use or universal destination of goods. The right to unemployment benefits is derived from the right to life.

Unemployment benefits, of course, are not the extent of the Roman welfare program. There are also "…the right to a pension and to insurance for old age and in case of accidents at work. Within the sphere of these principal rights, there develops a whole system of particular rights…."[24] As the number of Roman Catholic rights multiplies, the larger the government becomes, and the smaller the sphere of freedom shrinks. In addition to rights to welfare checks, unemployment grants, pensions, accident insurance, and old age insurance, governments must protect the disabled[25] as well. The Americans with Disabilities Act is similar to what the Vatican apparently had in mind when it advocated the "elimination of various obstacles" for the disabled in 1981.[26] Sometimes it takes the Roman Church-State years to get its policies enacted into law, but it usually succeeds.

23. John Paul II, *Laborem Exercens* (1981), 43.
24. John Paul II, *Laborem Exercens* (1981), 48. "…every man has the right to life, bodily integrity, and to the means which are suitable for the proper development of life; these are primarily food, clothing, shelter, rest, medical care, and finally the necessary social services. Therefore a human being also has the right to security in cases of sickness, inability to work, widowhood, old age, unemployment or in any other case in which he is deprived of the means of subsistence through no fault of his own" (John XXIII, *Pacem in Terris* [1963], 11).
25. "The various bodies involved in the world of labor, both the direct and the indirect employer, should therefore by means of effective and appropriate measures foster the right of disabled people to professional training and work…." (John Paul II, *Laborem Exercens* [1981], 53).
26. "Careful attention must be devoted to the physical and psychological working conditions of disabled people…and to the elimination of various obstacles…." (John Paul II, *Laborem Exercens* [1981], 53).

More basic than these interferences in the labor market is the Roman Church-State's policy of attacking business ownership itself. John XXIII, in his 1961 encyclical *Mater et Magistra*, asserted that "...it is today advisable as our predecessor [Pius XI, in *Quadragesimo Anno*, 1931] clearly pointed out, that work agreements be tempered in certain respects with partnership arrangements, so that 'workers and officials become participants in ownership or management, or share in some manner in profits.' "[27] Here the Roman Church-State is calling for non-owners – workers and government bureaucrats – to become owners or share in business profits. The distinction between sharing and stealing is, of course, drawn only by the consent of the property owner. If the property owner does not consent, if he is coerced by criminals, by the state, or by the Church-State, the action is not sharing, but stealing. That is precisely what the Roman Church-State advocates: legalized theft. It is theft of property from its owners under color of law. The Roman Church-State calls such legalized theft "sharing."

John XXIII repeatedly urged governments to intervene more and more in their economies. He suggested that new technologies would make such intervention easier, more effective, and more pervasive, and those technologies should be used to advantage by the public authorities. The goal of the Roman Church-State is a completely regulated economy:

> ...recent developments of science and technology provide additional reasons why, to a greater extent than heretofore, it is within the power of public authorities to reduce imbalances [between sectors, regions, and nations]. These same developments make it possible to keep fluctuations in the economy within bounds, and to provide effective measures for avoiding mass employment [*sic*]. Consequently it is requested again and again of public authorities responsible for the common good, that they intervene in a wide variety of economic affairs and that, in a more extensive and organized way than heretofore, they adapt institutions, tasks, means, and procedures to this end.[28]

27. John XXIII, *Mater et Magistra* (1961), 32. "...the good of the whole community must be safeguarded. By these principles of social justice, one class [capitalists] is forbidden to exclude the other [proletariat] from a share of the profits" (Pius XI, *Quadragesimo Anno* [1931], 30). Under the heading, "The uplifting of the proletariat," Pius XI declared that "Every effort, therefore, must be made that at least in the future a just share only of the fruits of production be permitted to accumulate in the hands of the wealthy...." (*Quadragesimo Anno* [1931], 33).

28. John XXIII, *Mater et Magistra* (1961), 54.

THE REDISTRIBUTIVE STATE AND INTERVENTIONISM

Because government is to intervene and interfere – to use the words of the Roman Church-State – in all aspects of the economy, government must engage in economic planning. John Paul II said that planning is a "must," a moral imperative:

> In order to meet the danger of unemployment and to ensure employment for all, the agents defined here as "indirect employer" [the civil authorities] must make provision for overall planning with regard to the different kinds of work by which not only the economic life but also the cultural life of a given society is shaped; they must also give attention to organizing that work in a correct and rational way. In the final analysis this overall concern weighs on the shoulders of the State, but it cannot mean one-sided centralization by the pubic authorities.[29]

Whatever "one-sided centralization" might be, it is to be avoided. Apparently the pope prefers two-sided centralization, or perhaps multilateral centralization. In any case, the Roman Church-State advocates and intends to participate in the centralization of power.

Planning is necessary because

> Individual initiative alone and the mere free play of competition could never assure successful development.... Hence programmes are necessary in order to "encourage, stimulate, coordinate, supplement and integrate" the activity of the individuals and intermediary bodies. It pertains to the public authorities to choose, even to lay down the objectives to be pursued, the ends to be achieved, and the means for attaining these, and it is for them to stimulate all the forces engaged in this common activity. But let them take care to associate private initiative and intermediary bodies with this work. They will thus avoid the danger of complete collectivization or of arbitrary planning....[30]

Capitalism, individual initiative and free competition, the infallible Church-State says, "could never assure successful development." Government programs are necessary in order to ensure such development. Through these programs the public authorities will choose, direct, regulate, and control all aspects of the economy. Of course, they will "associate" businesses and other non-governmental bodies in this overall planning and thus avoid "complete collectivization." Incomplete collectivization, otherwise known as fascism, is the goal. To make the

---

29. John Paul II, *Laborem Exercens* (1981), 43.
30. Paul VI, *Populorum Progressio* (1967), 33.

ECCLESIASTICAL MEGALOMANIA

Church-State's position clear, the pope attacked the heart of the capitalist system, the price system: "...prices which are 'freely' set in the market can produce unfair results. One must recognize that it is the fundamental principle of liberalism as the rule for commercial exchange which is questioned here."[31]

Ayn Rand pointed out that *Populorum Progressio*, the encyclical from which these quotations are taken, "was endorsed with enthusiasm by the Communist press the world over. 'The French Communist Party newspaper, *L'Humanité*, said the encyclical was "often moving" and constructive for highlighting the evils of capitalism long emphasized by Marxists,' reports *The New York Times* (March 30, 1967)."[32] The Communists, at least in this instance, were right.

The Roman Church-State, given its divine mission, understands itself to be the prime educator. Indeed, its central doctrine is the Magisterium – the teaching authority – of the Church. Pius XI, writing in his encyclical *On Christian Education of Youth* said: "...the Church is independent of any sort of earthly power as well in the origin as in the exercise of her mission as educator." Furthermore, "It is the duty of the State to protect in its legislation the prior rights...of the family as regards Christian education of its offspring, and consequently also to respect the supernatural rights of the Church in this same realm of Christian education."[33]

While others might have legal rights or moral rights or even natural rights, the Roman Church-State alone has supernatural rights. Because of these rights, the origin and exercise of ecclesiastical power in the field of education is independent of any earthly power. In fact, it is the duty of the government to acknowledge and respect the supernatural rights of the Roman Church-State in the field of education.

---

31. Paul VI, *Populorum Progressio* (1967), 58.

32. Ayn Rand, "Requiem for Man," in *Capitalism: The Unknown Ideal*, 316.

33. The State-Church's concern about education is not that the people be educated, but that it be the sole "educator." When it was in its power to educate the people, it failed to do so, preferring to keep them ignorant and obsequious. The Jesuit state in Paraguay is an illustration of the practice of the Church-State for a millennium. Mecham wrote: "The Jesuit plan of training and evangelization resulted, whether they intentionally desired it or not, in keeping the Indians [in Paraguay] as ignorant as possible of every duty but that of unquestioning, passive obedience" (J. Lloyd Mecham, *Church and State in Latin America: A History of Politico-Ecclesiastical Relations*. Chapel Hill: University of North Carolina Press, 1934, 235).

THE REDISTRIBUTIVE STATE AND INTERVENTIONISM

Because "All persons have an inalienable right to a quality education,"[34] "Government at all levels...has a responsibility to provide adequate professional and material resources to assist all children to attain a quality education and to safeguard their health and safety. This includes, but is not limited to, textbooks, transportation, appropriate health and safety services, economic assistance to those in need, and adequate information...."[35]

Article 797 of the Canon Law of the Roman Church-State states that "It is necessary that parents enjoy true freedom in selecting schools; the Christian faithful must therefore be concerned that civil society acknowledge this freedom for parents and also safeguard it with its resources in accord with distributive justice." This means that "true freedom" in education requires "civil society," that is, government, to subsidize religious schools. The Church-State made this even clearer when it said, "...policy decisions should allow for the existence of alternative educational systems including, but not limited to, charter schools; magnet schools; and public, private, and religious school choice programs, provided they offer quality programs and do not teach or practice intolerance or advocate illegal activity."[36] This reference to "school choice" means that the Roman Church-State favors voucher programs. Roman Catholic schools in the United States, from kindergarten to university, already receive hundreds of millions of dollars of tax subsidies, not through their tax exempt status, but through the provision of transportation, textbooks, teacher salaries, research grants, construction loans and grants, food, and so forth. Voucher programs, however, will permit Roman Catholic schools to receive hundreds of millions, perhaps billions, more tax dollars. And this, both the Roman

---

34. United States Catholic Conference, *Principles of Educational Reform in the United States*, 1995, 3. "The natural law also gives man the right to share in the benefits of culture, and therefore the right to a basic education and to technical and professional training" (John XXIII, *Pacem in Terris* [1963], 3).

35. United States Catholic Conference, *Principles of Educational Reform in the United States*, 7-8. "...the provision of a quality education for all children is the responsibility of all members of our civic community" (1). To coin a phrase, it takes a community to raise a child. One can see from these statements how flexible the principle of subsidiarity is: It allows the authorities, ecclesiastical or civil, to interfere in any aspect of society at any time. To believe that subsidiarity is a restraint on government action is to be blissfully ignorant of the meaning of Roman Catholic social thought.

36. United States Catholic Conference, *Principles of Educational Reform in the United States*, 8.

Church-State and its loyal defenders in conservative political circles tell us, is "true freedom."

The Roman Church-State endorses the same fascist approach to health care. "Our approach to health care is shaped by a simple but fundamental principle: 'Every person has a right to adequate health care.'... Health care is not a commodity; it is a basic human right... This right is explicitly affirmed in *Pacem in Terris* and is the foundation of our advocacy for health care reform."[37] The Roman bishops in the United States issued this statement in 1993, when the debate on health care reform was in high gear in Washington. It was intended to lend the moral authority of the Roman Church-State to the movement for the further socialization of health care in the United States. The American bishops, of course, were not acting on their own; they were acting in accordance with the fundamental principles and directives of the Roman Church-State. John Paul II had written in *Laborem Exercens* in 1981:

> Besides wages, various social benefits intended to ensure the life and health of workers and their families play a part here. The expenses involved in health care, especially in the cases of accidents at work, demand medical assistance should be easily available for workers, and that as far as possible, it should be cheap or even free of charge.[38]

The inalienable right to health care implies the inescapable duty of someone – a physician, a nurse, a pharmaceutical company, or a hospital – to provide that health care. The Roman Church-State realizes that, and maintains that it is the duty of those with the appropriate skills to provide health care. This is simply one application of the principle of the universal destination of goods. The rights advocated by the Roman Church-State require the enslavement of some people for the benefit of others. The Church-State seems to realize that this is the case, and advocates these rights for that reason. The Roman Church-State, from its inception, has been an advocate of slavery.

---

37. United States Catholic Conference, *A Framework for Comprehensive Health Care Reform: Protecting Human Life, Promoting Human Dignity, Pursuing the Common Good,* 1993, 1.

38. John Paul II, *Laborem Exercens* (1981), 47.

Eight

Has the Pope Beatified Ayn Rand?

DESPITE the Roman Catholic Church's strident and sustained crusade against political freedom and capitalism that has now lasted for more than a century, a small group of American Roman Catholic economists has begun to argue that the Roman Catholic Church now favors capitalism. Not only does the Roman Church-State favor capitalism *now*, according to these revisionists, it has *always* favored capitalism, we are told.[1] The opposite impression – the impression that the Roman Church-State was anti-capitalist – was created by "progressive leftists" who engaged in a "selective reading"[2] of the papal encyclicals. Among these revisionist Roman Catholic writers are Robert Sirico, a Paulist priest who is also the president of the Acton Institute in Grand Rapids, Michigan; and Michael Novak, a fellow of the American Enterprise Institute in Washington, D. C.[3]

Sirico argued, for example, that John Paul II's encyclical issued in commemoration of the hundredth anniversary of *Rerum Novarum* in 1991, *Centesimus Annus*, "represents a dramatic development in the encyclical tradition in favor of the free economy."[4] "More than any

---

1. Michael Novak explained that "one key point of this inquiry [his book] has been to show that the Catholic tradition also carries within it a powerful ethic of capitalism – indeed a fuller and deeper ethic than was available to the first Puritans" (*The Catholic Ethic and the Spirit of Capitalism*, New York: The Free Press, 1993, 232).

2. Sirico, "Catholicism's Developing Social Teaching," *The Freeman*, December 1991, 467. Sirico himself seemed to be of two minds on this question, for he also referred to the "left-wing trend" in Catholic social tradition (471).

3. Novak's book was written "In homage to Pope John Paul II," and, as one might expect from such a dedication, it is largely Roman Catholic propaganda.

4. Sirico, "Catholicism's Developing Social Teaching," *The Freeman*, December 1991, 462. If *Centesimus Annus* is a "dramatic development in favor of the free economy," then the encyclicals that went before must have been opposed to a free economy.

95

other church document," Sirico wrote, "this latest one celebrates the creativity of entrepreneurs and the virtues required for productivity."[5] Sirico asserted,"The pope affirms both the practical and moral legitimacy of profit, entrepreneurship, appropriate self-interest, productivity, and a stable currency."[6] Furthermore, *Centesimus Annus* is not only a "repudiation of the entire collectivist agenda, root and branch,...but [also] the warmest embrace of the free economy since the Scholastics."[7] "*Centesimus Annus* evidences the greatest depth of economic understanding and the most deliberate (and least critical) embrace of the system of free exchange on the part of the Catholic teaching authority in 100 years, and possibly since the Middle Ages...."[8] "[T]his encyclical constitutes the epitaph for liberation and collectivist movements in terms of any official ecclesiastical legitimacy."[9] It is "an uncompromising rejection of collectivism in its Marxist, Communist, socialist, and even welfare-statist manifestations."[10]

Now these are certainly dramatic claims for *Centesimus Annus*. One would expect such sweeping claims indicating dramatic[11] and almost revolutionary developments in Roman Catholic social thought to be supported by many quotations from the encyclical itself. Unfortunately, Sirico quoted only one complete sentence and one sentence fragment from the encyclical, a document of approximately 28,000 words. The

---

5. Sirico,"Catholicism's Developing Social Teaching," *The Freeman*, December 1991, 471.

6. Sirico,"Catholicism's Developing Social Teaching," *The Freeman*, December 1991, 471.

7. Sirico,"Catholicism's Developing Social Teaching," *The Freeman*, December 1991, 472. In his 1993 book Novak seemed to make less sweeping claims than Sirico. Novak wrote repeatedly that "Most assuredly, *Centesimus Annus* is no libertarian document – and precisely that, to many of us, is its beauty.... I want to stress that *Centesimus Annus* gives encouragement to social democrats and others of the moderate left..." (*The Catholic Ethic and the Spirit of Capitalism*, 138).

8. Sirico,"Catholicism's Developing Social Teaching," *The Freeman*, December 1991, 472.

9. Sirico,"Catholicism's Developing Social Teaching," *The Freeman*, December 1991, 473.

10. Sirico,"Catholicism's Developing Social Teaching," *The Freeman*, December 1991, 472.

11. "The latest installment in Catholic social teaching, and arguably its most dramatic development, comes in Pope John Paul II's *Centesimus Annus*, which commemorates Leo's encyclical [*Rerum Novarum*]" ("Catholicism's Developing Social Teaching," *The Freeman*, December 1991, 471).

sole complete sentence reads as follows: "By intervening directly and depriving society of its responsibility the social assistance state leads to a loss of human energies and an inordinate increase of public agencies, which are more dominated by bureaucratic ways of thinking than by concern for serving their clients, and which are accompanied by an enormous increase in spending."[12] The partial sentence Sirico quoted is a solitary reference to some of the virtues that compose the work ethic: "diligence, industriousness, prudence in taking reasonable risks, reliability and fidelity in interpersonal relationships, as well as courage in carrying out decisions which are difficult and painful but necessary, both for the overall working of a business and in meeting possible setbacks."[13] Any reader of Sirico's essay who actually reads the 1991 papal encyclical will be deeply disappointed, for virtually all of the claims that Sirico made are simply not supported by the statements of the encyclical itself.

Of course, some of Sirico's claims may be true. For example, when Sirico wrote that "*Centesimus Annus* evidences the greatest depth of economic understanding...on the part of Catholic teaching authority in 100 years," he may very well have been correct. Our survey of the teaching of official Roman Church-State social thought as expressed in the papal encyclicals and conciliar constitutions turned up little or no evidence of economic understanding. Instead, the Roman Church-State has shrilly denounced the market, self-interest, and capitalism on ethical grounds, and made sustained demands for government intervention to protect the "common good" and promote "social justice." Sirico's statement turns on a comparison between *Centesimus Annus* and previous encyclicals, so if the latest papal encyclical is less candid and forthright about, or less strident in, its criticism of capitalism, it might appear in a somewhat favorable light. And if the pope praises some of the "economic virtues," even though the praise is almost 500 years after Luther and Calvin, perhaps it is a sign of hope for economically conservative Roman Catholics like Mr. Sirico, who seem to be embarrassed by a Church-State that has been one of the world's longest and strongest proponents of anti-capitalist ideas.

12. Sirico, "Catholicism's Developing Social Teaching," *The Freeman*, December 1991, 471-472.
13. Sirico, "Catholicism's Developing Social Teaching," *The Freeman*, December 1991, 471.

Sirico claimed that "more than any other church document this latest one [*Centesimus Annus*] celebrates the creativity of entrepreneurs and the virtue required for productivity." This writer has not read all church documents, and neither, one supposes, has Mr. Sirico. In his essay Sirico discussed only one previous church document, *Rerum Novarum*, and furnished us with a creative misreading of that encyclical as well.[14] But despite his best efforts, *Rerum Novarum* is so obviously an anti-capitalist document that Sirico is finally embarrassed by it.[15] His desire to find something of economic value in the papal encyclicals seems to betray him into making statements that he cannot support. The many official Roman Church documents that this writer has read express the Roman Church-State's long-standing hatred for capitalism on moral grounds, a hatred that has now been clearly expressed by the Magisterium for over a century. P. T. Bauer accurately called these papal encyclicals "incompetent," "immoral," and "envy exalted."[16]

If Sirico's reading of *Centesimus Annus* is so misleading, what exactly did John Paul II say in the encyclical? Since *Centesimus Annus* was issued in commemoration of *Rerum Novarum*, the pope began by prais-

---

14. Sirico noted that his interpretation of *Rerum Novarum* is "not a prevalent one today. It [Sirico's interpretation] comes from a view of the world as expressed by classical liberals." Unfortunately for Sirico's interpretation, Leo XIII did not share the classical liberal view of the world, and *Rerum Novarum* itself rails against classical liberalism. To claim, therefore, as Sirico did, that *Rerum Novarum* lends itself to such an analysis is to misrepresent the encyclical (Sirico, "Catholicism's Developing Social Teaching," *The Freeman*, December 1991, 466).

15. Sirico admitted that Leo XIII erred "in a particular economic policy prescription, but not in his overall economic framework." Since that overall framework is a quasi-Marxist analysis of capitalism, one is baffled by Sirico's remark. It is telling that Sirico prefaced his discussion of *Rerum Novarum* with a long discussion of the Roman Church-State doctrine of papal infallibility, arguing that it does not apply to papal encyclicals. He apparently had hoped to avoid the problems that the claim of papal infallibility entailed for (1) his own economic views, which seem to be out of line with those of the Roman Church-State; and (2) what he regarded as dramatic differences in the views expressed from one papal encyclical to another. In so arguing, however, he subverted the Roman Church-State's claim to infallibility, for that claim rests on the alleged inadequacy and vagueness of Scripture, which consequently needs a living, clear, and infallible interpreter. But if the popes do not speak clearly and infallibly in their encyclicals, the Roman Church is in an even worse situation, and the Roman Catholic argument against the Reformed position that Scripture is its own proper interpreter collapses.

16. Peter T. Bauer, "Ecclesiastical Economics Is Envy Exalted," *This World*, Winter-Spring, 1982, 56-69.

ing *Rerum Novarum* as an "immortal document," and continued: "the vital energies rising from that root have not been spent with the passing of the years, but rather *have increased even more.*"[17] Continuing his praise for *Rerum Novarum* for several paragraphs, John Paul II asserted that "the validity of this teaching has already been pointed out in two Encyclicals published during my Pontificate: *Laborem Exercens*...and *Sollicitudo Rei Socialis*...."[18] John Paul II proposed a "re-reading" of *Rerum Novarum* "to discover anew the richness of the fundamental principles which it formulated...."[19] What are those fundamental principles? John Paul II, echoing Leo XIII a century before him, began with a quasi-Marxist analysis of capitalism. Please keep in mind that the quotations that follow are from the encyclical that Sirico and Novak have described as the most pro-capitalist document the Roman Church-State has ever written.

> 4.2 In the sphere of economics...new structures for the production of consumer goods had progressively taken shape [during the eighteenth and nineteenth centuries]. A new form of property had appeared – capital; and a new form of labor – labor for wages, characterized by high rates of production which lacked due regard for sex, age or family situation, and were determined solely by efficiency, with a view to increasing profits.
>
> 4.3 In this way labor became a commodity to be freely bought and sold on the market, its price determined by the law of supply and demand, without taking into account the bare minimum required for the support of the individual and his family. Moreover, the worker was not even sure of being able to sell "his own commodity," continually threatened as he was by unemployment, which, in the absence of any kind of social security, meant the specter of death by starvation.
>
> 4.4 The result of this transformation was a society "divided into two classes, separated by a deep chasm" [*Rerum Novarum*, 132].... Thus the prevailing political theory of the time [the nineteenth century] sought to promote total economic freedom by appropriate laws, or, conversely, by a deliberate lack of any intervention....
>
> 4.5 At the height of this clash, when people finally began to realize fully the very grave injustice of social realities in many places and the danger of a revolution fanned by ideas which were then called "social-

---

17. John Paul II, *Centesimus Annus* (1991), 1.2. Italics in the original.
18. John Paul II, *Centesimus Annus* (1991), 2.2.
19. John Paul II, *Centesimus Annus* (1991), 3.1.

ist," Pope Leo XIII intervened with a document which dealt in a systematic way with the "conditions of the workers...."

5.2 The Pope [Leo XIII] and the [Roman] Church...were confronted ...by a society which was torn by a conflict all the more harsh and inhumane because it knew no rule or regulation. It was the conflict between capital and labor....

5.3 In the face of a conflict which set man against man, almost as if they were "wolves," a conflict between the extremes of mere physical survival on the one side and opulence on the other, the Pope [Leo XIII] did not hesitate to intervene by virtue of his "apostolic office..."

5.4 In this way, Pope Leo XIII, in the footsteps of his Predecessors, created a lasting paradigm for the Church....

6.1 With the intention of shedding light on the conflict which had arisen between capital and labor, Pope Leo XIII affirmed the fundamental rights of workers.... "it may truly be said that it is only by the labor of the working-men that States grow rich."

6.2 Another important principle is undoubtedly that of the right to "private property...." The Pope is well aware that private property is not an absolute value, nor does he fail to proclaim the necessary complementary principles, such as the universal destination of the earth's goods.

6.3 On the other hand, it is certainly true that the type of private property which Leo XIII mainly considers is land ownership....

7.1 ...Pope Leo XIII's Encyclical [*Rerum Novarum*] also affirms other rights as inalienable and proper to the human person. Prominent among these...is the "natural human right" to form private associations. This means above all the right to establish professional associations for employers and workers, or of workers alone... [Neither Leo XIII nor John Paul II mentioned any right of employers to form associations for employers alone].

7.2 Together with this right, which – it must be stressed – the Pope [Leo XIII] explicitly acknowledges as belonging to "the working class," the Encyclical affirms just as clearly the right to the "limitation of working hours," the right to legitimate rest and the right of children and women to be treated differently with regard to the type and duration of work....

8.1 The Pope [Leo XIII] immediately adds another right which the worker has as a person. This is the right to a "just wage," which cannot be left to the "free consent of the parties...." This concept of relations between employers and employees, purely pragmatic and inspired by a thoroughgoing individualism, is severely censured in the Encyclical....

8.2 A workingman's wages should be sufficient to enable him to support himself, his wife and his children. "If through necessity or fear of a worse evil the workman accepts harder conditions because an employer or contractor will afford no better, he is made the victim of force and injustice."

8.3 Would that these words, written at a time when what has been called "unbridled capitalism" was pressing forward, should not have to be repeated today with the same severity. ...

10.1 *Rerum Novarum* criticizes two social and economic systems: socialism and liberalism.... "...wage-earners should be specially cared for and protected by the government."

This re-reading of *Rerum Novarum* by John Paul II preserved the Marxist flavor of the encyclical – an unsophisticated labor theory of value, the economic class structure of society, and the class struggle – and endorsed it. Leo XIII in 1891 and John Paul II in 1991 adopted a quasi-Marxist view of capitalism. Both John Paul II and Leo XIII also endorsed the fundamental principle of the "universal destination of goods," which holds that need makes all goods, both natural and manufactured, common, and that those who own goods must surrender them to those in need, or their goods will be rightfully taken from them by either the needy or by the public authorities.[20] To say of *Rerum Novarum*, as Sirico did, that it "provides one of the most finely honed defenses of the free market and private property order in the annals of Catholic, indeed Christian, social thought..."[21] is preposterous.

Later in *Centesimus Annus*, John Paul II endorsed the slogan of liberation theology; "the preferential option for the poor,"[22] and wrote, more ominously, that "The Pope does not, of course, intend to condemn every possible form of social conflict....The [1981] Encyclical *Laborem Exercens*, moreover, clearly recognized the positive role of conflict when it takes the form of a 'struggle for social justice....' "[23] These statements make Sirico's claim that *Centesimus Annus* "constitutes the epitaph for liberation and collectivist movements in terms of any official ecclesias-

20. "While the Pope proclaimed the right to private ownership, he affirmed with equal clarity that the 'use' of goods, while marked by freedom, is subordinated to their original common destination as created goods" (John Paul II, *Centesimus Annus* [1991], 30.2).
21. Sirico, "Catholicism's Developing Social Teaching," *The Freeman*, December 1991, 474.
22. John Paul II, *Centesimus Annus* (1991), 11.1.
23. John Paul II, *Centesimus Annus* (1991), 14.1.

tical legitimacy" false.[24] *Centesimus Annus* included a hardly veiled endorsement of liberation theology, and John Paul II endorsed liberation theology several times in other documents, as we have already seen. Liberation theology has continued to receive endorsement from the Roman Magisterium during the past twenty years, that is, during the reign of John Paul II.

Section 15 of *Centesimus Annus* endorsed all sorts of government intervention, and concluded with this paragraph:

> The Encyclical [*Rerum Novarum*] and the related social teaching of the Church had far reaching influence in the years bridging the nineteenth and twentieth centuries. This influence is evident in the numerous reforms which were introduced in the areas of social security, pensions, health insurance and compensation in the case of accidents, within the framework of greater respect for the rights of workers.

What was that far-reaching influence of *Rerum Novarum* to which John Paul II referred? In Europe *Rerum Novarum* granted the moral authority and the political support of the Roman Church-State and Roman Catholic voters to the rising tide of statism in all its forms except atheistic Communism: socialism, fascism,[25] and Nazism. In the

---

24. Nineteenth century Roman Catholic historian Lord Acton's comments about the Roman Catholic scholars of his day are timeless. He wrote a letter to von Döllinger explaining that his reading of history had convinced him that a common vice is "to defend one's cause by unfair or illicit means." Acton had studied, with "infinite credulity and trust" the most eminent Roman Catholic writers of his day. But he found that what they told him was "on many decisive questions, false." Acton came "very slowly and reluctantly indeed to the conclusion that they were dishonest." A special reason for their dishonesty was "the desire to keep up the credit of authority in the [Roman] Church." The Roman Catholic scholars ignored moral standards in their study of history, because "it is impossible honestly to apply a moral standard to history without discrediting the [Roman] Church in her collective action." In order that "men might believe the Pope, it was resolved to make them believe that vice is virtue and falsehood truth." This defect was not due to ignorance or incompetence. Acton found it in "the ablest, in the most learned, in the most plausible and imposing men" he knew. These men "who were outwardly defenders of religion," were actually "advocates of deceit and murder." The "great point was that these men justified things to which in the past the papacy stood committed. They wished men to think that those things had not happened, or that they were good. They preached falsehood and murder" (quoted in Hugh MacDougall, *The Acton-Newman Relations*, New York: Fordham University Press, 1962, 141-142). In his *History of Freedom*, Acton declared that the claims of the ultramontanists, the advocates of the infallibility of the pope, were based on "unremitting dishonesty in the use of texts."

25. The Roman Catholic scholar Karl Otmar von Aretin noted that "The papacy's

United States, it fueled the rise of the labor union movement,[26] the Progressive movement, and interventionism. Aaron I. Abell, Professor of History at the University of Notre Dame, sketched the influence of *Rerum Novarum* in the United States.[27]

In 1917 the hierarchy of the Roman Church-State in the United States formed the National Catholic War Council, the predecessor of the National Conference of Catholic Bishops. In 1919 the Council's Administrative Committee issued a plan for social reconstruction, written by John Augustus Ryan, a Jesuit. The plan, following the proposals of Ryan's 1906 book, *A Living Wage*, advocated social insurance against unemployment, sickness, invalidity, and old age; a federal child labor law; legal enforcement of labor's right to organize; public housing for the working classes; graduated taxes on inheritances, incomes, and excess profits; stringent regulation of public utility rates; government competition with monopolies; worker participation in business management, and so forth.[28] When Franklin Roosevelt was elected President in 1932, he asked Monsignor Ryan to join his administration, which Ryan did.

Fifty-four years ago Abell pointed out that "A social view of property…served as the entering wedge for much contemporary and future American Catholic participation in social reform."[29] Sirico as-

---

denial of the modern world, and in particular of democracy which guaranteed the freedom of the individual, favoured the emergence of fascist regimes in the 1920s" (*The Papacy and the Modern World*, Roland Hill, translator. New York: McGraw Hill Book Company, 1970, 8).

26. Sirico admitted that "*Rerum Novarum* became the springboard for the burgeoning labor movement in America and Europe" and that "To the [social] reformer's [sic] mind, Leo's encyclical gave them the support and recognition they needed to carry out their program" (Sirico, "Catholicism's Developing Social Teaching," *The Freeman*, December 1991, 467).

27. Abell, "The Reception of Leo XIII's Labor Encyclical in America, 1891-1919," *The Review of Politics*, October 1945. Abell's *American Catholicism and Social Action: A Search for Social Justice, 1865-1950*, is a detailed account of the social and political activities of both Roman Catholic laymen and officials in the United States.

28. The State of New York Joint Legislative Committee Investigating Seditious Activities (the Lusk Committee) published its opinion of the *Bishops' Program of Social Reconstruction* in 1920, referring to "a certain group in the Catholic Church with leanings toward Socialism, under the leadership of the Rev. Dr. Ryan…" (Abell, *American Catholicism and Social Action: A Search for Social Justice, 1865-1950*, University of Notre Dame Press, 1963, 205).

29. Abell, "The Reception of Leo XIII's Labor Encyclical in America, 1891-1919," *The Review of Politics*, October 1945, 471.

serted, contrary to the evidence, that this interpretation of *Rerum Novarum* "has over-emphasized the social view of property. This reflects a bias [in the interpreters] against individualism and self-interest...."[30] But, as we have seen, the bias against individualism and self-interest is the bias of the Roman Church-State, demonstrated through many quotations from papal encyclicals.[31] Sirico's alleged conspiracy of leftwing interpreters who have twisted the pope's "finely honed defense of private property" and capitalism into an endorsement of interventionism and social reform is a fantasy. It would be difficult to over-emphasize the bias of the Roman Church-State against private property, self-interest, and capitalism.[32]

Furthermore, that bias continues to be expressed by the Roman Church-State, even in the very encyclical that Sirico told us is an endorsement of capitalism.[33] After admitting that "the modern business economy has positive aspects,"[34] the pope wrote:

> Many other people, while not completely marginalized, live in situations in which the struggle for a bare minimum is uppermost. These are

---

30. Sirico, "Catholicism's Developing Social Teaching," *The Freeman*, December 1991, 467.

31. Even in *Centesimus Annus* the pope re-affirmed the hostility of the Roman Church-State to individualism: "In order to overcome today's widespread individualistic mentality, what is required is a concrete commitment to solidarity and charity..." (49.2).

32. Novak also attempted to put a spin on past encyclicals with these words: "As the last act of a play often changes the meaning of what went before, so in particular *Centesimus Annus* in 1991 cast new light on the preceding hundred years of papal social thought" (*The Catholic Ethic and the Spirit of Capitalism*, xv).

33. Economists sometimes forget Karl Marx's and Friedrich Engels' endorsement of the achievements of capitalism in *The Communist Manifesto*: "Modern industry has established the world market, for which the discovery of America paved the way. This market has given an immense development to commerce, to navigation, to communication by land.... It [the bourgeoisie] has accomplished wonders far surpassing Egyptian pyramids, Roman aqueducts, and Gothic cathedrals; it has conducted expeditions that put to shame all former Exoduses of nations and crusades.... The bourgeoisie, during its rule of scarcely one hundred years, has created more massive and more colossal productive forces than have all preceding generations together (*The Communist Manifesto*, Washington Square Press [1848] 1964, 60-65).

34. No doubt the "positive aspects" of the modern economy, though not listed by the pope, include the many government interventions in business and the economy long advocated by the Vatican. Such intervention seems to be the reason John Paul II distinguished between "early," "unbridled," and "primitive" capitalism, and the "modern business economy."

situations in which the rules of the earliest period of capitalism still flourish in conditions of "ruthlessness" in no way inferior to the darkest moments of the first phase of industrialization.... The human inadequacies of capitalism and the resulting domination of things over people are far from disappearing.[35]

Furthermore, John Paul II wrote,

It is right to speak of a struggle against an economic system, if the latter is understood as a method of upholding the absolute predominance of capital, the possession of the means of production and of the land.... In the struggle against such a system, what is being proposed as an alternative is not the socialist system, which in fact turns out to be State capitalism, but rather a society of free work.... Such a society is not directed against the market, but demands that the market be appropriately controlled by the forces of society and the State....[36]

Furthermore,

...it is unacceptable to say that the defeat of so-called "Real Socialism" leaves capitalism as the only model of economic organization.[37] ...if by "capitalism" is meant a system in which freedom in the economic sector is not circumscribed within a strong juridical framework which places it at the service of human freedom in its totality...then the reply [to the question, "Is capitalism the model for the Third World?"] is certainly negative.[38]

Building on the interventions that are already in place, the Roman Church-State wants more:

It is the task of the State to provide for the defense and preservation of common goods such as the natural and human environments, which cannot be safeguarded simply by market forces. Just as in the time of primitive capitalism the State had the duty of defending the basic rights of workers, so now, with the new capitalism, the State and all of society have the duty of defending those collective goods....[39]

Contrary to what Sirico alleged, there seem to be only two sentences in the entire encyclical that might appear to lend any support to

---

35. John Paul II, *Centesimus Annus* (1991), 33.2.
36. John Paul II, *Centesimus Annus* (1991), 35.2.
37. John Paul II, *Centesimus Annus* (1991), 35.4.
38. John Paul II, *Centesimus Annus* (1991), 42.2.
39. John Paul II, *Centesimus Annus* (1991), 40.1.

the market economy. One, as we have seen, is a mild criticism of bureaucratic ways of thinking and spending, which Sirico quoted. The other sentence, which Sirico did not quote, endorsed the "modern business economy" only on grounds of efficiency, not morality, as Sirico claimed, and the pope immediately qualified it:

> It would appear that, on the level of individual nations and of international relations, the free market is the most efficient instrument for utilizing resources and effectively responding to needs. But this is true only for those needs which are "solvent" insofar as they are endowed with purchasing power, and for those resources which are "marketable" insofar as they are capable of obtaining a satisfactory price. But there are many human needs which find no place on the market. It is a strict duty of justice and truth not to allow fundamental human needs to remain unsatisfied and not to allow those burdened by such needs to perish. [40]

Sirico provided neither quotations – nor even any citations – to support his sweeping assertion that the encyclical gave a moral endorsement of profit, self-interest, and a stable currency. This writer has found no such statements in the encyclical either. Therefore, I am forced to conclude that Sirico's assertion of a moral endorsement of capitalism by the Roman Church-State in *Centesimus Annus* is false. Perhaps Sirico was confused by John Paul II's reference to certain character traits as "virtues," namely industriousness, diligence, prudence, courage, and reliability, but endorsement of these character traits does not constitute an endorsement of profit, self-interest, and a stable currency, let alone capitalism. John Paul II tentatively ("It would appear") praised only the efficiency of the free market, and he did so only after the Communist systems of Europe had collapsed. But even that tentative praise was immediately weakened and qualified, and the paragraph concluded with the pope asserting, on *moral* grounds, the duty of the State "not to allow fundamental human needs to remain unsatisfied," as they would in a free market, even a market already regulated by government. This one tentative sentence about the efficiency of the market was buried in the middle of a document that repeatedly condemned real ("early," "unbridled," and "primitive") capitalism and repeatedly reaffirmed the Roman Church-State's commitment to her fundamental

---

40. John Paul II, *Centesimus Annus* (1991), 34.1.

social principles of the universal destination of goods, the primacy of need, and government regulation and control of the economy.

One can sympathize with a Roman Catholic who is embarrassed by the fact that his allegedly infallible Church has preached collectivism and condemned capitalism on moral grounds for more than a century. One can even understand such a Roman Catholic's desire to reinterpret any phrase from the pen of his infallible leader that might be made to favor capitalism and freedom. But neither our sympathy nor his embarrassment is an excuse for misrepresenting *Centesimus Annus* as a moral endorsement of capitalism. Sirico's claim that *Centesimus Annus* is "a repudiation of the entire collectivist agenda, root and branch" has no support in the text itself.

PART II
Autocracy Adored

∞

The Political Thought of the Roman Catholic Church

*Power tends to corrupt,
and absolute power corrupts absolutely.*

*John Emerich Edward Dalberg,
Lord Acton*

Nine

Lord Acton on Roman Catholic Political Thought

ONE OF THE greatest Roman Catholic historians of the nineteenth century, John Emerich Edward Dalberg, is better known to us as Lord Acton. Many have heard his warning, "Power corrupts." Actually, his exact words are: "Power tends to corrupt; absolute power corrupts absolutely." He wrote them in a letter to Mandell Creighton, and his words referred to the power of popes and kings. Acton wrote:

> I cannot accept your canon that we are to judge Pope and King unlike other men, with a favourable presumption that they did no wrong. If there is any presumption it is the other way, against holders of power, increasing as the power increases. Historic responsibility has to make up for the want of legal responsibility. Power tends to corrupt, and absolute power corrupts absolutely. Great men are almost always bad men, even when they exercise influence and not authority, still more when you superadd the tendency or the certainty of corruption by authority. There is no worse heresy than that the office sanctifies the holder of it....[1] For many years my view of Catholic controversy has been governed by the following chain of reasoning:
>
> 1. A crime does not become a good deed by being committed for the good of the church.
>
> 2. The theorist who approves the act is no better than the culprit who commits it.
>
> 3. The divine or historian who defends the theorist incurs the same blame....[2]

1. Acton to Creighton, April 5, 1887, Add. MSS, 6871; as quoted in Gertrude Himmelfarb, *Lord Acton: A Study in Conscience and Politics*. University of Chicago Press, 1952, 161.

2. Acton, Add. MSS, 5631; as quoted in Himmelfarb, *Lord Acton*, 162.

111

To commit murder is the mark of a moment, exceptional.
To defend it is constant, and shows a more perverted conscience.[3]

Acton was immensely learned, knew several languages, wrote prodigiously, and was a member of the Roman Catholic Church. As a historian Acton kept a notebook of his research on the Inquisition in which he wrote:

> The object of the Inquisition [was] not to combat sin – for sin was not judged by it unless accompanied by [theological] error. Nor even to put down error. For it punished untimely and unseemly remarks the same as blasphemy. Only unity. This became an outward, fictitious, hypocritical unity. The gravest sin was pardoned, but it was death to deny the *Donation of Constantine*. So men learned that outward submission must be given. All this [was] to promote authority more than faith. When ideas were punished more severely than actions – for all this time the Church was softening the criminal law, and saving men from the consequences of crime – and the *Donation* was put on a level with God's own law – men understood that authority went before sincerity.[4]

In 1868 Acton published a long essay in the *North British Review* about the St. Bartholomew's Massacre, which began in Paris, August 24, 1572, and spread throughout France. In the essay Acton argued that there was no evidence to absolve the Roman Church-State of premeditated murder. He argued that it was not only the facts that condemned the papacy for this heinous crime, but the whole body of casuistry developed by the Roman Church-State that made it an act of Christian duty and mercy to kill a heretic. Acton pointed out that only when the Roman Church-State could no longer rely on force but had to make its case before public opinion did it seek to explain away its murders. He wrote:

> The story is much more abominable than we all believed.... S. B. [St. Bartholomew's Massacre] is the greatest crime of modern times. It was committed on principles professed by Rome. It was approved, sanctioned, and praised by the papacy. The Holy See went out of its way to signify to the world, by permanent and solemn acts, how entirely it

---

3. Acton, Add. MSS, 4939; as quoted in Himmelfarb, *Lord Acton*, 162.

4. Acton, Add. MSS, 5536; as quoted in Himmelfarb, *Lord Acton*, 65. The primacy of unity and church authority is a constant theme of Roman Church-State political thought.

admired a king who slaughtered his subjects treacherously, because they were Protestants. To proclaim forever that because a man is a Protestant it is a pious deed to cut his throat in the night....[5]

Acton described the Ultramontanes – the proponents of papal infallibility led by the Jesuits – as "an organized conspiracy to establish a power which would be the most formidable enemy of liberty as well as of science throughout the world."[6] After studying the history of the Roman Church-State, Acton wrote:

> The papacy contrived murder and massacred on the largest and also on the most cruel and inhuman scale. They [the popes] were not only wholesale assassins but they made the principle of assassination a law of the Christian Church and a condition of salvation.... [The papacy is] the fiend skulking behind the Crucifix.[7]

No Protestant has surpassed Acton in the severity of his judgment of the papacy. Acton's denunciations of the persecutions and pretensions of the papacy and its defenders were frequent. He wrote that Pius IX

> covered with the white skull-cap of the *Syllabus* [*of Errors*] the overt acts of his predecessors, and invited the sanction of the Church for them at the [Vatican] Council [of 1870]. The papacy sanctions murder; the avowed defender and promoter of the papacy is necessarily involved in that sanction.... No man defends the papacy who has not accommodated his conscience to the idea of assassination.[8]

Exactly what form the papal fiend has taken will become clear in the chapters that follow.

---

5. Acton, Add. MSS 5004; as quoted in Himmelfarb, *Lord Acton*, 67.
6. Acton, January 1, 1870, *Correspondence*, 91; as quoted in Himmelfarb, *Lord Acton*, 104.
7. Acton, *Correspondence*, 55; as quoted in Himmelfarb, *Lord Acton*, 151.
8. Quoted in Hugh MacDougall, *The Acton-Newman Relations*, Fordham University Press, 1962, 142. Acton, of course, was not the first Roman Catholic to criticize the papacy; Dante had written in the fourteenth century in *De Monarchia* that "The crosier should not be joined with the sword." He denounced the claims of the papacy as "unscriptural, unhistorical, and illogical." In *The Divine Comedy, Paradiso*, xxvii, 40-60, Dante depicted Boniface VIII's papacy as a "sewer of blood and stench."

Ten

Roman Catholic Political Theory

To UNDERSTAND Acton's opinion of the papacy, we must recall the Roman Church-State's theory of ecclesiastical and political authority. The Roman Church-State traces its genealogy – and therefore its authority – back to Peter, an ecclesiastical and historical fantasy. Rather, it should trace its genealogy to two other men, Diotrephes and Constantine. F. A. Ridley argued that the proto-pope was Augustus:

> It is evident to anyone who can penetrate through fictions – inspired and otherwise – and see down to the bedrock of fact that as far as the real historical founder of the papacy can be said to be any single man, it was Augustus, the founder of the Roman Empire, and not Peter, the obscure fisherman of Galilee.... Had Augustus, and not Constantine, founded Constantinople to be the capital of the Roman Empire, the Roman See would probably never have emerged from the muck of provincial institutions.... The gradual evolution of the democratic State of Republican Rome into the theocratic despotism of the later Roman Caesars no doubt furnished a direct prototype for the evolution of the original Roman Presbytery into the monarchical papacy of later times.[1]

"Janus," the pen-name of the nineteenth century Roman Catholic historian Ignaz von Döllinger, wrote: "[Cardinal] Bellarmine acknowledged that without the forgeries of the pseudo-Isidore,...it would be impossible to make out even a semblance of traditional evidence" for the supremacy of the pope.[2] For nearly eight centuries the papacy did

---

1. F. A. Ridley, *The Papacy and Fascism*, London: Martin, Secker, Warburg, 1937, 31. John Henry, Cardinal Newman, referred to the Roman Church-State as the "residuary legatee" of the Roman Empire.

2. Quoted in Joseph S. Van Dyke, *Popery the Foe of the Church and of the Republic.* Second edition, New York: I. K. Funk and Company, 1871, 67.

trace its political power to Constantine, until Lorenzo Valla showed that the *Donation of Constantine* was a forgery, probably committed by the papacy itself to bolster its pretensions to political power.[3] The new Roman Emperors, however – nearly 500 years after Valla exposed the hoax – have yet to admit that their claim to political power and jurisdiction rests on forged documents.[4]

The notion of the pre-eminence of one man in the churches was not a late development. Christians sometimes resist the notion that the origins of the Roman Church-State might be found in the Bible. They should not. The New Testament clearly teaches that Antichrist was already at work at the time of the apostles.[5] His influence can be seen in such doctrines as forbidding to marry, forbidding to eat meat, free will, natural law, asceticism, and keeping the law as a condition of salvation.[6] The Roman Church-State structure might not have been completed for centuries – in fact, it is still not completed – but its beginnings can be traced to these doctrines and practices condemned in Scripture. The growth of the papacy itself is the history of the gradual triumph of the ecclesiastical megalomaniacs in the presbytery of Rome over their opponents, transforming Rome's original presbyterian government into an episcopalian government, then into an absolute monarchy, and finally a world empire.

In his third letter the Apostle John mentioned a man named Diotrephes. John reported:

> I wrote to the church, but Diotrephes, who loves to have the pre-eminence among them, does not receive us. Therefore, if I come, I will call to mind his deeds which he does, prating against us with malicious

---

3. See Appendix A.

4. Nowhere has the author found an admission by the papacy that the *Donation of Constantine* is a forged document. If the reader is aware of such an admission, please inform the author.

5. *1 John* 2:18; 4:3. Of course, it was not until the Roman Emperor was removed that the Roman Pope could emerge. Ridley commented: "This necessary fall of the Roman Empire, which paved the way for Papal supremacy in the West, was achieved in the fifth century…" (Ridley, *The Papacy and Fascism*, London: Martin, Secker, Warburg, 1937, 33).

6. Antichrist can be heard in the encyclicals of the present pope: "From the very lips of Jesus, the new Moses, man is once again given [in *Matthew* 19:17] the Commandments of the Decalogue. Jesus himself definitively confirms them and proposes them to us as the way and condition of salvation" (John Paul II, *Veritatis Splendor*, 12.2).

words. And not content with that, he himself does not receive the brethren, and forbids those who wish to, putting them out of the church.[7]

What Diotrephes was attempting to do on a local level even before the death of the Apostle John – the establishment of monepiscopal rule, that is, the rule of one man, as opposed to the plurality of presbyters (or bishops: the New Testament uses the terms interchangeably) – other church leaders would attempt in other local churches, and then at the metropolitan and regional levels, until, after several centuries, the bishop of Rome won the struggle for ecclesiastical power. There is no Biblical or historical evidence to show that the first pope was the Apostle Peter, as the Roman Church-State claims; Diotrephes was a proto-pope; he was an ambitious and anti-Christian church leader who loved to have pre-eminence, who prated against Christians with malicious words, and who expelled Christians from the church. His actions were opposed to the words of Christ: "You know that the rulers of the Gentiles lord it over them, and those who are great exercise authority over them. Yet it shall not be so among you...."[8]

In his first and second letters John had warned the early Christians that Antichrist was already working in the churches and the world.[9] But though Diotrephes was a precursor of the popes, the aggrandizement of the ancient Roman Church and its bishop and the development of a theory to justify papal power took centuries. There is nothing in the Scriptures that either expressly states or logically implies the primacy of the church of Rome or the office of pope in the Christian church. Far from being divinely instituted, the Roman Church-State is entirely a development of ambitious and sometimes unscrupulous men, their dupes, frauds, and forgeries.[10]

7. *3 John* 9-10.
8. *Matthew* 20:25-26.
9. See *1 John* 2:18, 22; 4:3; *2 John* 7.
10. "How the papacy lost its early innocence, degenerating into an absolute power, is the long and disreputable story of forgeries and fabrications, of which the *Donation of Constantine* in the eighth century and the *Isidorian Decretals* in the ninth were only the more flagrant episodes. Usurping the rights of the episcopacy and of the general councils, the papacy was finally driven to the principles and methods of the Inquisition to enforce its spurious claims and to the theory of infallibility to elevate it beyond all human control. [Ignaz von Döllinger in *The Pope and the Council*] piled high the sordid details of inventions and distorted texts, of Popes involved in contradiction and heresy, of historians falsifying history and theologians perverting theology" (Himmelfarb, *Lord Acton*, 97).

One of the more important forgeries supporting the claims of the Roman papacy was the *Donation of Constantine*. It was not discovered to be a forgery until the fifteenth century. For 700 years the infallible Roman Church-State and the authoritative pope had asserted its authenticity, based their claims to political power on it, and, as Acton reported, killed those who rejected their claims. Written most likely in the middle eighth century, the *Donation of Constantine* purported to convey a gift from the Roman Emperor Constantine to the bishop of Rome. Constantine moved the capital of the Roman Empire from Rome to Constantinople in A.D. 330. When he left, so the forgery goes, he gave

> to the holy apostles, my lords the most blessed Peter and Paul, and through them also to blessed Sylvester our father, supreme pontiff and universal pope of the city of Rome, and to the pontiffs, his successors who to the end of the world shall sit in the seat of blessed Peter, we grant and by this present we convey our imperial Lateran Palace, which is superior to and excels all palaces in the whole world; and further the diadem, which is the crown of our head; and the miter; as also the superhumeral, that is, the stole which usually surrounds our imperial neck; and the purple cloak and the scarlet tunic and all the imperial robes.... Wherefore, that the pontifical crown should not be made of less repute, but rather that the dignity of a more than earthly office and the might of its glory should be further adored – lo, we convey to the oft-mentioned and most blessed Sylvester, universal pope, both our palace, as preferment, and likewise all provinces, palaces, and districts of the city of Rome and Italy and of the regions of the West; and, bequeathing them to the power and sway of him and the pontiffs, his successors, we do (by means of fixed imperial decision through this our divine, sacred, and authoritative sanction) determine and decree that the same be placed at his disposal, and do lawfully grant it as a permanent possession to the holy Roman Church.[11]

Not only did the Roman Church-State claim on the basis of this fraudulent document that Constantine had given the western Roman Empire to the Church-State (clearly suggesting that the popes are the successors of Caesar, not of Peter), but also that Constantine had conveyed all the trappings of imperial power, including the stole, the crown,

---

[11]. Brian Tierney, *The Crisis of Church and State, 1050-1300*. Englewood Cliffs: Prentice-Hall, 1964, 21-22.

the cloak, and the tunic, which the popes still wear today. Despite the fact that the *Donation of Constantine* has been known to be a forgery for 500 years, it and other forgeries, such as the false *Decretals*, are so interwoven with the history and political theory of the Roman Church-State that the infallible Church-State has not repudiated them, because to do so might wreck its claim to both political power and infallibility.

Over the course of the centuries the Roman Church-State developed an elaborate rationalization for its pretensions to both ecclesiastical and political power. Its theory begins, oddly, with Scripture. Scripture teaches that all authority, political and ecclesiastical, is from God. The theologians of the Roman Church-State quoted *Romans* 13:1: "Let every soul be subject to the governing authorities, for there is no authority except from God, and the authorities that exist are appointed by God." They understood this passage to be a denial of any sort of republican or democratic ecclesiastical or civil theory. Political power and authority do not arise from the consent of the people, but from the delegation of God. Power and authority flow from the top down, not from the bottom up.

The next step in its artfully constructed political fantasy was to assert that God delegated this authority to one man: the bishop of Rome. Bernard of Clairvaux (1090-1153) stated the theory in these words:

> ...he who would deny that the sword belongs to thee [the pope] has not, as I conceive, sufficiently weighed the words of the Lord, where he said, speaking to Peter, "Put up *thy* sword into the scabbard" (*John* 18:11). For it is here plainly implied that even the material sword is thine, to be drawn at thy bidding, although not by thy hand. Besides, unless this sword also appertained to thee in some sense, when the disciples said to Christ, "Lord, behold, here are two swords" (*Luke* 22:38), he would never have answered as he did, "It is enough," but rather, "it is too much." We can therefore conclude that both swords, namely the spiritual and the material, belong to the Church, and that although only the former is to be wielded by her own hand, the two are to be employed in her service. It is for the priest to use the sword of the word, but to strike with the sword of steel belongs to the soldier, yet this must be by the authority and will of the priest and by the direct command of the emperor.... For the two swords are Peter's, to be drawn whenever necessary, the one by his own hand, the other by his authority.[12]

12. Tierney, *The Crisis of Church and State, 1050-1300*, 93-94.

ROMAN CATHOLIC POLITICAL THEORY

This theory of the two swords, so common during the Middle Ages, is based on an imaginative and convenient misinterpretation of *Luke* 22:38: "And they said, Lord, behold here are two swords. And he said unto them, It is enough." Brian Tierney, a noted Roman Catholic historian of the twentieth century, aptly wrote: "A whole inverted pyramid of political fantasy was erected on the basis of this one verse of Scripture."[13]

In 1075, a few years earlier than Bernard, one of the most ambitious popes, Gregory VII, previously known as Cardinal Hildebrand, had written the *Dictatus Papae*, from which these propositions are taken:

1. That the Roman Church was founded by God alone.
2. That the Roman Pontiff alone is rightly to be called universal.
3. That he alone can depose or reinstate bishops.
4. That his legate, even if of a lower grade, takes precedence in a council of bishops and may render a sentence of deposition against them.
5. That for him alone it is lawful to enact new laws according to the needs of the time....
6. That he alone may use the imperial insignia.
7. That the Pope is the only one whose feet are to be kissed by all princes.
8. That his bane alone is to be recited in the churches.
9. That his title is unique in the world.
10. That he may depose emperors.
18. That no sentence of his may be retracted by any one; and that he, alone of all, can retract it.
19. That he himself may be judged by no one.
22. That the Roman Church has never erred, nor ever, by the witness of Scripture, shall err to all eternity.
27. That the Pope may absolve subjects of unjust men from their fealty.[14]

In these sentences Gregory VII summarized the theory of papal power as it stood in the eleventh century. The papacy clearly was much different from its beginnings in Rome.

One of the most brilliant and audacious popes of the Middle Ages was Innocent III (1198-1216). Not only did he understand the funda-

---

13. Tierney, *The Crisis of Church and State, 1050-1300*, 8.
14. Tierney, *The Crisis of Church and State, 1050-1300*, 49-50.

mentals of Roman political thought, he stated them clearly and drew out some of their more important implications. In a sermon on the consecration of a pope, Innocent III wrote: "...Peter alone assumed the plenitude of power. You see then who is this servant set over the household, truly the vicar of Jesus Christ, successor of Peter, anointed of the Lord, a God of Pharaoh, set between God and man, lower than God but higher than man, who judges all and is judged by no one...." [15] According to official Roman Catholic political theory, the pope is a demi-god. The papacy's assertion of totalitarian theocracy is as pagan as the claims of the old Roman Emperors to which it bears some similarity. Roman Catholic historian Tierney attempted to excuse the totalitarian theocracy of the Roman Church-State by arguing that "it must be remembered that theocracy is a normal pattern of government."[16] The statement is true enough, if by "normal" we understand "usual," for even Christ had said that the Gentiles lord it over each other. But Christ went on to say, "It shall not be so among you."[17] The Gentiles exercise dominion over each other, but Christian leaders are to be servants, not lords. Christian political theory is not pagan political theory, but Roman Catholic political theory is pagan political theory.

In a letter to the patriarch of Constantinople (1199), Innocent III wrote: "...James, the brother of the Lord who 'seemed to be a pillar' (*Galatians* 1:19), content with Jerusalem alone...left to Peter not only the Universal Church but the whole world to govern...." [18] In a letter to Emperor Alexius of Constantinople (1201), Innocent III wrote: "...any one who fails to acknowledge Peter and his successors as pastors and teachers is outside his [Christ's] flock. We need hardly mention, since they are so well known, the words that Christ spoke to Peter and through Peter to his successors, 'Whatsoever you bind upon Earth, etc.' (*Matthew* 16:19), excepting nothing when he said, 'Whatsoever.'"[19]

In a letter to the archbishop of Ravenna (1198), Innocent III wrote: "Ecclesiastical liberty is nowhere better cared for than where the Roman church has full power in both temporal and spiritual affairs." [20]

---

15. Tierney, *The Crisis of Church and State, 1050-1300*, 132.
16. Tierney, *The Crisis of Church and State, 1050-1300*, 131.
17. *Matthew* 20:26.
18. Tierney, *The Crisis of Church and State, 1050-1300*, 132.
19. Tierney, *The Crisis of Church and State, 1050-1300*, 133.
20. Tierney, *The Crisis of Church and State, 1050-1300*, 132.

That is the meaning of *religious liberty* in the thought of the papacy down to the twentieth century: full power for the Roman Church-State in both temporal and spiritual affairs. Liberty is power.[21] In his 1198 letter *Sicut Universitatis Conditor*, Innocent III distinguished between spiritual and secular power, using the analogy, not original with him, of the Sun and the Moon.[22]

> Just as God, founder of the universe, has constituted two large luminaries in the firmament of heaven, a major one to dominate the day and a minor one to dominate the night, so he has established in the firmament of the Universal Church, which is signified by the name of heaven, two great dignities, a major one to preside, so to speak, over the days of the souls, and a minor one to preside over the night of the bodies. They are the pontifical authority and the royal power. Thus, as the Moon receives its light from the Sun and for this very reason is minor both in quantity and quality, in its size and in its effect, so the royal power derives from the pontifical authority the splendor of its dignity....

In his decretal *Venerabilem Fratrem* (1202), Innocent III repeated the argument that the temporal power is subservient to the spiritual power and the "very right and power" of the Emperor of the Holy Roman Empire comes from the pope.[23]

> [T]his right and power [of princes] has come to them from the Apostolic See, which had transferred the Roman Empire from the Greeks to the Germans in the person of Charlemagne....The right and authority to examine the persons elected as king – who is to be promoted to the office of emperor – belongs to us, who anoint, consecrate, and crown him.

Innocent III declared, "I have obtained from Peter the mitre for my priesthood and the crown for my royalty; he has made me vicar of Him upon whose vesture is written, King of Kings and Lord of Lords...."[24]

---

21. "Whenever there exists, or there is reason to fear, an unjust oppression of the people on the one hand, or a deprivation of the liberty of the church on the other, it is lawful to seek for such a change of government as will bring about due liberty of action" for the Roman Church (Leo XIII, *Libertas Praetantissimum, On Human Liberty* [1888], 51).
22. *Readings in Church History*, C. J. Barry, editor. Westminster, Maryland: The Newman Press, 1960, I, 438-439.
23. Barry, *Readings in Church History*, I, 437-438.
24. C. S. M. Walker, *The Gathering Storm*, 134.

The fact that the pope had granted authority to the emperor was an illustration of the plentitude of papal authority. Over the centuries this is how the argument has developed: Political power *per se* is not derived from Constantine, although direct jurisdiction over the Roman Empire is. Political power *per se* had been given to Peter by Jesus, and so it has descended from Peter through all the Roman popes.

In 1236, Gregory IX (1227-1241) wrote a letter to the Emperor, Frederick II, in which he argued that the *Donation of Constantine* was one basis of the temporal power of the papacy:

> [I]t is publicly obvious to the whole world that the aforesaid Constantine, who had received the exclusive monarchy over all parts of the world, decided as just...that as the vicar of the Prince of Apostles governed the empire of priesthood and of souls in the whole world, so he should also reign over things and bodies throughout the whole world; and...the Emperor Constantine humbled himself by his own vow and handed over the Empire to the perpetual care of the Roman Pontiff with the Imperial insignia and sceptres and the City and Duchy of Rome....Whence later in the aforesaid Charlemagne...the Apostolic See transferred the judgment-seat of the Empire to the Germans,...although reducing in nothing the substance of its own jurisdiction....[25]

Gregory appealed to the *Donation* as a grant of power so obvious and well-known that it ended all arguments about temporal power.

But the emperors, who coveted power themselves, soon argued that if the Roman Church-State had received the empire as a gift from Constantine, perhaps a later emperor could rescind the gift. To meet that argument, Innocent IV (1243-1254) in his 1246 encyclical *Eger Cui Levia*, expanded the Roman Church-State claim to political power from the specific case of the Holy Roman Empire to the general principle that *all* political power belongs by right to the pope:

> Whoever seeks to evade the authority of the Vicar of Christ...thereby impairs the authority of the Christ Himself. The King of kings has established us on Earth as his universal representative and has conferred full power on us; by giving to the prince of the apostles and to us the power of binding and loosing on Earth not only all men whatsoever, but also all things whatsoever....The power of temporal government cannot

25. Tierney, *The Crisis of Church and State, 1050-1300*, 144-145.

be exercised outside the church, since there is no power constituted by God outside her.... They are lacking in perspicacity and incapable of investigating the origin of things who imagine that the Apostolic See received from Constantine the sovereignty of the empire, whereas it had it previously, as is known, by nature and potentially. Our Lord Jesus Christ, Son of God, true man and true God...constituted to the benefit of the Holy See a monarchy not only pontifical but royal; he committed to the blessed Peter and his successors the reins of the empire both earthly and celestial, as is indicated by the plurality of the keys. Vicar of Christ has received the power to exercise his jurisdiction by the one over the Earth for temporal things, by the other in Heaven for spiritual things. In truth, when Constantine was joined to the Catholic church through the faith of Christ he humbly resigned to the church the inordinate tyranny that he had formerly exercised outside of it...and he received within the church from Christ's vicar, the successor of Peter, a duly ordered power of sacred rulership...and he who had formerly abused a power permitted to him afterwards exercised an authority bestowed on him.... For indeed the power of this material sword is implicit in the church, but it is made explicit through the emperor who receives it from the church.[26]

To meet the emperors' argument, the popes asserted that both political and ecclesiastical power had been given to Peter *alone*. In his *Decretales* (1250), Innocent IV wrote that "the emperor is the protector of the pope and takes an oath to him and holds the empire from him...."[27] Furthermore, "the pope, who is vicar of Jesus Christ, has power not only over Christians but also over all infidels, for Christ has power over all.... All men, faithful and infidels, are Christ's sheep by creation.... The pope has jurisdiction and power over all *de iure* though not *de facto*."[28]

Cardinal Hostiensis, a contemporary of Innocent IV, wrote that because the pope is to the emperor as the Sun is to the Moon, "the sacerdotal dignity is seven thousand, six hundred and forty-four and a half times greater than the royal, for we read in the fifth Book of the *Almagest* of Ptolemy, Proposition 18, 'It is clear that the magnitude of

---

26. *Twentieth Century Encyclopedia of Catholicism*. New York: Hawthorne Books, 1959, volume 77, pages 37-38.
27. Tierney, *The Crisis of Church and State, 1050-1300*, 153.
28. Tierney, *The Crisis of Church and State, 1050-1300*, 155-156.

the sun contains the magnitude of the moon seven thousand six hundred and forty-four and a half times.'"[29]

Boniface VIII (1294-1303) repeated, expanded on, and stated literally and forcefully this papal claim to absolute power in the bull *Unam Sanctam* (1302):

> We are taught by the words of the Gospel that in this church and in her power there are two swords, a spiritual one and a temporal one.... Certainly anyone who denies that the temporal sword is in the power of Peter has not paid heed to the words of the Lord when he said, "Put up thy sword into its sheath" (*Matthew* 26:52). Both then are in the power of the church, the spiritual and material swords; the one to be wielded for the church, the other by the church; the former by hand of the priest, the latter by the hand of kings and soldiers, but at the will and suffrance of the priest. For it is necessary that one sword should be under another and that the temporal authority should be subjected to the spiritual. For, while the apostle says, "There is no power but from God and those that are ordained of God" (*Romans* 13:1), they would not be ordained unless one sword was under the other and, being inferior, was led by the other to the highest things. For, according to the blessed Dionysius, it is the law of divinity for the lowest to be led to the highest through intermediaries. In the order of the universe all things are not kept in order in the same fashion and immediately, but the lowest are ordered by the intermediate and inferiors by superiors. But that the spiritual power excels any earthly one in dignity and nobility we ought the more openly to confess in proportion as spiritual things excel temporal ones.... For, the truth bearing witness, the spiritual power has to institute the earthly power and to judge it if it has not been good. So is verified the prophecy of *Jeremias* [1:10] concerning the church and the power of the church: "Lo, I have set thee this day over the nations and over kingdoms," etc.
>
> Therefore, if the earthly power errs, it shall be judged by the spiritual power; if a lesser spiritual power errs, it shall be judged by its superior; but if the supreme spiritual power errs, it can be judged only by God, not by man, as the apostle witnesses, "The spiritual man judgeth all things and he himself is judged by no man" (*1 Corinthians* 2:15).... Whoever, therefore, resists this power thus ordained by God, resists the ordination of God unless, like the Manicheans, he imagines that there are two beginnings, which we judge to be false and heretical, as Moses witnesses, for not "in the beginnings" but "in the beginning" God created Heaven

---

29. Tierney, *The Crisis of Church and State, 1050-1300*, 156.

and Earth (*Genesis* 1:1). Consequently we declare, state, define, and pronounce that it is altogether necessary to salvation for every human creature to be subject to the Roman pontiff.[30]

Boniface's argument for the subordination of civil authorities to the pope was based on the unity of the church. The organizational unity of the church requires not only that all theological persons and institutions be subject to the pope (Boniface had written: "if the Greeks or any others say that they were not committed to Peter and his successors, they necessarily admit that they are not of Christ's flock, for the Lord says in *John* that there is one sheepfold and one shepherd"), a position that proleptically condemned the Protestant Reformation of the sixteenth century, but also requires the subordination of all persons and institutions, including especially civil rulers, to the pope. Thus we see that in papal thought ecclesiastical unity is the foundation for political unity – that in fact ecclesiastical unity logically entails political unity, and political unity presupposes a prior ecclesiastical unity. Roman Catholic political theory is an integral part of Roman Catholic theology. The two are portions of the same system. When the Reformation occurred two centuries later, the Roman Church-State used this dogma in an effort to restore its ecclesiastical and political unity – to make all men subject to the pope – by force of arms. In the twentieth century, it has attempted to restore ecclesiastical unity both by force of arms and by unprecedented ecumenical overtures, as a prelude to a restored political unity.

Giles of Rome (died 1315) was the theoretician whose work *De Ecclesiastica Potestate* provided the theoretical foundations for the totalitarian papal claims of Boniface VIII. His arguments – some of his very sentences – were used by Boniface in *Unam Sanctam*. Giles, however, drew out more of the logical implications of the papal plentitude of power. For example, he argued that the pope owns everything on Earth:

> ...all temporal things are placed under the dominion and power of the church....The power of the supreme pontiff governs souls. Souls ought rightly to govern bodies.... But temporal things serve our bodies. It

---

30. Barry, *Readings in Church History*, I, 466-467. Tierney, *The Crisis of Church and State*, 1050-1300, 188-189. The last sentence, of course, made this doctrine definitive – a doctrine that cannot be changed by any subsequent pope.

follows then that the priestly power which governs souls also rules over bodies and temporal things.... No one can justly hold dominion over anything unless he is born again through the church.... It follows then that you should acknowledge that your heritage and all your lordship and every right of possession are yours more from the church and through the church and because you are a son of the church than from your carnal father or through him or because you are his son.... Although we say that the church is mother and mistress of all possessions and all temporalities, we do not thereby deprive the faithful of their lordships and possessions for...the church and the faithful each have a kind of lordship; but the church has a universal and superior lordship, the faithful a particular and inferior one.[31]

The faithful hold their properties and positions only by the sufferance of the Church-State, which has a universal and superior lordship. "The plentitude of power is in the spiritual sword." The popes applied this universal dominion to political power, and, by the same logic, universal dominion has important implications for the economic theory of the Roman Church-State as well.

Over the centuries other popes have reiterated this claim to total power, but rather than proceeding to a recital of such claims, let us turn to the political thought of Thomas Aquinas, since he also was writing in the thirteenth century, and since his works were subsequently endorsed by the Council of Trent and made the official philosophy of the Roman Church-State by Leo XIII in his 1879 encyclical *Aeterna Patris*.

---

31. Tierney, *The Crisis of Church and State, 1050-1300*, 198-200.

Eleven

The Political Thought of Thomas Aquinas

"Among the scholastic doctors," Leo XIII declared, "the chief and master of all towers Thomas Aquinas...."[1] "In the fields of ethics and politics," Tierney reported, "Thomistic teaching was strikingly successful from the outset, and his principal doctrines, which were in the main those of Aristotle, were assimilated into the most widely used manuals of law and moral theology in the fourteenth century."[2] It is Thomas' teaching that Leo XIII urged all Catholics everywhere to inculcate in the young, and to make the basis for Roman Catholic apologetics, philosophy, education, and action: "...we exhort you, venerable brethren, in all earnestness to restore the golden wisdom of St. Thomas, and to spread it far and wide for the defense and beauty of the Catholic faith....Let carefully selected teachers endeavor to implant the doctrine of Thomas Aquinas in the minds of the students...."

Leo XIII was neither the first nor the only pope to cite the authority of Thomas. In his book *St. Thomas Aquinas,* Jacques Maritain includes an appendix of "Papal Testimonies" to Thomas, a list that includes scores of references spanning eight centuries. In 1914, Pius X reiterated Leo XIII's injunction:

> So far as studies are concerned, it is Our will and We hereby explicitly ordain that the Scholastic philosophy be considered as the basis for

---

1. Leo XIII, *On the Restoration of Christian Philosophy, Aeterna Patris,* August 4, 1879. "But the chief and special glory of Thomas, one which he has shared with none of the Catholic doctors, is that the Fathers of Trent made it part of the order of the conclave to lay upon the altar, together with the code of Sacred Scripture and the decrees of the Supreme Pontiffs, the *Summa* of Thomas Aquinas, whence to see counsel, reason, and inspiration."

2. Tierney, *The Crisis of Church and State, 1050-1300,* 165.

scared studies.... We have in mind particularly the philosophy which has been transmitted to us by St. Thomas Aquinas. ... We renew and confirm them [all the enactments of Our Predecessor] and order them to be strictly observed by all concerned. Let Bishops urge and compel their observance in future....The same injunction applies also to Superiors of Religious Orders....The principles of philosophy laid down by St. Thomas Aquinas are to be religiously and inviolably observed.... The capital theses in the philosophy of St. Thomas are not to be placed in the category of opinions capable of being debated one way or another, but are to be considered as the foundations upon which the whole science of natural and divine things is based.... The experience of so many centuries has shown and every passing day more clearly proves the truth of the statement made by Our Predecessor John XXII: "He [Thomas Aquinas] enlightened the Church more than all the other Doctors together; a man can derive more profit from his books in one year than from a lifetime spent in pondering the philosophy of others...."[3]

The popes' injunctions did not go unheeded. Thomism flourished in the twentieth century, when some of the greatest students of Thomas published their works. Nearly sixty years ago, in 1941, Gordon Clark pointed out that

If one were to examine the list of books, articles, and periodicals published by Roman Catholic writers, one would be amazed at the wealth of productivity. The subject matter, not confined to theology as such, ranges through philosophy, anthropology, biology, education, history, and political science. Nor is it the mere quantity of the books that is significant. The strength of all this production lies in the fact that Romanism is attacking all these problems systematically. Whether the author writes on psychology or politics, the views expounded and advocated are the implications of the Thomistic system.... In the learned societies of our country, Romanist speakers are heard with respect, while orthodox Protestants are either rarely invited or else perhaps do not exist.[4]

---

3. Pius X, *Doctoris Angelici*, June 29, 1914; as quoted in Maritain, *St. Thomas Aquinas*, New York: Meridian Books [1931] 1958, 215-221.
4. Gordon H. Clark, "A Protestant Worldview," in *Against the World: The Trinity Review 1978-1988*, John Robbins, editor. The Trinity Foundation, 1996, 7.

What did Thomas write about politics? "The best regime of a community," according to Thomas, "is government by one person, which is made evident if we recall that the end for which a government exists is the maintenance of peace. Peace and unity of subjects is the goal of the ruler. But unity is more congruently the effect of one than of many."[5] In this argument and conclusion, Thomas relies on Aristotle, not the Bible, for the regime God constructed for the ancient Hebrews was a constitutional republic, not a monarchy. The sinful Israelites later demanded and got a monarchy, so that they would have a king like all the pagan nations around them. One of the greatest statements about government from ancient times is the warning about monarchy that God delivers to the Jews, through the prophet Samuel.[6] In this sequence – the movement from a decentralized republic to a centralized monarchy – the Roman Church-State imitated the ancient Israelites.

The Roman Church-State, of course, is based on the government of one man, the bishop of Rome. It is an absolute monarchy, in which the monarch holds his title for life. Furthermore, unity, which Thomas mentions as the desideratum of good government, is the motivation for one-man rule in the Roman Church-State. The pope, as absolute ruler of the Roman Church-State, represents the unity of the Roman Church-State on Earth.

While the Church-State is unified, there are, according to Thomas, two distinct powers, the spiritual and the temporal, possessed by a unified government:

> In order that spiritual matters might be kept separate from temporal ones, the ministry of this [spiritual] kingdom was entrusted not to earthly kings but to priests and especially to the highest of them, the successor of St. Peter, Vicar of Christ, the Roman Pontiff, to whom all kings must be subject just as they are subject to our Lord Jesus. For those to whom the care of an intermediate end pertains should be subject to him to whom the care of the ultimate end belongs and be directed by his rule.[7]

---

5. Thomas Aquinas, *The Political Ideas of St. Thomas Aquinas*. Dino Bigongiari, editor. New York: Hafner Publishing Company, 1953, xxvii. "Now it is manifest that what is itself one can more efficaciously bring about unity than a group of several....Therefore the rule of one man is more useful than the rule of many" (xxvii).

6. See *1 Samuel* 8.

7. Thomas Aquinas, "On Kingship," in *The Political Ideas of St. Thomas Aquinas*, 100.

The pope and only the pope stands in the place of Christ on Earth, and all men, including rulers, are subject to him: "In the pope the secular power is joined to the spiritual. He holds the apex of both powers, spiritual and secular, by the will of him who is priest and king unto eternity, king of kings and *Dominus Dominantium*."[8] No temporal ruler is a vicar of Christ. Moreover, all secular rulers are vassals of the pope. "In old Roman days," Thomas explained, "monarchs opposed Christ. But now kings comprehend and because of what they have learned, they serve Our Lord Jesus Christ in fear; and therefore, today kings are vassals of the church."[9]

Using an old analogy, Thomas argued that

> Secular power is subject to the spiritual power as the body is subject to the soul, and therefore it is not a usurpation of authority if the spiritual prelate interfere in temporal things concerning those matters in which the secular power is subject to him, or concerning those matters the care of which has been entrusted to him by the secular power.[10]

Therefore, not only are all men, including all rulers, subject to the power of the pope, but the pope can, whenever he sees fit, intervene in temporal matters directly and exercise the power that is always indirectly his.[11] Not only can the pope exercise temporal powers directly

---

8. Thomas Aquinas, *The Political Ideas of St. Thomas Aquinas*, xxxiv.
9. Thomas Aquinas, *Quaestiones Quodlibetales*, 11.19.
10. Thomas Aquinas, *The Political Ideas of St. Thomas Aquinas*, xxxiv.
11. Thomas provided explicit instructions on how lesser powers are subject to the jurisdiction of the pope, and how ordinary men are bound to obey the pope rather than their immediate superiors, should there happen to be a conflict: "Sometimes the inferior power emanates in its totality from the superior, in which case the entire potence of the former is founded upon the potence of the latter, so that obedience is due to the higher at all times and without exceptions. Such is the superiority of the Emperor's power over that of the Proconsul [quoted from St. Augustine]; such that of the Pope over all spiritual powers in the church, since the ecclesiastical hierarchies are ordained and disposed by him, and his power is in some manner the foundation of the church as it appears from *Matthew* 16. Hence we are required in all these things to obey him rather than the bishop or archbishop and to him the monk owes obedience in preference to his abbot. But two powers may be such that both arise from a third and supreme authority, and their relative rank then depends upon the will of this uppermost power. When this is the case, either one of the two subordinate authorities controls the other only in those matters in which its superiority has been recognized by the uppermost power. Of such nature is the authority exercised by rulers, by bishops, by archbishops, etc., over their subjects, for all of them have received it from the Pope and with it the conditions and limitations of its use" (*The Political Ideas of St. Thomas Aquinas*, xxxv).

and indirectly, he can excommunicate a ruler and thereby dissolve all obligations his subjects have to support and obey him, thus overthrowing governments at will. Thomas wrote:

> ...if someone commits the sin of unbelief he can be deprived of his right to rule by judicial sentence, just as for other failings.... Therefore, as soon as someone falls under a sentence of excommunication for apostasy from the faith, his subjects are *ipso facto* absolved from his rule and from the oath of fealty by which they were bound to him.[12]

In the sixteenth century, the Council of Trent declared that the pope has "all power on Earth.... All temporal power is his; the dominion, jurisdiction, and government of the whole Earth is his by divine right. All rulers of the Earth are his subjects and must submit to him." The views of *Unam Sanctam* are neither eccentric, exaggerated, nor merely medieval; they are the views of Thomas and the entire Church-State.

Long before the nineteenth century German philosopher G. W. F. Hegel thought of describing the State as God walking on Earth, the popes had made their claim to be God on Earth – the Vicar of Christ – a fundamental doctrine of Roman Church-State theology. Drawing on this centuries-old tradition, Leo XIII in the nineteenth century described himself in his encyclical letter on the reunion of Christendom as "We who hold upon this earth the place of God Almighty." The totalitarian systems of the twentieth century owe much more than has been recognized to the political thought and practice of the Roman Church-State.

The doctrine of the "plentitude of papal power" has been the unchanging teaching of the Roman Church-State. Its most recent *Catechism* expresses the totalitarian claim this way, omitting such details as might be inexpedient to mention in an age of democracy: "...the Roman Pontiff, by reason of his office as Vicar of Christ, and as pastor of the entire Church, has full, supreme, and universal power over the whole Church, a power which he can always exercise unhindered."[13] The Canon Law of the Roman Church-State provides that

> The bishop of the Church of Rome, in whom resides the office given in a special way by the Lord to Peter, first of the Apostles and to be

---

12. Thomas Aquinas, *Summa Theologiae,* ii-ii, Question 12, in *Basic Writings of Thomas Aquinas,* Anton C. Pegis, editor. New York: Random House, 1945.

13. *Catechism of the Catholic Church,* Liguori, Missouri: Liguori Publications, 1994, 882.

transmitted to his successors, is head of the college of bishops, the Vicar of Christ and Pastor of the Universal Church on Earth; therefore, in virtue of his office he enjoys supreme, full, immediate, and universal ordinary power in the Church which he can always freely exercise.[14]

The 1983 Canonists obligingly explain:

> Supreme power (*suprema*) means there is no power in the Church above this power. It is not subject to any other power on this Earth.... Vatican I applied this directly to the relationship between the Church and civil governments, some of which at that time claimed their approval was needed before papal decrees could affect citizens subject to them.... Full (*plena*) indicates supreme power is not parceled out, as if the pope had only a piece of supreme power. Supreme power is indivisible, for it is the power of Christ.... Ecclesial power is a spiritual reality unlimited by national boundaries or civil jurisdiction.... Universal (*universali*) power is unlimited by the confines of the diocese of Rome, its provinces, or even the Latin Church. It extends to the full communion of the Catholic Church in all its Ritual Churches....[15]

The coronation service of the popes includes the injunction to "Take thou the tiara adorned with the triple crown, and know that thou art the Father of princes and of kings, and art the Governor of the world."

---

14. Canon 331.

15. James Coriden, Thomas J. Green, and Donald E. Heintschel, editors. *The Code of Canon Law, A Text and Commentary*. Mahwah, New Jersey: Paulist Press, 1985.

Twelve

Persecution, Inquisition, and Slavery

THE ROMAN Church-State's absolute monarchy, in opposition to which the civil monarchs of England and France adopted and developed the theory of the divine right of kings, became the first totalitarian power in the West, and the mother of twentieth century totalitarianism. The Roman Church-State insisted on unity, conformity, and loyalty from everyone; dissenters were to be corrected, and if contumacious, killed. Thomas Aquinas stated the Roman Church-State theory justifying legalized murder and wars of aggression:

> There are some unbelievers such as the Gentiles and the Hebrews who have never accepted the Christian faith. These should in no way be forced to believe.... Appropriate force may be used by the faithful to prevent them from interfering with the faith through blasphemy or evil inducements, or open persecution. This is the reason that Christians often make war on unbelievers, not to force them to believe...but to prevent them from interfering with the Christian faith. However, there are other unbelievers, such as heretics and all apostates who once accepted and professed the faith. These are to be compelled, even by physical force, to carry out what they promised and to hold what they once accepted.[1]

Of course, Thomas was not the first defender of state-sanctioned murder; the Roman Church-State had already been practicing and defending murder. The Lateran Council of 1139, for example, a century before Thomas, urged secular powers to punish heresy. Pope

---

1. Thomas Aquinas, *Summa Theologiae*, ii-ii, Question 10, Article 8, in *Basic Writings*.

Alexander III (1159-1181) and the Lateran Council of 1179 urged the use of force and held out rewards such as two years' remission of penance for those who murdered heretics. The Crusades, the wars of aggression waged by the Roman Church-State during the Middle Ages, were justified by the same rationale.

Two centuries after Thomas, Martin V (1417-1431) ordered the King of Poland to exterminate the Hussites. The pope wrote to the king:

> Know that the interests of the Holy See, and those of your crown, make it a duty to exterminate the Hussites. Remember that these impious persons dare proclaim principles of equality; they maintain that all Christians are brethren and that God has not given to privileged men the right of ruling the nations; they hold that Christ came on Earth to abolish slavery; they call the people to liberty, that is to the annihilation of kings and priests. While there is still time, then, turn your forces against Bohemia; burn, massacre, make deserts everywhere, for nothing could be more agreeable to God, or more useful to the cause of kings, than the extermination of the Hussites.

During the centuries between Thomas and the twentieth, the political thought of the Roman Church-State did not substantially change. In the thirteenth century, the Roman Church-State exterminated the Albigenses in southern France:

> From 1202 to 1226 the papacy sent army after army to the South of France to crush the Albigensian heretics and to punish their supporters. The Albigensian Crusades were religious wars and like all religious wars they were bloody and cruel. They began with a calculated act of terror, the massacre of Beziers; they ended with the establishment of the Inquisition, one of the most effective means of thought control that Europe has ever known. They were completely successful: The losing faith, the Albigensian heresy, was exterminated.[2]

Ignaz von Döllinger, one of the most prominent Roman Catholic historians of the nineteenth century, wrote:

> Through the influence of Gratian...and unwearied activity of the Popes and their legates since 1183, the view of the Church had been...[that] every departure from the teaching of the Church, and every important opposition to any ecclesiastical ordinances, must be punished with death,

---

2. Joseph R. Strayer, Preface to *The Albigensian Crusades*. Ann Arbor: University of Michigan Press, 1992 [1971].

and the most cruel of deaths, by fire.... Both the initiation and carrying out of this new principle must be ascribed to the Popes alone.... It was the Popes who compelled bishops and priests to condemn the heterodox to torture, confiscation of their goods, imprisonment, and death, and to enforce these executions of this sentence on the civil authorities, under pain of excommunication. From 1200 to 1500 the long series of Papal ordinances on the Inquisition, ever increasing in severity and cruelty, and their whole policy towards heresy, runs on without a break. It is a rigidly consistent system of legislation; every pope confirms and improves upon the devices of his predecessor.... It was only the absolute dictation of the Popes and the notion of their infallibility in all questions of Evangelical morality, that made the Christian world...[accept] the Inquisition, which contradicted the simplest principles of Christian justice and love to our neighbor, and would have been rejected with universal horror in the ancient church.[3]

During this same period, and into the twentieth century, the Roman Church-State was becoming more and more explicitly committed to the idea of a world government, headed by a temporal ruler who received his authority from the pope and who was subservient to the pope.[4] Nothing in recent years has changed that fundamental position of the Roman Church-State; indeed, recent popes have reiterated the need for a world government.

Protestant American clergymen, as well as a few theological liberals, once recognized what the Roman Church-State is, as can be seen from this quotation from a sermon delivered by Tunis Wortman in 1800, "A Solemn Address to Christians and Patriots":

> If you are real Christians, anxious for the honor and purity and interest of the Christian church, you will feel a steady determination to preserve it from corruption. Unless you maintain the pure and primitive spirit of Christianity, and prevent the cunning and intrigue of statesmen from mingling with it institutions, you will become exposed to a renewal of the same dreadful and enormous scenes which have not only disgraced the annals of the Church, but destroyed the peace, and sacrificed the lives of millions. It is by such scenes and by such dreadful crimes that Christianity has suffered; by such fatal and destructive enormities which, since the days of Constantine, have been perpetrated without intermission,

---

3. Ignaz von Döllinger, *The Pope and the Council*. London, 1869, 190-193.

4. The pope is "...the highest authority on earth,..." according to Pius XI in his 1931 encyclical *Quadragesimo Anno*, 7.

that the church has become debased and polluted, in language similar to that of Joshua, we have reason to exclaim there is an accursed thing within the tabernacle. The blood of many an innocent Abel has stained the ephod, the vestments and the altar. Religion has suffered more from the restless ambition and impiety of the church of Rome than from all the writings of a Voltaire, a Tindal, a Volney, or even the wretched blasphemies of Paine. We have years and volumes – we have a world of experience before us, in the sufferings and miseries of ages – a ready lesson too impressive to be resisted: both as Christians and as men, we are powerfully conjured to reject all attempts to promote an union, between the church and the state – the very idea of such an union is insupportable. Neither directly nor indirectly should we suffer it to be effected.... The church of Rome arose from the smallest beginnings. She commenced her career with professions of mildness, clemency and moderation, displaying at first the innocence and the harmlessness of the dove: she afterwards discovered [disclosed] the horrid fangs of the serpent, and exercised the unrelenting barbarity of a crocodile. The successors of St. Peter, no longer spiritual bishops, became a race of tyrants, more ferocious than Nero, or Domitian, and more pampered than Eliogabalus himself.[5]

From its inception until the twentieth century, the Roman Catholic Church has endorsed slavery. John Francis Maxwell, a Roman Catholic priest whose book bears the *nihil obstat* of John Pledger and the *imprimatur* of Cyril Cowderoy, Archbishop of Southwark (England), summarized the position of the Roman Church-State in these words:

---

5. Tunis Wortman, "A Solemn Address to Christians and Patriots," in Ellis Sandoz, editor, *Political Sermons of the American Founding Era, 1730-1805*. Indianapolis: Liberty Fund, 1991. Another sermon by Samuel Sherwood included these paragraphs: "I would observe with all judicious commentators and expositors that have wrote on the subject, that popery, or the reign and kingdom of the man of sin, the old serpent, the dragon, its rise and progress and its downfall and overthrow is the greatest, the most essential, and the most striking part of this revelation of St. John.... Among all his crafty and diabolical inventions, popery, which exalts the principal leaders and abettors of it...seems most cunningly devised and best adapted to answer its purpose, and has proved the most formidable engine of terror and cruelty to the true members of Christ's church, and this has been the chief subject of prophecy since the coming of Christ, and was foretold by some of the prophets under the Jewish dispensation.... As power has been the greatest enemy, and the greatest corrupter of Christianity, we may rationally conclude that more prophecies relate to that, than to any other distant event" (Samuel Sherwood, "The Church's Flight into the Wilderness," 1776, in Sandoz, *Political Sermons of the American Founding Era, 1730-1805*).

PERSECUTION, INQUISITION, AND SLAVERY

Since the sixth century and right up until the twentieth century it has been common Catholic teaching that the social, economic and legal institution of slavery is morally legitimate provided that the master's title of ownership is valid and provided that the slave is properly looked after and cared for, both materially and spiritually. This institution of genuine slavery, whereby one human being is legally owned by another, and is forced to work for the exclusive benefit of his owner in return for food, clothing and shelter, and may be bought, sold, donated or exchanged, was not merely tolerated but was commonly approved of in the Western Latin Church for over 1400 years.[6]

This teaching, which Maxwell described as a "disaster," has been whitewashed by modern Roman Catholic historians who want to "defend the good name of the Catholic Church."[7]

Since the early beginnings (in the eighteenth century) of the modern anti-slavery movement, a few Catholic historians have done their best to whitewash the past history of this common teaching of the Popes, Councils, Church Fathers, Bishops, canonists and moralists on slavery....[8]

The whitewashing, however, was not done merely by a few Roman Catholic historians, but by the popes themselves. For example, Leo XIII, author of *Rerum Novarum*, wrote in 1890:

From the beginning, almost nothing was more venerated in the Catholic Church which embraces all men with motherly love, than the fact that she looked to see a slavery eased and abolished which was oppressing so many people....; she undertook the neglected cause of the slaves and stood forth as a strenuous defender of liberty, although she conducted her campaign gradually and prudently so far as times and circumstances permitted...; nor did this effort of the Church to liberate slaves weaken in the course of time; indeed the more slavery flourished from time to time, the more zealously she strove. The clearest historical documents are evidence for this...and many of our predecessors including St. Gregory the Great, Hadrian I, Alexander III, Innocent III, Gregory IX, Pius II, Leo X, Paul III, Urban VIII, Benedict XIV, Pius VII and Gregory XVI, made every effort to ensure that the institution of

---

6. John Francis Maxwell, *Slavery and the Catholic Church: The History of Catholic Teaching Concerning the Moral Legitimacy of the Institution of Slavery*. Chichester and London: Barry Rose Publishers, 1975, 10.
7. Maxwell, *Slavery and the Catholic Church*, 10.
8. Maxwell, *Slavery and the Catholic Church*, 10.

slavery should be abolished where it existed and that its roots should not revive where it had been destroyed.⁹

This last statement provoked even the Roman Catholic priest Maxwell to demur with the "greatest respect": "this is historically inaccurate." Maxwell pointed out that "In his earlier letter of 1888 he [Leo XIII] had made selective use of a number of documents written by these same 12 Popes to suggest that there had been a constant 'anti-slavery' tradition in the Catholic Church."¹⁰ Such subreption is not unique to Leo XIII, of course; the papacy had been rewriting history at least as early as the eighth century when it forged the *Donation of Constantine*. Maxwell provided some of the historical evidence demonstrating the lies of Leo.

Maxwell traced the failure of the Roman Church-State to correct itself or to be corrected on the subject of slavery to several factors, including

(1) the principle of the continuity and irreformability of doctrine;¹¹

(2) the influence of theological censorship, which for the past 400 years has restricted theological expression and discussion;¹²

(3) the placing of anti-slavery writings by Roman Catholic laymen on the Index of Prohibited Books in the nineteenth century;

(4) the uncritical adoption and approval of the principles of pagan Roman civil law concerning slavery;

(5) the "long-continued misunderstanding of the meaning of the natural moral law;"

(6) a misunderstanding of the effects of slavery; and

(7) a misunderstanding of Scripture.¹³

---

9. Leo XIII, *Catholicae Ecclesiae*, November 20, 1890; as quoted in Maxwell, *Slavery and the Catholic Church*, 117.

10. Maxwell, *Slavery and the Catholic Church*, 117.

11. This is one of the fundamental principles of the Roman Catholic system, stated innumerable times in its official documents.

12. Of course, censorship has been a characteristic of the Roman Church-State from its inception as well, not merely during the last 400 years. The 1983 revision of the Code of Canon Law abolished the Index of Prohibited Books (*censura repressiva*), but prior censorship, *censura praevia*, is retained. Of course, there is nothing to prevent the revival of the Index at any time.

13. In 1873 Pius IX attached an indulgence to a prayer for the "wretched Ethiopians in Central Africa that almighty God may at length remove the curse of Cham [*Genesis* 9:25-27] from their hearts."

PERSECUTION, INQUISITION, AND SLAVERY

Maxwell cited several examples of the Roman Church-State's advocacy and practice of slavery. The ninth Council of Toledo (655) decreed that the children of priests who had remained neither celibate nor chaste would become permanent slaves of the Church. In 1012 the Council of Pavia issued a similar decree. These decrees were incorporated into the Canon Law of the Roman Church-State. In 1089 at the Synod of Melfi, Urban II enforced clerical celibacy by granting secular authorities the power to enslave the wives of priests. This decree was also incorporated into the Church-State's Canon Law.

At the beginning of the thirteenth century, Aristotle's works were translated into Latin and began to influence the thinking of the Roman Church-State, principally through the work of Thomas Aquinas. In the *Politics*, Aristotle had written concerning slavery:

> [I]t is clearly natural and beneficial to the body that it should be ruled by the soul.... Tame animals have a better nature than wild, and it is better for all such animals that they should be ruled by man because they then get the benefit of preservation.... We may thus conclude that all men who differ from others as much as the body differs from the soul, or an animal from a man...all such are by nature slaves, and it is better for them...to be ruled by a master. A man is thus by nature a slave if he is capable of becoming...the property of another, and if he participates in reason to the extent of apprehending it in another, though destitute of it himself.... But the use which is made of the slave diverges but little from the use made of tame animals; both he and they supply their owner with bodily help in meeting his daily requirements.... It is thus clear that, just as some are by nature free, so other are by nature slaves, and for these latter the condition of slavery is both beneficial and just.[14]

Thomas Aquinas accepted this Aristotelian view of slavery, believing that slavery was "beneficial to human life."

In the fifteenth and sixteenth centuries, exercising their *plenitudo potestatis*, the popes granted the kings of Portugal and Spain

> ...full and free permission to invade, search out, capture and subjugate the Saracens and pagans and any other unbelievers and enemies of Christ wherever they may be, as well as their kingdoms, duchies, counties, principalities, and other property...and to reduce their persons into

---

14. Aristotle, *Politics*, Ernest Barker, translator. Oxford University Press, 1946, L.I.5, 11-14.

perpetual slavery, and to apply and appropriate and convert to the use and profit of yourself and your successors...in perpetuity, the above-mentioned kingdoms, duchies, counties, principalities, and other property and possessions and suchlike goods....[15]

This was done because the popes were "justly desiring that whatsoever concerns the integrity and spread of the faith, for which Christ our God shed his blood, shall flourish in the virtuous souls of the faithful...." In 1493, the same papal permission to slaughter, loot, subjugate, and enslave was granted to Spain not just for campaigns against Africa, but for campaigns against the newly discovered Americas as well. Maxwell remarked that "Portugal and Spain were understood by the Holy See to be at war with the enemies of Christendom – the Negroes of West Africa and the 'Indians' of America – wherever they may be."[16]

In 1548, Paul III issued a *motu proprio*, dealing with slavery in Rome:

By reason of our pastoral office, we gladly attend to the troubles of individual Christians, as far as we can with God's help; and having regard to the fact that the effect of a multitude of slaves is that inherited estates are enriched, agricultural property is better looked after and cities are extended, and desiring to provide security against loss for the people as well as their profit, of our own free will we approve and confirm the above-mentioned enactments and orders...; and nevertheless, as a greater precaution [we decree] that each and every person of either sex, whether Roman or non-Roman, whether secular or clerical, and no matter of what dignity, status, degree, order, or condition they be, may freely and lawfully buy and sell publicly any slaves whatsoever of either sex, and make contracts about them as is accustomed to be done in other places, and publicly hold them as slaves and make use of their work, and compel them to do the work assigned to them. And with Apostolic authority, by the tenor of these present documents, we enact and decree in perpetuity that slaves who flee to the Capitol and appeal for their liberty shall in no wise be freed from the bondage of their servitude, but that <u>notwithstanding their flight and appeal of this sort they shall be returned in slavery to their owners, and if it seems proper they shall be punished</u> as runaways; and we very strictly forbid our beloved sons who for the time being are *conservatori* of the said city to presume by their authority to emancipate the aforesaid slaves – who flee as previously described and

15. As quoted in Maxwell, *Slavery and the Catholic Church*, 53.
16. Maxwell, *Slavery and the Catholic Church*, 56.

appeal for their liberty – from the bondage of their slavery, irrespective of whether they were made Christians after enslavement, or whether they were born in slavery even from Christian slave parents....[17]

From the fifteenth to the eighteenth centuries the popes themselves owned galley-slaves for their naval squadron.

In 1866, the Vatican issued the following statement on slavery and slave trading:

> [S]lavery itself, considered as such in its essential nature, is not at all contrary to the natural and divine law, and there can be several just titles of slavery and these are referred to by approved theologians and commentators of the sacred canons.... From this it follows that it is not contrary to the natural and divine law for a slave to be sold, bought, exchanged or donated, provided that in this sale, purchase, exchange, or gift, the due conditions are strictly observed which the approved authors likewise describe and explain. Among these conditions the most important ones are that the purchaser should carefully examine whether the slave who is put up for sale has been justly or unjustly deprived of his liberty, and that the vendor should do nothing which might endanger the life, virtue, or Catholic faith of the slave who is to be transferred to another's possession.[18]

Maxwell concludes his summary of Roman Catholic moral teaching on slavery with these words:

> If Adolf Hitler has decided to inquire from the Catholic authorities, between 1933 and 1945, whether the institution of slavery in labour camps for condemned criminals was morally legitimate, and whether it was morally right to enslave foreign non-Christian prisoners in just warfare and use them to work in German factories, there is regrettably little doubt that he would have received the reply that there was a "probable opinion" in the affirmative.[19]

---

17. As quoted in Maxwell, *Slavery and the Catholic Church*, 75. American Chief Justice Roger Taney, author of the decision in the famous *Dred Scott* case, was a Roman Catholic.
18. As quoted in Maxwell, *Slavery and the Catholic Church*, 78-79.
19. Maxwell, *Slavery and the Catholic Church*, 124.

Thirteen

The Nineteenth Century

HAVING taken a position favoring authoritarian world government, the Roman Church-State in the nineteenth century turned its attention to attacking capitalism and limited government. For centuries the Roman Church-State had used every means at its disposal in a desperate effort to end the Reformation and the religious, political, and economic freedom it had brought to millions of Christians and their neighbors.[1] An institution of the old aristocracy, the Roman Church-State allied herself with kings and the old nobility in an effort to regain control of Europe. Its efforts were futile. The Reformation could not be stamped out, although millions lost their lives in the persecutions and wars that Rome began in its desperate attempt *ecrasez l'infâme* of Protestantism. Capitalism, the economic system of Christianity, gradually replaced feudalism and guild socialism, the medieval economic system of Romanism. After their most violent efforts had failed to destroy the Reformation, the popes continued to breathe out threats against all who disagreed with them. On December 8, 1864, Pius IX issued the encyclical *Quanta Cura*, containing a *Syllabus of Errors*, not Roman errors, of course, but a vitriolic condemnation of all modernity,

---

1. Leo XIII blamed everything bad on the Reformation: "In truth, sudden uprisings and the boldest rebellions immediately followed in Germany the so-called Reformation, the authors and leaders of which, by their new doctrines, attacked at the very foundation religious and civil authority; and this with so fearful an outburst of civil war and with such slaughter that there was scarcely any place free from tumult and bloodshed. From this heresy there arose in the last century the false philosophy…. Hence we have reached the limit of horrors, to wit, Communism, Socialism, Nihilism, hideous deformities of the civil society of men and almost its ruin" (*Diuturnum Illud, Of Civil Government*, 1881; in Gerard F. Yates, editor, *Papal Thought on the State: Excerpts from Encyclicals and Other Writings of Other Recent Popes.* New York: Appleton-Century Crofts, 1958, 8-9).

both the Reformation and its fruits, and the humanist ideas and institutions that developed from the Renaissance.

Pius IX roared against pantheism, naturalism, rationalism, indifferentism, Protestantism, freedom, and other theological, philosophical, and political errors. Here are a few of Pius IX's own words stating in a positive way some of the principles of Roman Catholic political thought:

> 15. No man is free to embrace and profess that religion which he believes to be true, guided by the light of reason.
>
> 17. The eternal salvation of any out of the true Church of Christ [the Roman Church-State] is not even to be hoped for.
>
> 18. Protestantism is not another and diversified form of the one true Christian religion in which it is possible to please God equally as in the [Roman] Catholic Church.
>
> 19. The [Roman] Church is a true, perfect, and entirely free association; she enjoys peculiar and perpetual rights conferred upon her by her divine founder, and it neither belongs to the civil power to define what are these rights of the [Roman] Church, nor the limits within which she may exercise them.
>
> 21. The [Roman] Church has the power to define dogmatically the religion of the [Roman] Catholic Church to be the only true religion.
>
> 22. The obligation which securely binds [Roman] Catholic teachers and writers is not limited to those things which are proposed by the infallible judgment of the [Roman] Church as dogmas of faith for belief by all.
>
> 23. The Roman Pontiffs and Ecumenical Councils have never exceeded the limits of their power, or usurped the rights of Princes, much less committed errors in defining matters of faith and morals.
>
> 24. The [Roman] Church has the power of employing force and of exercising direct and indirect temporal power.
>
> 34. The doctrine which equaled the Roman Pontiff to an absolute Prince, acting in the Universal [Roman] Church, is not a doctrine which prevailed merely in the Middle Ages.
>
> 54. Kings and Princes are not only not exempt from the jurisdiction of the [Roman] Church, but are subordinate to the Church in litigated questions of jurisdiction.
>
> 55. The [Roman] Church ought to be in union with the State, and the State with the [Roman] Church.
>
> 57. Philosophical principles, moral science, and civil laws may and must be made to bend to Divine and Ecclesiastical authority [of the Roman Church-State].

ECCLESIASTICAL MEGALOMANIA

77. It is necessary even in the present day that the [Roman] Catholic religion shall be held as the only religion of the State, to the exclusion of all other forms of worship.

80. The Roman Pontiff cannot and ought not reconcile himself to, or agree with, progress, Liberalism, and Modern Civilization.

Six years later, after Pius IX had rigged the first Vatican Council so that it would officially declare him infallible,[2] William Gladstone, Prime Minister of England, wrote a pamphlet titled, *The Vatican Decrees and Their Bearing on Civil Allegiance after 1870*. In his pamphlet Gladstone wrote: "With this decree, the claims of Innocent III over mankind have been resurrected in the nineteenth century – like some mummy picked out of its dusty sarcophagus."[3] In 1885 the Jesuit-trained Leo XIII, the pope credited with being the most far-sighted of the past two centuries in the area of social teaching, endorsed and repeated Pius IX's *Syllabus of Errors*:

To the like effect, also, as occasion presented itself, did Pius IX brand publicly many false opinions which were gaining ground, and afterward ordered them to be condensed in summary form in order that in this sea of error Catholics might have a light which they might safely follow. It will suffice to indicate a few of them [errors]: ...The [Roman] Church must be separated from the State, and the State from the [Roman] Church.... ...It is untrue that the civil liberty of every form of worship, and the full power given to all of openly and publicly manifesting whatsoever opinions and thought, lead to the more ready corruption of the minds and morals of the people....[4]

Now these statements are not from the thirteenth century, but were made only a hundred years ago. The Roman Church-State has not changed its spots, even in the past century, although it has become even more clever, less candid, and more subtle, than it has been in the past. John Paul II agrees: "... the Church's [social] teaching...has remained

---

2. See Geddes MacGregor, *The Vatican Revolution*, and Henry Hudson, *Papal Power: Its Origin and Development*. "Vatican I was the first wholly and officially secret Ecumenical Council in history and the first without significant lay representation" (Richard N. Ostling, *Secrecy in the Church: A Reporter's Case for the Christian's Right to Know.* New York: Harper and Row, 1974, 82).

3. Quoted in Anthony Rhodes, *The Power of Rome in the Twentieth Century*, 16.

4. Leo XIII, *Immortale Dei, The Christian Constitution of States* (1885), 23.

144

unchanged throughout the centuries within the context of different historical experiences."⁵

After the Roman Church-State lost the Papal States and its three million subjects to a newly unified Italy in 1870, the pope hunkered down in the Vatican and hurled curses at the world. It was not until the coronation of Leo XIII in 1878 that the Roman Church-State began its intellectual and political ascendancy that has continued throughout the twentieth century. Building on the developed political thought of the Roman Church-State, Leo XIII issued the encyclical *Immortale Dei, The Christian Constitution of States*, in 1885. In it he appealed to the now centuries old analogy of soul and body.⁶ This "orderly connection" had been disrupted by the Reformation, which Leo XIII condemned repeatedly. He wrote:

> It is part of this theory that all questions that concern religion are to be referred to private judgment; that everyone is to be free to follow whatever religion he prefers, or none at all if he disapprove of all. From this the following consequences logically follow: that the judgment of each one's conscience is independent of all law; that the most unrestrained opinions may be openly expressed as to the practice or omission of Divine Worship; and that everyone has an unbounded license to think whatever he chooses and to publish abroad whatever he thinks.⁷

"Doctrines such as these," Leo wrote, appealing to the tradition of the Roman Church-State,

> ...the Roman Pontiffs...have never allowed to pass uncondemned. Thus Gregory XVI in his Encyclical Letter "Mirari Vos," of date August 15, 1832, inveighed with weighty words against the sophisms which even in his time were being publicly inculcated – namely, that no preference should be shown for any particular form of worship; that it is right for individuals to form their own personal judgments about religion; that each man's conscience is his sole and all-sufficing guide; and that it is lawful for every man to publish his own views, whatever they may be and even to conspire against the State.⁸

---

5. John Paul II, *On Human Labor, Laborem Exercens* (1981), 26.
6. "The Almighty, therefore, has appointed the charge of the human race between two powers.... There must, accordingly, exist between these two powers, a certain orderly connection, which may be compared to the union of soul and body in man..." (Leo XIII, *Immortale Dei* [1885], in Yates, *Papal Thought on the State*, 17).
7. Leo XIII, *Immortale Dei* [1885], in Yates, *Papal Thought on the State*, 40.
8. Leo XIII, *Immortale Dei* [1885], in Yates, *Papal Thought on the State*, 23.

The result of this state of affairs is an intolerable interference with the Roman Church-State's liberty, said Leo.

> Now when the State rests on foundations like those just named – and for the time being they are greatly in favor – it readily appears into what and how unrightful a position the Church is driven. For when the management of public business is in harmony with doctrines of such a kind, the Catholic religion is allowed a standing in civil society equal only, or inferior, to societies alien from it; no regard is paid to the laws of the [Roman] Church, and she who, by the order and commission of Jesus Christ, has the duty of teaching all nations, finds herself forbidden to take any part in the instruction of the people.... They who administer the civil power...defiantly put aside the most sacred decrees of the [Roman] Church.... They treat the [Roman] Church with such arrogance that, rejecting entirely her title to the nature and rights of a perfect society, they hold that she differs in no respect from other societies in the State....[9]

The Roman Church-State denounced equality before the law, for the simple reason that no other society on Earth is in fact its equal. Leo XII wrote:

> The cause of all these evils [of modernity] lies principally in this: that men have despised and rejected the holy and august authority of the [Roman] Church, which, in the name of God, is placed over the human race.... We declare that we shall never cease to contend for the full obedience to our authority, for the removal of all obstacles put in the way of our full exercise of our ministry and power, and for our restoration to that condition of things in which the provident design of the Divine Wisdom had formerly placed the Roman pontiff.... Not only because the [possession of] civil sovereignty is necessary for the protecting and preserving of the full liberty of the spiritual power, but because, moreover – a thing in itself evident – whenever there is a question of the temporal principality of the Holy See, then the interests of the public good and the salvation of the whole of human society are involved.[10]

---

9. Leo XIII, *Immortale Dei* [1885], in Yates, *Papal Thought on the State*, 20.
10. As quoted in R. W. Thompson, *The Footprints of the Jesuits*, 339-343.

Fourteen

The Magisterium

WE MUST emphasize the fundamental teaching of the Roman Church-State that it is both infallible and the authority on political and economic matters. Some people labor under the mistaken idea that only when the pope speaks on matters of faith and morals, narrowly considered, does he claim to be infallible and his statements binding on ordinary Catholic laymen. Now the question of when the pope is infallible or fallible does not affect our analysis of Roman Catholic political and economic thought; the content of that thought does not change. But the issue of the pope's infallibility and how it is treated by some Roman Catholic writers suggest that they want us to think of the pope as some harmless, eccentric, and ineffective man in Italy who speaks for no one but himself. That, however, is not the teaching of the Roman Church-State, and any Roman Catholic who suggests it is is either misinformed or disingenuous.

The Roman Church-State has made a different and much more encompassing claim. In his encyclical *Quadragesimo Anno*, Pius XI said: "But before proceeding to discuss these problems, We lay down the principles long since clearly established by Leo XIII, that it is Our right and Our duty to deal authoritatively with social and economic problems."[1] The 1983 revision of the Canon Law (which is the latest revision) contains the following language: "To the Church belongs the right always and everywhere to announce moral principles, including those pertaining to the social order, and to make judgments on any human affairs to the extent that they are required by the fundamental

---

1. Pius XI, *Quadragesimo Anno* (1931), 21. Pius XI was probably referring to Leo XIII's statement in *Duties of the Christian Citizen*, 1890, "...politics...are inseparably bound up with the laws of morality and religious duties."

rights of the human person or the salvation of souls."[2] Virtually nothing is excluded by the phrase "faith and morals." Joseph Cardinal Ratzinger explained this in a letter to Professor Charles Curran of Catholic University in Washington, D.C., in August 1986:

> [T]he teaching of the Second Vatican Council...clearly does not confine the infallible Magisterium purely to matters of faith nor to solemn definitions. *Lumen Gentium* states: "...when, however, they [the bishops] even though spread throughout the world, but still maintaining the bond of communion between themselves and with the successor of Peter, and authentically teaching on matters of faith or morals, are in agreement that a particular position ought to be held as definitive, then they are teaching the doctrine of Christ in an infallible manner."...In any case, the faithful must accept not only the infallible Magisterium. They are to give the religious submission of intellect and will to the teaching which the Supreme Pontiff or the college of bishops enunciate on faith or morals when they exercise the authentic Magisterium, even if they do not intend to proclaim it with a definitive act.[3]

Leo XIII had explained the status of encyclicals at the end of the nineteenth century: You priests, he wrote, must display your

> ...priestly zeal and pastoral vigilance in kindling in the souls of your people the love of our holy religion, in order that they may thereby become more closely and heartily attached to this Chair of truth and justice, accept all its teachings with the deepest assent of mind and will, and unhesitatingly reject all opinions, even the most widespread, which they know to be in opposition to the doctrines of the Church.[4]

The editor of *The Encyclicals of John Paul II* explained the authority of papal pronouncements:

---

2. Canon 747.
3. Joseph Cardinal Ratzinger, as quoted in Jean Evangelauf, "Catholic U. Professor, Barred from Teaching Theology, Vows to Fight," *The Chronicle of Higher Education*, September 3, 1986, 44-47. Ratzinger elaborated on the doctrine of the Magisterium in "Commentary on 'Ad Tuendam Fidem.'" There he wrote: "Every believer, therefore, is required to give firm and definitive assent to these truths, based on faith in the Holy Spirit's assistance to the Church's magisterium, and on the Catholic doctrine of the infallibility of the [universal and ordinary] magisterium in these matters" (*The Pope Speaks: the Church Document's Bimonthly*, Volume 43, Number 6, November/December 1998, 333).
4. As quoted in R. W. Thompson, *The Footprints of the Jesuits*, 343.

The authority of an encyclical does not depend on the reasons the Pope gives for his teaching. If reasonable arguments determined a document's authority, observes Frances Sullivan, "papal teaching would have no more claim on the assent of Catholics than it does on the assent of anyone else who might happen to read an encyclical." When the Successor of Peter publishes an encyclical, he teaches in Christ's name and is guided by the Holy Spirit. He is not acting as a theologian whose authority depends on the strength of the arguments adduced in order to uphold a certain judgment. Because of the divine assistance promised to Peter and his successors (*cf. Mt* 16:18-19; *Lk* 22:31-32; *Jn* 21:15-17), the teaching of the Bishop of Rome enjoys an authority that goes beyond the force of his argumentation.... What Pius XII asserted about the authority of papal encyclicals also remains valid: "The teaching contained in encyclical letters cannot be dismissed on the pretext that the popes do not exercise in them the supreme power of their teaching authority.[5] Rather, such teaching belongs to the ordinary Magisterium, of which it is true to say: 'He who hears you, hears Me' " (*Lk* 10:16)....[6]

The pope, let me repeat, claims to be God on Earth.[7]

---

5. Although he did not dismiss the teaching of Leo XIII, Paulist priest Robert Sirico, president of the Acton Institute, said the pope fell into error in *Rerum Novarum*. Sirico's discussion of the Magisterium, however, was designed to give himself, and the pope, plenty of room to squirm: "...the teaching authority itself recognizes certain boundaries to its competence and has outlined, very generally, the parameters of that competence. There are times when the boundaries may be obscure and where they may overlap fields outside its immediate mission, but this merely makes the business of interpreting these documents more challenging; it does not vitiate the church's claim for them" (Robert A. Sirico, "Catholicism's Developing Social Teaching," *The Freeman*, December 1991, 462). Not only did Sirico's view vitiate the Roman Church-State's pretensions to infallibility, it destroys at one fell swoop the entire Roman Catholic argument against the Protestant position. The Roman Church-State promised to give us a clear and infallible interpretation of Scripture. Now Sirico has told us that the interpretation of these papal interpretations is "challenging." It seems that the Bible is much more perspicuous than the pronouncements of ecclesiastical megalomaniacs in Rome; the Bible is, in fact, its own infallible interpreter. For a further discussion of Sirico's views, see chapter 8.

6. J. Michael Miller, editor. *The Encyclicals of John Paul II*. Huntington, Indiana: Our Sunday Visitor, 1996, 20. Sirico's contention that the encyclicals "make no claim to infallibility as such" is therefore, beside the point. "He who hears you, hears Me."

7. Here is the statement of Vicar General Preston in New York, January 1, 1888: "Every word that Leo [XIII] speaks from his high chair is the voice of the Holy Ghost and must be obeyed.... It is said that politics is not within the province of the Church, and that the church has only jurisdiction in matters of faith. You say, 'I will receive my faith from the Pontiff, but I will not receive my politics from him.' This assertion is

ECCLESIASTICAL MEGALOMANIA

The Second Vatican Council declared:

> The Roman Pontiff, head of the college of bishops, enjoys this infallibility in virtue of his office, when, as supreme pastor and teacher of all the faithful...he proclaims in an absolute decision a doctrine pertaining to faith and morals. For that reason his definitions are rightly said to be irreformable...in no way in need of the approval of others, and do not admit of appeal to any other tribunal. ...the faithful, for their part, are obliged to submit to their bishop's decision, made in the name of Christ, in matters of faith and morals, and to adhere to it with a ready and respectful allegiance of mind. This loyal submission of the will and intellect must be given, in a special way, to the authentic teaching authority of the Roman Pontiff even when he does not speak ex cathedra in such wise, indeed, that his supreme teaching authority be acknowledged with respect, and that one sincerely adhere to decisions made by him....[8]

So embarrassed Roman Catholic intellectuals cannot squirm out of agreeing with what the encyclicals say. Even though the pope might not explicitly claim infallibility every time he publishes an encyclical, he does speak authoritatively, which means that every Roman Catholic is required to yield "loyal submission of will and intellect."

---

disloyal and untruthful.... You must not think as you choose; you must think as Catholics" (Quoted in Josiah Strong, *Our Country*, 63). In addition to speaking as God, the pope is the owner of all ecclesiastical property: "By virtue of his primacy in governance the Roman Pontiff is the supreme administrator and steward of all ecclesiastical goods" (Canon 1273).

8. Second Vatican Council, *Lumen Gentium* (1964), 25.

Fifteen

Solidarity, Subsidiarity, and the Common Good

"THE PRINCIPLE of solidarity," says the *Catechism of the Catholic Church*, "is a direct demand of human and Christian brotherhood." That, of course, is not a definition of the word. Sometimes the principle of solidarity is called "friendship" or "social charity," and it is a major aspect of "social justice."[1] Nor is that a definition. Not given to clear definitions, or in this case, any definition at all, the *Catechism* continues: "Solidarity is manifested in the first place by the distribution of goods and remuneration for work. It also presupposes the effort for a more just social order where tensions are better able to be reduced and conflicts more readily settled by negotiation."[2]

> Socio-economic problems can be resolved only with the help of all the forms of solidarity: solidarity of the poor among themselves, between rich and poor, of workers among themselves, between employers and employees in a business, solidarity among nations and peoples. International solidarity is a requirement of the moral order; world peace depends in part upon this. The virtue of solidarity goes beyond material goods.... Solidarity is an eminently Christian virtue. It practices the sharing of spiritual goods even more than material ones.[3]

This idea seems to be a vague assertion of ethical and economic collectivism. At least it has something to do with virtue, it is a "requirement of the moral order," and it is "sharing" involving material goods. Such vague collectivist notions are very useful to the Roman Church-

---

1. *Catechism of the Catholic Church* (1994), 1939.
2. *Catechism of the Catholic Church* (1994), 1940.
3. *Catechism of the Catholic Church* (1994), 1941, 1942, 1948.

State in building its arguments for domestic interventionism and world government.

When certain Roman Catholics have run for political office in the United States, they have asserted the principle of subsidiarity during their campaigns as the reason why they, as good sons of the Roman Church-State, can oppose some federal intervention in state matters, or some state intervention in local matters. They assert that the Roman Church-State endorses some sort of federal or decentralized system.

According to the Roman Church-State, subsidiarity

> ...is a fundamental principle of social philosophy, unshaken and unchangeable.... The state should leave to these smaller groups the settlement of business of minor importance. It will thus carry out with greater freedom, power, and success the tasks belonging to it, because it alone can effectively accomplish these, directing, watching, stimulating and restraining....[4]

According to Pius XI, the state should delegate some matters, those of minor importance, to smaller groups within the state and society. This will free the state to carry out its more important duties with greater power and success. Those most important duties are directing, watching, stimulating, and restraining the smaller groups within society. Far from being a restraint on state power, subsidiarity enhances state power. Furthermore, that increased state power is to be used to monitor all aspects of society, to direct them to ends and purposes chosen by the highest authority within the state, to stimulate and restrain them so that they follow the directions issued by higher authority. Thus subsidiarity is not a restriction on the power of government at all, but merely a principle of efficient management designed to make the most effective use of the government's power and resources.

One example of how the doctrine of subsidiarity works in practice may be found in the New Deal. David O'Brien reported that "Interested Catholics found in papal teaching ample justification for government action. Applying the principle of subsidiarity, few could see any alternative to stronger intervention by the national government into the nation's economic life."[5] Rather than being an obstacle to centralization, subsidiarity is the reason for centralization of power.

4. Pius XI, *Quadragesimo Anno* (1931), 40-41.
5. David O'Brien, *Public Catholicism*, 173.

SOLIDARITY, SUBSIDIARITY, AND THE COMMON GOOD

The principle of subsidiarity is the fiction by which conservative Roman Catholic laymen try to reconcile their Church-State's obvious authoritarianism with their own desire for freedom. They refer to statements such as this in *Catechism of the Catholic Church:* "The principle of subsidiarity is opposed to all forms of collectivism. It sets limits for state intervention. It aims at harmonizing the relationships between individuals and societies. It tends toward the establishment of true international order."[6] *How* it does all these things, we are not told. *That* it does them is asserted dogmatically. *What* the limits are, we are not told. *That* there are limits is asserted as an ipsedixitism. *That* the principle is opposed to all forms of collectivism is asserted for the faithful to believe; *why* or *how* it is so opposed is neither argued nor stated. Believing these statements requires implicit faith.

In another place the *Catechism* continues:

> The teaching of the [Roman] Church has elaborated the principle of subsidiarity, according to which "a community of a higher order should not interfere in the internal life of a community of a lower order, depriving the latter of its functions, but rather should support it in case of need and help to co-ordinate its activity with the activities of the rest of society, always with a view to the common good."[7]

Few bother to ask Roman Catholic political candidates how, exactly, this principle of subsidiarity is supposed to limit power in a political or ecclesiastical structure in which power flows from the top down. Who is to judge when a "community of a higher order" is interfering too much with a "community of a lower order"? The lower order community cannot judge. The lower order community is, according to Roman Catholic political thought, monitored, directed, stimulated, and restrained by the higher order community. The lower order community understands only its own interests and acts in their behalf, while the higher order community understands the common good, and acts in its behalf. All judgments about what constitutes too much interference must always be made by the higher order community, which alone has the common good in view. The authority to judge such matters is inherent in the definition of the term "higher order." The body does not judge the soul; the soul judges the body. The child does

---

6. *Catechism of the Catholic Church* (1994), 1885.
7. *Catechism of the Catholic Church* (1994), 1883.

not judge the parents; the parents judge the child. The ordinary Catholic layman – even the cardinals – does not judge the pope; the pope is judged by no one.

Furthermore, the principle of subsidiarity itself neither implies nor sets forth any criteria for deciding when interference is unwarranted; that decision is entirely at the discretion of the higher order community. The principle itself, as presented in the *Catechism of the Catholic Church*, mandates that the higher order community "should support it [the lower order community] in case of need." What this "need" might be, we are not told. What the "support" might be, we are not told. As we have seen in Part 1, in the economic thought of the Roman Church-State, "need," "common good," and "social justice" are the mantras that authorize both governments and individuals to commit various crimes and sins.

The *Catechism of the Catholic Church* also declares that the higher order community "should help to coordinate its [the lower order community's] activity with the activities of the rest of society." That function requires the higher order community to act as the planner and director of all the subordinate communities in society. That is why the principle of subsidiarity, according to the *Catechism*, "tends toward the establishment of a true international order." But in discussing international order, we are getting ahead of our story, and we must postpone our discussion of the Roman Church-State's advocacy of world government until chapter nineteen.

It is quite clear that in asserting the principle of subsidiarity, the Roman Church-State is not espousing the decentralized and federal system mandated by Scripture[8] and reflected in the United States Constitution, but merely its own hierarchical structure in which the higher orders, at their discretion, control the lower orders, and the power of the highest order, the papacy, controls all, and is controlled by no one. The pope, who is the highest authority on Earth, permits lesser men to exercise the power he has received from Peter and in turn delegated to them under the principle of "subsidiarity." He directs, monitors, restrains, and stimulates so that all do his bidding. There is little accommodation needed between the principle of subsidiarity and the theory behind the fascist regimes of the twentieth century.

8. See E. C. Wines, *Commentaries on the Laws of the Ancient Hebrews*. Philadelphia and London: William S. and Alfred Martin, James Nisbet and Company, 1859.

SOLIDARITY, SUBSIDIARITY, AND THE COMMON GOOD

In his 1961 encyclical *Mater et Magistra,* John XXIII explained how the principle of subsidiarity justifies intervention by government in the economy: "But in this matter [economic affairs]...it is necessary that public authorities take active interest.... This intervention of public authorities that encourages, stimulates, regulates, supplements, and complements, is based on the principle of subsidiarity...."[9] The papacy has a much different understanding of the principle of subsidiarity than some American Roman Catholic laymen seem to have, and in the Roman Church-State, it is the papacy, not the laymen, that is both authoritative and infallible. The doctrine of subsidiarity is one of the Roman Church-State's subterfuges to achieve big government; it is not a limit on the power of government.

Now, whoever wields political power must wield it, the Roman Church-State asserts again and again, for the "common good." The term appears scores of times in the papal encyclicals, in the *Catechism of the Catholic Church,* and in statements issued by the other bishops. We are told:

> First, the common good presupposes respect for the person as such. In the name of the common good, public authorities [that is, civil governments] are bound to respect the fundamental and inalienable rights of the human person.... In particular, the common good resides in the conditions for the exercise of the natural freedoms indispensable to the development of the human vocation, such as the right to act according to a sound norm of conscience and to safeguard...privacy, and rightful freedom also in matters of religion.[10]

The *Catechism* here endorses "inalienable rights," a concept that is logically incoherent and incompatible with justice, as I have demonstrated elsewhere,[11] saying that all civil governments must respect the fundamental and inalienable rights of the human person.[12] Lest anyone mistake the pope for, say, Thomas Jefferson, the Roman Church-State qualifies its apparent endorsement of freedom by noting that the

---

9. John XXIII, *Mater et Magistra, On Christianity and Social Progress* (1961), 52-53.
10. *Catechism of the Catholic Church* (1994), 1907.
11. See John W. Robbins, *Without a Prayer: Ayn Rand and the Close of Her System.* The Trinity Foundation, 1997, 180-214.
12. It was not only the American framers but also the French Revolutionaries who used the rhetoric of rights, but while the words were the same, the meanings were not.

common good resides in the conditions for the exercise of natural freedoms. In other places, the Roman Church-State explains that without such conditions, freedom is meaningless. Therefore, the common good is prior to, more important than, and more fundamental than freedom.

Even this statement from the *Catechism* seems to say much more about freedom than it actually says. For example, it is not freedom of conscience that the Roman Church-State wants to protect, but "the right of acting according to a sound norm of conscience." Who decides what a "sound norm of conscience" is? The infallible Church-State. Who decides what "rightful freedom also in matters of religion" is? The infallible Church-State. Many Church-State pronouncements are worded in this ambiguous way, so that the casual reader, not familiar with the whole political and economic thought of the Roman Church-State, reads them carelessly, not realizing that every word, phrase, and sentence are carefully weighed and measured in order to disclose and to conceal exactly what the Church-State intends. The Soviet Constitution of 1936, written and adopted by the government of one of the bloodiest rulers of the twentieth century, Joseph Stalin, also protected freedom of religion and conscience.[13] It is only when one understands how that sentence in the 1936 Constitution fits into the Communist system that you can understand that what Stalin meant by the phrase "freedom of religion" is not what the framers meant by the phrase "free exercise of religion" in the First Amendment to the United States Constitution. Equivocation has always been an indispensable tool of those who wish to conceal their intentions or their ideas.[14]

The language of Chapter X of the 1936 Soviet Constitution, on the Fundamental Rights and Duties of Citizens, is similar to statements issued by the Roman Church-State. Article 118 provided that "Citizens of the U.S.S.R. have the right to work, that is, the right to guaranteed employment and payment for their work.... The right to work is ensured by ...the abolition of unemployment." Article 199 provided that "Citizens of the U.S.S.R. have the right to rest and leisure. The

---

13. *Communism in Action: A Documentary History*, Henry M. Christman, editor. New York: Bantam Books, 1969, 114-116.

14. Perhaps the best essay on the subject is still George Orwell's "Politics and the English Language."

right to rest and leisure is ensured by the establishment of the eight-hour day for factory and office workers...." Article 120 mandated that "Citizens of the U.S.S.R. have the right to maintenance in old age and also in cases of sickness and disability...." Article 121 provided that "Citizens of the U.S.S.R. have the right to education. This right is ensured by universal and compulsory elementary education; by free education up to and including the seventh grade; by a system of state stipends for students of higher educational establishments who excel in their studies...." Article 122 asserted that "Women in the U.S.S.R. are accorded equal rights with men in all spheres of economic, government, cultural, political and other public activity. The possibility of exercising these rights is ensured by women being accorded an equal right with men to work, payment for work, rest and leisure, social insurance and education, and by state protection of mother and child, state aid to mothers of large families and unmarried mothers, maternity leave with full pay, and the provision of a wide network of maternity homes, nurseries, and kindergartens." Article 124 provided that "freedom of religious worship...is recognized for all citizens." Article 125 provided that the "citizens of the U.S.S.R. are guaranteed by law: (a) freedom of speech; (b) freedom of the press; (c) freedom of assembly...; (d) freedom of street processions and demonstrations." In all these rights, Communism and Catholicism are similar.

The Roman Church-State recognizes the right of men to pursue truth. But who has a monopoly on truth? The popes have told us that: "...the Chair of Peter, [is] that sacred depository of all truth..."[15] and "...the doctrine of the Church, which alone in the social as in all other fields can offer real light and assure salvation...."[16]

---

15. Pius XI, *Quadragesimo Anno* (1931), 5.
16. Pius XI, *On Atheistic Communism* (1937), 59. Sometimes "Evangelicals" in the United States assert that on many if not on most points of doctrine the Roman Church-State teaches the same things that Protestants teach, by which they mean: The Roman Church-State agrees with the Bible. They are quite mistaken. Here is what the *Pastoral Statement on Biblical Fundamentalism* (1987) said about the Bible: "Biblical fundamentalists are those who present the Bible, God's inspired Word, as the only necessary source for teaching about Christ and Christian living." "A further characteristic of Biblical fundamentalism is that it tends to interpret the Bible as being always without error, or as literally true in a way quite different from the Catholic Church's teaching on the inerrancy of the Bible. For some Biblical fundamentalists, inerrancy extends even to scientific and historical matters. The Bible is represented without regard for its histori-

"Second," the *Catechism* says,

> the common good requires the social well-being and development of the group itself. Development is the epitome of all social duties. Certainly, it is the proper function of authority to arbitrate, in the name of the common good, between various particular interests; but it should make accessible to each what is needed to lead a truly human life: food, clothing, health, work, education and culture, suitable information, the right to establish a family, and so on. [17]

---

cal context and development." "With Vatican II we believe that 'the books of Scripture must be acknowledged as teaching firmly, faithfully and without error that truth which God wanted put into the sacred writings for the sake of our salvation' (*Constitution on Divine Revelation*, no. 11). We do not look upon the Bible as an authority for science or history. We see truth in the Bible as not to be reduced solely to literal truth, but also to include salvation truths expressed in varied literary forms." "We observed in Biblical fundamentalism an effort to try to find in the Bible all the direct answers for living – though the Bible itself nowhere claims such an authority." Another official Vatican document, *The Interpretation of the Bible in the Church*, told us that "The fundamentalist approach [to Biblical interpretation] is dangerous..." (19). In these statements, the Roman Church-State denied the sufficiency, the infallibility, the inerrancy, the historical and scientific accuracy, and the literal truth of the Bible. Add to this the Roman doctrines that there are 73 books of Scripture, that the Church-State wrote, canonized, approved, and authenticates Scripture, and that the Church-State is the only authentic and authoritative interpreter of Scripture, and it is clear that Roman Catholicism and Protestantism have nothing in common on the doctrine of Scripture. In Christianity it is the Scriptures that have a systematic monopoly on truth. In Romanism, it is the Church. The issue remains: *sola Scriptura versus sola Ecclesia*. Furthermore, it is fundamentalism, that is, Protestantism, which the Vatican characterized as "dangerous." To my knowledge, no other movement, social or political (unless it is capitalism) has been denounced by the Roman Church-State as "dangerous" in the last 25 years. Those who say that Protestantism has much in common with Roman Catholicism are culpably mistaken. If one were to examine every doctrine that Christianity allegedly has in common with Roman Catholicism, he would find the same divergence that we have found in the doctrine of Scripture. Churchgoers are easily fooled by the similarity of phrases without understanding how the meaning of words, phrases, sentences, and even paragraphs is modified by the system of which they are a part. The Roman Church-State uses this apparent agreement in doctrine to convince other churches and individuals into joining it: "This Church constituted and organized in the world as a society, subsists in the Catholic Church, which is governed by the successor of Peter and by the Bishops in communion with him, although many elements of sanctification and of truth are found outside of its visible structure. These elements, as gifts belonging to the Church of Christ, are forces impelling toward catholic unity" (Second Vatican Council, *Lumen Gentium* [November 21, 1964]).

17. *Catechism of the Catholic Church* (1994), 1908.

SOLIDARITY, SUBSIDIARITY, AND THE COMMON GOOD

The common good becomes the reason for extensive government intervention into the economy. Not only does the government – which is the sole temporal representative of the "common good" – "arbitrate" among the "particular interests," but it also has the duty of providing the conditions of freedom: food, clothing, health, work, education, culture, information, the right to establish a family, and so on. The common good, which can be determined only by government, since all other groups (except, of course, the Roman Church-State) are of a lower order and represent only particular interests, is the great fiction by which the State defends its control of society.[18] Look at the list again: food, clothing, health, work, education, culture, information: Little is omitted. And what is overlooked in this list is found in other encyclicals. In Roman Catholic political thought, the government acts for the common good; government itself is not seen as a particular interest; it alone is concerned with the public welfare. It was one of the greatest achievements of the American framers – as expressed, for example, in *Federalist* Number 10 – to regard governors not as above factions or politics, not as motivated by disinterested benevolence, but as themselves factions advancing particular interests. Governors are not above faction, pure and public-spirited, as the Roman Church-State pretends, but are themselves factions. Because men do not change their nature when they assume public office, the fundamental desideratum in constructing a government is a system of checks and balances to array factions within the government against each other, so that government itself may be restrained. But an absolute monarchy such as the Roman Church-State knows nothing of limiting the power of governors, and nothing of freedom.[19]

18. "Political power, which is the natural and necessary link for ensuring the cohesion of the social body, must have as its aim the achievement of the common good. While respecting the legitimate liberties of individuals, families, and subsidiary groups, it acts in such a way as to create, effectively and for the well-being of all, the conditions required for attaining man's true and complete good, including his spiritual end" (Paul VI, *Apostolic Letter on the Coming Eightieth, Octogesima Adveniens* [1971], 46). Notice that this statement clearly implies the union of church and state, for the political power provides the conditions required to attain spiritual goals.

19. John Hughes, bishop of New York in the early nineteenth century, reflected the ecclesiology of the Church-State when he thundered: "I will suffer no man in my diocese I cannot control." Francis Patrick Kenrick, bishop of Philadelphia, commented on "how hard it is to uphold sacred rights when laymen meddle in the affairs of the church." "In 1829, meeting for the first time as a council legislating for the American

Aristotle is also the source for the Roman Church-State's idea of the common good: "Each human community possesses a common good which permits it to be recognized as such; it is in the political community that its most complete realization is found. It is the role of the state to defend and promote the common good of civil society, its citizens, and intermediate bodies."[20] This statement from the *Catechism of the Catholic Church* could have been plagiarized from the *Politics*.[21]

---

church, the [Roman Catholic] bishops decided to eliminate, as fast as the law would allow, all forms of effective lay participation and instead ensure that the title to church property was placed under the effective control of the bishop. It took years to find the favorable political climate in each state to allow for such control in law, but strong bishops now insisted that title be turned over to them before new churches would be blessed. Older churches were denied pastoral services, even in some cases placed under interdict, if they refused to recognize the absolute control of the bishops.... The church, it seemed, while affirming republican values of self-government and individual responsibility in public life, all but totally rejected those principles in organizing the church's internal affairs" (David O'Brien, *Public Catholicism*, 26). At the very time the bishops were grabbing control of the American Catholic churches from trustees and meddlesome laymen, "they set forth directly their commitment to American institutions and republican principles, affirming 'a milder, a better, a more Christian-like principle, that of genuine religious liberty...'" (O'Brien, *Public Catholicism*, 30).

20. *Catechism of the Catholic Church* (1994), 1910.

21. Gordon Clark wrote of Aristotle: "Now if Plato's theory is a form of communism, perhaps Aristotle could be called fascist. The important thing is that they are both totalitarian" (*A Christian View of Men and Things,* The Trinity Foundation [1952] 1998, 109).

Sixteen

Fascism and Nazism

ONE OF THE topics rarely discussed in polite society is the Roman Church-State's role in supporting the fascist and Nazi regimes of the twentieth century. That support is not accidental, but flows from the social teaching and ecclesiastical structure of the Roman Church-State. Christopher Dawson, a Roman Catholic historian, wrote that Roman Catholicism:

> ...is by no means hostile to the authoritarian ideal of the State. Against the liberal doctrines of the divine right of majorities and the unrestrained freedom of opinion the [Roman] Church has always maintained the principles of authority and hierarchy and a high conception of the prerogatives of the State. [Roman Catholic social ideas] have far more affinity with those of fascism than with those of either Liberalism or Socialism. [They] correspond much more closely, at least in theory, with the Fascist conception of the functions of the "leader" and the vocational hierarchy of the Fascist state than they do with the system of parliamentary democratic party government....[1]

Occasionally the media report some new development in the continuing story of Vatican collaboration with Fascists and Nazis, but these brief mentions are almost always followed by thundering silence. The Roman Church-State has done its best to cover up its complicity in supporting some of the most notorious dictators of the twentieth century,[2] but sometimes publicity just cannot be avoided, despite the best

---

1. Christopher Dawson, *Religion and the Modern State*, New York, 1936, 135-136.
2. A partial list of twentieth-century Roman Catholic dictators would include: Adolf Hitler, Germany, 1933-1945; Benito Mussolini, Italy, 1922-1943; Francisco Franco, Spain, 1936-1975; Antonio Salazar, Portugal, 1932-1968; Juan Peron, Argentina, 1946-1955; Ante Pavelic, Croatia, 1941-1945; Engelbert Dollfuss and Kurt von Schuschnigg,

efforts of the Vatican spinmeisters. The Associated Press carried one such story in 1998:

> The Vatican may have helped leaders of the Nazi-backed Fascist regime in Croatia escape after World War II with plundered gold and other valuables from Holocaust victims, an U.S. report concluded Tuesday. "It seems unlikely that they were entirely unaware of what was going on," the report said of Pope Pius XII and his advisers, who helped run a Rome pontifical college where war criminals took sanctuary.
>
> The Vatican connection was raised in the second U.S. report on Nazi gold, a document focusing on how neutral nations provided Germany with materials for weapons and goods during World War II. Stuart Eizenstadt, Undersecretary of State for Economics, urged the Vatican to search its records on Croatia's Ustasha regime, which may have escaped with up to $80 million.
>
> "Answers may only exist in Vatican and Croatian and Serbian archives," Eizenstadt said. "A full accounting should be made." Eizenstadt said Vatican officials told him such a search would be difficult. Previously Vatican officials said they could not find any Nazi gold-related records.[3]

The Roman Church-State has repeatedly refused to open up its own archives on these matters. The evidence outside the Vatican's archives indicates that the papacy encouraged, supported, and collaborated with both the Mussolini and Hitler regimes, as well as setting up its own totalitarian state in Croatia during the war.[4]

Since the Roman Church-State is itself an authoritarian institution in which none of the rulers is elected by the people, in which power

---

Austria, 1932-1934. Under Dollfuss, Austrian parliamentary democracy was abolished and Austria became a Roman Catholic corporativist state. Von Schuschnigg continued the corporativism of Dollfuss until the Nazi *Anschluss*, which Austrian Cardinal Innitzer welcomed.

3. Associated Press wire story, *Johnson City* [Tennessee] *Press*, June 3, 1998. Whether those Serbian archives will survive the war started by NATO in March 1999 is a difficult question.

4. "Mussolini's Fascist regime bent over backwards to give special dispensations to the Holy See on matters of taxes.... [Such arrangements were made secretly.] I myself was cabled at least twice by my [United] Stateside editors to lay off the subject of the Vatican's finances. The editors 'justified' the censorship by explaining that the local archdiocese...would use its considerable clout and good standing with the publication's owner, who would then very likely carpet the offending editor" (Nino Lo Bello, *The Vatican Papers*, New English Library, 212).

flows from the top down, and in which there is to be no disagreement with the leadership, it has shown an affinity for civil governments that reflect its own totalitarian and authoritarian structure, governments made in its own image. Writing in the *New Individualist Review* in 1965, Stephen J. Tonsor pointed out the hostility of the Roman Church-State to Republican Germany after World War I, and its support for Nazi Germany:

> There is the fact that German Catholicism was hostile to the Weimar Republic; that it marshaled its great power against the ideological and social pluralism, the liberalism, the democracy, the secular tone of Weimar Germany. The Church's vision was dominated by the ideal of an authoritarian state whose object was the promotion of virtue and true religion....[5]

Despite its hostility to the Weimar Republic, the Roman Catholic Church in Germany flourished during those years. Subsidized by the government, by 1930, there were twenty million Catholics in Germany, led by twenty thousand Catholic priests. New monasteries, new schools, new houses for religious orders were being rapidly built. In 1931, Karl Bachem, historian of the Roman Catholic Center Party, gloated, "Never yet has a Catholic country possessed such a developed system of all conceivable Catholic associations as today's Catholic Germany."[6] The Center Party, started in 1870 in opposition to Bismarck's *Kulturkampf*, was an ally of the Socialist Party in Germany during the 1920s.

The fountainhead and stronghold of the Nazi movement in Germany was Bavaria in south Germany, Roman Catholic Germany, not Protestant north Germany. German Roman Catholics joined the Nazi Party *en masse* and enthusiastically supported the Hitler regime. Over half of Hitler's troops were Roman Catholic. At the height of his power in 1942, Hitler ruled over the largest Roman Catholic population in the world. They were accustomed to authoritarian government in their religious lives, which made them unquestioning and enthusiastic supporters of authoritarian civil governments as well.[7]

---

5. Stephen J. Tonsor, "The View from London Bridge," *New Individualist Review*, Summer 1965, 671.

6. As quoted in Lewy, *The Catholic Church and Nazi Germany*, McGraw-Hill, 1964, 5.

7. The Nazi military oath posed no problem for German Roman Catholics accustomed to taking orders from an ecclesiastical Führer. "The text of this military oath, as included in the *Katholisches Gesangbuch*, edited by Chaplain Felix Groos for distribu-

ECCLESIASTICAL MEGALOMANIA

Of course, Roman Catholic laymen were simply following the example and the instructions of their religious leaders. Pius XI was the first head of state to recognize Hitler's government in 1933. Pius XI praised Hitler in public, even before he extended official recognition to the Hitler regime. In 1933, Pius XI told Hitler's Vice Chancellor Fritz von Papen, also a Roman Catholic, "how pleased he was that the German Government now had at its head a man uncompromisingly opposed to Communism...."[8] Not only did Pius XI's 1931 encyclical *Quadragesimo Anno* influence Franklin Roosevelt's New Deal,[9] it apparently persuaded German Chancellor Franz von Papen to bring Hitler to power in Germany. Von Aretin reported that

> Ideas about the corporate state, as developed in the encyclical *Quadragesimo Anno*, were having their effect on Germany too and at a critical moment weakened the democratic substance of the Centre party. One German Catholic who was particularly influenced by these ideas was Franz von Papen, who became chancellor on June 1, 1932. His authoritarian views contributed to the breakup of the Weimar Republic, and it was his support that enabled Hitler to take over as chancellor on 30 January 1933.[10]

---

tion to Catholic servicemen under the auspices of the Military Bishop, reads: 'I swear before God this sacred oath that I will render unconditional obedience to the Führer of the German nation and Volk, Adolf Hitler, the Supreme Commander of the Armed Forces, and that, as a brave soldier, I will be ready at all times to stake my life in fulfillment of this oath'" (Gordon Zahn, *German Catholics and Hitler's Wars*. University of Notre Dame Press [1962] 1989, 56).

8. Fritz von Papen, *Memoirs*. London: 1952, 279; as quoted in Dave Hunt, *A Woman Rides the Beast*, 59.

9. "As Catholic leaders mobilized for social justice they were in a position to evaluate the New Deal recovery and reform measures. Few denied that the New Deal's grandiose plan, the National Industrial Recovery Act, resembled, superficially at least, the vocational group system outlined in the Pope's recent encyclical. Through industrial codes – 731 in all – the act sought 'to induce and maintain united action of labor and management under adequate governmental sanction and supervision.' " If labor were given a greater voice in the code authorities, John Ryan, the leading Roman Catholic economist in the United States, believed that the program "would become substantially the same as the occupational groups mentioned by Pope Pius XI [in *Quadragesimo Anno*]" (Abell, *American Catholicism and Social Action: A Search for Social Justice*, 248-249). Ryan regarded the NRA as a "complete break with the system of free enterprise and competition." "With greater representation and authority provided for labor, they [the code authorities] could readily be developed into an industrial system which could be in complete accord with the social order proposed by the Holy Father" (as quoted in O'Brien, *Public Catholicism*, 172).

10. Von Aretin, *The Papacy and the Modern World*, 206. The Weimar government was

FASCISM AND NAZISM

On July 20, 1933, the Roman Church-State signed a treaty with Hitler guaranteeing the loyalty of German Roman Catholics to the Hitler regime.[11] One of the Roman Catholic bishops in Germany, Berning, published a book stressing the link between Roman Catholicism and German patriotism and sent a copy to Hitler "as a token of my devotion." German Monsignor Hartz praised Hitler for having saved Germany from "the poison of Liberalism [and] the pest of Communism." The Roman Church-State military bishop endorsed the Nazi goal of *Lebensraum*. It was no wonder, then, that the Roman Catholic publicist Franz Taeschner praised "the Führer, gifted with genius," and declared that he had "been sent by providence in order to achieve the fulfillment of Catholic social ideas."[12]

Tonsor wrote:

> [I]n accommodating to National Socialism through the Concordat of July 1933, the [Roman] Church put its stamp of approval upon a criminal regime and opened the way for recognition of that regime within Germany and abroad. The cooperation of the [Roman] Church went well beyond the Concordat. The [Roman State] Church played an important role in the Saar referendum, in the re-militarization of the Rhineland, in the Austrian *Anschluss*, in the German war effort, 1939-1945, and in the "crusade against Soviet Bolshevism." The Catholic press in Germany was frequently little more than an extension of

---

heavily Roman Catholic. There were three Roman Catholic Chancellors, and Roman Catholics held half of the Weimar cabinet posts.

11. Leo XIII explained the significance of such concordats in his 1885 encyclical, *Immortale Dei*: "There are, nevertheless, occasions when another method of concord is available, for the sake of peace and liberty: We mean when rulers of the State and the Roman Pontiff come to an understanding touching some special matter. At such times the Church gives signal proof of her motherly love by showing the greatest possible kindliness and indulgence..." (*Immortale Dei*, 17). Leo XIII anticipated the objection that concordats unified church and state: "If in any State the Church retains her own right – and this with the approval of the civil law, owing to an agreement publicly entered into by the two powers – men forthwith begin to cry out that matters affecting the Church must be separated from those of the State..." (*Immortale Dei*, 20-21). Of course, the Roman Church-State is unconcerned about such objections, for it rejects the idea that church and state ought to be separate. The pope is head of both state and church.

12. Guenther Lewy, *The Catholic Church and Nazi Germany*. 161-162. Under the terms of a 1929 Concordat, the government of Germany collected a church tax from its citizens, half of which went to the Roman Church-State in Germany, and half to the Vatican. Hitler kept that tax in force throughout his regime.

ECCLESIASTICAL MEGALOMANIA

Goebbels' propaganda ministry, and German bishops and priests often spoke the party Chinese of the Nazis.[13]

Tonsor continued:

> Ultimately the worst sins of the German Catholic Church and of the Papacy were those of omission; the failure to speak out against racism, persecution, the violation of the peace, murder on a scale hitherto unknown in human history, in morally unambiguous terms. To be sure, there were infrequent statements from the German bishops and the Papacy, but they were couched in the muted and esoteric language of encyclical Latin. If Jesus Christ has spoken this language he might have been appointed to the Sanhedrin.[14]

Contrary to Tonsor, however, the worst political sin of the Roman Church-State was not its failure to speak out unambiguously against the Nazi regime, its wars of aggression, and its legalized murder of millions – after all, as Acton and others have pointed out, those were things that the Roman Church-State itself had theologically justified. No, perhaps its worst political sin was the active support that the Roman Church-State gave to the Hitler and Mussolini regimes.[15] Of course, the Roman Church-State did not then and does not now recognize its moral turpitude in this matter or any other.

An American Roman Catholic writer, Gordon Zahn, in a 1962 book, *German Catholics and Hitler's Wars*, showed that

> The German Catholic supported Hitler's wars not only because such support was required by the Nazi rulers but also because his religious leaders formally called upon him to do so.... [B]y example and open encouragement, the Catholic press and the Catholic organizations gave their total commitment to the nation's cause....[16]

---

13. Tonsor, "The View from London Bridge," *New Individualist Review*, Summer 1965, 672.

14. Tonsor, "The View from London Bridge," *New Individualist Review*, Summer 1965, 672.

15. Pius XI referred to Mussolini as "a man free of the prejudices of the 'Liberal' school, a man in whose eyes their laws and orders, or rather disorders, are monstrous and misshapen" (Anthony Rhodes, *The Vatican in the Age of the Dictators, 1922-1945*. London: Hodder and Stoughton, 1973, 25). The Papacy had been railing against classical liberalism for more than a century.

16. Gordon Zahn, *German Catholics and Hitler's Wars*, 56. Zahn wrote: "...something of an aura of legitimacy to Hitler's foreign policy of aggrandizement and aggression was provided [by the pastoral letters of the Catholic Church]" (68).

166

FASCISM AND NAZISM

The political thought of the Roman Church-State, in which the interests of the individual are sacrificed for the common good, found an echo in the political thought of the Nazis. The 1933 Fulda Pastoral Letter from the German Catholic bishops read: "Only if the individual sees himself as a part of an organism and places the common good ahead of individual good will his life once again be marked by the humble obedience and joyous service that Christian Faith demands...."[17] In the Pastoral Letter, the Roman Church-State's own authoritarian structure was offered to German Catholics as a model to support the their submission to the Hitler government.

Adolf Hitler himself was a Roman Catholic. Hitler had been reared in a traditional Catholic family. As a child and youngster little Adolf had regularly attended Mass, had served as an acolyte during Mass, had hoped to become a priest, and had attended school in a Benedictine monastery at Lambach, Austria. It was at the monastery Hitler first discovered the Hindu swastika that he later adopted as the symbol of his National Socialist movement.[18] As an adult, Hitler remained a member in good standing in the Roman Church-State. At no time did officials of the Church-State excommunicate him. When the German military plotted to assassinate Hitler in 1944, and the plot failed, the Roman Church-State in Germany offered a *Te Deum* to thank God for the Führer's escape.

As for Benito Mussolini, the Roman Catholic fascist dictator of Italy, in his first speech in the Chamber of Deputies on June 21, 1921, a year before he became *Il Duce*, he said:

> I affirm here that the Latin and imperial tradition of Rome is represented by Catholicism.... I think and affirm that the only universal idea that today exists in Rome, is that which shines from the Vatican.... I thus think that, if the Vatican definitely renounces its temporal claims [to the former papal states]..., Italy...ought to furnish the Vatican with material

---

17. Zahn, *German Catholics and Hitler's Wars*, 74.
18. Walter Laquer noted that "Nazism contained a pagan element, and Italian fascism featured an anticlerical trend, but they appeared only at the margins of these movements. Once in power, the fascist states were eager not to jeopardize their relations with the [Roman] Church. On the other hand, the clergy played a crucial role in fascist or pro-fascist regimes and movements" (Walter Laquer, *Fascism: Past, Present, Future*. New York: Oxford University Press, 1996, 148).

aid.... Because the development of Catholicism in the world...is of both interest and pride for us who are Italians....[19]

On February 5, 1922, while standing in St. Peter's Square on the third day of the conclave that elected Pius XI, and just nine months before his own elevation to office, Mussolini remarked, "It is incredible that our Liberal Governments could have failed to see that the universality of the papacy, heir of the universality of the Roman Empire, represents the greatest glory of Italian history and tradition."[20] Seven years later, Mussolini's plans were executed in the Lateran Agreements of 1929:

> [H]is policy of [political] reconciliation [with the Roman Church-State] culminated in the Lateran treaties of 1929, in which Italy solved the "Roman question," which had long plagued it, by recognizing the extraterritorial status of the Vatican. The Catholic Church, on the other hand, committed itself to collaborate with the fascist regime, which in turn recognized Catholicism as the "dominant faith"[21]

Some commentators have suggested that the establishment of the Roman Catholic Church as the State Church of Italy contradicted the irreligious doctrines of the fascists. Binchy argued that

> this view is hardly correct. Fascism proclaims itself to be Catholic, in the sense that Catholicism is one of the many elements in its composition.... By establishing Catholicism as the State Church it ensures the observance of its own fundamental dogma, "everything within the State, nothing outside the State."[22]

The Lateran Treaties of 1929 restored the political status of the Roman Church-State by recognizing its sovereignty over Vatican City, an area of 108 acres within the city of Rome. According to Laquer,

> The pope himself repeatedly referred to Mussolini as a man sent by divine providence and offered his full support for Mussolini's foreign political adventures. Even in the conflicts of the 1930s..., the [Roman] Church's complaints were directed not against Fascism as such, but merely against its attempt to curtail the Church's prerogatives.[23]

---

19. Peter C. Kent, *The Pope and the Duce: The International Impact of the Lateran Agreements*, New York: St. Martin's Press, 1981, 6.
20. D. A. Binchy, *Church and State in Fascist Italy*, Oxford University Press [1941] 1970, 100.
21. Walter Laquer, *Fascism: Past, Present, Future*, 41.
22. Binchy, *Church and State in Fascist Italy*, 359.
23. Laquer, *Fascism: Past, Present, Future*, 41-42.

After he became *Il Duce*, Mussolini made notes of a meeting with Pius XI in which he quoted the pope as saying,

> I am happy that compatibility has been re-established between the Fascist Party and Catholic Action. If even, the difficulties have disappeared for the Catholics. But I do not see, in the whole of Fascist doctrine – with its affirmation of the principles of order, authority, and discipline – anything contrary to Catholic conceptions.[24]

The Roman Church-State supported Mussolini's campaign against Ethiopia during the 1930s. Ridley reported that

> This imperialistic enterprise [the conquest of Ethiopia, 1935-1936] was openly favoured by the Papacy in spite of its wantonly aggressive character and flagrant barbarities against unarmed civilians…. The Papacy publicly applauded the imperialistic desire for expansion of this "peaceful nation" [Italy], high Italian prelates transformed themselves into jingoistic recruiting-sergeants, and the final climax of the war, or, to speak more accurately, of the mass murder of unarmed primitives by modern science, the capture of Addis Ababa and the flight of the Negus, was celebrated at the Pope's order by thanksgiving services and the ringing of bells in all the churches of Italy. The Pope, in fact, was only repeating the historic thanksgiving that Gregory XIII (1572-1585) had ordered to celebrate the famous massacre of the French Protestants on St. Bartholomew's Eve, August 24, 1572 – an event greeted in Rome with similar rejoicings.[25]

Ridley pointed out that in the seventeenth century the Ethiopian Empire had expelled the Jesuits, and the Ethiopian Coptic Church had always resisted Roman Catholic ecclesiastical imperialism. The conquest of the Empire by Mussolini brought one more recalcitrant church and people under the influence of Rome.

Not only did the Roman Church-State support Hitler and Mussolini, it also created its own fascist state in Croatia. Laquer tells us that "One species of fascism with a time-honored past had a recent revival and may have a promising future in some parts of the world. This is clerical fascism…."[26]

---

24. Kent, *The Pope and the Duce*, 192-193.
25. Ridley, *The Papacy and Fascism*, 195-196.
26. Laquer, *Fascism: Past, Present, Future*, 147. "Historical fascism and clerical fascism share an economic doctrine or, more accurately, an absence of an economic doctrine.

Avro Manhattan, a former reporter for the British Broadcasting Company, reports that in Croatia

> ...the [Roman] Catholic Church [erected] a State in complete accord with all her tenets. The result was a monster standing upon the armed might of twin totalitarianisms: the totalitarianism of a ruthless Fascist State and the totalitarianism of Catholicism.... What gives to such a creature of Vatican diplomacy its peculiar importance is that here we have an example of the Catholic Church's implementing all her principles, unhampered by opposition, or by fear of world opinion. The uniqueness of the Independent Catholic State of Croatia lies precisely in this: that it provided a model in miniature of what the Catholic Church, had she the power, would like to see in the West and, indeed, everywhere. As such it should be carefully scrutinized....[27]

A fascist named Ante Pavelic was installed as head of the Ustasha regime in Croatia in 1941. The Roman Church-State archbishop issued a Pastoral Letter ordering the Croatian clergy to support the new Ustasha government. During the years in which the Ustasha government existed, a Franciscan monk, Miroslav Filipovic, managed the Jasenovac concentration camp for two years, during which time he directed the extermination of not less than 100,000 victims, mostly Serbs who were members of the Orthodox Church. Laquer reported that "The Croat State in Ustasha...provides a good example of the dual impact of religion and fascism resulting in state terrorism unprecedented even by Balkan standards."[28] Roman Church-State "Priests figured prominently among the... fascists; meetings were preceded by church services, and religious flags were carried in the fascist processions...."[29]

The Roman Catholic Lo Bello provided more details:

> After Yugoslavia's capitulation [to Germany in 1941], the new state of Croatia was formed, and this gave rise to a band of Catholic fanatics, the Ustashi, who decided to eliminate all non-Catholics in Croatia. Thus all men, women and children who were Jews, Gypsies, or Orthodox Serbs were slaughtered by the thousand. In one morning alone, inside an

---

They both reject materialist socialism but favor a 'just social order.' They are against Western-style capitalism but do not oppose the ownership of private property. Since they do not trust the markets, they dabble in state capitalism" (152).

27. Avro Manhattan, *The Vatican's Holocaust*, Ozark Books, 1986, 9.
28. Laquer, *Fascism: Past, Present, Future*, 148.
29. Laquer, *Fascism: Past, Present, Future*, 151.

FASCISM AND NAZISM

Orthodox Church in the Village of Glina, the Ustashi brutally murdered more than 700 Serbs. The killings not only had the backing of the local Roman Catholic priests, but were carried out by a large number of priests and friars leading the killer gangs. Even more terrible were the Catholic priests who became concentration camp directors and carried out the torture and murder of thousands of people.... [One of them was] the monk Miroslav Filipovac, a Franciscan who was made Commandant of the Jasenovac concentration camp, which equaled Dachau in horror and who was responsible for the deaths of 40,000 people.[30]

The Yugoslav chapter of the International Red Cross, having full documentation of the Roman Catholic holocaust in Croatia, sent a courier to Rome to deliver the documentation and persuade the pope to forbid any further murders. Among the documents the Red Cross courier carried was a letter from the former Minister of the Kingdom of Yugoslavia. The Red Cross courier, after being repeatedly rebuffed by the Vatican bureaucracy, handed the documentation including the Minister's letter addressed to the pope, directly to Pius XII at a public audience. The letter read, in part:

> Your Grace, I write this to you as man to man, as a Christian to a Christian. Since the first day of the Independent Croatian State, the Serbs have been massacred and this massacring has continued to this day.... Why do I write this to you? Here is why: in all these unprecedented crimes, worse than pagan, our Catholic Church has also participated in two ways. First a large number of priests, clerics, friars and organized Catholic youth actively participated in all these crimes, but more terrible even, Catholic priests became camp and group commanders and as such ordered or tolerated the horrible tortures, murders and massacres of a baptized people. None of this could have been done without the permission of their bishops.... It is the duty of the Church to raise its voice: first because it is a Church of Christ; second, because it is powerful....

The letter was signed by Privislav Grizogono, former Minister of the Kingdom of Yugoslavia, and dated February 8, 1942.[31]

Pius XII ignored the documents. The Vatican bureaucracy consulted with the Croatian ambassador, who claimed the Communists had com-

---

30. Nino Lo Bello, *The Vatican Papers*. England: New English Library, 1982, 26.
31. Lo Bello, *The Vatican Papers*, 27-28.

171

mitted the atrocities. Between 1941 and 1945, the Roman Church-State in Croatia murdered an estimated 700,000 Orthodox Serbs and 90,000 Jews and gypsies. The Vatican neither defrocked nor excommunicated anyone responsible for the holocaust.[32]

R. J. Rummell wrote:

> The Roman Catholic Ustashi set about to brutally murder them [Serbian Orthodox] sometimes after vicious torture; they were slaughtered like pigs. Burned to death in their churches, hunted down individually and shot, and hung, cut, or sawed to death; they suffered every device to cause pain and steal their life. To give some examples:
>
> At Korenica hundreds of persons were killed, but before they died many of them had their ears and noses cut off and then they were compelled to graze in the meadow. The tortures the most frequently applied were beatings, severing of limbs, goring of eyes and breaking of bones. Cases are related of men being forced to hold red-hot bricks, dance on barbed wire with naked feet, and wear a wreath of thorns. Needles were stuck in fingers under nails, and lighted matches held under their noses.
>
> Of the murders on the large scale in the village of Korito 104 peasants were severely tortured, tied in bundles and thrown in a pit… then gasoline was poured over all the bodies and ignited.[33]
>
> Forty students were smothered and then burnt.…[T]he Ustashi drove a hot iron rod into a man's head. Sometimes women were quartered, and to vary the spectacle, arms instead of legs were torn off.[34]

The torture and murder were the result of the teaching of the Roman Church-State, as Acton had said.

> The Ustashi soon found that killing and disposing of millions of Serbs was less easy than they thought. They also tried to deport hundreds of thousands to Serbia…. Consistently, this was done with great cruelty

---

32. Instead of denouncing fascism and Nazism, the Vatican repeated its denunciations of capitalism. In a radio broadcast on September 1, 1944, Pius XII condemned capitalism because it is "contrary to natural law" (as quoted by Norbert Mette, "Socialism and Capitalism in Papal Social Teaching" in *Rerum Novarum: One Hundred Years of Catholic Social Teaching*, John Coleman and Gregory Baum, editors. Philadelphia and London: Trinity Press International and SCM press, 1991, 30).

33. Edmond Paris, *Genocide in Satellite Croatia. 1941-1945: A Record of Racial and Religious Persecutions and Massacres.* Lois Perkins, translator. Chicago: The American Institute for Balkan Affairs, 1961, 106.

34. Paris, *Genocide in Satellite Croatia*, 134-145.

and loss of life. They also sought to forcibly convert remaining Serbs from their Orthodox faith to Catholicism.... Croatian rulers, which included at the highest levels the Croatian Catholic hierarchy, some of whom actually participated in the killing, were determined to fully Catholicize and homogenize Croatia.... Said one Ustashi priest, the Reverend Dijonisije Jurichev, "In this country, nobody can live except Croatians. We know very well how to deal with those that oppose conversion [to the Roman Catholic faith]. I personally have put an end to whole provinces, killing everyone – chicks and men alike. It gives me no remorse to kill a small child when he stands in the path of the Ustasha."[35]

Rummell provided us with a summary of the estimates of Orthodox Serbs murdered by the Roman Catholic Croatian regime, and compared it to other deadly regimes of the twentieth century:

> Hitler's troubleshooter in the Balkans, Hermann Neubacher, put the dead at 750,000 overall. Tito claimed the number killed (which he attributed to the Nazis) to be at least 500,000 in three months of 1941; Chetnik estimates were 600,000 to 800,000, with Mihailovic himself preferring the 600,000 estimate as of late 1942; and Serbian estimates give the toll as 750,000. Some of the killers themselves thought they murdered 1 million....When the number of Jews and Gypsies murdered is included,... this is more than twice the democide risk for Europeans, including Jews, living under Nazi occupation; and much greater still than the risk of being killed by their own government of citizens living in the Soviet Union or Communist China, or of those living under Japanese occupation during World War II.[36]

We can only conclude that one of the most brutal and inhuman regimes of the twentieth century – not just the medieval millennium – is the Roman Church-State.

---

35. R. J. Rummell, *Death by Government*. New Jersey: Transaction Publishers, 1995, 340ff.
36. Rummell, *Death by Government*, 345.

Seventeen

Totalitarianism

Although we have neither the time nor the space to develop the thesis here, the Roman Church-State devised much of the theory on which secular twentieth century totalitarian regimes have been based, as well as acting as a model for them. The practices and policies we associate with secular totalitarianism – thought control, coerced adherence to the Party line, domestic espionage, denunciation by friends, family, and acquaintances, midnight arrests, secret prisons, secret police, secret trials, forfeiture of property, censorship, the leadership principle, an infallible leader, an infallible party, wars of aggression, wars of extermination, anti-Semitism, the big lie technique, propaganda – these are also the things that have characterized the theory and practice of the Roman Church-State for centuries.

> When Pius IX made the profound observation,... "I am tradition," he summed up the silent revolution which the decree of papal infallibility had effectually accomplished. Henceforth, the "Leader" principle was dogmatically accepted in the Roman Catholic Church in all its implications; truth and tradition become the will of the papal leader, who is not guided by the dead hand of the past, but by the living needs of the present.[1]

Now the Roman Church-State did not invent all these policies; it adapted many of them from pagan governments; but it has been one of the most egregious practitioners of these policies for the past millennium. The Nazi regime lasted twelve years. The Communists ruled Russia for seventy years. The Roman Church-State has been exercising dominion over governments and peoples for more than a millennium.

1. Ridley, *The Papacy and Fascism*, 121.

TOTALITARIANISM

In a 1943 book, *Crusade for Pan Europe,* Count Coundenhove-Kalergi explained the fascist nature of the Roman Catholic system:

> There is no reason for a basically anti-Fascist attitude on the part of [Roman] Catholicism. [Roman] Catholicism is the fascist form of Christianity of which Calvinism represents its democratic wing. The [Roman] Catholic hierarchy rests fully and securely on the leadership principle with infallible pope in supreme command for a lifetime.... This constitutional – not moral – analogy between fascism and [Roman] Catholicism offers the key to the fact that in Europe as well as in America, [Roman] Catholic nations follow fascist doctrine more willingly than Protestant nations, which are the main strongholds of democracy. Even in Germany the fascist movement did not come from the Protestant North but from the [Roman] Catholic South, not from Berlin, but from Munich. Like Hitler himself, most other leaders of Nazism have a [Roman] Catholic and not a Protestant background. It is obvious that the [Roman] Catholic Church will prefer the democratic system in states where she forms a minority, because she depends on tolerance there. For a [Roman] Catholic nation she seems to prefer a system of moderate fascism....[2]

Forty years later, Armando Valladares gave us a graphic account of the Roman Church-State's activities in Cuba following the Communist Revolution there in 1959:

> Ever since Castro's triumph, [Roman] Catholic priests [in Cuba] had followed the development of the Revolution with great concern. As soon as they saw that it was going down the path to Marxism, they denounced it, and from their pulpits alerted their parishioners to the approaching danger. On May 8, 1960, all Cuban bishops signed a pastoral letter condemning Communism. All the schools were seized by the government, including [Roman] Catholic and Protestant schools, and all religious instruction was abolished. On June 26, 1961, the *Marques de Comillas* docked at the port of La Coiruna in Spain with hundreds of lay and clerical leaders who had been expelled from Cuba. On September 17, 1961, Castro exiled another 136 Catholic priests. The Cuban government's hostility undoubtedly had its effect, because from that time onward the attitude of the [Roman] Catholic Church in Cuba made a 180-degree turn. The artificer of the new relationship was

---

2. Count Coundenhove-Kalergi, *Crusade for Pan Europe.* New York: Putnams, 1943, 173; as quoted in Paul Blanshard, *Freedom and Catholic Power in Spain and Portugal,* 257.

Monsignor Cesar Zacchi, the Vatican's ambassador to Cuba, who made his first appearance declaring that Cuba was pagan before the Revolution but a believer under Communism....

[A] pastoral letter appeared, signed by most of the Cuban bishops.... In the letter the American blockade of Cuba was condemned and the people of Cuba were asked to work to help the Revolution in pulling the country up from underdevelopment. The letter blamed poverty and scarcity not on the Communist system and its defects, but on the American blockade. It was obvious from the way the situation was handled that the leadership of the [Roman] church in Cuba and the Cuban government were collaborating.

Before the letter was read in the churches, the Political Police in coordination with the Committees for the Defense of the Revolution organized cliques which would go into the [Roman] churches to applaud the pastoral letter. The Cuban authorities knew about its contents beforehand, but the parish priests did not. The priests received the letter in sealed envelopes, with instructions not to open it until they read it at the principal masses that Sunday.... Not only their parishioners but also they themselves were taken by surprise....

The Vatican Nuncio [Zacchi] appeared in a photograph with Castro and at many parties and meetings. He was forever making declarations. In one he asked the young people to join the Communist militia and help Castro defend the Revolution against enemy aggression. These enemies were the anti-Communists. The most exalted of all the declarations made by Monsignor Zacchi was the one which painted Castro as a man with deep Christian values. Castro soon gave the Papal Nuncio his own brand-new bus to transport seminarians to farms where they would work "voluntarily" to help the Revolution.... At that time there existed what was called the Havana Cordon. This was a wide farm strip which surrounded the capital, where following Castro's personal directions thousands of fruit and coffee trees and vegetables were planted.... Saturdays and Sundays the government mobilized tens of thousands of people to labor in those fields. The people hated the Havana Cordon; it was maintained by slave labor. Monsignor Zacchi went with Castro to have his photo made as he held a hoe in the Havana Cordon. He declared that the Havana Cordon was a "demonstration of the enthusiasm of the Cuban people." ...In return for his favor, on December 14, 1967, Castro was guest of honor at Monsignor Zacchi's episcopal consecration.... After the expulsion of the priests and Zacchi's arrival, never again did the [Roman] Catholic Church in Cuba raise its voice against the crimes and tortures or demand that the firing squads be abolished. During that time it was not only a silent church, but something much worse, a church of complicity.[3]

Valladares called the Roman Church-State a "church of complicity" that supported and collaborated with Castro's Communist regime. From his account, we can see that the Roman Church-State did not hesitate to betray even its own parish priests who had denounced Communism. Collaboration with the Castro regime – and the legal privileges one could obtain from such collaboration – were more important to the Roman Church-State than adhering to it own denunciations of Communism in the 1930s.

For centuries the Roman Church-State has expressed its opposition to freedom – freedom of thought, freedom of speech, freedom of teaching and education, freedom of the press, and freedom of religion. Leo XIII, the first pope to write extensively on the social teaching of the Roman Church-State at the end of the nineteenth century, addressed all these issues in his various encyclicals. Let us discuss freedom of religion first.

The Roman Church-State has always held that there ought to be no separation of the institutions of church and state. Leo XIII wrote:

> On the question of the separation of the Church and State the same Pontiff [Gregory XVI] writes as follows: "Nor can we hope for happier results, either for religion or for the civil government, from the wishes of those who desire that the Church be separated from the State, and the concord between the secular and ecclesiastical authority be dissolved. It is clear that these men, who yearn for a shameless liberty, live in dread of an agreement which has always been fraught with good, and advantageous alike to sacred and civil interests."[4]

Freedom of religion, Leo XIII wrote, is a false freedom: "...liberty of so false a nature [liberty of worship] is greatly hurtful to the true liberty of both rulers and their subjects. Religion, of its essence, is wonderfully helpful to the State."[5] Not only is such freedom false and hurtful, it is forbidden by justice and by reason: "First," the infallible Leo wrote,

---

3. Armando Valladares, *Against All Hope: The Prison Memoirs of Armando Valladares*. New York: Alfred A. Knopf, 1987, 282-283.
4. Leo XIII, *Immortale Dei* (1885), 23.
5. Leo XIII, *Libertas Praestantissimum* (1888), 44.

177

...let us examine that liberty in individuals which is so opposed to the virtue of religion, namely the liberty of worship, as it is called.... Justice therefore forbids, and reason itself forbids, the State to be godless; or to adopt a line of action which would end in godlessness – namely, to treat the various religions (as they call them) alike, and to bestow upon them promiscuously equal rights and privileges.[6]

In order to make sure that he was not misunderstood, Leo XIII also attacked liberty of conscience: "Another liberty is widely advocated, namely, liberty of conscience. If by this is meant that every one may, as he chooses, worship God or not, it is sufficiently refuted by the arguments already adduced."[7] The denial of freedom of religion and liberty of conscience has been the policy of the Roman Church-State whenever it has had the opportunity to put its principles into practice. As we have seen, one of the bases for such a denial is unity. When the Roman Church-State was criticized for persecuting Christians in Spain who wanted to worship as required by the Bible, the Spanish bishops responded by explaining that religious unity is the foundation of social order. The Metropolitan Conference of Bishops said:

> It is most surprising to find that outside of Spain there are Catholics who contest Catholic unity.... Pope Leo XIII did not sanction toleration except when required by circumstances, to avoid greater evils; he further stated that, the greater the toleration granted the less perfect is the society. Let us Spanish Catholics refrain from criticizing those of our brothers who, forming a minority in some countries, seek protection under the standard of freedom; but let us also refrain from granting, on principle, the same rights to falsehood as to truth. And let Catholics of all countries, if they wish to remain faithful to papal teaching, refrain from accusing the Catholics of Spain – the country which has had the privilege of preserving its unity of faith – of having an intransigent or reactionary spirit, because they defend that Catholic unity. It is not possible to have faith in the Catholic Church without considering Catholic unity to be an ideal for every state and nation.[8]

Just as the Roman Church-State denies freedom of religion, so it denies freedom of the press:

---

6. Leo XIII, *Libertas Praestantissimum* (1888), 42-43.
7. Leo XIII, *Libertas Praestantissimum* (1888), 48.
8. As quoted in Jacques Delpech, *The Oppression of Protestants in Spain*, Boston: Beacon Press, 1955, 33.

We must now consider briefly liberty of speech and liberty of the press. It is hardly necessary to say that there can be no such right as this.... For right is a moral power which...it is absurd to suppose that nature has accorded indifferently to truth and falsehood, to justice and injustice. Men have a right freely and prudently to propagate throughout the State what things soever are true and honorable, so that as many as possible may possess them; but lying opinions, than which no mental plague is greater, and vices which corrupt the heart and moral life, should be diligently repressed by public authority, lest they insidiously work the ruin of the State. The excesses of an unbridled intellect, which unfailingly end in the oppression of the untutored multitude, are no less rightly controlled by the authority of the law than are the injuries inflicted by violence upon the weak. And this all the more surely, because by far the greater part of the community is either absolutely unable, or able only with great difficulty, to escape from illusions and deceitful subtleties, especially such as flatter the passions. If unbridled license of speech and of writing be granted to all, nothing will remain sacred and inviolate....[9]

Here is another quotation from Leo XIII's 1885 encyclical *Immortale Dei*:

So, too, the liberty of thinking, and of publishing, whatsoever each one likes, without any hindrance, is not in itself an advantage over which society can wisely rejoice. On the contrary, it is the fountainhead and origin of many evils.... Whatever, therefore, is opposed to virtue and truth, may not rightly be brought temptingly before the eye of man, much less sanctioned by the favor and protection of the law. A well-spent life is the only passport to heaven, whither all are bound, and on this account the State is acting against the laws and dictates of nature whenever it permits the license of opinion and of action to lead minds astray from truth, and souls away from the practice of virtue. To exclude the [Roman State] Church, founded by God Himself, from the business of life, from the power of making laws, from the training of youth, from domestic society, is a grave and fatal error.[10]

The theology – specifically the soteriology – of the Roman Church-State directly affects its political views. Leo XIII wrote that "a well-

9. Leo XIII, *Libertas Praestantissimum* (1888), 44-45.
10. Leo XIII, *Immortale Dei* (1885), 22. The Index of Prohibited Books was abolished in the 1983 revision of the Canon Law. It could, of course, be reinstated in a future revision. Prior censorship was kept in force.

spent life is the only passport to heaven," and in order to ensure lives are well spent, governments must deny freedom of religion and of the press. Of course, a person's well-spent life is not a passport to Heaven at all, let alone "the only passport."[11] The focus of the Roman Church-State on good works as the way to Heaven results in its authoritarian structure and its totalitarian philosophy. The Biblical doctrine of justification by faith alone on the basis of the imputed righteousness of Christ alone, rediscovered by the Reformers in the sixteenth century, is the foundation of political freedom.[12] Later, in our discussion of world government, we will see how the soteriological universalism of the Roman Church-State, which is also obvious in this quotation, influences its views of government.

Leo XIII continued:"...the unrestrained freedom of thinking and of openly making known one's thoughts is not inherent in the rights of citizens and is by no means to be reckoned worthy of favor and support."[13] Furthermore, "A like judgement must be passed upon what is called liberty of teaching.... the liberty of which we have been speaking is greatly opposed to reason.... a liberty which the State cannot grant without failing in its duty." [14]

Now a few embarrassed American Roman Catholics might object that Leo XIII wrote a century ago, and that the Roman Church-State has changed in the twentieth century, especially since Vatican II. They might quote the following words from the Second Vatican Council:

> This Vatican Council declares that the human person has a right to religious freedom. This freedom means that all men are to be immune from coercion on the part of individuals or of social groups and of any human power, in such wise that no one is to be forced to act in a manner contrary to his own beliefs, whether privately or publicly, whether alone or in association with others, within due limits."[15]

---

11. There has been only one well-spent life in the history of the human race: the 33 years of Jesus Christ.

12. For excellent theological discussions of the doctrine of justification by faith alone, see Charles Hodge, *Justification by Faith Alone* (Trinity Foundation, 1994) and Horatius Bonar, *The Everlasting Righteousness* (Trinity Foundation, 1994).

13. Leo XIII, *Immortale Dei* (1885), 24.

14. Leo XIII, *Libertas Praestantissimum* (1888), 45.

15. *Declaration on Religious Freedom*, promulgated by Paul VI, December 7, 1965.

Please note, however, the strange way this statement is worded. There is, of course, the final and portentous phrase, "within due limits." What are those limits? One must turn to the social encyclicals of the papacy to find out, and those are the encyclicals from which we have already been quoting at length. Second, notice that this religious freedom, which the Vatican Council presumes to confer on all men, is freedom from coercion by individuals, social groups, and human powers. It is not freedom from coercion by the Roman Church-State, which is an infallible divine institution. Leo XIII said that he (and all the popes) – by virtue of his office – was God on Earth. This endorsement of religious liberty, in other words, is far less than it seems to be at first glance. It is the freedom to be Roman Catholic – and that is all it is. Whenever the Roman Church-State speaks in favor of liberty in general or religious liberty in particular, it means its own liberty, not yours or mine.[16]

Thus, those embarrassed folks who ask us to believe that while the Roman Church-State from the sixth through the twentieth centuries may have been opposed to freedom, the Church-State at the end of the twentieth century is a friend of freedom, simply do not understand the political and ecclesiastical doctrines, the political and ecclesiastical policies, or the strategy of the Roman Church-State. The Church-State favors only its own liberty, while denying liberty to all others. Sometimes it is amusing to see what mental contortions embarrassed defenders of Roman Catholicism will go through to argue that their beloved Mother Church is not really a dominatrix, a fiend skulking behind the crucifix, to use Acton's phrase. Of course, it would be inaccurate to deny that the Roman Church-State has changed in the past century, but it would be irrelevant to assert it. The Church-State is always changing as circumstances change, yet always the same – *semper eadem*. Its tactics change; its strategy remains. The Roman Church-State itself forbids us to disagree with the authoritative popes, whose words I have quoted by the thousands.

Leo XIII was candid enough to tell us what is really going on when the Roman Church-State seems to be adopting a less violent or less totalitarian position. Leo XIII wrote: "And although in the extraordi-

---

16. Gregory XVI in *Mirari Vos* (August 15, 1832) denounced freedom of conscience as an "insane folly," freedom of the press as "a pestiferous error, which cannot be sufficiently detested" (von Döllinger, *The Pope and the Council*, 21).

nary condition of these times the Church usually acquiesces in certain modern liberties, not because she prefers them in themselves, but because she judges it expedient to permit them, she would in happier times exercise her own liberty...."[17] Thus, happier times for the Roman Church-State mean sadder times for everyone else. Then the Roman Church-State will be able to put into practice its own principles, and it will not have to acquiesce in certain modern liberties for expedient reasons.[18]

To cite but one example, the Church-State's treatment of the Bible itself. The present Canon Law of the Roman Church-State provides that "...writings to be published by the Christian faithful which touch upon faith or morals [must] be submitted to their [the bishops'] judgment...."[19] Even the Bible is not exempt from the totalitarian control of the Roman Church-State at the "extraordinary" present time:

> Books of the Sacred Scriptures cannot be published unless they have been approved either by the Apostolic See or by the conference of bishops; for their vernacular translations to be published it is required that they likewise be approved by the same authority and also annotated with necessary and sufficient explanations."[20]

These are not the rules of the thirteenth century; they are the present Canon Law of the Roman Church-State. Under pressure from freedom-loving peoples of the world, the Church-State has yielded a little on censorship; but even at the end of the twentieth century, it outlaws the publication of the Bible unless approved by the pope and accompanied by "necessary and sufficient explanations." The Roman Church-State dares to censor God himself.

17. Leo XIII, *Libertas Praestantissimum* (1888), 50. "From what has been said, it follows that it is quite unlawful to demand, to defend, or to grant unconditional freedom of thought, of speech, of writing, or of worship, as if these were so many rights given by nature to man.... It likewise follows that freedom in these things may be tolerated wherever there is just cause; but only with such moderation as will prevent its degenerating into license and excess.... liberty is to be regarded as legitimate in so far only as it affords greater facility for doing good, but no farther" (51).
18. The Roman Catholic Swiss theologian Hans Küng once remarked: "The Curia would like to burn me at the stake as a heretic, but the twentieth century has given me a stay of execution. The Lord never gave His permission for the kind of Church government we've been getting since the third century A.D. when our Church left the hands of Jesus Christ" (as quoted by Lo Bello, *The Vatican Papers*, 166).
19. Canon 823.
20. Canon 825.

Eighteen

Strategy for Subverting a Republic

NOT BEING a republic or a democracy, but an absolute monarchy that believes in a medieval class structure, the Roman Church-State has been challenged by the age of democracies.[1] During the modern age, the age shaped in part by the Reformation, its economic system, capitalism, and its political system, constitutional republicanism, the papacy realized that it would not be able to exercise its full powers for the time being. Leo XIII, who considered the situation "extraordinary," as indeed it is in the history of the world, wrote: "And although in the extraordinary condition of these times the Church usually acquiesces in certain modern liberties, not because she prefers them in themselves, but because she judges it expedient to permit them, she would in happier times exercise her own liberty...."[2] Realizing that it could not hope, for the time being, to direct political affairs as it had at one time, the Roman Church-State, speaking through Leo XIII, expressed its policy thus:

> Yet with the discernment of a true mother, the Church weighs the great burden of human weakness, and well knows the course down

---

1. "Again, it is not of itself wrong to prefer a democratic form of government, if only the Catholic doctrine be maintained as to the origin and exercise of power" (Leo XIII, *Libertas Praestantissimum* [1888], 51). The popes feel it is necessary to state explicitly and repeatedly that it is not wrong to prefer a democratic or a republican government. They do not feel that it is necessary to make such statements about absolute monarchies or dictatorships. Those forms of government are similar to Rome's own autocratic government, and have its tacit approval. Rome's moral reassurance must be given only to those who favor republics and democracies, not to those who favor monarchies and authoritarian governments.

2. Leo XIII, *Libertas Praestantissimum* (1888), 50.

which the minds and actions of men are in this our age being borne. For this reason, while not conceding any right to anything save what is true and honest, she does not forbid public authority to tolerate what is at variance with truth and justice, for the sake of avoiding some greater evil, or of obtaining or preserving some greater good.[3]

In 1902 the Congregation for Extraordinary Ecclesiastical Affairs issued this directive to the Christian Democratic Party in Italy:

In the pursuit of its programme Christian Democracy is bound to act in accordance with the authority of the Church, in complete submission and obedience to the bishops and their representatives. In all matters concerning the religious interests and actions of the Church in society, Catholic journalists and writers are expected to submit their reason and will to bishops and pope.[4]

In mid-twentieth century Monsignor Ronald Knox of England reiterated Leo XIII's strategy for Roman Catholic operations in a republic:

[A] body of Catholic patriots entrusted with the Government of a Catholic State will not shrink even from repressive measures in order to perpetuate the secure domination of Catholic principles among their fellow-countrymen. It is frequently argued that if Catholics have at the back of their system such notions of "toleration," it is unreasonable in them to complain when a modern State restricts, in its turn, the political or educational liberty, which they themselves wish to enjoy. What is sauce for the goose is sauce for the gander. The contention is ill conceived. For when we demand liberty in the modern State, we are appealing to its own principles, not to ours.[5]

Monsignor John Ryan, the Roman Catholic architect of the New Deal, put the matter in these words:

---

3. Leo XIII, *Libertas Praestantissimum* (1888), 49. "...the tolerance of evil which is dictated by political prudence should be strictly confined to the limits which its justifying cause, the public welfare, requires" (50).

4. As quoted in von Aretin, *The Papacy and the Modern World*, 124-125.

5. Ronald Knox, *Beliefs of Catholics* [1927] 1949; as quoted in Paul Blanshard, *Freedom and Catholic Power in Spain and Portugal*, 115. It was such subtlety and subreption that led Pascal to denounce the casuistry of the Jesuits in his *Provincial Letters*: "O what an execrable system is this, and how utterly corrupt in all its main points and principles...."

STRATEGY FOR SUBVERTING A REPUBLIC

But constitutions can be changed, and non-Catholic sects may decline to such a point that the political proscription of them may become feasible and expedient. What protection would they have then against a Catholic State? The latter could logically tolerate only such religious activities as were confined to members of the dissenting groups. It could not permit them to carry on general propaganda nor accord their organizations certain privileges that had formerly been extended to all religious corporations, for example, exemption from taxation.[6]

In 1948, the Jesuit Cavalli explained Roman Church-State political strategy in *La Civilta Cattolica*:

> The Roman Catholic Church, convinced, through its divine prerogatives, of being the only true church, must demand the right of freedom for herself alone, because such a right can only be possessed by truth, never by error.... In a state where the majority of the people are Catholic, the Church will require that legal existence be denied to error, and that if religious minorities actively exist, they shall have only a de facto existence without opportunity to spread their beliefs.[7]

Realizing that, for the time being, the Church-State would have to tolerate democratic governments, Leo XIII and his successors appealed to Roman Catholic laymen to advance the cause of the Church-State. For example, Leo XIII wrote:

> First and foremost it is the duty of all Catholics worthy of the name and wishful to be known as most loving children of the Church, to reject without swerving whatever is inconsistent with so fair a title; to make use of popular institutions, so far as can honestly be done, for the advancement of truth and righteousness; to strive that liberty of action shall not transgress the bounds marked out by nature and the law of God; to endeavor to bring back all civil society to the pattern and form of Christianity which we have described....[8]

These laymen, of course, are known as the "pope's divisions." To the extent that they obey the pope, rather than think for themselves or be guided by Scripture, they constitute a fifth column in every nation on Earth. They are the means by which the papacy has advanced its politi-

---

6. As quoted in O'Brien, *Public Catholicism*, 165.
7. April 3, 1948; as quoted in Delpech, *The Oppression of Protestants in Spain*.
8. Leo XIII, *Immortale Dei* (1885), in Yates, 28.

cal agenda in the United States for 200 years. In *Pacem in Terris*, his 1963 encyclical, John XXIII wrote that Catholics active in social, economic and political affairs must always make decisions

> ...in accordance with the principles of the natural law, with the social doctrine of the [Roman] Church, and with the directives of ecclesiastical authorities. For it must not be forgotten that the [Roman] Church has the right and the duty not only to safeguard the principles of ethics and religion, but also to intervene authoritatively with Her children in the temporal sphere, when there is a question of judging the application of those principles to concrete cases.[9]

---

9. John XXIII, *Pacem in Terris* (1963), 160. Was John writing for the benefit of President Kennedy? Leo XIII wrote a letter to Cardinal Gibbons of Baltimore dated January 22, 1899: "...the Church will not tolerate, in America or elsewhere, any Catholic organization which does not partake of the Church's universal character, nor recognize the absolute authority of the Roman Pontificate" (as quoted in Rhodes, *The Power of Rome in the Twentieth Century*, 138).

Nineteen

World Government

WHAT THE Roman Church-State accomplished on a small scale during the Middle Ages is what it desires to achieve on a global scale in the coming millennium. If it fails to reach its goal within the next hundred years, it will not quit. It will continue to work relentlessly for world power, even if it should take another millennia or two.

In its social encyclicals of the twentieth century, the Roman Church-State has frequently called for world government. One of the major documents issued by the Second Vatican Council, *Gaudium et Spes*, is typical:

> It is our clear duty, therefore, to strain every muscle in working for the time when all war can be completely outlawed by international consent. This goal undoubtedly requires the establishment of a universal public authority acknowledged as such by all and endowed with the power to safeguard on the behalf of all, security, regard for justice, and respect for rights.[1]

This "universal public authority" is necessary for several reasons; here the Roman Church-State mentions three: security, justice, and rights. One of the more significant reasons for world government is to manage the world economy and redistribute goods from the rich nations to the poor nations. John Paul II wrote in 1987 to express his "insistence on the 'most serious duty' incumbent on the more developed nations 'to help the developing countries.' "[2]

The "common good" is the great fiction used by the Roman Church-State to justify government control of society and economy. It is also

---

1. Second Vatican Council, *Gaudium et Spes* (1965), 82.
2. John Paul II, *Sollicitudo Rei Socialis* (1987), 7; the quote is from Paul VI, *Populorum Progressio* (1967).

useful in arguing for a world government, as many popes have done. The *Catechism of the Catholic Church* points out that "Human interdependence is increasing and gradually spreading throughout the world."[3] The unity of the human family, embracing people who enjoy equal natural dignity, implies a universal common good. This good calls for an organization of the community of nations able to "provide for the different needs of men...food, hygiene, education...."[4]

All of this is driven by the theological premise that "The members of mankind share the same basic rights and duties, as well as the same supernatural destiny."[5]

> Because all men are joined together by reason of their common origin, their redemption by Christ, and their supernatural destiny, and are called to form one Christian family, We appealed in the Encyclical *Mater et Magistra* to economically developed nations to come to the aid of those which were in the process of development.[6]

The Roman Church-State's grand design for world government rests on the fundamental theological assumption of the spiritual unity of the human race: "Since it is world justice which is in question here, the unity of the human family...must first of all be seriously affirmed. Christians find a sign of this solidarity in the fact that all human beings are destined to become in Christ sharers in the divine nature."[7]

The Roman Church-State sees itself as an unique institution that alone can accomplish this global unification: "Moreover, since in virtue of her mission and nature she is bound to no particular form of human culture, nor to any political, economic or social system, the [Roman State] Church by her very universality can be a very close bond between diverse human communities and nations, provided these trust

---

3. The Roman Church-State sees the tendency toward unity in many areas, and it welcomes them all as contributing to its grand plan: "The Church recognizes that worthy elements are found in today's social movements, especially an evolution toward unity, a process of wholesome socialization and of association in civic and economic realms. The promotion of unity belongs to the innermost nature of the Church, for she is, 'thanks to her relationship with Christ, a sacramental sign and an instrument of intimate union with God, and of the unity of the whole human race' " (*Gaudium et Spes* [1965], 42).

4. *Catechism of the Catholic Church* (1994), 1911.

5. Paul VI, *Octogesima Adveniens* (1971), 16.

6. John XXIII, *Pacem in Terris* (1963), 121.

7. Second General Assembly of the Synod of Bishops, *Justice in the World* (1971), 17.

her and truly acknowledge her right to true freedom in fulfilling her mission."[8]

Few people understand the importance of the Roman Church-State in contemporary international affairs. When the United States appointed an ambassador to the Roman Church-State in 1984 during the Reagan administration, the Senate Committee on Foreign Affairs commented on the diplomatic significance of the Roman Church-State in its Report on the bill:

> The Vatican is an important player on the world stage. It maintains a diplomatic presence and has wide influence and access to important areas of great interest to the United States, such as Eastern Europe, Central America, Africa, and the Middle East. Vatican diplomats, widely regarded as among the most skilled in the world, play an active role in international political affairs....

Nino Lo Bello reported that:

> Whatever the true figures [for the numbers of intelligence agents] are for either the CIA or the KGB, neither of them has as many secret agents in the field as the Vatican. Without doubt, the Vatican runs the world's most efficient and most elaborate spy system with agents in just about every country in the world and certainly in every capital city, no matter how small.... The papal James Bonds, or pontifical 007s, came into being in 1910 under the rule of Pope Pius X and were put into full global operation during the administrations of Pope Benedict XV (1914-1922) and Pope Pius XI (1922-1939). The group of espionage agents came to be known by the popes as *Sodalitium pianum*, and it includes every priest, nun, monk, brother or Catholic secular worker anywhere on Earth. All of them understand that if he or she hears of anything or sees anything that the Vatican or the Pope should know about, they should communicate it to an immediate superior who will in turn get the crucial information to the closest diocese or archdiocese – from whence the said information will be swiftly communicated to Rome....
> The numerical extent of the Pope's world spy network can be calculated by citing official Catholic figures for 1981. There are nearly 260,000 diocesan priests, more than 120,000 regular priests, approximately 65,000 seminarians, over 210,000 male religious, and well over 950,000 nuns – not to mention an untold number of secular workers which runs to well over 2.5 million people.[9]

8. Second Vatican Council, *Gaudium et Spes* (1965), 42.
9. *The Vatican Papers*, 110.

ECCLESIASTICAL MEGALOMANIA

Martin A. Lee, writing for the *National Catholic Reporter* in 1983, reported that James Jesus Angleton, who ran counter-intelligence operations in Rome during World War II for the Office of Strategic Services, the forerunner of the Central Intelligence Agency, later became head of the CIA's Vatican Desk. There, Angleton was in charge of

> an extensive spy network that included priests behind the iron curtain who passed information on a regular basis to the office of the papal secretariat which, in turn, maintained a liaison relationship with the CIA.... As chief of the CIA's super-secret counter-intelligence staff, Angleton was involved in a wide range of covert operations.... In the late 1940s he recommended that the CIA finance Catholic Action.... Catholic Action played a pivotal role in the 1948 Italian elections, as the Christian Democrats (funded heavily by the CIA) defeated the Communist Party and socialist parties in Italy.[10]

The Senate Committee Report continued:

> Less well known...are the Vatican's day to day but very important activities related to issues across the whole spectrum of American concerns, including immigration policy, refugee resettlement, food and medicine distribution, narcotics control, and education.... The committee noted that diplomatic recognition focuses on the Pope as chief of state of Vatican City and not on his office as leader of the Roman Catholic Church....[11]

The last sentence quoted is, of course, a fiction, for the State of Vatican City is only 108 acres and had a population in 1994 of only 474. In size and population, Vatican City is the world's smallest state (assuming one does not count the Knights of Malta),[12] dwarfed by both San Marino and Liechtenstein.[13] The United States sends ambassadors nei-

---

10. Martin A. Lee, "Who Are the Knights of Malta?" *National Catholic Reporter*, October 14, 1983, 5. The Vatican keeps in contact with its agents by many means, including Vatican Radio: "[D]uring the early morning hours of each weekday the office of the Vatican's Secretary of State broadcasts messages – many of them in code – to priests, nuncios, apostolic delegates and cardinals in all parts of the world" (Nino Lo Bello, *The Vatican Papers*, 119)

11. Senate Committee on Foreign Relations, *Executive Report 98-21*, February 27, 1984.

12. 1998 population of Vatican City: 860; size: 0.44 square kilometers, about two-thirds the area of the Mall in the District of Columbia.

13. 1998 population of San Marino: 25,000; area: 60 square kilometers; 1998 population of Liechtenstein: 32,000; area: 160 square kilometers. San Marino is 120 times as large as Vatican City; Liechtenstein is 320 times as large.

ther to the Principality of Liechtenstein nor to the Republic of San Marino. The only reason the State of Vatican City is significant is that it is the headquarters of the Roman Church-State, the Vatican, just as the Kremlin was the headquarters of the Soviet Union. The Committee Report itself betrays the real intention of the Senate by elsewhere and repeatedly referring to the new United States ambassador as the ambassador to "The Holy See," not to Vatican City. Thomas J. Reese pointed out that

> The Secretariat of State conducts the foreign relations of Vatican City, but foreign ambassadors are accredited not to Vatican City but to the Holy See. Thus even if the pope lost Vatican City as a sovereign state, as head of the Catholic church he could still exchange diplomatic representatives with countries.[14]

The Holy See, embodying spiritual and temporal sovereignty, "appears," in the words of the *New Catholic Encyclopedia*, "somewhat as an anomaly in international law" – that is, as the only "religious institution engaged in diplomatic intercourse." In 1957 the United Nations and the Holy See agreed to discontinue the usage "Vatican City" and to speak of "The Holy See."[15] The statement in the Senate Report quoted above was apparently designed to placate and mislead those who opposed sending an ambassador to the Roman Church-State as being a violation of the principle of separation of church and state.[16]

This "anomaly," as the *New Catholic Encyclopedia* called the Roman Church-State, has taken every opportunity to advance its goal of world government. Paul VI in 1967 included an entire section titled "Toward an Effective World Authority" in his encyclical *Populorum Progressio*:

> This international collaboration on a worldwide scale requires institutions that will prepare, coordinate, and direct it until finally there is established an order of justice which is universally recognized.... Who does not see the necessity of thus establishing progressively a world

---

14. Reese, *Inside the Vatican*, 19.
15. Charles Whittier, Congressional Research Service, Library of Congress, "Relations Between the United States and the Holy See, 1797-1977," 7.
16. John Adams expressed his opinion that "congress [sic] will probably never send a Minister to His Holiness [the pope] who can do them [Congress] no service, upon condition of receiving a Catholic legate or nuncio...[a representative of] an ecclesiastical tyrant..." (quoted by Whittier, "Relations Between the United States and the Holy See, 1797-1977").

authority, capable of acting effectively in the juridical and political sectors? [17]

"There is a need," wrote Paul VI in *Octogesimo Adveniens*, "to establish a greater justice in the sharing of goods, both within national communities and on the international level."[18] John Paul II elaborated, reasserting the Church-State's doctrines of solidarity and the universal destination of goods:

> When interdependence becomes recognized in this way, the correlative response as a moral and social attitude, as a "virtue," is solidarity. This then is not a feeling of vague compassion or shallow distress at the misfortunes of so many people, both near and far. On the contrary, it is a firm and persevering determination to commit oneself to the common good...because we are all really responsible for all. This determination is based on the solid conviction that what is hindering full development is that desire for profit and that thirst for power already mentioned.[19]

In addition to the theological reasons why the world must be unified, world government is necessary because

(a) the moral order demands it:

> Today the universal common good poses problems of world-wide dimensions, which cannot be adequately tackled or solved except by the efforts of public authority endowed with a wideness of powers, structure, and means of the same proportions: that is, of public authority which is in a position to operate in an effective manner on a world-wide basis. The moral order itself, therefore, demands that such a form of public authority be established.[20]

(b) in order to manage the environment: "The concepts of an ordered universe and a common heritage both point to the necessity of

---

17. Paul VI, *Populorum Progressio* (1967), 78.
18. Paul VI, *Octogesimo Adveniens* (1971), 43. Monsenor Alfonso Lopez Trujillo, Secretary General of the Latin American Bishops Conference (CELAM), asserted that "The United States and Canada are rich because the peoples of Latin America are poor. They have built their wealth on top of us" (quoted in Malcom Deas, "Catholics and Marxists," *London Review of Books*, March 19, 1981).
19. John Paul II, *Sollicitudo Rei Socialis* (1987), 38.
20. John XXIII, *Pacem in Terris*, 1963, 137.

a more internationally coordinated approach to the management of the earth's goods."[21]

(c) to control multi-national corporations:

Under the driving force of new systems of production...the multinational enterprise, which by the concentration and flexibility of their means can conduct autonomous strategies which are largely independent of the national political powers and therefore not subject to control from the point of view of the common good....[22]

(d) to end international free trade:

The teaching of Leo XIII in *Rerum Novarum* is always valid: if the positions of the contracting parties are too unequal, the consent of the parties does not suffice to guarantee the justice of their contract... What was true of the just wage for the individual is also true of international contracts: an economy of exchange can no longer be based solely on the law of free competition, a law which in its turn, too often creates an economic dictatorship. Freedom of trade is fair only if it is subject to the demand of social justice.[23]

(e) to transfer massive amounts of wealth from rich nations to poor nations:

...the duty of human solidarity – the aid that the rich nations must give to developing countries; the duty of social justice....the duty of universal charity....[24] We must repeat once more that the superfluous wealth of rich countries should be placed at the service of poor nations.[25]

Let the aims of the Second Development Decade be fostered. These include the transfer of a precise percentage of the annual income of the richer countries to the developing nations, fairer prices for raw materials, the opening of the markets of the richer nations, and in some fields, preferential treatment for exports of manufactured goods from the developing nations. These aims represent first guidelines for a graduated taxation of income as well as for an economic and social plan for the entire world. We grieve whenever richer nations turn their backs on this ideal of worldwide sharing and responsibility. We hope that no such weakening of international solidarity will take away their force....[26]

21. John Paul II, *The Ecological Crisis: A Common Responsibility* (December 8, 1989), 9.
22. Paul VI, *Octogesima Adveniens* (1971), 44.
23. Paul VI, *Populorum Progressio* (1967), 59.
24. Paul VI, *Populorum Progressio* (1967), 44.
25. Paul VI, *Populorum Progressio* (1967), 49.
26. *Justice in the World* (1971), 21.

(f) to foster development and save the peace:

> Government officials, it is your concern to mobilize your people to form a more effective world solidarity, and above all to make them accept the necessary taxes on their luxuries and their wasteful expenditures, in order to bring about development and to save the peace.[27]

(g) and because national governments are incapable of ensuring the universal common good:

> ...under the present circumstances of human society both the structure and form of governments as well as the power which public authority wields in all the nations of the world, must be considered inadequate to promote the universal common good.[28]

In the judgment of the Roman Church-State, the United Nations is, at the present time, the likeliest vehicle to achieve the political and economic world unification that the Roman Church-State desires. Pius XII proclaimed that the United Nations

> ought also to have the right and the power of forestalling all military intervention of one nation state in another, whatever the pretext under which it is effected, and also the right and power of assuming, by means of a sufficient police force, the safeguarding of order in the state which is threatened....We desire the authority of the United Nations strengthened, especially for effecting general disarmament, which we have so much at heart.[29]

The Church-State has been lavish in its moral support for the United Nations. John XXIII referred to the Universal Declaration of Human Rights as "An act of the highest importance performed by the United Nations Organization...approved in the General Assembly of December 10, 1948."[30]

---

27. Paul VI, *Populorum Progressio* (1967), 84.

28. John XXIII, *Pacem in Terris* (1963), 135. John XXIII called for governments not only to be given greater power, but also to undergo structural change so that they might use that increased power more effectively. There is an entire section in *Pacem in Terris* titled: "Insufficiency of modern states to ensure the universal common good."

29. Quoted in Anne Fremantle, "The Papacy and Social Reform: The Great Encyclicals," in *The Papacy: An Illustrated History from St. Peter to Paul VI,* Christopher Hollis, editor. New York: Macmillan, 1964, 248-249. The book bears both a *nihil obstat* and an *imprimatur*.

30. John XXIII, *Pacem in Terris* (1963), 143.

It is therefore our ardent desire that the United Nations Organization – in its structure and in its means – may become ever more equal to the magnitude and nobility of its tasks, and may the time come as quickly as possible when every human being will find therein an effective safeguard for the rights which derive directly from his dignity as a person, and which are therefore universal, inviolable and inalienable rights.[31]

Ayn Rand was right when she wrote in 1967: "The Catholic Church has never given up the hope to re-establish the medieval union of church and state, with a global state and a global theocracy as its ultimate goal."[32]

The Roman Church-State is a hybrid – a monster of ecclesiastical and political power. Its political thought is totalitarian, and whenever it has had the opportunity to apply its principles, the result has been bloody repression. If, during the last 30 years, it has softened its assertions of full, supreme, and irresponsible power, and has murdered fewer people than before, such changes in behavior are not due to a change in its ideas, but to a change in its circumstances. Lord Acton noted a century ago that it was only when the Roman Church-State faced public opinion that disapproved of Church-State-sanctioned murder that it slowed its persecutions and attempted to speak with a voice less bloodthirsty. The Roman Church-State in the twentieth century, however, is an institution recovering from a mortal wound. If and when it regains its full power and authority, it will impose a regime more sinister than any the planet has yet seen.

---

31. John XXIII, *Pacem in Terris* (1963), 145.
32. Ayn Rand, "Requiem for Man," in *Capitalism: The Unknown Ideal*, 315.

Twenty

2000: Jubilee, Punctuated by Apologies

ON MARCH 16, 1998, Cardinal Edward Idris Cassidy, President of the Commission for Religious Relations with Jews, released a document titled "We Remember: A Reflection on the Shoah by the Commission for Religious Relations with Jews." Before the document's release, rumors in the press were that the Vatican would apologize for its part in fostering the Holocaust or shielding Nazi war criminals. When it did not do so, there was a storm of criticism about the document and the failure of the Vatican to apologize fully. Reading "We Remember" can give some insight into what the Roman Church-State was saying and what it probably will never say.

"We Remember" opens with a quotation from *Tertio Millennio Adveniente*, an apostolic letter issued by John Paul II:

> It is appropriate that, as the second millennium of Christianity draws to a close, the Church should become more fully conscious of the sinfulness of her children, recalling all those times in history when they departed from the spirit of Christ and His Gospel and, instead of offering to the world the witness of a life inspired by the values of faith, indulged in ways of thinking and acting which were truly forms of counterwitness and scandal.[1]

A careful reading of this sentence discloses the distinction the pope makes between the "Church" and "her children." The two are not the same. The Church is to become more conscious of "the sinfulness of her children," for it was the children, not the Roman Church-State,

---

1. John Paul II, *Tertio Millennio Adveniente* (November 10, 1994), 33; as quoted in *The Pope Speaks: The Church Documents Bimonthly*, July/August 1998, 243.

that "departed from the spirit of Christ and His Gospel" and "indulged in ways of thinking and acting which were truly forms of counterwitness and scandal." The pope is compelled to draw this distinction between the Roman Church and her children, because Roman Catholic doctrine teaches that the Church is infallible. The Roman Church cannot err, let alone depart from the Spirit of Christ. Further on, "We Remember" quotes from a speech that John Paul II gave to the Symposium on the Roots of Anti-Judaism on October 31, 1997:

> In the Christian world – I do not say on the part of the Church as such – erroneous and unjust interpretations of the New Testament regarding the Jewish people and their alleged culpability have circulated for too long, engendering feelings of hostility towards this people.[2]

Here one can see the pope's distinction between the Roman Church and the "Christian world." The Roman Church remains pure and pristine; it was someone else in the "Christian world" that was to blame for the anti-Semitism.[3] The Commission states: "We deeply regret the errors and failures of those sons and daughters of the Church....At the end of this millennium the Catholic Church desires to express her deep sorrow for the failures of her sons and daughters of every age. This is an act of repentance...."[4] Of course, it is not an act of repentance at all. The Roman Church – by its own dogma – has nothing of which to repent. The very title of document issued by Cassidy's Commission was "We Remember," not "We Repent." It is an acknowledgment, however inadvertent, that the Roman Church-State is the mother of men who have murdered in "every age."

---

2. *The Pope Speaks*, July/August 1998, 245.

3. The Roman Church-State erroneously refers to anti-Semitism as anti-Judaism. Presumably it does so in an effort to be precise, for there are Semites who are not Jews. But the terms are not equivalent. *Anti-Semitism* is a racist term; *anti-Judaism* is a religious term. All Christians, all Muslims, all secular humanists (to offer only three examples), simply because they believe their views are exclusively true, espouse anti-Judaism, just as all Communists espouse anti-capitalism, and all capitalists, anti-communism. The switch in terms confuses race with religion. One indicates a hostility to persons; the other an hostility to ideas. This confusion in the mind of the Roman Church-State may indicate why it historically was both anti-Semitic and anti-Judaic. During the sixteenth and seventeenth centuries, for example, Protestant rulers offered protection to Jews persecuted by Roman Catholic rulers and the Roman Church-State. The same was true in the 1930s and 1940s.

4. *The Pope Speaks*, July/August 1998, 248-249.

ECCLESIASTICAL MEGALOMANIA

The press is again filled with rumors that the Vatican is drafting more apologies to be issued during the year 2000, the "Great Jubilee" on the Roman Church-State calendar. Such apologies are expected to cover various sins in its past: the condemnation of Martin Luther, the Inquisition, the St. Bartholomew Massacre, the Holocaust, persecution of dissenters, and so on. Such apologies are meaningless gestures and posturing, for their only possible meaning to the Roman Church-State is better public relations. The Church claims to be infallible.

Instead of repentance, what is almost certain to come forth from the City on Seven Hills in 2000 are calls for more redistribution of wealth, domestically, but especially globally; the cancellation of international debts owed by lesser developed countries; and a reaffirmation of the collectivist economic doctrines – social justice, the common good, and the universal destination of goods – that the Roman Church-State has taught for centuries. The Roman Church-State is, to use its own word, irreformable.

Until the Roman Church-State abandons the theology and philosophy that preclude it from repenting, until it repudiates the doctrines that have justified its use of force and violence, either directly or through proxies, and until it dismantles its entire apparatus of command, coercion, and control that has enabled it to inflict harm on its many victims, ecclesiastical apologies, or, more accurately, "remembrances," are both duplicitous and disingenuous. The world might as well forgive an "apologetic" yet intact and unrepentant fascist, Nazi, or Communist regime its sins and crimes. Furthermore, many of the victims of the Roman Church-State are gone; they alone, not the present generation, could forgive the Roman Catholic Church, but they cannot do so. The Roman Church is morally required to seek forgiveness from its victims, but its victims are dead. Therefore, the Roman Church-State cannot be forgiven. It is not within our poor power to act on behalf of its victims. And it is not within the poor power of the Roman Church-State to repent for her "sons."

The world will know that Rome is genuinely repentant only when its mind changes (for that is what the word *repentance* means), and the world will know that its mind has changed only when its theology, monarchy, episcopacy, economic thought, and political pretensions have been explicitly repudiated. Anything less than such a repudiation is merely another subterfuge in a long tradition of frauds, forgeries, and deceptions intended to mislead the world.

Appendices

∞

The Donation of Constantine
The Vatican Decree of 1870

Appendix A

The Donation of Constantine

IN HIS introduction to the *Donation of Constantine* and Lorenzo Valla's exposé of the document as an ecclesiastical forgery, Christopher Coleman wrote:

> For centuries the Papacy was the strongest institution in western Europe. While its control at any one time rested principally on the power it actually possessed and on the ability of its representatives, legal theories and historical documents played a not inconsiderable part in its rise and decline. Of these documents the *Donation of Constantine* was perhaps the most spectacular, even though it was not the most important. It was cited by no less than ten Popes of whom we know, to mention no lesser writers, in contentions for the recognition of papal control, and contributed not a little to the prestige of the Papacy.... In the full text of the *Donation,*... one found many features distinctive of Italian documents on the eighth century, and a number that apparently are peculiar to the chancellery of Stephen II (III), Bishop of Rome 752-757, and of Paul I (757-767), more particularly the latter.... In short, the language of the *Donation* seems to point to the papal chancellery as the place of its origin, and the pontificate of Paul I (757-767) as the most probable time.... The papacy was then cutting loose from the Emperor at Constantinople and ignoring his representatives in Italy, as well as developing its own independent policy toward Italian territory, toward the Lombards, and toward the Franks. The aim of the forger seems to have been the characteristically medieval one of supplying documentary warrant for the existence of the situation which had developed through a long-drawn-out revolution, namely, the passage of imperial prerogatives and political control in Italy from the Emperor to the papacy. Hence, along with general statements of papal primacy, and of gifts of property, detailed and explicit stress is laid upon the granting of imperial power to

the Pope, and upon the right of the Roman clergy to the privileges of the highest ranks of Roman society.[1]

The Roman Church-State, more than 500 years after Valla demonstrated the *Donation* to be a forgery, one of many forgeries and hoaxes that compose its history and buttress its claims to power and authority, still has not acknowledged the *Donation* to be a forgery. The same ecclesiastical megalomania that led the Roman Church-State to make its outrageous claims to infallible spiritual authority ensures that it will not and cannot genuinely repent of its sins and lies, but only of its getting caught in them. What follows are Christopher Coleman's introduction to Valla's *Discourse*, the *Donation* itself, and the full text of Valla's exposure of the lie.

Translator's Introduction

The *Donation of Constantine* – the most famous forgery in European history; papal authority – since the triumph of Christianity the most perennial question of European society; historical criticism – one of the most comprehensive, most alluring, and most baffling enterprises of the modern mind; Lorenzo Valla – the greatest of the professional Italian humanists; these lines of study have converged, accidentally perhaps, to call forth the following pages. Much of the subject matter which might properly form their introduction I have already treated more fully in an earlier work,[2] and a brief statement will suffice here.

The *Donation of Constantine (Constitutum Constantini)*, written probably not long after the middle of the eighth century, became widely known through its incorporation in the *Pseudo-Isidorian Decretals* (about 847-853). Parts of it were included in most of the medieval collections of canon law; Anselm's, Deusdedit's and Gratian's great work (the *Decretum*, or *Concordia discordantium canonum*). It purports to reproduce a legal document in which the Emperor Constantine the Great, reciting his baptism and the cure of his leprosy at the hands of Sylvester, Bishop of Rome 314-336, confirmed the privilege of that pontiff as head of all

1. Christopher B. Coleman, *The Treatise of Lorenzo Valla on the Donation of Constantine*. New York: Russell and Russell [1922] 1971, 2, 6-7.

2. C. B. Coleman, *Constantine the Great and Christianity, three phases: the historical, the legendary, and the spurious*. Columbia University Studies in History, Economics and Public Law, vol. LX, no. 1. Columbia University Press, and Longmans, Green & Co., New York, 1914.

the clergy and supreme over the other four patriarchates, conferred upon him extensive imperial property in various parts of the world, especially the imperial Lateran palace, and the imperial diadem and tiara, and other imperial insignia; granted the Roman clergy the rank of the highest Roman orders and their privileges; gave Sylvester and his successors freedom in consecrating men for certain orders of the clergy; it tells how he, Constantine, recognized the superior dignity of the Pope by holding the bridle of his horse; grants Sylvester Rome, all of Italy, and the western provinces, to remain forever under the control of the Roman See; and states his own determination to retire to Byzantium in order that the presence of an earthly emperor may not embarrass ecclesiastical authority. This remarkable document was almost universally accepted as genuine from the ninth to the fifteenth century.

The question of the position of the bishop of Rome in the Christian Church lacks but a few generations of being as old as Christianity itself. His relation to secular governments became an acute problem as soon as the imperial government broke down in Italy, and has remained so to the present moment. For centuries the Papacy was the strongest institution in western Europe. While its control at any one time rested principally on the power it actually possessed and on the ability of its representatives, legal theories and historical documents played a not inconsiderable part in its rise and decline. Of these documents the Donation of Constantine was perhaps the most spectacular, even though it was not the most important. It was cited by no less than ten Popes of whom we know, to mention no lesser writers, in contentions for the recognition of papal control, and contributed not a little to the prestige of the Papacy. On the other hand, when its spuriousness became known, the reaction against it, as in Luther's case, contributed powerfully to the revolt from Rome. Its century-long influence entitles it to a respect difficult for any one who now reads it to feel. And Valla's discussion of it contains many interesting reflections on the secular power of the Papacy, perhaps the most interesting expression in this connection of fifteenth century Italian humanism.

Among the achievements of modern historical criticism Valla's work was a conspicuous pioneer. Its quality and its importance have often been exaggerated, and as often underestimated. It is some satisfaction to make it more generally available in the original text and translation, so that the reader may judge for himself. A critical appraisal would have to take into account that Nicholas Cusanus some seven years earlier in his *De Concordantia Catholica* covered part of the same ground even better than Valla did, and anticipated some of his arguments. But Valla's treatise is more exhaustive, is in more finished and effective literary form, and in effect established for the world generally the proof of the falsity of the Donation. Moreover, for the first time, he used effectively the method of studying the usage of words in the variations of their meaning and application, and other devices of internal criticism which are the tools of historical criticism today. So, while Valla's little book may seem slight beside later masterpieces of investigation and beside systematic treatises in larger fields, it is none the less a landmark in the rise of a new science. I speak from personal experience in adding that it is still useful in college in promoting respect for, and development in, critical scholarship.

As to Valla himself the words of Erasmus will bear repetition: "Valla, a man who with so much energy, zeal and labor, refuted the stupidities of the barbarians, saved half-buried letters from extinction, restored Italy to her ancient splendor of eloquence, and forced even the learned to express themselves henceforth with more circumspection."[3] The Italian Renaissance is much extolled among us, – and so little known. A short time ago diligent search revealed no copy of Valla's works in the United States, and many libraries had none of his separate writings. The same is doubtless true in the case of other great names in the Renaissance. Meanwhile, there are those whose profession it is to teach European history and who are utterly unacquainted with medieval and later Latin.

The best life of Valla is that by Girolamo Mancini.[4] There is no satisfactory account of him in English. Valla wrote his *Discourse on the Forgery of the Alleged Donation of Constantine* (*Declamatio de falso credita et ementita donatione Constantini*, also referred to as *Libellus*, and *Oratio*) in 1440, when he was secretary to Alfonso, king of Aragon, Sicily, and Naples. It may well be considered as part of the campaign which that king was conducting against Pope Eugenius IV in furtherance of his claims to Italian territories.

There has hitherto been no satisfactory text of this treatise. The first printed edition, that of Ulrich von Hutten, in 1517, is excessively rare,

---

3. F. M. Nichols, ed., *Epistles of Erasmus*. Longmans, Green & Co., New York, 1901.
4. *Vita di Lorenzo Valla* (Florence, 1891).

and it, as well as its numerous reprints, is defective in places. The same is true of the text in the collected works of Valla, the *Opera*, printed at Basle, 1540, 1543 (?). The only English edition, by Thomas Godfray (London, 1525 ?), is rare and of no great merit. A modern French edition by Alcide Bonneau (*La Donation de Constantin*, Paris, 1879) gives the text with a French translation and a long introduction. It is based on the 1520 reprint of Hutten's edition, is polemical, uncritical, and admittedly imperfect. A modern edition with translation into Italian (*La dissertazione di Lorenzo Valla su la falsa e manzognera donazione di Costantino* tradotta in Italiano da G. Vincenti, Naples, 1895) is out of print.

My text is based on the manuscript *Codex Vaticanus* 5314, dated December 7, 1451, the only complete manuscript of the treatise I have been able to find. I have collated this with Hutten's text as found in one of the earliest, if not the earliest, reprint (contained in the little volume *De Donatione Constantini quid veri habeat*, etc., dated 1520 in the Union Theological Seminary library copy, but corresponding closely to the one dated 1518 in E. Bocking's edition of the works of Ulrich von Hutten, vol. 1, p. 18), and have occasionally used readings from Hutten's text or later ones, such as that of Simon Schard,[5] but in every instance I have indicated the *MS* reading. I have used uniform, current spelling and punctuation, and have used my own judgment in paragraphing.

Preceding Valla's treatise I reprint, with a translation, the text of the *Donation* as given, with the omission of long sections, in Gratian's *Decretum*, or *Concordia discordantium canonum*, which was the form Valla used and on which he based his criticism. I take it from A. Friedberg's edition of the *Corpus Iuris Canonici*, volume I, columns 342-345. The full text of the *Donation* is best given by Karl Zeumer, in the *Festgabe für Rudolf von Gneist* (Julius Springer, Berlin, 1888), pages 47-59, reprinted among other places in my *Constantine the Great and Christianity*, pp. 228-237. The document may be studied to advantage also in the *Decretales Pseudo-Isidorianae et Capitula Angiliamni*, ed. Hinschius (Leipsic, 1863). An English translation, from Zeumer's text, is in E. F. Henderson's *Select Historical Documents of the Middle Ages*, pages 319-329.

In the translation of passages of the *Donation* I have, so far as possible, used the words of Henderson's translation. In quotations from the Bible

---

5. *Syntagma tractatuum de imperiali iurisdictione*, etc., Strassburg, 1609; first published under a similar title at Basle, 1566.

I have used the *King James Version*. In translating Valla's quotations from the *Donation* I have usually, though not always, followed him in giving words their classical and not their medieval meaning.

The *Donation of Constantine* grew out of the legends about Sylvester I, Bishop of Rome, as well as out of legends about Constantine. These are described at length in *Constantine the Great and Christianity*. The most familiar form of the Sylvester-Constantine legend is that of Mombritius' *Sanctuarium, sive Vitae collectae, ex codibus*, Milan, *c.* 1470, volume II, folio 279: Paris, 1910, volume II, pages 508-531.

Present-day scholarship is not in entire agreement on all points connected with the *Donation of Constantine*. The following summary, however, may be hazarded. The problem of modern criticism of course, is, not to establish the spuriousness of the *Donation* – that has long been obvious – but to locate the origin of the document as closely as possible.

The development of the Sylvester-Constantine legend was worked out best by Döllinger (*Papstfabeln des Mittelalters*, Munich, 1863: ed., J. Friedrich, Stuttgart, 1890) and by Duchesne (in his edition of the *Liber Pontificalis*, vol. 1, 1886, pp. cvii-cxx). These have shown the existence at Rome, as early as the last of the sixth century, of the story which forms most of the narrative part of the *Donation*, and gave the forger the whole of his background.

The earliest known manuscript of the document is in the *Codex Parisiensis Lat.* 2778, in the *Collectio Sancti Dionysii*, found in the monastery of St. Denis, in France. The collection contains documents dating from the last years of the eighth century, though it may have been put together later. The collected *Pseudo-Isidorian Decretals*, in which the *Donation* was virtually published to the world, in the middle of the ninth century, also came out in France. French writers of the ninth century, also, were the first, so far as we know, to refer to the *Donation*. Such facts help to fix the date of the forgery, but under the circumstances they do not fix the place as France. Rather they are merely another illustration of the well-known leadership of France in learning and politics during the ninth century.

Linguistic peculiarities of the document have been most exhaustively treated by one of the greatest of critical historians, Paul Scheffer-Boichorst,[6] not to speak of briefer studies by Döllinger, Brunner, and

---

6. *Neue Forschungen uber die Konstantinische Schenkung, in mittheilungen d. Instituts für*

THE DONATION OF CONSTANTINE

others. In the full text of the *Donation*, as for instance the one published by Zeumer, are found many features distinctive of Italian documents of the eighth century, and a number that apparently are peculiar to the chancellery of Stephen II (III), Bishop of Rome 752-757, and of Paul I (757-767), more particularly the latter. (Some of these do not occur in the passages and the text which Valla used; that is, in his copy of Gratian's *Decretum*.) This is true in varying degrees of particularity of the form or usage of the following words: *synclitus* (for *senatus*) in §15; *banda* (for *vexillum*) in §14; *censura* (*diploma*) in §17; *constitutum* (*decretum*) in §§17 and 18; *retro* (applied to the future) in §§1 and 19; *largitas* (*possessio*) in §13; *consul* and *patricius* (as mere designations of rank) in §15; *vel* (*et*) in §§11, 12, 13, 16, 19; *seu* (*et*) in §§14 and 17; *satraps* (as a Roman official) in §§8, 11, and 19; and *inluminator* in §7 in some manuscripts. The following phrases, also, are more or less distinctive: *Deo amabilis* in §1; *Deo vivo qui nos regnare precipit* in §19; *uno ex eadem sancta Trinitate* in §1; *principem apostolorurn vel eius vicarios firmos apud Deum adesse patronos* in §11; *pro concinnatione luminariorum* in §13; *et subscriptio imperialis* in §20; *propriis manibus roborantes* in §20; *religiosus clericus* in §15. The first part of §4; *Tres itaque formae... hominem*, is very similar to part of a letter of Paul I's in 757. In short, the language of the *Donation* seems to point to the papal chancellery as the place of its origin, and the pontificate of Paul I (757-767) as the most probable time.

That also seems to offer the situation and environment which would most naturally call forth the document as we have it. This is well brought out by Ludo Moritz Hartmann in his *Geschichte Italiens im Mittelalter*,[7] and by Erich Caspar in his *Pippin und die romische Kirche*.[8] The Papacy was then cutting loose from the emperor at Constantinople and ignoring his representatives in Italy, as well as developing its own independent policy toward the Lombards, and toward the Franks. The aim of the forger seems to have been the characteristically medieval one of supplying documentary warrant for the existence of the situation which had developed through a long-drawn-out revolution, namely, the passage of imperial prerogatives and political control in Italy from the Emperor to the Papacy. Hence, along with general statements of

---

oster. Geschichtsforschung, vol. X (1889), pp. 325 *et seq.*, XI (1890), pp. 128 *et seq.* Reprinted in his *Gesammelte Schriften in der Historische Studien of E. Eberling*, vol. XLII.

7. II, ii (Leipsic, 1903), pp. 218-231.
8. Berlin, 1914, pp. 185-189.

209

papal primacy, and of gifts of property, detailed and explicit stress is laid upon the granting of imperial honors, the imperial palace, and imperial power to the Pope, and upon the right of the Roman clergy to the privileges of the highest ranks of Roman society. Legal confirmation was thus given for riding roughshod over the vestiges and memories of the imperial regime in Italy and for looking to the Papacy as the source of all honors and dignities. Furthermore we know that Paul I was extremely devoted to the memory of Sylvester, and so it may well have been under his influence that this document came into existence with its tribute to Sylvester's personal character and historic significance.

The Donation of Constantine

As given in part one, division XCVI, chapters XIII and XIV of Gratian's *Decretum*, or *Harmony of the Canons.*
PALEA[9]

CHAPTER XIII. CONCERNING THE SAME [10]

The Emperor Constantine yielded his crown, and all his royal prerogatives in the city of Rome, and in Italy, and in western parts to the Apostolic [See]. For in the Acts of the Blessed Sylvester (which the Blessed Pope Gelasius in the Council of the Seventy Bishops recounts as read by the catholic, and in accordance with ancient usage many churches he says follow this example) occurs the following:
PALEA

CHAPTER XIV. CONCERNING THE SAME

The Emperor Constantine the fourth day after his baptism conferred this privilege on the Pontiff of the Roman church, in the whole Roman world priests should regard him as their head, as judges do the king. In this privilege among other things is this; "We – together with all our satraps, and the whole senate and my nobles, and also all the

---

9. The meaning of this word in this connection is unknown. The chapters to which it is prefixed are for the most part supposed to have been early marginal annotations afterwards incorporated in the text of the *Decretum*. *Cf.* Friedberg, *Corpus Iuris canonici*, vol. I, Prolegomena, p. lxxxvi.

10. The subject of chapters xi and xii is, "The Emperors must be under the Pontiffs, not over them." Chapters xiii and xiv continue the same subject.

people subject to the government of glorious Rome – considered it advisable, that as the Blessed Peter is seen to have been constituted vicar of the Son of God on the earth, so the Pontiffs who are the representatives of that same chief of the apostles, should obtain from us and our empire the power of a supremacy greater than the clemency of our earthly imperial serenity is seen to have conceded to it, choosing that same chief of the apostles and his vicars to be our constant intercessors with God. And to the extent of our earthly imperial power, we have decreed that his holy Roman church shall be honored with veneration, and that more than our empire and earthly throne the most sacred seat of the Blessed Peter shall be gloriously exalted, we giving to it power, and dignity of glory, and vigor, and honor imperial. And we ordain and decree that he shall have the supremacy as well over the four principal seats Alexandria, Antioch, Jerusalem, and Constantinople, as also over all the churches of God in the whole earth. And Pontiff, who at the time shall be at the head of the holy Roman church itself, shall be more exalted than, and chief over, all the priests of the whole world, and according to his judgment everything which is provided for the service of God and for the stability of the faith of Christians is to be administered. *And below:*

§1. On the churches of the blessed apostles Peter and Paul, for the providing of the lights, we have conferred landed estates of possessions, and have enriched them with different objects and through our sacred imperial mandate we have granted him of our property in the east as well as in the west, and even in the northern and the southern quarter; namely, in Judea, Greece, Asia, Thrace, Africa, and Italy and the various islands; under this condition indeed, that all shall be administered by the hand of our most blessed father the supreme Pontiff, Sylvester, and his successors. *And below:*

§2. And to our Father, the Blessed Sylvester, supreme Pontiff and Pope universal, of the city of Rome, and to all the Pontiffs, his successors, who shall sit in the seat of the Blessed Peter even unto the end of the world, we by this present do give our imperial Lateran palace, then the diadem, that is, the crown of our head, and at the same time the tiara and also the shoulder-band – that is, the strap that usually surrounds our imperial neck; and also the purple mantle and scarlet tunic, and all the imperial raiment; and also the same rank as those presiding over the imperial cavalry, conferring also even the imperial scepters, and at the same time all the standards, and banners, and the different ornaments, and all the pomp of our imperial eminence, and the glory of our power.

§3. We decree moreover, as to the most reverend men, the clergy of different orders who serve that same holy Roman church, that they have that same eminence, distinction, power and excellence, by the glory of which it seems proper for our most illustrious senate to be adorned; that is, that they be made patricians and consuls, and also we have proclaimed that they be decorated with the other imperial dignities. And even as the imperial militia is adorned, so also we decree that the clergy of the holy Roman church be adorned. And even as the imperial power is adorned with different offices, of chamberlains, indeed, and door-keepers, and all the guards, so we wish the holy Roman church also to be decorated. And in order that the pontifical glory may shine forth most fully, we decree this also; that the horses of the clergy of this same holy Roman church be decorated with saddle-cloths and linens, that is of the whitest color, and that they are to so ride. And even as our senate uses shoes with felt socks, that is, distinguished by white linen, so the clergy also should use them, so that, even as the celestial orders, so also the terrestrial may be adorned to the glory of God.

§4. Above all things, moreover, we give permission to that same most holy one our Father Sylvester and to his successors, from our edict, that he may make priest whomever he wishes, according to his own pleasure and counsel, and enroll him in the number of the religious clergy [i.e., regular, or monastic, clergy; or, perhaps, the cardinals], let no one whomsoever presume to act in a domineering way in this.

§5. We also therefore decreed this, that he himself and his successors might use and bear upon their heads – to the praise of God for the honor of the Blessed Peter – the diadem, that is, the crown which we have granted him from our own head, of purest gold and precious gems. But since he himself, the most blessed Pope, did not at all allow that crown of gold to be used over the clerical crown which he wears to the glory of the Blessed Peter, we placed upon his most holy head, with our own hands, a glittering tiara of dazzling white representing the Lord's resurrection, and holding the bridle of his horse, out of reverence for the Blessed Peter, we performed for him the duty of groom, decreeing that all his successors and they alone, use this same tiara in processions in imitation of our power.

§6. Wherefore, in order that the supreme pontificate may not deteriorate, but may rather be adorned with glory and power even more than is the dignity of an earthly rule; behold, we give over and relinquish to the aforesaid our most blessed Pontiff, Sylvester, the universal Pope, as well our palace, as has been said, as also the city of Rome, and all the provinces, places and cities of Italy and the western regions, and we decree by this our godlike and pragmatic sanction that they are to be controlled by him and by his successors, and we grant that they shall remain under the law of the holy Roman church.

§7. Wherefore we have perceived it to be fitting that our empire and the power of our kingdom should be transferred in the regions of the East, and that in the province of Byzantia, in the most fitting place, a city should be built in our name, and that our empire should there be established, for where the supremacy of priests and the head of the Christian religion has been established by the heavenly Emperor, it is not right that there an earthly emperor should have jurisdiction.

§8. We decree, moreover, that all these things, which through this our sacred imperial [charter] through other godlike decrees we have established and confirmed, remain inviolate and unshaken unto the end of the world. Wherefore, before the living God who commanded us to reign, and in the face of his terrible judgment, we entreat, through this our imperial sanction, all the emperors our successors, and all the nobles, the satraps also, the most glorious senate, and all the people in the whole world, now and in all times still[11] to come subject to our rule, that no one of them in any way be allowed either to break these [decrees], or in any way overthrow them. If any one, moreover – which we do not believe – prove a scorner or despiser in this matter, he shall be subject and bound over to eternal damnation, and shall feel the holy ones of God, the chief of the apostles, Peter and Paul, opposed to him in the present and in the future life, and he shall be burned in the lower Hell and shall perish with the devil and all the impious. The page, moreover, of this our imperial decree, we, confirming it with our own hands, did place above the venerable body of the Blessed Peter, chief of the apostles. Given at Rome on the third day before the Kalends of April, our master the august Flavius Constantine, for the fourth time, and Gallicanus, most illustrious men, being consuls.

11. *Retro* was used at Rome in the latter part of the eighth century with the peculiar meaning of "still" or "again." This is one of the clues to the date and place of the document. Henderson's translation is erroneous.

The Discourse of Lorenzo Valla on the Forgery of the Alleged Donation of Constantine

I have published many books, a great many, in almost every branch of learning. Inasmuch as there are those who are shocked that in these I disagree with certain great writers already approved by long usage, and charge me with rashness and sacrilege, what must we suppose some of them will do now! How they will rage against me, and if opportunity is afforded how eagerly and how quickly they will drag me to punishment! For I am writing against not only the dead, but the living also, not this man or that, but a host, not merely private individuals, but the authorities. And what authorities! Even the supreme pontiff, armed not only with the temporal sword as are kings and princes, but with the spiritual also, so that even under the very shield, so to speak, of any prince, you cannot protect yourself from him; from being struck down by excommunication, anathema, curse. So if he was thought to have both spoken and acted prudently who said, "I will not write against those who can write 'Proscribed,'" how much more would it seem that I ought to follow the same course toward him who goes far beyond proscription, who would pursue me with the invisible darts of his authority, so that I could rightly say, "Whither shall I go from thy spirit, or whither shall I flee from thy presence?"[12] Unless perhaps we think the supreme pontiff would bear these attacks more patiently than would others. Far from it; for Ananias, the high priest, in the presence of the tribune who sat as judge, ordered Paul when he said he lived in good conscience to be smitten on the mouth; and Pashur, holding the same rank, threw Jeremiah into prison for the boldness of his speech. The tribune and the governor, indeed, were able and willing to protect the former, and the king the latter, from priestly violence. But what tribune, what governor, even if he wanted to, could snatch me from the hands of the chief priest if he should seize me?

But there is no reason why this awful, twofold peril should trouble me and turn me from my purpose; for the supreme pontiff may not bind nor loose any one contrary to law and justice. And to give one's

---

12. *Ps.* cxxxix,7.

life in defense of truth and justice is the path of the highest virtue, the highest honor, the highest reward. Have not many undergone the hazard of death for the defense of their terrestrial fatherland? In the attainment of the celestial fatherland (they attain it who please God, not men), shall I be deterred by the hazard of death? Away then with trepidation, let fears far remove, let doubts pass away. With a brave soul, with utter fidelity, with good hope, the cause of truth must be defended, the cause of justice, the cause of God.

Nor is he to be esteemed a true orator who knows how to speak well, unless he also has the courage to speak. So let us have the courage to accuse him, whoever he is, that commits crimes calling for accusation. And let him who sins against all be called to account by the voice of one speaking for all. Yet perhaps I ought not to reprove my brother in public, but by himself. Rather, "Them that sin" and do not accept private admonition "rebuke before all, that others also may fear."[13] Or did not Paul, whose words I have just used, reprove Peter to his face in the presence of the church because he needed reproof? And he left this written for our instruction. But perhaps I am not a Paul that I should reprove a Peter. Yea, I am a Paul because I imitate Paul. Just as, and this is far greater, I become one in spirit with God when I diligently observe his commandments. Nor is any one made immune from chiding by an eminence which did not make Peter immune, and many others possessed of the same rank; for instance, Marcellus,[14] who offered a libation to the gods, and Celestine [I] who entertained the Nestorian heresy, and certain even within our own memory whom we know were reproved, to say nothing of those condemned, by their inferiors, for who is not inferior to the Pope?[15]

It is not my aim to inveigh against any one and write so-called Philippics against him – be that villainy far from me – but to root out error from men's minds, to free them from vices and crimes by either admonition or reproof. I would not dare to say [that my aim is] that others, taught by me, should prune with steel the papal see, which is Christ's vineyard, rank with overabundant shoots and compel it to bear rich grapes instead of meager wildings. When I do that, is there any one

---

13. *I Tim.* v, 20.
14. Valla's error for Marcellinus. The whole story is apocryphal.
15. A reference to the reforming councils of the fifteenth century.

who will want to close either my mouth or his own ears, much less propose punishment and death? If one should do so, even if it were the Pope, what should I call him, a good shepherd, or a deaf viper which would not choose to heed the voice of the charmer, but to strike his limbs with its poisonous bite?

I know that for a long time now men's ears are waiting to hear the offense with which I charge the Roman pontiffs. It is, indeed, an enormous one, due either to supine ignorance, or to gross avarice which is the slave of idols, or to pride of empire of which cruelty is ever the companion. For during some centuries now, either they have not known that the *Donation of Constantine* is spurious and forged, or else they themselves forged it, and their successors, walking in the same way of deceit as their elders, have defended as true what they knew to be false, dishonoring the majesty of the pontificate, dishonoring the memory of ancient pontiffs, dishonoring the Christian religion, confounding everything with murders, disasters and crimes. They say the city of Rome is theirs, theirs the kingdom of Sicily and of Naples,[16] the whole of Italy, the Gauls, the Spains, the Germans, the Britons, indeed the whole West; for all these are contained in the instrument of the *Donation* itself.[17] So all these are yours, supreme pontiff? And it is your purpose to recover them all? To despoil all kings and princes of the West of their cities or compel them to pay a yearly tribute, is that your plan?

I, on the contrary, think it fairer to let the princes despoil you of all the empire you hold. For, as I shall show, that *Donation* whence the supreme pontiffs will have their right derived was unknown equally to Sylvester and to Constantine.

But before I come to the refutation of the instrument of the *Donation* which is their one defense, not only false but even stupid, the right order demands that I go further back. And first, I shall show that Constantine and Sylvester were not such men that the former would choose to give, would have the legal right to give, or would have it in his power to give those lands to another, or that the latter would be willing to accept them or could legally have done so. In the second

---

16. Valla was in the service of the king of Sicily and of Naples when he wrote this.

17. The phrase "Italy and the western provinces," in the *Donation of Constantine*, meant to the writer of that document the Italian peninsula, including Lombardy, Venetia, Istria, and adjacent islands. Other countries probably did not occur to him as part of the Roman Empire. Valla, however, followed the current interpretation.

place, if this were not so, though it is absolutely true and obvious, [I shall show that in fact] the latter did not receive nor the former give possession of what is said to have been granted, but that it always remained under the sway and empire of the Caesars. In the third place, [I shall show that] nothing was given to Sylvester by Constantine, to an earlier Pope (and Constantine had received baptism even before that pontificate), and that the grants were inconsiderable, for the mere subsistence of the Pope. Fourth, that it is not true either that a copy of the *Donation* is found in the *Decretum* [of Gratian], or that it was taken from the *History of Sylvester*; for it is not found in it or in any history, and it is composed of contradictions, impossibilities, stupidities, barbarisms and absurdities. Further, I shall speak of the pretended or mock donation of certain other Caesars. Then by way of redundance I shall add that even had Sylvester taken possession, nevertheless, he or some other pontiff having been dispossessed, possession could not be resumed after such a long interval under either divine or human law. Last [I shall show] that the possessions which are now held by the supreme pontiff could not, in any length of time, be validated by prescription.

And so to take up the first point, let us speak first of Constantine, then of Sylvester.

It would not do to argue a public and *quasi*-imperial case without more dignity of utterance than is usual in private cases. And so speaking as in an assembly of kings and princes, as I assuredly do, for this oration of mine will come into their hands, I choose to address an audience, as it were, face to face. I call upon you kings and princes, for it is difficult for a private person to form a picture of a royal mind; I seek your thought, I search your heart, I ask your testimony. Is there any one of you who, had he been in Constantine's place, would have thought that he must set about giving to another out of pure generosity the city of Rome, his fatherland, the head of the world, the queen of states, the most powerful, the noblest and the most opulent of peoples, the victor of the nations, whose very form is sacred, and betaking himself thence to an humble little town, Byzantium; giving with Rome Italy, not a province but the mistress of provinces; giving the three Gauls; giving the two Spains; the Britons; the whole West; depriving himself of one of the two eyes of his empire? That any one in possession of his senses would do this, I cannot be brought to believe.

What ordinarily befalls you that is more looked forward to, more pleasing, more grateful, than for you to increase your empires and kingdoms, and to extend your authority as far and as wide as possible? In this, as it seems to me, all your care, all your thought, all your labor, night and day is expended. From this comes your chief hope of glory, for this you renounce pleasures; for this you subject yourselves to a thousand dangers; for this your dearest pledges; for this your own flesh you sacrifice with serenity. Indeed, I have neither heard nor read of any of you having been deterred from an attempt to extend his empire by loss of an eye, a hand, a leg, or any other member. Nay, this very ardor and this thirst for wide dominion is such that whoever is most powerful, him it thus torments and stirs the most. Alexander, not content to have traversed on foot the deserts of Libya, to have conquered the Orient to the farthest ocean, to have mastered the North, amid so much bloodshed, so many perils, his soldiers already mutinous and crying out against such long, such hard campaigns, seemed to himself to have accomplished nothing unless either by force or by the power of his name he should have made the West also, and all nations, tributary to him. I put it too mildly; he had already determined to cross the ocean, and if there was any other world, to explore it and subject it to his will. He would have tried, I think, last of all to ascend the heavens. Some such wish all kings have, even though not all are so bold. I pass over the thought how many crimes, how many horrors have been committed to attain and extend power, for brothers do not restrain their wicked hands from the stain of brothers' blood, nor sons from the blood of parents, nor parents from the blood of sons. Indeed, nowhere is man's recklessness apt to run riot further nor more viciously. And to your astonishment, you see the minds of old men no less eager in this than the minds of young men, childless men no less eager than parents, kings than usurpers.

But if domination is usually sought with such great resolution, how much greater must be the resolution to preserve it! For it is by no means so discreditable not to increase an empire as to impair it, nor is it so shameful not to annex another's kingdom to your own as for your own to be annexed to another's. And when we read of men being put in charge of a kingdom or of cities by some king or by the people, this is not done in the case of the chief or the greatest portion of the empire, but in the case of the last and least, as it were, and that with the understanding that the recipient should always recognize the donor as his sovereign and himself as an agent.

Now I ask, do they not seem of a base and most ignoble mind who suppose that Constantine gave away the better part of his empire? I say nothing of Rome, Italy, and the rest, but the Gauls where he had waged war in person, where for a long time he had been sole master, where he had laid the foundations of his glory and his empire! A man who through thirst for dominion had waged war against nations, and attacking friends and relatives in civil strife had taken the government from them, who had to deal with remnants of an opposing faction not yet completely mastered and overthrown; who waged war with many nations not only by inclination and in the hope of fame and empire but by very necessity, for he was harassed every day by the barbarians; who had many sons, relatives and associates; who knew that the Senate and the Roman people would oppose this act; who had experienced the instability of conquered nations and their rebellions at nearly every change of ruler at Rome; who remembered that after the manner of other Caesars he had come into power, not by the choice of the Senate and the consent of the populace, but by armed warfare; what incentive could there be so strong and urgent that he would ignore all this and choose to display such prodigality?

They say, it was because he had become a Christian. Would he therefore renounce the best part of his empire? I suppose it was a crime, an outrage, a felony, to reign after that, and that a kingdom was incompatible with the Christian religion! Those who live in adultery, those who have grown rich by usury, those who possess goods which belong to another, they after baptism are wont to restore the stolen wife, the stolen money, the stolen goods. If this be your idea, Constantine, you must restore your cities to liberty, not change their master. But that did not enter into the case; you were led to do as you did solely for the glory of your religion. As though it were more religious to lay down a kingdom than to administer it for the maintenance of religion! For so far as it concerns the recipients, that *Donation* will be neither honorable nor useful to them. But if you want to show yourself a Christian, to display your piety, to further the cause, I do not say of the Roman church, but of the Church of God, now of all times act the prince, so that you may fight for those who cannot and ought not to fight, so that by your authority you may safeguard those who are exposed to plots and injuries. To Nebuchadnezzar, to Cyrus, to Ahasuerus, and to many other princes, by the will of God, the mystery of the truth was revealed;

but of none of them did God demand that he should resign his government, that he should give away part of his kingdom, but only that he should give the Hebrews their liberty and protect them from their aggressive neighbors. This was enough for the Jews; it will be enough for the Christians also. You have become a Christian, Constantine? Then it is most unseemly for you now as a Christian emperor to have less sovereignty than you had as an infidel. For sovereignty is an especial gift of God, to which even the gentile sovereigns are supposed to be chosen by God.

But he was cured of leprosy! Probably, therefore, he would have wished to show his gratitude and give back a larger measure than he had received.. Indeed! Naaman the Syrian, cured by Elisha, wished merely to present gifts, not the half of his goods, and would Constantine have presented the half of his empire? I regret to reply to this shameless story as though it were undoubted and historical, for it is a reflection of the story of Naaman and Elisha; just as that other story about the dragon is a reflection of the fabulous dragon of Bel.[18] But yielding this point, is there in this story any mention made of a "donation"? Not at all. But of this, more later.

He was cured of leprosy? He took on therefore a Christian spirit; he was imbued with the fear of God, with the love of God; he wished to honor him. Nevertheless I cannot be persuaded that he wished to give away so much; for, so far as I see, no one, either pagan, in honor of the gods, or believer, in honor of the living God, has resigned his empire and given it to priests. In sooth, of the kings of Israel none could be brought to permit his people to go, according to the former custom, to sacrifice at the temple in Jerusalem; for fear lest, moved by that solemn religious ceremony and by the majesty of the temple, they should return to the king of Judah from whom they had revolted. And how much more is Constantine represented to have done! And that you may not flatter yourself with the cure of leprosy, [let me say that] Jeroboam was the first one chosen by God to be king of Israel and indeed from a very low estate, which to my mind is more than being healed of leprosy;

---

18. In many versions of the *Life of Sylvester* there is a marvelous story of an enormous serpent, finally subdued by the saint. *Cf. infra*, p. 143; Coleman, *Constantine the Great and Christianity*, pp. 161 *et seq.*; Mombritius, *Sanctuarium, Sive Vitae collectae ex codibus* (Milan, *c.* 1479), v, ii, pp. 279 *et seq.*, also Paris edition, 1910. For the story of Bel and the Dragon, *cf.* the book of that name in the *Apocrypha*.

nevertheless he did not presume to entrust his kingdom to God. And will you have Constantine give to God a kingdom which he had not received from him, and that, too, when he would offend his sons (which was not the case with Jeroboam), humiliate his friends, ignore his relatives, injure his country, plunge everybody into grief, and forget his own interests!

But if, having been such a man as he was, he had been transformed as it were into another man, there would certainly not have been lacking those who would warn him, most of all his sons, his relatives, and his friends. Who does not think that they would have gone at once to the emperor? Picture them to yourself, when the purpose of Constantine had become known, trembling, hastening to fall with groans and tears at the feet of the prince, and saying:

"Is it thus that you, a father hitherto most affectionate toward your sons, despoil your sons, disinherit them, disown them? We do not complain of the fact that you choose to divest yourself of the best and largest part of the empire so much as we wonder at it. But we do complain that you give it to others to our loss and shame. Why do you defraud your children of their expected succession to the empire, you who yourself reigned in partnership with your father? What have we done to you? By what disloyalty to you, to our country, to the Roman name or the majesty of the empire, are we deemed to deserve to be deprived of the chiefest and best part of our principality; that we should be banished from our paternal home, from the sight of our native land, from the air we are used to, from our ancient ties! Shall we leave our household gods, our shrines, our tombs, exiles, to live we know not where, nor in what part of the earth?

"And we, your kindred, your friends, who have stood so often with you in line of battle, who have seen brothers, fathers, sons, pierced and writhing under hostile sword, and have not been dismayed at the death of others, but were ourselves ready to seek death for your sake, why are we now deserted one and all by you! We who hold the public offices of Rome, who govern or are destined to govern the cities of Italy, the Gauls, the Spains, and other provinces, are all of us to be deposed? Are all of us to be ordered into private life? Or will you compensate us elsewhere for this loss? And how can you, when such a large part of the world has been given to another? Will your majesty put the man who had charge of a hundred peoples over one? How could you have conceived such a plan? How is it that you have suddenly become oblivious of your subjects, so that you have no consideration for your friends, nor your kindred, nor your sons? Would that it had been our lot, your Majesty, while your honor and your victory were unimpaired, to fall in battle, rather than to see this!

"You have the power, indeed, to do with your empire what you will, and even with us, one thing however excepted, which we will resist to the death; we will not give up the worship of the immortal gods — just for the sake of a conspicuous example to others, that you may know how much that bounty of yours will be worth to the Christian religion. For if you do not give your empire to Sylvester, we are willing to be Christians with you, and many will imitate us. But if you do give it, not only will we not endure to become Christians, but you will make the name hateful, detestable, execrable to us, and you will put us in such a position that at last you will pity our life and our death, nor will you accuse us, but only yourself, of obstinacy."

Would not Constantine, unless we would have him totally devoid of humanity, if he were not moved of his own accord, have been moved by this speech? But if he had not been willing to listen to these men, would there not have been those who would oppose this act with both word and deed? Or would the Senate and the Roman people have thought that they had no obligation to do anything in a matter of such importance? Would it not have put forward some orator "distinguished in character and service," as Virgil says, who would hold forth to Constantine as follows:

"Your Majesty, if you are heedless of your subjects and of yourself, nor care to give your sons an inheritance, nor your kindred riches, nor your friends honors, nor to keep your empire intact, the Senate and the Roman people at least cannot be heedless of its rights and its dignity. How come you to take such liberties with the Roman Empire, which has been built up, not from your blood, but from ours! Will you cut one body into two parts, and out of one kingdom make two kingdoms, two heads, two wills, and as it were, reach out to two brothers swords with which to fight over their inheritance! We give to states which have deserved well of this city the rights of citizenship, so that they may be Roman citizens; you take away from us the half of the empire, so that they will not know this city as their mother. In beehives, if two kings are born, we kill the weaker one; but in the hive of the Roman Empire, where there is one prince, and that the best, you think that another must be introduced, and that the weakest one, not a bee, but a drone.[19]

"We see a sore lack of prudence on your part, your Majesty. For what will happen, if either during your life or after your death, war should be waged by barbarian tribes against the part of the empire which you are alienating, or against the other, which you leave for yourself? With what military force, with what resources can we go to meet them? Even now with the troops of the whole empire we have scarcely enough power; shall we have enough then? Or will this part be forever at peace with that? In my opinion it cannot be, for Rome will want to rule and the other part will not want to be subject. Nay, even in your lifetime, shortly, when the old officials are removed and new ones put in their places, when you withdraw to your kingdom and fare far forth and another is ruling here, will not all interests be different, that is, diverse and contrary? Usually when a kingdom is divided between two brothers, at once the hearts of the people also are divided, and war arises from within sooner than from foreign enemies. That that will happen in this empire, who does not see it? Or do you not know that it was chiefly on this ground that the patricians once said that they would rather die before the eyes of the Roman people than allow the motion to be carried that part of the Senate and part of the plebeians should be sent to live at Veii and that the Roman people should have two cities in common; for if in one city there were so many dissentions, how would it be in two cities? So in our time, if there are so many disorders in one empire, your own knowledge and your labors are a witness, how will it be in two empires!

"Come now, do you think that when you are engaged in wars, there will be men here willing or able to bear you aid? Those who will be in command of our soldiers and cities will always shrink from arms and warfare, as will he who appoints them. Indeed, will not either the Roman legions or the provinces themselves try to despoil this man, so inexperienced in ruling and so inviting to violence, hoping that he will neither fight back nor seek revenge? By Hercules! I believe they will not remain in allegiance a single month, but immediately, at the first news of your departure they will rebel. What will you do? What plan will you follow when you are pressed with a twofold and even a manifold

---

19. I have made two English paragraphs of the rather long Latin one. [Coleman]

war? The nations which we have conquered we can scarcely hold; how can we withstand them if in addition we have war with free peoples?

"As for your interests, your Majesty, that is for you to see to. But this ought to concern us no less than you. You are mortal; the Empire of the Roman people ought to be immortal, and so far as in us lies, it will be, and not the Empire alone but respect for it as well. Shall we, forsooth, accept the government of those whose religion we despise; shall we, rulers of the world, serve this altogether contemptible being! When the city was captured by the Gauls the aged Romans did not suffer their beards to be stroked by the victors. Will all these men of senatorial, praetorian, tribunician, consular and triumphal rank now suffer those to rule them, upon whom as upon guilty slaves they themselves have heaped every kind of contumely and punishment! Will those men create magistrates, govern provinces, wage war, pass sentences of death upon us? Will the Roman nobility take wages under them, hope for honors and receive rewards at their hands? What greater, what deeper wound can we receive? Do not think, your Majesty, that the Roman blood has so degenerated as to endure this with equanimity and not deem it a thing to be avoided by fair means or foul. By my faith, not even our women would suffer it, but they would rather burn themselves with their dear children and their household gods, for Carthaginian women should not be braver than Roman.

"To be sure, your Majesty, if we had chosen you king, you would have a great measure of control over the Roman Empire indeed, yet not such that you could in the least diminish its greatness, for then we who should have made you king, by that same token would order you to abdicate your kingdom. How much less then could you divide the kingdom, alienate so many provinces, and deliver even the capital of the kingdom over to a man who is a stranger and altogether base. We put a watch-dog over the sheepfold, but if he tries rather to act like a wolf, we either drive him out or kill him. Now will you, who have long been the watch-dog of the Roman fold and defended it, at the last in unprecedented manner turn into a wolf?

"But you must know, since you compel us to speak harshly in defense of our rights, that you have no right over the Empire of the Roman people, for Caesar seized the supreme power by force; Augustus was the heir of his wrongdoing and made himself master by the ruin of the opposing factions; Tiberius, Gaius, Claudius, Nero, Galba, Otho,

THE DONATION OF CONSTANTINE

Vitellius, Vespasian, and the rest, in the same way or nearly so, made spoil of our liberty; and you also became ruler by expelling or killing others. I say nothing of your being born out of wedlock.

"Wherefore, to speak our mind, your Majesty; if you do not care to keep the government of Rome, you have sons, and by the law of nature, with our permission, also, and on our motions, you may substitute one of them in your place. If not, it is our purpose to defend the public honor and our personal dignity. For this is no less an act of violence against the Quirites than was once the rape of Lucretia, nor will there fail us a Brutus to offer himself to this people as a leader against Tarquinius for the recovery of liberty. We will draw our swords first upon those whom you are putting over us, and then upon you, as we have done against many emperors and for lighter reasons."

This would surely have prevailed on Constantine, unless we deem him made of stone or wood. And if the people would not have said this, it could be believed that they spoke among themselves and vented their rage in about these words. Let me go on a step and say that Constantine wished to benefit Sylvester, the one whom he would subject to the hatred and the swords of so many men that he, Sylvester, would scarcely have survived, I think, a single day. For it seemed that when he and a few others had been removed, all trace of such a cruel outrage and insult would have been obliterated from the breasts of the Romans.

Let us suppose, however, if possible, that neither prayers, nor threats, nor any argument availed aught, and that still Constantine persisted and was not willing to yield through persuasion the position he had taken. Who would not acknowledge himself moved by the speech of Sylvester, that is, if the event had ever actually occurred? It would doubtless have been something like this:

"Most worthy prince and son, Caesar, though I cannot but like and embrace your piety, so abject and effusive, nevertheless you have fallen somewhat into error in offering gifts to God and immolating victims, and I am not at all surprised at it, for you are still a novice in the Christian service. As once it was not right for the priest to sacrifice every sort of beast and animal and fowl, so now he is not to accept every sort of gift. I am a priest and pontiff, and I ought to look carefully at what I permit to be offered on the altar, lest perchance there be offered, I do not say an unclean animal, but a viper or a serpent. And this is what you would do. But if it were your right to give a part of the Empire including Rome, queen of the world, to another than your sons, a thing I do not at all approve; if this people, if Italy, if the other nations, should suffer themselves to be willing to submit to the government of those whom they hate and whose religion, snared by the enticements of this world, they have hitherto spit upon — an impossible supposition; if you nevertheless think I am to be given anything, my most loving son, I could not by any argument be brought to give you my assent, unless I were to be false to myself, to forget my station, and well-nigh deny my Lord Jesus. For your gifts, or if you wish, your payments, would tarnish and utterly ruin my honor and purity and holiness and that of all my successors, and would close the way to those who are about to come to the knowledge of the truth.

"Elisha was not willing, was he, to accept a reward when Naaman the Syrian was cured of the leprosy? Should I accept one when you are cured? He rejected presents; should I allow kingdoms to be given to me? He was unwilling to obscure the prophetic office; could I obscure the office of Christ, which I bear in me? But why did he think that the prophetic office would be obscured by his receiving gifts? Doubtless because he might seem to sell sacred things, to put the gift of God out at usury, to want the patronage of men, to lower and lessen the worth of his benefaction. He preferred, therefore, to make princes and kings his beneficiaries rather than to be himself their beneficiary, or even to allow mutual benefactions. For, as says the Lord, 'It is more blessed to give than to receive.'[20] I am in the same case, only so, more whom the Lord taught, saying, 'Heal the sick, cleanse the lepers, raise the dead, cast out devils: freely ye have received, freely give.'[21] Shall I commit such a disgrace, your Majesty, as not to follow the precepts of God; as to tarnish my glory? 'It will be better,' says Paul, 'for me to die than that any man should make my glorying void.'[22] Our glory is to honor our ministry in the sight of God, as Paul also said; 'I speak to you Gentiles, as I am the apostle of the Gentiles, I magnify mine office.'[23]

"Your Majesty, should even I be both an example and a cause for the apostasy of others, I, a Christian, a priest of God, pontiff of Rome, vicar of Christ! For how, indeed, will the blamelessness of priests remain

20. *Acts* xx, 35.
21. *Matt.* x, 8.
22. *I Cor.* ix, 15.
23. *Rom.* xi, 13.

untouched amid riches, magistracies, and the management of secular business? Do we renounce earthly possessions in order to attain them more richly, and have we given up our own property in order to possess another's and the public's? Shall we have cities, tributes, tolls? How then can you call us 'clergy' if we do this? Our portion, or our lot, which in Greek is called *kleros,* is not earthly, but celestial. The Levites, also clergy, were not allotted a portion with their brethren, and do you command us to take even our brothers' portion!

"What are riches and dominions to me who am commanded by the voice of the Lord not to be anxious for the morrow, and to whom he said; 'Lay not up for yourselves treasures upon earth, possess not gold nor silver nor money in your purses,'[24] and 'It is harder for a rich man to enter into the kingdom of heaven, than for a camel to go through the eye of a needle.'[25] Therefore he chose poor men as his ministers, and those who left all to follow him, and was himself an example of poverty. Even so is the handling of riches and of money, not merely their possession and ownership, the enemy of uprightness. Judas alone, he that had the purses and carried the alms, was a liar, and for the love of money, to which he had become accustomed, chided and betrayed his Master, his Lord, his God. So I fear, your Majesty, lest you change me from a Peter into a Judas.

"Hear also what Paul says: 'We brought nothing into this world and it is certain we can carry nothing out. And having food and raiment, let us be therewith content. But they that will be rich fall into temptation and a snare of the devil, and into many foolish and hurtful lusts, which drown men in destruction and perdition. For the love of money is the root of all evil, which while some coveted after, they erred from the faith, and pierced themselves through with many sorrows. But thou, O man of God, flee these things.'[26] And you command me, your Majesty, to accept what I ought to shun as poison!

"And consider besides, for prudence' sake, your Majesty, what chance would there be in all this for divine service? To certain who complained that their destitute were neglected in the daily distribution, the apostles answered that it was not reason that they should leave the word

---

24. Quoted, freely, from *Matt.* vi, 19 and *Luke* x, 4.
25. Quoted, freely, from *Matt.* xix, 24; *Mk.* x, 25; *Luke* xviii, 25.
26. *I Tim.* vi, 7-11.

of God, and serve tables.[27] Yet to feed widows, how different is that from exacting tolls, running the treasury, hiring soldiers, and engaging in a thousand other cares of this sort! 'No man that warreth for God entangleth himself with the affairs of this life,'[28] says Paul. Did Aaron and others of the tribe of Levi take care of anything except the tabernacle of the Lord? And his sons, because they had put strange fire in their censers, were consumed by fire from heaven. And you order us to put the fire of worldly riches, forbidden and profane, in our sacred censers, that is, our priestly duties! Did Eleazar, did Phinehas, did the other priests and ministers, either of the tabernacle or of the temple, administer anything except what pertained to the divine service? I say did they administer, nay, could they have administered anything, if they wished to fulfil their own duty? And if they did not wish to, they would hear the curse of the Lord, saying, 'Cursed be they that do the work of the Lord deceitfully.'[29] And this curse, though it impends over all, yet most of all it impends over the pontiffs.

"Oh what a responsibility is the pontifical office! What a responsibility it is to be head of the church! What a responsibility to be appointed over such a great flock as a shepherd at whose hand is required the blood of every single lamb and sheep lost; to whom it is said, 'If thou lovest me more than these, as thou sayest, feed my lambs.' Again, 'If thou lovest me, as thou sayest, feed my sheep.' And a third time, 'If thou lovest me, as thou sayest, feed my sheep.'[30] And you order me, your Majesty, to shepherd also goats and swine, which cannot be herded by the same shepherd!

"What! you want to make me king, or rather Caesar, that is ruler of kings! When the Lord Jesus Christ, God and man, king and priest, affirmed himself king, hear of what kingdom he spoke: 'My kingdom,' he said, 'is not of this world; if my kingdom were of this world, then would my servants fight.'[31] And what was his first utterance and the oft-repeated burden of his preaching, but this: 'Repent, for the kingdom of heaven is at hand.'[32] 'The kingdom of God is at hand for him for whom

27. *Acts* vi, 2.
28. *II Tim.* ii, 4.
29. *Jer.* xlviii, 10, quoted freely.
30. Free quotations from *John* xxi, 15-17.
31. *John* xviii, 36.
32. *Matt.* iv., 17.

the kingdom of heaven is prepared.' When he said this, did he not make clear that he had nothing to do with secular sovereignty? And not only did he not seek a kingdom of this sort, but when it was offered him, he would not accept it. For once when he learned that the people planned to take him and make him king, he fled to the solitude of the mountains. He not only gave this to us who occupy his place as an example to be imitated, but he taught us by precept: 'The princes of the Gentiles exercise dominion over them, and they that are great exercise authority upon them. But it shall not be so among you; but whosoever will be great among you, let him be your minister; and whosoever will be chief among you, let him be your servant; even as the Son of man came not to be ministered unto, but to minister, and to give his life a ransom for many.'[33]

"Know this, your Majesty; God formerly established judges over Israel, not kings; and he hated the people for demanding a king for themselves. And he gave them a king on account of the hardness of their hearts, but only because he permitted their rejection, which he revoked in the new law. And should I accept a kingdom, who am scarcely permitted to be a judge? 'Or do ye not know,' says Paul, 'that the saints shall judge the world? And if the world shall be judged by you, you are not the ones to judge the smallest matters. Know ye not that we shall judge angels? How much more things that pertain to this life! If then ye have judgments of things pertaining to this life, set them to judge who are least in the church.'[34] But judges merely gave judgment concerning matters in controversy, they did not levy tribute also. Should I do it, with the knowledge that when Peter was asked by the Lord, 'Of whom do the kings of the earth take custom or tribute? of their own children or of strangers?' and answered 'Of strangers,' the Lord said, 'Then are the children free.'[35] But if all men are my children, your Majesty, as they certainly are, then will all be free; nobody will pay anything. Therefore your Donation will be no good to me, and I shall get nothing out of it but labor which I am least able to do, as also I am least justified in doing it.

33. *Matt.* xx, 25-28.
34. *I Cor.* vi, 2-5, distorted in punctuation and meaning. Paul argues that cases should be settled inside the church, and that even the humblest Christians are competent to act as judges; Valla quotes him to show that church leaders are not to be judges.
35. Quotations are from *Matt.* xvii, 25-26.

"Nay more, I should have to use my authority to shed blood in punishing offenders, in waging wars, in sacking cities, in devastating countries with fire and sword. Otherwise I could not possibly keep what you have given me. And if I do this am I a priest, a pontiff, a vicar of Christ? Rather I should hear him thunder out against me, saying, 'My house shall be called of all nations the house of prayer, but ye have made it a den of thieves.'[36] 'I am not come into the world,' said the Lord, 'to judge the world, but to save it.'[37] And shall I who have succeeded him be the cause of men's death, I to whom in the person of Peter it was said, 'Put up again thy sword into his place, for all they that take the sword shall perish with the sword'?[38] It is not permitted us even to defend ourselves with the sword, for Peter wished only to defend his Lord, when he cut off the servant's ear. And do you command us to use the sword for the sake of either getting or keeping riches?

"Our authority is the authority of the keys, as the Lord said, 'I will give unto thee the keys of the kingdom of Heaven: and whatsoever thou shalt bind on Earth shall be bound in Heaven: and whatsoever thou shalt loose on Earth shall be loosed in Heaven.'[39] 'And the gates of Hell shall not prevail against it.'[40] Nothing can be added to this authority, nor to this dignity, nor to this kingdom. He who is not contented therewith, seeks something more from the devil, who dared even to say to the Lord, 'I will give thee all the kingoms of the world, if thou wilt fall to the earth and worship me.'[41] Wherefore, your Majesty, by your leave let me say it, do not play the part of the devil to me by ordering Christ, that is, me, to accept the kingdoms of the world at your hand. For I prefer rather to scorn than to possess them.

"And, to speak of the unbelievers, future believers though, I hope, do not transform me for them from an angel of light into an angel of darkness. I want to win their hearts to piety, not impose a yoke upon their necks; to subject them to me with the sword of the Word of God, not with a sword of iron, that they should not be made worse than they are, nor kick, nor gore me, nor, angered by my mistake, blaspheme the

36. *Mk.* xi, 17.
37. *John* xii, 47.
38. *Matt.* xxvi, 52.
39. *Matt.* xvi, 19.
40. *Matt.* xvi, 18.
41. *Matt.* iv, 8-9, free quotation.

name of God. I want to make them my most beloved sons, not my slaves; to adopt them, not cast them out; to have them born again, not to seize them out of hand; to offer their souls a sacrifice to God, not their bodies a sacrifice to the devil. 'Come unto me,' says the Lord, 'for I am meek and lowly in heart. Take my yoke upon you, and ye shall find rest for your souls. For my yoke is easy and my burden is light.'[42]

"Finally, to come to an end at last, in this matter accept that sentence of his, which he spoke as though to me and to you; 'Render unto Caesar the things which are Caesar's; and unto God, the things that are God's.'[43] Accordingly, therefore, your Majesty, you must not surrender the things that are yours, and I must not accept the things that are Caesar's; nor will I ever accept though you offer them a thousand times."

To this speech of Syvester's, worthy of an apostolic hero, what could there be further for Constantine to bring out in opposition? Since the case stands thus, do not they who say that the Donation took place do violence to Constantine when they would have him rob his own familyand tear the Roman Empire asunder? Do they not do violence to the Senate and the Roman people, to Italy, and to the whole West, which according to them allowed the government to be changed contrary to law and justice? Do they not do violence to Sylvester, who according to them accepted a gift not befitting a holy man? violence to the supreme pontificate, when they think that it would take charge of earthly kingdoms and rule over the Roman Empire? Verily, all this tends to show plainly that Constantine, in the face of so many obstacles, would never have thought of giving practically the whole Roman state to Sylvester, as they say he did.

Proceed to the next point; to make us believe in this "donation" which your document recites, something ought still to be extant concerning Sylvester's acceptance of it. There is nothing concerning it extant. But it is believable, you say, that he recognized this "donation." I believe so, too; that [if it was given] he not only recognized it, but sought it, asked for it, extorted it with his prayers; that is believable. But why do you reverse the natural conjecture and then say it is believable? For the fact that there is mention of the donation in the document of

---

42. *Matt.* xi, 28-30, with the phrases transposed.
43. *Matt.* xxii, 21.

the deed is no reason for inferring that it was accepted; but on the contrary, the fact that there is no mention [anywhere] of an acceptance is reason for saying that there was no donation. So you have stronger proof that Sylvester refused the gift than that Constantine wished to give it, and a benefaction is not conferred upon a man against his will. Indeed, we must suspect not so much that Sylvester refused the grants as that he tacitly disclosed that neither could Constantine legally make them nor could he himself legally accept.

O avarice, ever blind and ill-advised! Let us suppose that you may be able to adduce even genuine documents for the assent of Sylvester, not tampered with, authentic: even so, were the grants actually made which are found in such documents? Where is any taking possession, any delivery? For if Constantine gave a charter only, he did not want to befriend Sylvester, but to mock him. It is likely, you say, that any one who makes a grant, gives possession of it, also. See what you are saying; for it is certain that possession was not given, and the question is whether the title was given! It is likely that one who did not give possession did not want to give the title either.

Or is it not certain that possession was never given? To deny it is the sheerest impudence. Did Constantine ever lead Sylvester in state to the Capitol amid the shouts of the assembled Quirites, heathen as they were? Did he place him on a golden throne in the presence of the whole Senate? Did he command the magistrates, each in the order of his rank, to salute their king and prostrate themselves before him? This, rather than the giving of some palace such as the Lateran, is customary in the creation of new rulers. Did he afterwards escort him through all Italy? Did he go with him to the Gauls? Did he go to the Spains? Did he go to the Germans, and the rest of the West? Or if they both thought it too onerous to traverse so many lands, to whom did they delegate such an important function, to represent Caesar in transferring possession and Sylvester in receiving it? Distinguished men, and men of eminent authority, they must have been: and nevertheless we do not know who they were. And how much weight there is here in these two words, *give* and *receive*! To pass by ancient instances, I do not remember to have seen any other procedure when any one was made lord of a city, a country, or a province; for we do not count possession as given until the old magistrates are removed and the new ones substituted. If then Sylvester had not demanded that this be done, nevertheless the dignity of Constantine required that he show that he gave possession not in words, but in fact, that he ordered officers to retire and others to be substituted by Sylvester. Possession is not transferred when it remains in the hands of those who had it before, and the new master dares not remove them.

But grant that this also does not stand in the way, that, notwithstanding, we assume Sylvester to have been in possession, and let us say that the whole transaction took place though not in the customary and natural way. After Constantine went away, what governors did Sylvester place over his provinces and cities, what wars did he wage, what nations that took up arms did he subdue, through whom did he carry on this government? We know none of these circumstances, you answer. So! I think all this was done in the nighttime, and no one saw it at all!

Come now! Was Sylvester ever in possession? Who dispossessed him? For he did not have possession permanently, nor did any of his successors, at least till Gregory the Great, and even he did not have possession. One who is not in possession and cannot prove that he has been disseized certainly never did have possession, and if he says he did, he is crazy. You see, I even prove that you are crazy! Otherwise, tell who dislodged the Pope? Did Constantine himself, or his sons, or Julian, or some other Caesar? Give the name of the expeller, give the date, from what place was the Pope expelled first, where next, and so in order. Was it by sedition and murder, or without these? Did the nations conspire together against him, or which first? What! Did not one of them give him aid, not one of those who had been put over cities or provinces by Sylvester or another Pope? Did he lose everything in a single day, or gradually and by districts? Did he and his magistrates offer resistance, or did they abdicate at the first disturbance? What! Did not the victors use the sword on those dregs of humanity, whom they thought unworthy of the Empire, to revenge their outrage, to make sure of the newly won mastery, to show contempt for our religion, not even to make an example for posterity? Did not one of those who were conquered take to flight at all? Did no one hide? Was no one afraid? O marvelous event! The Roman Empire, acquired by so many labors, so much bloodshed, was so calmly, so quietly both won and lost by Christian priests that no bloodshed, no war, no uproar took place; and not less marvelous, it is not known at all by whom this was done, nor when, nor how, nor how long it lasted! You would think that Sylvester reigned in sylvan shades, among the trees, not at Rome nor among men, and that he was driven out by winter rains and cold, not by men!

Who that is at all widely read, does not know what Roman kings, what consuls, what dictators, what tribunes of the people, what censors, what aediles were chosen? Of such a large number of men in times so long past, none escapes us. We know also what Athenian commanders there were, and Theban, and Lacedemonian; we know all their battles on land and sea. Nor are the kings of the Persians unknown to us; of the Medes; of the Chaldeans; of the Hebrews; and of very many others; nor how each of these received his kingdom, or held it, or lost it, or recovered it. But how the Roman Empire, or rather the Sylvestrian, began, how it ended, when, through whom, is not known even in the city of Rome itself. I ask whether you can adduce any witnesses of these events, any writers. None, you answer. And are you not ashamed to say that it is likely that Sylvester possessed – even cattle, to say nothing of men!

But since you cannot [prove anything], I for my part will show that Constantine, to the very last day of his life, and thereafter all the Caesars in turn, did have possession [of the Roman Empire], so that you will have nothing left even to mutter. But it is a very difficult, and, I suppose, a very laborious task, forsooth, to do this! Let all the Latin and the Greek histories be unrolled, let the other authors who mention those times be brought in, and you will not find a single discrepancy among them on this point. Of a thousand witnesses, one may suffice; Eutropius, who saw Constantine, who saw the three sons of Constantine who were left masters of the world by their father, and who wrote thus in connection with Julian, the son of Constantine's brother: "This Julian, who was subdeacon in the Roman church and when he became Emperor returned to the worship of the gods, seized the government, and after elaborate preparations made war against the Parthians; in which expedition I also took part."[44] He would not have kept silent about the donation of the Western Empire [had it been made], nor would he have spoken as he did a little later about Jovian, who succeeded Julian: "He made with Sapor a peace which was necessary, indeed, but dishonorable, the boundaries being changed and a part of the Roman Empire being given up, a thing which had never before happened since the

---

44. Eutropius, *Breviarum ab urbe condita*, X, xvi, 1.

Roman state was founded; no, not even though our legions, at the Caudine [Forks] by Pontius Telesinus, and in Spain at Numantia, and in Numidia, were sent under the yoke, were any of the frontiers given up."[45]

Here I would like to interrogate you, most recent, though deceased, Popes, and you, Eugenius, who live, thanks only to Felix.[46] Why do you parade the *Donation of Constantine* with a great noise; and all the time, as though avengers of a stolen Empire, threaten certain kings and princes; and extort some servile confession or other from the Emperor when he is crowned, and from some other princes, such as the king of Naples and Sicily? None of the early Roman pontiffs ever did this, Damasus in the case of Theodosius, nor Syricius in the case of Arcadius, nor Anastasius in the case of Honorius, nor John in the case of Justinian, nor the other most holy Popes respectively in the case of the other most excellent Emperors: rather they always regarded Rome and Italy and the provinces I have named as belonging to the Emperors. And so, to say nothing of other monuments and temples in the city of Rome, there are extant gold coins of Constantine's after he became a Christian, with inscriptions, not in Greek, but in Latin letters, and of almost all the Emperors in succession. There are many of them in my possession with this inscription for the most part, under the image of the cross, "*Concordia orbis* [The Peace of the World]." What an infinite number of coins of the supreme pontiffs would be found if you ever had ruled Rome! But none such are found, neither gold nor silver, nor are any mentioned as having been seen by any one. And yet whoever held the government at Rome at that time had to have his own coinage: doubtless the Pope's would have borne the image of the Savior or of Peter.

Alas for man's ignorance! You do not see that if the *Donation of Constantine* is authentic nothing is left to the Emperor, the Latin Emperor, I mean. Ah, what an Emperor, what a Roman king, he would be, when if any one had his kingdom and had no other, he would have nothing at all! But if it is thus manifest that Sylvester did not have possession, that is, that Constantine did not give over possession, then there will be no doubt that he [Constantine], as I have said, did not give

---

45. *Ibid.*, X, xvii, 1 and 2.
46. The antipope elected by the Council of Basle in 1439. This reference is one of the clues to the date of Valla's treatise.

even the right to possess. That is, unless you say that the right was given, but that for some reason possession was not transferred. In that case he manifestly gave what he knew would never in the least exist; he gave what he could not transfer; he gave what could not come into the possession of the recipient until after it was nonexistent; he gave a gift which would not be valid for five hundred years, or never would be valid. But to say or to think this is insanity.

But it is high time, if I am not to be too prolix, to give the adversaries' cause, already struck down and mangled, the mortal blow and to cut its throat with a single stroke. Almost every history worthy of the name speaks of Constantine as a Christian from boyhood, with his father Constantius, long before the pontificate of Sylvester; as, for instance, Eusebius, author of the *Church History*, which Rufinus, himself a great scholar, translated into Latin, adding two books on his own times.[47] Both of these men were nearly contemporary with Constantine. Add to this also the testimony of the Roman pontiff who not only took part, but the leading part in these events, who was not merely a witness but the prime mover, who narrates, not another's doings, but his own. I refer to Pope Melchiades, Sylvester's immediate predecessor. He says: "The church reached the point where not only the nations, but even the Roman rulers who held sway over the whole world, came together into the faith of Christ and the sacraments of the faith. One of their number, a most devout man, Constantine, the first openly to come to belief in the Truth, gave permission to those living under his government, throughout the whole world, not only to become Christians, but even to build churches, and he decreed that landed estates be distributed among these. Finally also the said ruler bestowed immense offerings, and began the building of the temple which was the first seat of the blessed Peter, going so far as to leave his imperial residence and give it over for the use of the blessed Peter and his suc-

---

47. Valla's statement about Eusebius' *Church History* is slightly overdrawn. Some passages, while not definitely saying that Constantine was a Christian from boyhood would naturally be construed as implying this, especially when taken in connection with the chapter headings in use long before Valla's time; e.g. ix, 9, §§1-12. In his *Life of Constantine*, I, 27-32, however, Eusebius tells the story of the Emperor's conversion in the campaign against Maxentius in 312 by the heavenly apparition, thus implying that he was not previously a Christian. Valla does not seem to have known of this latter work. Nor is he aware of the passage in Jerome, *Chron. ad. ann.*, 2353, that Constantine was baptized near the end of his life by Eusebius of Nicomedia.

cessors."[48] You see, incidentally, that Melchiades does not say that anything was given by Constantine except the Lateran palace, and landed estates, which Gregory mentions very frequently in his register. Where are those who do not permit us to call into question whether the *Donation of Constantine* is valid, when the "donation" both antedated Sylvester and conferred private possessions alone?

But though it is all obvious and clear, yet the deed of gift itself, which those fools always put forward, must be discussed.

And first, not only must I convict of dishonesty him who tried to play Gratian and added sections to the work of Gratian, but also must convict of ignorance those who think a copy of the deed of gift is contained in Gratian; for the well-informed have never thought so, nor is it found in any of the oldest copies of the *Decretum*. And if Gratian had mentioned it anywhere, he would have done so, not where they put it, breaking the thread of the narrative, but where he treats of the agreement of Louis [the Pious]. Besides, there are two thousand passages in the *Decretum* which forbid the acceptance of this passage; for example, that where the words of Melchiades, which I have cited above, are given. Some say that he who added this chapter [the *Donation of Constantine*] was called Palea,[49] either because that was his real name or because what he added of his own, compared with Gratian, is as straw [*palea*] beside grain. However that may be, it is monstrous to believe that the compiler of the *Decretum* either did not know what was interpolated by this man, or esteemed it highly and held it for genuine. Good! It is enough! We have won! First, because Gratian does not say what they lyingly quote; and more especially because on the contrary, as can be seen in innumerable passages, he denies and disproves it; and last, because they bring forward only a single unknown individual, of not the least authority, so very stupid as to affix to Gratian what cannot be harmonized with his other statements. This then is the author you

48. This is an extract from a spurious letter purporting to be from Melchiades, or Miltiades; as palpable a forgery as the *Donation of Constantine* itself. The whole letter is given in Migne, P.L., viii, column 566. For the question when Constantine became a Christian, and of his relations with the Popes and the church, *cf.* Coleman, *Constantine the Great and Christianity*, with references to sources and literature.

49. A number of chapters in Gratian's *Decretum* added after Gratian have this word at their head, the one containing the *Donation of Constantine* among them. *Cf.* Friedberg's edition of the *Decretum Gratiani*, prima pars, dist. xcvi, c. xiii, in his *Corpus Iuris Canonici*, Leipsic, 1879-1881.

bring forward? On his sole testimony you rely? His charter, in a matter of such importance, you recite as confirmation against hundreds of kinds of proof? But I should have expected you to show gold seals, marble inscriptions, a thousand authors.

But, you say, Palea himself adduces his author, shows the source of his narrative, and cites Pope Gelasius and many bishops as witnesses; it is, he says, "from the *Acts* of Sylvester (which the blessed Pope Gelasius in the Council of the Seventy Bishops recounts as read by the catholic, and in accordance with ancient usage many churches he says follow this example) which reads: 'Constantine...,etc,' "[50] Considerably earlier, where books to be read and books not to be read are treated, he had said also; "The *Acts* of the blessed Sylvester, chief priest though we know not the name of him who wrote it, we know to be read by many of the orthodox of the city of Rome, and in accordance with ancient usage the churches follow this example."[51] Wonderful authority this, wonderful evidence, irrefutable proof! I grant you this, that Gelasius in speaking of the Council of the Seventy Bishops said that. But did he say this, that the deed of gift is to be read in the *Acts* of the most blessed Sylvester? He says, indeed, only that the *Acts* of Sylvester are read, and that in Rome, and that many other churches follow her authority. I do not deny this, I concede it, I admit it, I also stand up with Gelasius as a witness to it. But what advantage is this to you except that you may be shown to have deliberately lied in adducing your witnesses? The name of the man who interpolated this ["Donation" of yours] is not known, and he is the only one who says this [that the *Donation* is in the *Acts* of Sylvester]; the name of the man who wrote the history of Sylvester is not known and he is the only one cited as witness, and that erroneously. And good men and prudent as you are, you think this is enough and more than enough evidence for such an important transaction! Well! how Your judgment differs from mine! Even if this grant were contained in the *Acts* of Sylvester, I should not think it was to be considered genuine, for that history is not history, but fanciful and most shameful fiction, as I shall later show; nor does any one else of any authority whatever make mention of this grant. And even James of

---

50. *Decretum Gratiani*, Prima pars, dist. xcvi, c. xiii; in Friedberg, *Corpus iuris canonici*, vol. II, p. 342.

51. *Ibid.*, Pars prima, dist. xv, c. iii, Palea 19; in Friedberg, vol. II.

THE DONATION OF CONSTANTINE

Voragine, though as an archbishop disposed to favor the clergy, yet in his *Acts of the Saints*[52] preserved silence on the *Donation of Constantine* as fictitious and not fit to figure in the *Acts* of Sylvester; a conclusive judgment, in a way, against those, if there were any, who would have committed it to writing.

But I want to take the forger himself, truly a "straw" man without wheat, by the neck, and drag him into court. What do you say, you forger? Whence comes it that we do not read this grant in the *Acts* of Sylvester? This book, forsooth, is rare, difficult to get, not owned by the many but rather kept as the Fasti once were by the pontifices, or the Sibylline books by the Decemvirs! It was written in Greek, or Syriac, or Chaldee! Gelasius testifies that it was read by many of the orthodox; Voragine mentions it; we also have seen thousands of copies of it, and written long ago; and in almost every cathedral it is read when Sylvester's Day comes around.[53] Yet nevertheless no one says that he has read there what you put in it; no one has heard of it; no one has dreamt of it. Or is there perhaps some other history of Sylvester? And what can that be? I know no other, nor do I understand that any other is referred to by you, for you speak of the one which Gelasius says is read in many churches. In this, however, we do not find your grant. But if it is not found in the *Life of Sylvester*, why do you declare that it is? How did you dare to jest in a matter of such importance, and to make sport of the cupidity of silly men?

But I am foolish to inveigh against the audacity of this [forger], instead of inveighing against the insanity of those who give him credence. If any one should say that this had been recorded for remembrance among the Greeks, the Hebrews, the barbarians, would you not bid him name his author, produce his book, and the passage, to be explained by a reliable translator, before you would believe it? But now your own language, and a very well-known book are involved, and either you do not question such an incredible occurrence, or when you do not find it written down you have such utter credulity as to believe that it is written down and authentic! And, satisfied with this title, you move Heaven and Earth, and, as though no doubt existed, you pursue with the terrors of war and with other threats those who do not believe

---

52. *Cf.* Voragine, *Golden Legend*, trans. by Wm. Caxton, rev. by Ellis (London, 1900).
53. December 31.

you! Blessed Jesus, what power, what divinity there is in Truth, which unaided defends itself without any great struggle from all falsehoods and deceits; so that not undeservedly, when contention had arisen at the court of king Darius as to what was most powerful, and one said one thing and another another, the palm was awarded to Truth.[54]

Since I have to do with priests and not with laymen, I suppose I must seek ecclesiastical precedents. Judas Maccabaeus, when he had sent ambassadors to Rome and obtained a friendly alliance from the Senate, took pains to have the terms of the alliance engraved on brass and carried to Jerusalem. I pass by the stone tables of the Decalogue, which God gave to Moses. And this *Donation of Constantine*, so magnificent and astounding, cannot be proved by any copies, in gold, in silver, in brass, in marble, or even in books, but only, if we believe it, on paper, or parchment. According to Josephus, Jubal, the inventor of music, when the elders expressed the opinion that the world was to be destroyed, once by water, and again by fire, inscribed his teaching on two columns, one of brick against the fire, and one of stone against the flood, which columns still remained at the time of Josephus, as he himself writes, so that his benefaction to men might always continue. And among the Romans, while still rustic and country bred, when writing was inadequate and rare, the laws of the Twelve Tables nevertheless were engraved on brass, and though the city was stormed and burned by the Gauls they were afterwards found unharmed. Thus careful foresight overcomes the two mightiest forces known to man, namely, long lapse of time and the violence of fortune. Yet Constantine signed a donation of the world on paper alone and with ink, though the very inventor of the fabulous story makes him say that he thought there would not be lacking those who with unholy greed would set aside this *Donation!* Do you have this fear, Constantine, and do you take no precaution lest those who would snatch Rome from Sylvester should also steal the charter?

Why does Sylvester do nothing for himself? Does he leave everything thus to Constantine? Is he so careless and lazy in such an important matter? Does he not look ahead at all for himself, for his church, for posterity? See to whom you commit the administration of the Roman Empire; in the midst of such an important transaction, fraught

---

54. A reference to the story of the three young men in the bodyguard of Darius; *cf.* I *Esdras* iii and iv.

THE DONATION OF CONSTANTINE

with so much either of gain or of peril, he goes sound asleep! For let the charter ever be lost, he will not be able, at least as time goes on, to prove the granting of the "privilege."[55]

"The page of the privilege" this crazy man calls it [i.e., the *Donation of Constantine*]. And do you (let me controvert him as though he were present) call the gift of the Earth a "privilege"; do you want it written thus in the document; and do you want Constantine to use that kind of language? If the title is ridiculous, what shall we think the rest of it is?

"The Emperor Constantine the fourth day after his baptism conferred his privilege on the pontiff of the Roman church, that in the whole Roman world priests should regard him as their head, as judges do the king." This sentence is part of the *History* [*Life*] *of Sylvester*,[56] and it leaves no doubt where [nor why] the document gets its title "privilege." But, in the manner of those who fabricate lies, he begins with the truth for the purpose of winning confidence in his later statements, which are false, as Sinon says in Virgil:

> "... Whate'er
> My fate ordains, my words shall be sincere:
> I neither can nor dare my birth disclaim;
> Greece is my country, Sinon is my name."[57]

This first; then he put in his lies. So our Sinon does here; for when he had begun with the truth, he adds:

> In this privilege, among other things, is this: "We — together with all our satraps and the whole Senate and the nobles also, and all the people subject to the government of the Roman church[58] — considered it advisable that, as the blessed Peter is seen to have been constituted vicar of God on the Earth so the pontiffs who are the representatives of that same chief of the apostles, should obtain from us and our Empire the power of a supremacy greater than the clemency of our earthly imperial serenity is seen to have conceded to it."

---

55. In the following section my translation of the phrases of the *Donation* is harmonized so far as possible with the translation in E. F. Henderson, *Select Historical Documents of the Middle Ages*.

56. *Cf.* Coleman, *Constantine the Great and Christianity*, p. 224, II. 8 *et seq.*

57. Virgil, *Aeneid*, ii, 77-78. Dryden's translation.

58. The text of the *Donation* which Valla used, though apparently in a copy of Gratian's *Decretum* extant in his time, differs here and in a number of the other places, from the texts which we have, whether in Gratian's *Decretum*, or in the *Pseudo-Isidorian Decretals*.

O thou scoundrel, thou villain! The same history [the *Life of Sylvester*] which you allege as your evidence, says that for a long time none of senatorial rank was willing to accept the Christian religion, and that Constantine solicited the poor with bribes to be baptized. And you say that within the first days, immediately, the Senate, the nobles, the satraps, as though already Christians, with the Caesar passed decrees for the honoring of the Roman church! What! How do you want to have satraps come in here? Numskull, blockhead! Do the Caesars speak thus; are Roman decrees usually drafted thus? Whoever heard of satraps being mentioned in the councils of the Romans?[59] I do not remember ever to have read of any Roman satrap being mentioned, or even of a satrap in any of the Roman provinces. But this fellow speaks of the Emperor's satraps, and puts them in before the Senate, though all honors, even those bestowed upon the ruling prince, are decreed by the Senate alone, or with the addition "and the Roman people." Thus we see carved on ancient stones or bronze tablets or coins two letters, "S.C.," that is "By decree of the Senate," or four, "S.P.Q.R.," that is, "The Senate and the Roman People." And according to Tertullian, when Pontius Pilate had written to Tiberius Caesar and not to the Senate concerning the wonderful deeds of Christ, inasmuch as magistrates were supposed to write concerning important matters to the Senate, the Senate gave way to spite and opposed Tiberius' proposal that Jesus be worshipped as a God, merely on account of its secret anger at the offense to senatorial dignity.[60] And, to show how weighty was the authority of the Senate, Jesus did not obtain divine worship.

What now! Why do you say "nobles" ["optimates"]? Are we to understand that these are leading men in the republic; then why should they be mentioned when the other magistrates are passed by in silence? Or are they the opposite of the "popular" party which curries favor with the people; the ones who seek and champion the welfare of every aristocrat and of the "better" elements, as Cicero shows in one of his orations? Thus we say that Caesar before the overthrow of the republic

---

59. The word *satrap* was in fact applied to higher officials at Rome only in the middle of the eighth century. Scheffer-Boichorst, *Mitteilungen des Institus f. osterreichesche Geschichtsforschung*, x (1889), p. 315.

60. Tertullian tells this apocryphal story in his *Apology*, chaps. 5 and 21. For a translation of letters alleged to have been written to Tiberius by Pilate, see *Nicene and Post-Nicene Fathers*, ed. Philip Schaff (New York, 1890-1897), vol. VIII, pp. 459-463.

had been a member of the "popular" party, Cato of the "optimates." The difference between them Sallust explained. But the "optimates" are not spoken of as belonging to the [Emperor's] council, any more than the "popular" party, or other respectable men are.

But what wonder that the "optimates" belonged to the council, when, if we believe this fellow, "all the people," and the people "subject to the Roman church" at that, acted officially with the Senate and the Caesar![61] And what people are these? The Roman people? But why not say the Roman people, rather than the "people subject"? What new insult is this to the Quirites of whom the great poet sings: "Do thou, O Roman, take care to rule the peoples with imperial sway!"[62] Can those who rule other peoples, themselves be called a subject people? It is preposterous! For in this, as Gregory in many letters testifies, the Roman ruler differs from the others, that he alone is ruler of a free people. But be this as it may. Are not other peoples also subject? Or do you mean others also? How could it be brought to pass in three days that all the people subject to the government of the Roman church gave assent to that decree? Though did every Tom, Dick, and Harry give his judgment? What! would Constantine, before he had subjected the people to the Roman pontiff, call them subject? How is it that those who are called subjects are said to have been in authority in the making of the decree? How is it that they are said to have decreed this very thing, that they should be subject and that he to whom they are already subject should have them as his subjects? What else do you do, you wretch, other than admit that you have the will to commit forgery, but not the ability?

> Choosing that same prince of the apostles, or his vicars, to be our constant intercessors with God. And, to the extent of our earthly imperial power, we have decreed that his holy Roman church shall be honored with veneration: and that more than our empire and earthly throne, the most sacred seat of the blessed Peter shall be gloriously exalted; we giving to it power and glory, and dignity, and vigor and honor imperial.

---

61. Valla's argument in this paragraph is partly based on the defective text of the *Donation* which he used, *cf. supra*, p. 85, note 2. Zeumer's text would be translated, "all the Roman people who are subject to the glory of our rule," and Friedberg's, "all the people subject to the glorious rule of Rome."

62. Virgil, *Aeneid*, vi, 852.

Come back to life for a little while, Firmianus Lactantius, stop this ass who brays so loudly and outrageously. So delighted is he with the sound of swelling words, that he repeats the same terms and reiterates what he has just said. Is it thus that in your age the secretaries of the Caesars spoke, or even their grooms? Constantine chose them not "as his intercessors" but "to be his intercessors." The fellow inserted that "to be" [*esse*] so as to get a more elegant rhythm. A fine reason! To speak barbarously so that your speech may run along more gracefully, as if indeed, anything can be graceful in such filthiness. "Choosing the prince of the apostles, or his vicars": you do not choose Peter, and then his vicars, but either him, excluding them, or them, excluding him.[63] And he calls the Roman pontiffs "vicars" of Peter, either as though Peter were living, or as though they were of lower rank than was Peter. And is not this barbarous; "from us and our empire"?[64] As if the empire had a mind to give grants, and power! Nor was he content to say "should obtain," without also saying "conceded," though either one would have sufficed. And that "constant intercessors,"[65] is very elegant indeed! Doubtless he wants them "constant" so that they may not be corrupted by money nor moved by fear. And "earthly imperial power"; two adjectives without a conjunction. And "be honored with veneration": and "clemency of our imperial serenity";[66] it smacks of Lactantian eloquence to speak of "serenity" and "clemency," instead of grandeur and majesty, when the power of the Empire is concerned! And how inflated he is with puffed-up pride; as in that phrase "gloriously exalted" by "glory, and power, and dignity, and vigor, and imperial honor"! This seems to be taken from the *Apocalypse*, where it says, "Worthy is the Lamb that was slain, to receive power, and divinity and wisdom, and strength, and honor and blessing."[67] Frequently, as will be shown later, Constantine is made to arrogate to himself the titles of God, and to try to imitate the language of the sacred scriptures, which he had never read.

63. The conjunction "seu" in classical Latin meant, as Valla insists, "or"; in the eighth century it was often used with the meaning "and." The forger of the *Donation* used it in the latter sense. Valla did not see the significance of this usage for dating the forgery.
64. *Cf. supra*, p. 85, note 2.
65. *Cf. supra*, p. 85, note 2.
66. "firmos patronos" – this use of "firmus" characterizes the style of Pope Paul I (757-767). See Scheffer-Boichorst, *op. cit.*, p. 311.
67. *Rev.* v, 12; with variations.

And we ordain and decree that he shall have the supremacy as well over the four seats, Alexandria, Antioch, Jerusalem, and Constantinope, as also over all the churches of God in the whole Earth. And the pontiff also, who at the time shall be at the head of the holy Roman church itself, shall be more exalted than, and chief over, all the priests of the whole world; and, acording to his judgment everything which is to be provied for the service of God, and for the faith or the stability of the Christians is to be administered.

I will not speak hre of the babarisms in [the forger's]language when he says "chief over the priests" instead of chief of the priests; when he puts in the same sentence "extiterit" and "existat" [confusing meanings, moods and tenses); when, having said "in the whole Earth," he adds again "of the whole world," as though he wished to include something else, or the sky, which is part of the world, though a good part of the Earth even was not under Rome; when he distinguishes between providing for "the faith" of Christians and providing for their "stability," as though they could not coexist;[68] when he confuses "ordain" and "decree," and when, as though Constantine had not already joined with the rest in making the decree, he has him now ordain it, and as though he imposes a punishment, decree [confirm] it, and confirm it together with the people. [That, I pass by.] But what Christian could endure this [other thing], and not, rather, critically and severely reprove a Pope who endures it, and listens to it willingly and retails it; namely, that the Roman See, though it received its primacy from Christ, as the Eighth Synod declared according to the testimony of Gratian and many of the Greeks, should be represented as having received it from Constantine, hardly yet a Christian, as though from Christ? Would that very modest ruler have chosen to make such a statement, and that most devout pontiff to listen to it? Far be such a grave wrong from both of them!

How in the world – this is much more absurd, and impossible in the nature of things – could one speak of Constantinople as one of the patriarchal sees, when it was not yet a patriarchate, nor a see, nor a Christian city, nor named Constantinople, nor founded, nor planned! For the "privilege" was granted, so it says, the third day after Constantine became a Christian; when as yet Byzantium, not Constantinople, occu-

---

68. Part of this criticism rests upon the peculiarities of the text of the *Donation* which Valla used.

pied that site. I am a liar if this fool does not confess as much himself. For toward the end of the "privilege" he writes:

> Wherefore we have perceived it to be fitting that our empire and our royal power should be transferred in the regions of the East; and that in the province of Bizantia [*sic*], in the most fitting place, a city should be built in our name; and that our empire should there be established.

But if he was intending to transfer the empire, he had not yet transferred it; if he was intending to establish his empire there, he had not yet established it; if he was planning to build a city, he had not yet built it. Therefore he could not have spoken of it as a patriarchal see, as one of the four sees, as Christian, as having this name, nor as already built. According to the history (the *Life of Sylvester*) which Palea cites as evidence, he had not yet even thought of founding it. And this beast, whether Palea or some one else whom Palea follows, does not notice that he contradicts this history, in which it is said that Constantine issued the decree concerning the founding of the city, not on his own initiative, but at a command received in his sleep from God, not at Rome but at Byzantium, not within a few days [of his conversion] but several years after, and that he learned its name by revelation in a dream.[69] Who then does not see that the man who wrote the "privilege" lived long after the time of Constantine, and in his effort to embellish his falsehood forgot that earlier he had said that these events took place at Rome on the third day after Constantine was baptized? So the trite old proverb applies nicely to him, "Liars need good memories."

And how is it that he speaks of a province of "Byzantia," when it was a town, Byzantium by name? The place was by no means large enough for the erection of so great a city; for the old city of Byzantium was included within the walls of Constantinople. And this man says the [new] city is to be built on the most fitting place in it! Why does he choose to put Thrace, in which Byzantium lies, in the East, when it lies to the north? I suppose Constantine did not know the place which he had chosen for the building of the city, in what latitude it was, whether it was a town or a province, nor how large it was!

> On the churches of the blessed apostles Peter and Paul, for the providing of the lights, we have conferred landed estates of possessions, and

---

69. *Cf.* Coleman, *Constantine the Great and Christianity*, pp. 148-151, 161-164.

have enriched them with different objects; and through our sacred imperial mandate, we have granted them of our property in the east as well as in the west; and even in the north and in the southern quarter; namely, in Judea, Greece, Asia, Thrace, Africa and Italy and the various islands; under this condition indeed, that all shall be administered by the hand of our most blessed father the supreme pontiff, Sylvester, and his successors.

O you scoundrel! Were there in Rome churches, that is, temples, dedicated to Peter and Paul? Who had constructed them? Who would have dared to build them, when, as history tells us, the Christians had never had anything but secret and secluded meeting-places? And if there had been any temples at Rome dedicated to these apostles, they would not have called for such great lights as these to be set up in them; they were little chapels, not sanctuaries; little shrines, not temples; oratories in private houses, not public places of worship. So there was no need to care for the temple lights, before the temples themselves were provided.

And what is this that you say? You make Constantine call Peter and Paul blessed, but Sylvester, still living, "most blessed"; and call his own mandate, pagan as he had been but a little while before, "sacred"! Is so much to be donated "for the providing of the lights" that the whole world would be impoverished? And what are these "landed estates," particularly "landed estates of possessions"? The phrase "possessions of landed estates" is good usage; "landed estates of possessions" is not. You give landed estates, and you do not explain which landed estates. You have enriched "with different objects," and you do not show when nor with what objects. You want the corners of the Earth to be administered by Sylvester, and you do not explain how they are to be administered. You say these were granted earlier? Then why do you say that you have now begun to honor the Roman church, and to grant it a "privilege"? Do you make the grant now; do you enrich it now? Then why do you say "we have granted" and, "we have enriched"? What are you talking about; what is in your mind, you beast? (I am speaking to the man who made up the story, not to that most excellent ruler, Constantine.)

But why do I ask for any intelligence in you, any learning, you who are not endowed with any ability, with any knowledge of letters, who say "lights" for lamps, and "be transferred in the regions of the east" instead of "be transferred to the regions of the east," as it should be? And what next? Are these "quarters" of yours really the four quarters of the world? What do you count as eastern? Thrace? It lies to the north, as I have said. Judea? It looks rather toward the south, for it is next to Egypt. And what do you count as western? Italy? But these events occurred in Italy and no one living there calls it western; for we say the Spains are in the west; and Italy extends, on one hand to the south and on the other to the north, rather than to the west. What do you count as north? Thrace? You yourself choose to put it in the east. Asia? This alone includes the whole east, but it includes the north also, like Europe. What do you count as southern? Africa, of course. But why do you not specify some province? Perhaps you think even the Ethiopians were subject to the Roman Empire! And anyway Asia and Africa do not come into consideration when we divide the Earth into four parts and enumerate the countries of each, but when we divide it into three, Asia, Africa, Europe; that is, unless you say Asia for the province of Asia, and Africa for that province which is next to the Gaetuli, and I do not see why they, especially, should be mentioned.

Would Constantine have spoken thus when he was describing the four quarters of the Earth? Would he have mentioned these countries, and not others? Would he have begun with Judea, which is counted as a part of Syria and was no longer "Judea" after the destruction of Jerusalem (for the Jews were driven away and almost exterminated, so that, I suppose, scarcely one then remained in his own country, but they lived among other nations)? Where then was Judea? It was no longer called Judea, and we know that now that name has perished from the Earth. Just as after the driving out of the Canaanites the region ceased to be called Canaan and was renamed Judea by its new inhabitants, so when the Jews were driven out and mixed tribes inhabited it, it ceased to be called Judea.

You mention Judea, Thrace, and the islands, but you do not think of mentioning the Spains, the Gauls, the Germans, and while you speak of peoples of other tongues, Hebrew, Greek, barbarian you do not speak of any of the provinces where Latin is used. I see: you have omitted these for the purpose of including them afterwards in the Donation. And why were not these many great provinces of the East sufficient to bear the expense of providing the lights without the rest of the world contributing!

I pass over the fact that you say these are granted as a gift, and therefore not, as our friends say, in payment for the cure of the leprosy. Otherwise – well, any one who classes a gift as a payment is ill-bred.

> To the blessed Sylvester, his [Peter's] vicar, we by this present do give our imperial Lateran palace, then the diadem, that is, the crown of our head, and at the same time the tiara and also the shoulder-band – that is, the strap that usually surrounds our imperial neck; and also the Purple mantle and scarlet tunic, and all the imperial raiment; and the same rank as those presiding over the imperial cavalry; conferring also on him the imperial scepters, and at the same time all the standards and banners and the different imperial ornaments, and all the pomp of our imperial eminence and the glory of our power.
>
> And we decree also, as to these men of different rank, the most reverend clergy who serve the holy Roman church, that they have that same eminence of distinguished power and excellence, by the glory of which it seems proper for our most illustrious Senate to be adorned; that is, that they be made patricians, consuls – and also we have proclaimed that they be decorated with the other imperial dignities. And even as the imperial militia stands decorated, so we have decreed that the clergy of the holy Roman church be adorned. And even as the imperial power is ordered with different offices, of chamberlains, indeed, and door-keepers and all the bed-watchers, so we wish the holy Roman church also to be decorated. And, in order that the pontifical glory may shine forth most fully, we decree also that the holy clergy of this same holy Roman church may mount mounts adorned with saddlecloths and linens, that is, of the whitest color; and even as our Senate uses shoes with felt socks, that is, they [the clergy] may be distinguished by white linen, and that the celestial [orders] may be adorned to the glory of God, just as the terrestrial are adorned.

O holy Jesus! This fellow, tumbling phrases about in his ignorant talk – will you not answer him from a whirlwind? Will you not send the thunder? Will you not hurl avenging lightnings at such great blasphemy? Will you endure such wickedness in your household? Can you bear this, see this, let it go on so long and overlook it? But you are long-suffering and full of compassion. Yet I fear lest this your long-suffering may rather be wrath and condemnation, such as it was against those of whom you said, "So I gave them up unto their own hearts' lust:

and they walked in their own counsels,"[70] and elsewhere, "Even as they did not like to retain me in their knowledge, I gave them over to a reprobate mind, to do those things which are not convenient."[71] Command me, I beseech thee, O Lord, that I may cry out against them, and perchance they may be converted.

O Roman pontiffs, the model of all crimes for other pontiffs! O wickedest of scribes and Pharisees, who sit in Moses' seat and do the deeds of Dathan and Abiram! Will the raiment, the habiliments, the pomp, the cavalry, indeed the whole manner of life of a Caesar thus befit the vicar of Christ? What fellowship has the priest with the Caesar? Did Sylvester put on this raiment; did he parade in this splendor; did he live and reign with such a throng of servants in his house? Depraved wretches! They did not know that Sylvester ought to have assumed the vestments of Aaron, who was the high priest of God, rather than those of a heathen ruler.

But this must be more strongly pressed elsewhere. For the present, however, let us talk to this sycophant about barbarisms of speech; for by the stupidity of his language his monstrous impudence is made clear, and his lie.

"We give," he says, "our imperial Lateran palace": as though it was awkward to place the gift of the palace here among the ornaments, he repeated it later where gifts are treated. "Then the diadem;" and as though those present would not know, he interprets, "that is, the crown." He did not, indeed, here add "of gold," but later, emphasizing the same statements, he says, "of purest gold and precious gems." The ignorant fellow did not know that a diadem was made of coarse cloth or perhaps of silk; whence that wise and oft-repeated remark of the king, who, they say, before he put upon his head the diadem given him, held it and considered it long and exclaimed, "O cloth more renowned than happy! If any one knew you through and through, with how many anxieties and dangers and miseries you are fraught, he would not care to pick you up; no, not even if you were lying on the ground!" This fellow does not imagine but that it is of gold, with a gold band and gems such as kings now usually add. But Constantine was not a king, nor would he have dared to call himself king, nor to adorn himself with royal ceremony.

---

70. *Ps.* lxxxi, 12.
71. *Rom.* i, 28, with the person of the verb changed.

He was Emperor of the Romans, not king. Where there is a king, there is no republic. But in the republic there were many, even at the same time, who were "imperatores" [generals]; for Cicero frequently writes thus, "Marcus Cicero, imperator, to some other imperator, greeting": though, later on, the Roman ruler, as the highest of all, is called by way of distinctive title the Emperor.

"And at the same time the tiara and also the shoulder-band – that is the strap that usually surrounds our imperial neck." Who ever heard "tiara" [*phrygium*] used in Latin? You talk like a barbarian and want it to seem to me to be a speech of Constantine's or of Lactantius'. Plautus, in the *Menaechmi*, applied "phrygionem" to a designer of garments; Pliny calls clothes embroidered with a needle "phrygiones" because the Phrygians invented them; but what does "phrygium" mean? You do not explain this, which is obscure; you explain what is quite clear. You say the "shoulderband" is a "strap," and you do not perceive what the strap is, for you do not visualize a leather band, which we call a strap, encircling the Caesar's neck as an ornament. [It is of leather], hence we call harness and whips "straps": but if ever gold straps are mentioned, it can only be understood as applying to gilt harness such as is put around the neck of a horse or of some other animal. But this has escaped your notice, I think. So when you wish to put a strap around the Caesar's neck, or Sylvester's, you change a man, an Emperor, a supreme pontiff, into a horse or an ass.

"And also the purple mantle and scarlet tunic." Because Matthew says "a scarlet robe," and John "a purple robe,"[72] this fellow tries to join them together in the same passage. But if they are the same color, as the Evangelists imply, why are you not content, as they were, to name either one alone; unless, like ignorant folk today, you use "purple" for silk goods of a whitish color? The "purple" [*pupura*], however, is a fish in whose blood wool is dyed, and so from the dye the name has been given to the cloth, whose color can be called red, though it may rather be blackish and very nearly the color of clotted blood, a sort of violet. Hence by Homer and Virgil blood is called purple, as is porphyry, the color of which is similar to amethyst; for the Greeks call purple "porphyra." You know perhaps that scarlet is used for red; but I would swear that you do not know at all why he makes it

---

72. *Matt.* xxvii, 28; *John* xix, 2.

"coccineum" when we say "coccum," or what sort of a garment a "mantle" [*chlamys*] is.

But that he might not betray himself as a liar by continuing longer on the separate garments, he embraced them all together in a single word, saying, "all the imperial raiment." What! even that which he is accustomed to wear in war, in the chase, at banquets, in games? What could be more stupid than to say that all the raiment of the Caesar befits a pontiff!

But how gracefully he adds, "and the same rank as those presiding over the imperial cavalry." He says "seu" ["or" for "and"].[73] He wishes to distinguish between these two in turn, as if they were very like each other, and slips along from the imperial raiment to the equestrian rank, saying – I know not what! He wants to say something wonderful, but fears to be caught lying, and so with puffed cheeks and swollen throat, he gives forth sound without sense.

"Conferring also on him the imperial sceptres." What a turn of speech! What splendor! What harmony! What are these imperial sceptres? There is one sceptre, not several; if indeed the Emperor carried a sceptre at all. Will now the pontiff carry a sceptre in his hand? Why not give him a sword also, and helmet and javelin?

"And at the same time all the standards and banners." What do you understand by "standards" [*signa*]? "Signa" are either statues (hence frequently we read "signa et tabulas" for pieces of sculpture and paintings – for the ancients did not paint on walls, but on tablets) or military standards (hence that phrase "Standards, matched eagles"[74]). In the former sense small statues and sculptures are called "sigilla." Now then, did Constantine give Sylvester his statues or his eagles? What could be more absurd? But what "banners" [*banna*[75]] may signify, I do not discover. May God destroy you, most depraved of mortals, who attribute barbarous language to a cultured age!

"And different imperial ornaments." When he said "banners," he thought he had been explicit long enough, and therefore he lumped

---

73. Here as was common in medieval Latin, "seu" is the equivalent of "et," and means "and." Valla's criticism is correct, but might go further in fixing the time of the forgery. *Cf. supra*, p. 91, note 1.

74. Lucan, *Pharsalia*, i, 7.

75. In our best texts of the *Donation* this word is "banda," used in the eighth century for "colors" or "flags."

the rest under a general term. And how frequently he drives home the word "imperial," as though there were certain ornaments peculiar to the Emperor over against the consul, the dictator, the Caesar!

"And all the pomp of our imperial eminence, and the glory of our power." "He discards bombast and cubit-long words,[76] This king of kings, Darius, the kinsman of the gods,"[77] never speaking save in the plural! What is this imperial "pomp"; that of the cucumber twisted in the grass, and growing at the belly? Do you think the Caesar celebrated a triumph whenever he left his house, as the Pope now does, preceded by white horses which servants lead saddled and adorned? To pass over other follies, nothing is emptier, more unbecoming a Roman pontiff than this. And what is this "glory"? Would a Latin have called pomp and paraphernalia "glory," as is customary in the Hebrew language? And instead of "soldiers" [*milites*] you say soldiery [*militia*[78]] which we have borrowed from the Hebrews, whose books neither Constantine nor his secretaries had ever laid eyes on!

But how great is your munificence, O Emperor, who deem it not sufficient to have adorned the pontiff, unless you adorn all the clergy also! As an "eminence of distinguished power and excellence," you say, they are "made patricians and consuls." Who has ever heard of senators or other men being made patricians? Consuls are "made," but not patricians. The senators, the conscript fathers, are from patrician (also called senatorial), equestrian, or plebeian families as the case may be. It is greater, also, to be a senator than to be a patrician; for a senator is one of the chosen counselors of the Republic, while a patrician is merely one who derives his origin from a senatorial family. So one who is a senator, or of the conscript fathers, is not necessarily forthwith also a patrician. So my friends the Romans are now making themselves ridiculous when they call their praetor "senator," since a senate cannot consist of one man and a senator must have colleagues, and he who is now called "senator" performs the function of praetor. But, you say, the title of patrician is found in many books.[79] Yes; but in those which

---

76. Horace, *Ars Poetica*, l. 97.

77. Julius Valeriu, *Res Gestae Alexandri*, i, 37.

78. At Rome in the eighth century, the time of the forgery, "militia" indicated a civil rank, rather than soldiers.

79. The allusion is to the title of Patrician given to Pippin and to his sons as defenders of the Roman See.

speak of times later than Constantine; therefore the "privilege" was executed after Constantine.

But how can the clergy become consuls?[80] The Latin clergy have denied themselves matrimony; and will they become consuls, make a levy of troops, and betake themselves to the provinces allotted them with legions and auxiliaries? Are servants and slaves made consuls? And are there to be not two, as was customary; but the hundreds and thousands of attendants who serve the Roman church, are they to be honored with the rank of general? And I was stupid enough to wonder at what was said about the Pope's transformation! The attendants will be generals; but the clergy soldiers. Will the clergy become soldiers or wear military insignia, unless you share the imperial insignia with all the clergy? [I may well ask] for I do not know what you are saying. And who does not see that this fabulous tale was concocted by those who wished to have every possible license in the attire they were to wear? If there are games of any kind played among the demons which inhabit the air I should think that they would consist in copying the apparel, the pride and the luxury of the clergy, and that the demons would be delighted most by this kind of masquerading.

Which shall I censure the more, the stupidity of the ideas, or of the words? You have heard about the ideas; here are illustrations of his words. He says, "It seems proper for our Senate to be adorned" (as though it were not assuredly adorned), and to be adorned forsooth with "glory." And what is being done he wishes understood as already done; as, "we have proclaimed" for "we proclaim": for the speech sounds better that way. And he puts the same act in the present and in the past tense; as, "we decree," and "we have decreed." And everything is stuffed with these words, "we decree," "we decorate," "imperial," "imperial rank," "power," "glory." He uses "extat" for "est," though "extare" means to stand out or to be above; and "nempe" for "scilicet" [that is, "indeed" for "to wit"]; and "concubitores" [translated above, bed-watchers] for "contubernales" [companions or attendants]. "Concubitores" are literally those who sleep together and have intercourse; they must certainly be understood to be harlots. He adds those with whom he may sleep,

---

80. The office of consul as it existed in the Republic and the Empire disappeared in the time of the German invasions. The word was later applied quite differently, to a group, practically a social class, at Rome.

I suppose, that he may not fear nocturnal phantoms.[81] He adds "chamberlains"; he adds "door-keepers."

It is not an idle question to ask why he mentions these details. He is setting up, not an old man, but a ward or a young son, and like a doting father, himself arranges for him everything of which his tender age has need, as David did for Solomon! And that the story may be filled in every respect, horses are given the clergy – lest they sit on asses' colts in that asinine way of Christ's! And they are given horses, not covered nor saddled with coverings of white, but decorated with white color. And what coverings! Not horse-cloths, either Babylonian or any other kind, but "mappulae" [translated above, saddle-cloths] and "lintearnina" [linen cloths or sheets, translated above, linen]. "Mappae" [*serviettes*] go with the table, "linteamina" with the couch. And as though there were doubt as to their color, he explains, "that is to say, of the whitest color." Talk worthy of Constantine; fluency worthy of Lactantius; not only in the other phrases, but also in that one, "may mount mounts"!

And when he had said nothing about the garb of senators, the broad stripe, the purple, and the rest, he thought he had to talk about their shoes; nor does he specify the crescents [which were on their shoes], but "socks" or rather he says "with felt socks," and then as usual he explains, "that is, with white linen," as though socks were of linen! I cannot at the moment think where I have found the word "udones" [socks], except in Valerius Martial, whose distich inscribed "Cilician Socks" runs: "Wool did not produce these, but the beard of an ill-smelling goat. Would that the sole in the gulf of the Cinyps might lie."[82] So the "socks" are not linen, nor white, with which this two-legged ass says, not that the feet of senators are clad, but that senators are distinguished.

And in the phrase "that the terrestrial orders may be adorned to the glory of God, just as the celestial," what do you call celestial, what terrestrial? How are the celestial orders adorned?[83] You may have seen what glory to God this is. But I, if I believe anything, deem nothing

---

81. Where Valla's text of the *Donation* reads "concubitorum," Zeumer's reads "excubiorum" [guards].

82. Martial XIV, 141 (140).

83. Valla for this part of his criticism uses the rather unintelligible order of words found in most texts of the *Donation*, instead of the more intelligible order which he used in his earlier quotations. *Cf.* pp. 102, 103.

more hateful to God and to the rest of humanity than such presumption of clergy in the secular sphere. But why do I attack individual items? Time would fail me if I should try, I do not say to dwell upon, but to touch upon them all.

> Above all things, moreover, we give permission to the blessed Sylvester and his successors, from our edict, that he may make priest whomever he wishes, according to his own pleasure and counsel, and enroll him in the pious number of the religious clergy [i. e., regular clergy; or perhaps cardinals]: let no one whomsoever presume to act in a domineering way in this.[84]

Who is this Melchizedek that blesses the patriarch Abraham? Does Constantine, scarcely yet a Christian, give to the man by whom he was baptized and whom he calls blessed, authority to make priests? As though Sylvester had not and could not have done it before! And with what a threat he forbids any one to stand in the way! "Let no one, whomsoever, presume to act in a domineering way in this matter." What elegant diction, too! "Enroll in the pious number of the religious"; and "clericare," "clericorum," "indictu," and "placatus"!

And again he comes back to the diadem:

> We also therefore decreed this, that he himself and his successors might use, for the honor of the blessed Peter, the diadem, that is the crown, which we have granted him from our own head, of purest gold and precious gems.

Again he explains the meaning of diadem, for he was speaking to barbarians, forgetful ones at that. And he adds "of purest gold," lest perchance you should think brass or dross was mixed in. And when he has said "gems," he adds "precious," again fearing lest you should suspect them of being cheap. Yet why did he not say most precious, just as he said "purest gold"? For there is more difference between gem and gem, than between gold and gold. And when he should have said "distinctum gemmis," he said "ex gemmis." Who does not see that this was taken from the passage, which the gentile ruler had not read, "Thou

---

84. Valla's text of the *Donation* in this paragraph differs greatly from Zeumer's, Hinschius', and Friedberg's. It is not very clear in any of the texts whether the intent is to give the Pope power to take any one whomsoever into the clergy and thus relieve him from civil and military duties, or to prevent the Roman nobility from forcing their way into ecclesiastical offices against the will of the Pope.

settest a crown of precious stone on his head"?[85] Did the Caesar speak thus, with a certain vanity in bragging of his crown, if indeed the Caesars were crowned, but cheapening himself by fearing lest people would think that he did not wear a crown "of purest gold and precious gems," unless he said so?

Find the reason why he speaks thus: "for the honor of the Blessed Peter." As though, not Christ, but Peter, were the chief corner-stone on which the temple of the church is built; an inference he later repeats! But if he wanted to honor him so much, why did he not dedicate the episcopal temple at Rome to him, rather than to John the Baptist?

What? Does not that barbarous way of talking, show that the rigmarole was composed, not in the age of Constantine, but later; "decernimus quod uti debeant"[86] for the correct form "decernimus ut utantur"? Boors commonly speak and write that way now; "Iussi quod deberes venire" for "Iussi ut venires." And "we decreed," and "we granted," as though it were not being done now, but had been done some other time!

> But he himself, the blessed Pope, did not allow that crown of gold to be used over the clerical crown which he wears to the glory of the most blessed Peter.

Alas for your singular stupidity, Constantine! Just now you were saying that you put the crown on the Pope's head for the honor of the blessed Peter; now you say that you do not do it, because Sylvester refuses it. And while you approve his refusal, you nevertheless order him to use the gold crown; and what he thinks he ought not to do, that you say his own successors ought to do![87] I pass over the fact that you call the tonsure a crown, and the Roman pontiff "Pope," although that word had not yet begun to be applied to him as a distinctive title.

---

85. *Ps.* xxi, 3, with variation.
86. Valla does not, here, quote his own text of the *Donation* correctly.
87. This singular confusion about the crown in the *Donation* is explained by Brunner, *Festgabe für Rudolf von Gneist*, pp. 25 *et seq.*, as giving the pope the possession, but not the use of the imperial crown, thus paving the way for his prerogative of conferring the crown upon Louis the Pious in 816. Scheffer-Boichorst takes the whole episode as an attempt of the forger to glorify Sylvester by having the emperor honor him with the imperial crown, and having the Pope display the clerical humility (and pride) of rejecting it.

But we placed upon his most holy head, with our own hands, a glittering tiara of the most dazzling white, representing the Lord's resurrection. And holding the bridle of his horse, out of reverence for the blessed Peter, we performed for him the duty of squire; decreeing that all his successors, and they alone, use this same tiara in processions in imitation of our power.

Does not this fable-fabricator seem to blunder, not through imprudence, but deliberately and of set purpose, and so as to offer handles for catching him? In the same passage he says both that the Lord's resurrection is represented by the tiara, and that it is an imitation of Caesar's power; two things which differ most widely from each other. God is my witness, I find no words, no words merciless enough with which to stab this most abandoned scoundrel; so full of insanity are all the words he vomits forth. He makes Constantine not only similar in office to Moses, who at the command of God honored the chief priest, but also an expounder of secret mysteries, a most difficult thing even for those long versed in the sacred books. Why did you not make Constantine supreme pontiff while you were about it, as many emperors have been, that he might more conveniently transfer his attire to the other high priest? But you did not know history. And I give thanks to God on this very score, that he did not permit this utterly vicious scheme to be suggested save to an exceedingly stupid man. Subsequent considerations also show this. For he suggests the fact that Moses performed for Aaron, seated on a horse, the duty of squire [*dextratoris*], and that in the midst not of Israel, but of the Canaanites and the Egyptians, that is, of an heathen state, where there was not so much a secular government as one of demons and demon-worshipping peoples.

Wherefore, in order that the supreme pontificate may not deteriorate, but may rather be adorned with glory and power even more than is the dignity of an earthly rule; behold, we give over and relinquish to the most blessed pontiff and universal Pope, Sylvester, as well our palace as also the city of Rome and all the provinces, places and cities of Italy or[88] of the western regions; and by our pragmatic sanction we have decreed that they are to be controlled by him and by his successors, and that they remain under the law of the holy Roman church.

88. Valla's text of the *Donation* here has "sive" for "seu," *cf. supra*, p. 91, note 1.

We have already, in the oration of the Romans and that of Sylvester, said a good deal about this.[89] Here it is in place to say that no one would have thought of including all the nations in a single word of a grant; and that a man who had earlier followed out the minutest details of straps, the shoes, the linen horsecloths, would not have thought of omitting to cite by name provinces which now have separate kings or rulers equal to kings, and more than one to each. But this forger, of course, did not know which provinces were under Constantine, and which were not. For certainly not all were under him. When Alexander died, we see all the countries enumerated one by one in the division among the generals. We see the lands and rulers which were under the government of Cyrus, whether voluntarily or by conquest, named by Xenophon. We see the names of the Greek and barbarian kings, their lineage, their country, their bravery, their strength, their excellence, the number of their ships and the approximate number of their men, included by Homer in his catalog. And not only did many Greeks follow his example, but our Latin authors also, Ennius, Virgil, Lucan, Statius, and others. By Joshua and Moses in the division of the promised land, even all the little villages were described. And you refuse to enumerate even provinces! You name only the "western provinces."[90] What are the boundaries of the west; where do they begin; where do they end? Are the frontiers of west and east, south and north, as definite and fixed as those of Asia, Africa and Europe? Necessary words you omit, you heap on superfluous ones. You say, "provinces, places and cities." Are not provinces and cities, "places"? And when you have said provinces you add cities, as though the latter would not be understood with the former. But it is not strange that a man who gives away so large a part of the Earth should pass over the names of cities and of provinces, and as though overcome with lethargy not know what he says. "Of Italy or of the western regions," as though he meant "either...or" when he means "both";[91] speaking of "provinces... of the... regions," when it should

---

89. *Cf. supra*, pp. 41 *et seq.*, 49 *et seq.*

90. This phrase as used in the *Donation* probably meant Lombardy, Venetia, and Istria; i.e. practically northern, as distinct from peninsular, Italy. *Cf. supra*, p. 27, note 2, also Döllinger, *Papstfabeln* (ed. Friedrich), p. 122, note. In classical Latin it would have been, as Valla insists, a vague term.

91. *Cf. supra*, pp. 91, 109.

ECCLESIASTICAL MEGALOMANIA

rather be the regions of the provinces; and using the gerundive, "permanendas," for the future infinitive (*permansuras*).

> Wherefore we have perceived it to be fitting that our empire and our royal power should be transferred in the regions of the East; and that in the province of Byzantia [*sic*], in the most fitting place, a city should be built in our name; and that our empire should there be established.

I pass over the fact that in saying "a city should be built" [he uses the word for "the state" instead of "the city"], and cities, not states, are built; and the fact that he says "the province of Byzantia."[92] If you are Constantine, give the reason why you should choose that as the best place for founding your city. For that you should "transfer" yourself elsewhere after giving up Rome, was not so much "fitting" as necessary. You should neither call yourself Emperor when you have lost Rome and deserved least from the Roman name whose meaning you destroy; nor call yourself "royal," for no one before you has done so – unless you call yourself a king because you have ceased to be a Roman![93] But you allege a reason sound and honorable: "For where the chief of [all] priests and the head of the Christian religion has been established by the heavenly Emperor, it is not right that there an earthly Emperor should have jurisdiction."

O stupid David, stupid Solomon, stupid Hezekiah, Josiah, and all the other kings, stupid all and irreligious, who persisted in dwelling in the city of Jerusalem with the chief priests, and did not yield them the whole city! Constantine in three days is wiser than they could be in their whole life. And you call [the Pope] a "heavenly Emperor" because he accepts an earthly empire; unless by that term you mean God (for you speak ambiguously) and mean that an earthly sovereignty of priests was by him established over the city of Rome and other places, in which case you lie.

> We decreed, moreover, that all these things which through this sacred imperial [charter] and through other godlike decrees we establish and confirm, remain inviolate and unshaken unto the end of the world.

A moment ago, Constantine, you called yourself earthly; now you call yourself divine and sacred. You relapse into paganism and worse

---

92. *Cf. supra*, p. 95.
93. King [*rex*] was a forbidden title at Rome after the time of the Tarquins.

THE DONATION OF CONSTANTINE

than paganism. You make yourself God, your words sacred, and your decrees immortal; for you order the world to keep your commands "inviolate and unshaken." Do you consider who you are: just cleansed from the filthiest mire of wickedness, and scarcely fully cleansed? Why did you not add, "Till Heaven and Earth pass, one jot or one tittle shall in no wise pass from this 'privilege' "?[94] The kingdom of Saul, chosen by God, did not pass on to his sons; the kingdom of David was divided under his grandson, and afterward destroyed. And by your own authority you decree that the kingdom which you give over without God, shall remain even until the end of the world! Whoever taught you that the world is to pass away so soon? For I do not think that at this time you had faith in the poets, who alone bear witness to this. So you could not have said this, but some one else passed it off as yours.

However, he who spoke so grandly and loftily, begins to fear, and to distrust himself, and so takes to entreating:

> Wherefore, before the living God, who commanded us to reign, and in the face of his terrible judgment, we entreat all the emperors our successors, and all the nobles, the satraps also and the most glorious Senate, and all the people in the whole world, likewise also for the future, that no one of them, in any way, be allowed either to break this, or in any way overthrow it.

What a fair, what a devout adjuration! It is just as if a wolf should entreat by his innocence and good faith the other wolves and the shepherds not to try to take away from him, or demand back, the sheep which he has taken and divided among his offspring and his friends. Why are you so afraid, Constantine? If your work is not of God it will be destroyed; but if it is of God it cannot be destroyed. But I see! You wished to imitate the *Apocalypse,* where it says: "For I testify unto every man that heareth all the words of the prophecy of this book, If any man shall add unto these things, God shall add unto him the plagues that are written in this book. And if any man shall take away from the words of the book of this prophecy, God shall take away his part out of the book of life, and out of the holy city."[95] But you had never read the *Apocalypse;* therefore these are not your words.

94. A parody on *Matt.* v, 18.
95. *Rev.* xxii, 18-19.

If any one, moreover – which we do not believe – prove a scorner in this matter, he shall be condemned and shall be subject to eternal damnation; and shall feel the holy apostles of God, Peter and Paul, opposed to him in the present and in the future life. And he shall be burned in the lower Hell and shall perish with the devil and all the impious.

This terrible threat is the usual one, not of a secular ruler, but of the early priests and flamens, and nowadays, of ecclesiastics. And so this is not the utterance of Constantine, but of some fool of a priest who, stuffed and pudgy, knew neither what to say nor how to say it, and, gorged with eating and heated with wine, belched out these wordy sentences which convey nothing to another, but turn against the author himself. First he says, "shall be subject to eternal damnation," then as though more could be added, he wishes to add something else, and to eternal penalties he joins penalties in the present life; and after he frightens us with God's condemnation, he frightens us with the hatred of Peter, as though it were something still greater. Why he should add Paul, and why Paul alone, I do not know. And with his usual drowsiness he returns again to eternal penalties, as though he had not said that before. Now if these threats and curses were Constantine's, I in turn would curse him as a tyrant and destroyer of my country, and would threaten that I, as a Roman, would take vengeance on him. But who would be afraid of the curse of an overly avaricious man, and one saying a counterfeit speech after the manner of actors, and terrifying people in the role of Constantine? This is being a hypocrite in the true sense, if we press the Greek word closely; that is, hiding your own personality under another's.

The page,[96] moreover, of this imperial decree, we, confirming it with our own hands, did place above the venerable body of the blessed Peter.[97]

Was it paper or parchment, the "page" on which this was written? Though, in fact, we call one side of a leaf, as they say, a page; for instance, a pamphlet [?] has ten leaves, twenty pages.

---

96. "Pagina" in medieval Latin often meant "document."

97. In the *Liber Pontificalis* (ed. Duchesne, i, 454) the keys of Ravenna and other cities included in the so-called *Donation of Pippin* are said to have been placed in "the confession of St. Peter" (i.e., before his tomb). This association seems to have been common in the eighth century.

THE DONATION OF CONSTANTINE

But oh! the unheard of and incredible thing [that Constantine did]! I remember asking some one, when I was a youth, who wrote the book of *Job*; and when he answered, "Job himself," I rejoined, "How then would he mention his own death?" And this can be said of many other books, discussion of which is not appropriate here. For how, indeed can that be narrated which has not yet been done; and how can that which [the speaker] himself admits was done after the burial, so to say, of the records, be contained in the records? This is nothing else than saying that "the page of the privilege" was dead and buried before it was born and yet never returned from death and burial; and saying expressly that it was confirmed before it had been written, and not with one hand alone at that, but with both of the Caesar's hands! And what is this "confirming"? Was it done with the signature of the Caesar, or with his signet ring? Surely, hard and fast that – more so by far than if he had entrusted it to bronze tablets! But there is no need of bronze inscription, when the charter is laid away above the body of the blessed Peter. But why do you here suppress Paul, though he lies with Peter, and the two could guard it better than if the body of one alone were present?

You see the malicious artfulness of the cunning Sinon![98] Because the *Donation of Constantine* cannot be produced, therefore he said that the "privilege" is not on bronze but on paper records; therefore he said that it lies with the body of the most holy apostle, so that either we should not dare to seek it in the venerable tomb, or if we should seek it, we would think it rotted away. But where then was the body of the blessed Peter? Certainly it was not yet in the temple where it now is, not in a place reasonably protected and safe. Therefore the Caesar would not have put the "page" there. Or did he not trust the "page" to the most blessed Sylvester, as not holy enough, not careful nor diligent enough? O Peter! O Sylvester! O holy pontiffs of the Roman church! to whom the sheep of the Lord were entrusted, why did you not keep the "page" entrusted to you? Why have you suffered it to be eaten by worms, to rot away with mold? I presume that it was because your bodies also have wasted away. Constantine therefore acted foolishly. Behold the "page" reduced to dust; the right conferred by the "privilege" at the same time passes away into dust.

---

98. *Cf. supra*, p. 85.

And yet, as we see, a copy of the "page" is shown. Who then was so bold as to take it from the bosom of the most holy apostle? No one did it, I think. Whence then the copy? By all means some ancient writer ought to be adduced, one not later than the time of Constantine. However, none such is adduced, but as it happens some recent writer or other. Whence did he get it? For whoever composes a narrative about an earlier age, either writes at the dictation of the Holy Spirit, or follows the authority of former writers, and of those, of course, who wrote concerning their own age. So whoever does not follow earlier writers will be one of those to whom the remoteness of the event affords the boldness to lie. But if this story is to be read anywhere, it is not consistent with antiquity any more than that stupid narrative of the glossator Accursius about Roman ambassadors being sent to Greece to get laws agrees with Titus Livius and the other best writers.

> Given at Rome, on the third day before the Kalends of April, Constantine Augustus consul for the fourth time, and Gallicanus consul for the fourth time.[99]

He took the next to the last day of March so that we might feel that this was done in the season of holy days, which, for the most part, come at that time. And "Constantine consul for the fourth time, and Gallicanus consul for the fourth time." Strange if each had been consul thrice, and they were colleagues in a fourth consulship! But stranger still that the Augustus, a leper, with elephantiasis (which disease is as remarkable among diseases, as elephants are among animals), should want to even accept a consulship, when king Azariah, as soon as he was affected with leprosy, kept himself secluded, while the management of the kingdom was given over to Jotham his son;[100] and almost all lepers have acted similarly. And by this argument alone the whole "privilege" is confuted outright, destroyed, and overturned. And if any one disputes the fact that Constantine must have been leprous before he was consul, he should know that according to physicians this disease develops gradually, that according to the known facts of antiquity the consulate is an annual office and begins in the month of January; and these events are said to have taken place the following March.

---

99. In the best text of the *Donation* this is not called the fourth consulship of Gallicanus. In any case, however, the date is impossible; no such consulship as this is known.

100. *II Kings* xv, 5.

Nor will I here pass over the fact that "given" is usually written on letters, but not on other documents, except among ignorant people. For letters are said either to be given one (*illi*) or to be given to one (*ad illum*); in the former case [they are given] to one who carries them, a courier for instance, and puts them in the hand of the man to whom they are sent; in the latter case [they are given] to one in the sense that they are to be delivered to him by the bearer, that is [they are given to] the one to whom they are sent. But the "privilege," as they call it, of Constantine, as it was not to be delivered to any one, so also it ought not to be said to be "given." And so it should be apparent that he who spoke thus lied, and did not know how to imitate what Constantine would probably have said and done. And those who think that he has told the truth, and defend him, whoever they are, make themselves abetters and accessories in his stupidity and madness. However, they have nothing now with which to honorably excuse their opinion, not to speak of defending it.

Or is it an honorable excuse for an error, to be unwilling to acquiesce in the truth when you see it disclosed, because certain great men have thought otherwise? Great men, I call them, on account of their position, not on account of their wisdom or their goodness. How do you even know whether those whom you follow, had they heard what you hear, would have continued in their belief, or would have given it up? And moreover it is most contemptible to be willing to pay more regard to man than to Truth, that is, to God. [I say this] for some men beaten at every argument are wont to answer thus: "Why have so many supreme pontiffs believed this *Donation* to be genuine?" I call you to witness, that you urge me where I would not, and force me against my will to rail at the supreme pontiffs whose faults I would prefer to veil. But let us proceed to speak frankly, inasmuch as this case cannot be conducted in any other way.

Admitting that they did thus believe and were not dishonest; why wonder that they believed these stories where so much profit allured them, seeing that they are led to believe a great many things, in which no profit is apparent, through their extraordinary ignorance? Do you not, at Ara Coeli, in that most notable temple and in the most impressive place, see the fable of the Sibyl and Octavian[101] depicted by the

---

101. This apocryphal story ran that the sibyl prophesied of Christ, and that Augustus erected an altar to him.

authority, they say, of Innocent III, who wrote it and who also left an account of the destruction of the Temple of Peace on the day of the Savior's birth, that is, at the delivery of the Virgin?[102] These stories tend rather to the destruction of faith, by their falsity, than to the establishment of faith, by their wonders. Does the vicar of Truth dare to tell a lie under the guise of piety, and consciously entangle himself in this sin? Or does he not lie? Verily, does he not see that in perpetrating this he contradicts the most holy men? Omitting others, Jerome cites the testimony of Varro that there were ten Sibyls, and Varro wrote his work before the time of Augustus. Jerome also writes thus of the Temple of Peace: "Vespasian and Titus, after the Temple of Peace was built at Rome, dedicated the vessels of the temple [of the Jews] and all manner of gifts in her shrine, as the Greek and Roman historians tell." And this ignorant man, alone, wants us to believe his libel, barbarously written at that, rather than the most accurate histories of ancient and most painstaking authors!

Since I have touched on Jerome, I will not suffer the following insult to him to be passed by in silence. At Rome, by the authority of the Pope, with the candles ever burning, as though for a relic of the saints, is shown a copy of the Bible, which they say is written in the hand of Jerome. Do you seek proof? Why, there is "much embroidered cloth and gold," as Virgil says, a thing which indicates rather that it was not written by the hand of Jerome. When I inspected it more carefully, I found that it was written by order of a king, Robert, I think, and in the handwriting of an inexperienced man.

Similarly – there are indeed ten thousand things of this sort at Rome – among sacred objects is shown the panel portrait of Peter and Paul, which, after Constantine had been spoken to by these apostles in his sleep, Sylvester produced in confirmation of the vision. I do not say this because I deny that they are portraits of the apostles (would that the letter sent in the name of Lentulus about the portrait of Christ were as genuine, instead of being no less vicious and spurious than this "privilege" which we refuted), but because that panel was not produced for Constantine by Sylvester. At that story my mind cannot restrain its astonishment.

---

102. The Temple of Peace was built by Vespasian and was not destroyed until it was burned down in the time of Commodus.

THE DONATION OF CONSTANTINE

So I will briefly discuss the Sylvester legend, because the whole question hinges on this; and, since I have to do with Roman pontiffs, it will be in order to speak chiefly of the Roman pontiff so that from one example an estimate of the others may be formed. And of the many absurdities told in this [legend] I shall touch upon one alone, that of the serpent,[103] in order to show that Constantine had not been a leper. And verily the *Life of Sylvester* (*Gesta Silvestri*), according to the translator, was written by Eusebius,[104] a Greek, always the readiest people at lying, as Juvenal's satirical judgment runs: "Whatever in the way of history a lying Greek dares tell."[105]

Whence came that dragon? Dragons are not engendered in Rome. Whence, too, his venom? In Africa alone, on account of its hot climate, are there said to be pest-producing dragons. Whence, too, so much venom that he wasted with pestilence such a spacious city as Rome; the more remarkable that the serpent was down in a cavern so deep that one descended to it by a hundred and fifty steps? Serpents, excepting possibly the basilisk, inject their poison and kill, not with their breath, but with their bite. Cato, fleeing from Caesar through the very midst of the African deserts with such a large force as he had, did not see any of his company slain by the breath of a serpent, either on the march or in camp; nor do the natives think the air pestilential on account of serpents. And if we believe at all in the stories, the Chimaera, the Hydra and Cerberus have all often been seen and touched without injury.

Why hadn't the Romans already slain it instead [of waiting for Sylvester]? They couldn't, you say? But Regulus killed a much larger serpent in Africa on the banks of the Bagradas. And it was very easy indeed to kill the one at Rome; for instance, by closing the mouth of the cavern. Or didn't they want to? Ah, they worshipped it as a god, I suppose, as the Babylonians did? Why then, as Daniel is said to have

---

103. This episode in the *Gesta*, or *Actus*, or *Vita*, *Silvestri*, as may be gathered from Valla's subsequent discussion, involves an enormous serpent, dwelling in a cave under the Tarpeian rock, devastating the entire city of Rome with his poisonous breath, appeased only by maidens being given to him to devour, and finally bound forever in his cave by Sylvester. For references, *cf.* Coleman, *Constantine, etc.* pp. 161, 168.

104. Apparently Valla assumes that the *Gesta Silvestri* was written by a Greek named Eusebius, but not Eusebius of Caesarea, author of the *Church History*. *Cf.*, however, Coleman, *Constantine*, pp. 161-168.

105. *Satura*, x, 174-175.

killed that serpent,[106] had not Sylvester killed this one when he had bound him with a hempen thread, and destroyed that brood forever? The reason the inventor of the legend did not want the dragon slain was that it might not be apparent that he had copied the narrative of Daniel. But if Jerome, a most learned and accurate translator, Apollinaris, Origen, Eusebius and others affirm the story of Bel to be apocryphal, if the Jews in their original of the Old Testament do not know it; that is, if all the most learned of the Latins, most of the Greeks, and certain of the Hebrews, condemn that as a legend, shall I not condemn this adumbration of it, which is not based on the authority of any writer, and which far surpasses its model in absurdity?

For who had built the underground home for the beast? Who had put it there and commanded it not to come out and fly away (for dragons fly, as some say; even though others deny it)? Who had thought out that kind of food for him? Who had directed that women, virgins at that, devoted to chastity, go down to him, and only on the Kalends? Or did the serpent remember what day was the Kalends? And was he content with such scant and occasional food? And did not the virgins dread such a deep cavern, and a beast so monstrous and greedy? I suppose the serpent wheedled them, as they were women, and virgins, and brought him his victuals; I suppose he even chatted with them. What if, pardon the expression, he even had intercourse with them; for both Alexander and Scipio are said to have been born by the embrace of a dragon, or a serpent, with their mothers! Why, if food were afterward denied him, would he not have come out then, or have died?

O the strange folly of men who have faith in these senile ravings! How long now had this been going on? When did the beginning occur? Before the advent of the Savior, or after? As to this, nothing is known. We should be ashamed! We should be ashamed of these silly songs, and this frivolity worse than dangerous! A Christian, who calls himself a son of truth and light, should blush to utter things which not only are not true, but are not credible.

But, they say, the demons obtained this power over the heathen, so as to mock them for serving the gods. Silence, you utter ignoramuses, not to call you utter rascals, you who always spread such a veil over your stories! True Christianity does not need the patronage of falsehood; it

---

106. *Cf.* the story of Bel and the Dragon in the *Apocrypha*.

is maintained satisfactorily by itself, and by its own light and truth, without those lying and deceitful fables – unmitigated insults to God, to Christ, and to the Holy Spirit. Would God thus have given the human race over into the power of demons, to be seduced by such evident, such imposing miracles, that he might well-nigh be accused of the injustice of turning sheep over to wolves, and that men should have good excuse for their errors? But if so much license was once given demons, even more would be given them now among infidels; which is by no means the case, nor are any legends of this sort told by them.

Passing by other peoples, I will speak of the Romans. Among them the miracles reported are few, and they early and obscure. Valerius Maximus tells that that chasm in the middle of the forum when Curtius, armed and spurring on his horse, plunged into it, closed again, and returned forthwith to its former state.[107] Again, the [effigy of] Juno Moneta, it was asked in jest, by a certain Roman soldier at the capture of Veii, whether it wanted to move to Rome, replied that it did.[108]

Titus Livius, an earlier and more authoritative writer, knows neither of these stories. For he has it that the chasm was permanent, not a sudden opening but an old one, there before the founding of the city, and called Curtius' Pond, because Mettius Curtius, a Sabine, fleeing from an attack by the Romans, had hidden in it; and that the Juno did not reply, but nodded assent, and it was added to the story afterwards that she had spoken.[109] And about the nod also, it is evident that they lied, either by interpreting the movement of image when they pulled it away as made by its own accord, or by pretending in the same joking way in which they asked the question that the hostile, conquered, stone goddess nodded assent. Indeed, Livy does not say that she nodded, but that the soldiers exclaimed that she nodded. Such stories, too, good writers do not defend as facts, but excuse as tradition. For even as this same Livy says, "This indulgence is to be granted antiquity, that by mingling the human and the divine it may make the beginnings of cities more august."[110] And elsewhere: "But in connection with events of such ancient times, if probabilities should be accepted as facts, no harm would be done. These stories are more suited to the display of a

---

107. *Factorum et dictorum memorabilium libri novem*, V, vi, 2.
108. *Ibid.*, I, viii, 3.
109. Livy, VII, 6, incorrectly summarized.
110. Livy, Preface, 7.

stage which delights in wonders, than to sober belief; it is not worth while either to affirm or to refute them."[111]

Terentius Varro, an earlier, more learned and, I think, more authoritative writer than these two, says there were three accounts of Curtius' Pond given by as many writers; one by Proculus, that this pond was so called for a Curtius who cast himself into it; another by Piso, that it was named for Mettius the Sabine; the third by Cornelius, and he adds Luctatius as his associate in the matter, that it was for Curtius the consul, whose colleague was Marcus Genutius.[112]

Nor should I have concealed that Valerius cannot be altogether criticized for speaking as he does, since a little later he earnestly and seriously adds: "And I do not ignore the fact that as to human eyes and ears perceiving the movement and the voice of immortal gods, our judgment is rather confused by wavering opinion; but because what is said is not new but the repetition of traditions, the authors may lay claim to credence."[113] He spoke of the voice of the gods on account of the Juno Moneta,[114] and on account of the statue of Fortune which is represented to have twice spoken in these words, "With due form have you seen me, matrons; with due form have you dedicated me."[115]

But our own story-tellers every once in a while bring in talking idols of which the heathen themselves, and the worshippers of the idols, do not speak; rather they deny them more earnestly than the Christians affirm them. Among the heathen the very few wonders which are told make their way not by the belief of writers, but by the sanction of their antiquity, as something sacred and venerable; among our writers wonders more recent are narrated, wonders of which the men of those times did not know.

I neither disparage admiration for the saints, nor do I deny their divine works, for I know that faith, as much of it as a grain of mustard seed, is able even to remove mountains. Rather I defend and uphold them, but I do not allow them to be confused with ridiculous legends. Nor can I be persuaded that these writers were other than either infidels, who did this to deride the Christians in case these bits of fiction handed

---

111. Livy, V, 21, 9.
112. Terentius Varro, *De Lingua Latina*, lib. V, 148-150.
113. Valerius Maximus, *Factorum et Dictorum Memorabilium*, lib. i, viii, 7.
114. *Ibid.*, i, viii, 3.
115. *Ibid.*, i, viii, 4, with the substitution of "seen" for "given."

THE DONATION OF CONSTANTINE

out by crafty men to the ignorant should be accepted as true, or else believers with a zeal for God, to be sure, but not according to knowledge, men who did not shrink from writing shameless accounts not only of the acts of the saints but even of the mother of God, and indeed of Christ himself, nor from writing pseudo-gospels. And the supreme pontiff calls these books apocryphal as though it were no blemish that their author is unknown, as though what was told were credible, as though they were sacred, tending to establish religion; so that now there is no less fault on his part in that he approves evils, than on the part of the one who devised them. We detect spurious coins, we pick them out and reject them; shall we not detect spurious teaching? Shall we retain it, confuse it with the genuine and defend it as genuine?

But I, to give my frank opinion, deny that the *Acts* of Sylvester is an apocryphal book; because, as I have said, a certain Eusebius is said to have been its author; but I think it is false and not worth reading, in other parts as well as in what it has to say about the serpent, the bull,[116] and the leprosy, to refute which I have gone over so much ground. For even if Naaman was leprous, should we forthwith say that Constantine also was leprous? Many writers allude to it in Naaman's case; that Constantine the head of the whole Earth had leprosy no one mentioned; at least none of his fellow citizens, but perhaps some foreigner or other, to be given no more credence than that other fellow who wrote about wasps building their nest in Vespasian's nostrils, and about the frog taken from Nero at birth, whence they say the place was called the Lateran, for the frog (*rana*) is concealed (*latere*) there in its grave.[117] Such stuff neither the wasps themselves, nor frogs, if they could speak, would have uttered! [I pass over the statement that boys' blood is a remedy for leprosy, which medical science does not admit;[118]] unless they attribute this to the Capitoline gods, as though they were wont to talk and had ordered this to be done!

---

116. In a disputation between Sylvester and Jewish rabbis the rabbis are said to have killed a bull by shouting the sacred name, Jehovah, and Sylvester is said to have brought him to life by whispering the name of Christ. *Cf.* Coleman, *Constantine the Great, etc.*, p. 163.

117. These stories were to be found, among other places, in the *Mirabilia urbis Romae*, a guidebook to Rome dating from the twelfth century. English translation by F. M. Nichols, *The Marvels of Rome* (London and Rome 1889), pp. 19-20.

118. This clause, though not in the *MS* or Hutten, seems necessary to the sense of the following clause, so I have translated it from Bonneau's text. In the *Vita Silvestri* we

ECCLESIASTICAL MEGALOMANIA

But why should I wonder that the pontiffs are not informed on these points, when they do not know about their own name! For they say that Peter is called Cephas because he was the head of the apostles, as though this noun were Greek, from κεφαλή, and not Hebrew, or rather Syriac; a noun which the Greeks write κηφᾶς, and which with them means rock (*Petrus*), and not head! For "petrus," "petra," (rock) is a Greek noun. And "petra" is stupidly explained by them through a Latin derivation, as from "pede trita" (trodden by foot)! And they distinguish "metropolitan" from "archbishop," and claim that the former is so called from the size of the city, though in Greek it is not called μετρόπολις; but μητρόπολις, that is, the mother-state or city. And they explain "patriarch" as "pater patrum" (father of fathers); and "papa" (pope) from the interjection "pape" (indeed); and "orthodox" as from the words meaning "right glory"; and they pronounce "Simonem" (Simon) with a short middle vowel, though it should be read with a long one, as are "Platonem" (Plato) and "Catonem" (Cato). And there are many similar instances which I pass, lest for the fault of some of the supreme pontiffs I should seem to attack all. These instances had to be given so that no one should wonder that many of the Popes have been unable to detect that the *Donation of Constantine* was spurious; though, in my opinion this deception originated with one of them.

But you say, "Why do not the Emperors, who were the sufferers from this forgery, deny the *Donation of Constantine*, instead of admitting it, confirming it and maintaining it?" A great argument! A marvelous defense! For of which Emperor are you speaking? If of the Greek one, who was the true Emperor, I will deny the admission; if of the Latin, I will confess it, and with pleasure. For who does not know that the Latin Emperor was gratuitously established by a supreme pontiff, Stephen I think, who robbed the Greek Emperor because he would not aid Italy, and established a Latin Emperor; so the Emperor thus received more from the Pope than the Pope from the Emperor?[119] Oh, of course, Achilles and Patroclus divided the Trojan spoils between themselves alone on some such terms. The words of Louis [the Pious] seem to me

---

are told that the pagan priests ordered Constantine to bathe in infants' blood in order to cure himself of leprosy. *Cf.* Coleman, *Constantine the Great, etc.* p. 162.

119. It will be remembered that Valla wrote this while in the service of the King of Naples, who was in conflict with imperial as well as with papal claims.

to imply just this when he says, "I, Louis, Roman Emperor, Augustus, ordain and grant, by this compact of our confirmation, to you, blessed Peter, prince of the apostles, and through you to your vicar, the supreme pontiff, lord Paschal [I], and to his successors forever, to hold, just as from our predecessors until now you have held, under your authority and rule, the Roman state with its duchy, with all its towns and villages, its mountain districts, sea coasts and harbors, and all cities, forts, walled towns, and estates in the districts of Tuscany."[120]

Do you, Louis, make a pact with Paschal? If these are yours, that is, the Roman Empire's, why do you grant them to another? If they are his and are held in his own possession, what sense is there in your confirming them? How little of the Roman Empire will be yours if you lose the very head of the Empire? From Rome the Roman Emperor takes his name. What! Are your other possessions yours or Paschal's? Yours, you will say, I suppose. Therefore, the *Donation of Constantine* is not valid at all; that is, if you possess what was given by him to the pontiff. If it is valid, by what right does Paschal give you the rest [of the Empire], retaining for himself only what he possesses? What does your excessive prodigality toward him at the expense of the Roman Empire mean, or his toward you? Therefore, deservedly do you call it a "compact," something like collusion.

"But what shall I do?" you will say. "Shall I try to recover by force what the Pope has in his possession? But he, alas, has now become more powerful than I. Shall I seek to regain it by law? But my right is only such as he is willing for it to be. For I came to the throne, not through an inherited title, but by a compact that if I wish to be Emperor I should promise the Pope in turn such and such considerations. Shall I say that Constantine did not of the Empire? But that way I should be arguing the cause of the Greek Emperor, and I should rob myself of all imperial dignity. For the Pope says he makes me Emperor with this very thing in view, as a kind of vicar of his; and unless I bind myself, he will not make me Emperor; and unless I obey I shall have to abdicate. If only he gives me the throne I will acknowledge everything, I will agree to everything. Only; take my word for it, if I had Rome and Tuscany in my possession, I would act quite differently and Paschal

---

120. A forgery of the eleventh century. *Cf.* E. Emerton, *Medieval Europe*, p. 55.

would sing me that old song of the *Donation,* spurious in my opinion, in vain. As things are, I yield what I neither have nor hope to have. To question the right of the Pope is not my concern but that of the Emperor yonder at Constantinople."

I quite excuse you, Louis, and every other ruler similarly placed. What must we suspect of the compact of other Emperors with the supreme pontiffs, when we know what Sigismund did, a ruler otherwise most excellent and courageous, but at that time affected and weakened by age? We saw him, hedged in throughout Italy, with a few retainers, living from day to day at Rome, and he would, indeed, have perished with hunger, had not Eugenius fed him – but not for nothing, for he extorted the *Donation* from him. When he had come to Rome to be crowned Emperor of the Romans, he could not get the Pope to crown him, except by confirming the *Donation of Constantine* and by granting anew all that it contained. What more contradictory than for him to be crowned Roman Emperor who had renounced Rome itself, and that by the man whom he both acknowledges and, so far as he can, makes master of the Roman Empire; and [for the Emperor] to confirm the *Donation* which, if genuine, leaves none of the Empire for the Emperor! It is a thing which, as I think, not even children would have done. So it is not strange that the Pope arrogates to himself the coronation of the Caesar, which ought to belong to the Roman people.

If you, O Pope, on the one hand can deprive the Greek Emperor of Italy and the western provinces, and on the other you create a Latin Emperor, why do you resort to "compacts"? Why do you divide the Caesar's estate? Why do you transfer the Empire to yourself?

Wherefore, let whoever is called Emperor of the Romans know that in my judgment he is not Augustus, nor Caesar, nor Emperor unless he rules at Rome; and unless he takes up the recovery of the city of Rome, he will plainly be forsworn. For those earlier Caesars, and Constantine first of them, were not forced to take the oath by which the Caesars are now bound; but rather the oath that, so far as it lay in human power, they would not diminish the extent of the Roman Empire, but would diligently add to it.

Yet not for this reason are they called Augusti, namely that they ought to augment the Empire, as some in whose knowledge of Latin is imperfect; for he is called Augustus, as consecrated, from "avium gustus" (the taste, or appetite, of the birds), a customary step in consulting the omens; and this derivation is supported by the language of the Greeks, among whom the Augustus is called Σεβαστός, from which Sebastia gets its name. Better might the supreme pontiff be called Augustus from "augere" (to augment), except for the fact that when he augments his temporal he diminishes his spiritual power. Thus it is a fact that the worse the supreme pontiff is, the more he exerts himself to defend this *Donation*. Take the case of Boniface VIII, who deceived Celestine by means of pipes fixed in the wall.[121] He both writes concerning the *Donation of Constantine*, and he despoils the French king; and, as though he wished to put the *Donation of Constantine* in execution, he decrees that the kingdom itself belonged to and was subject to the Roman church. This decretal his successors, Benedict and Clement, revoked outright, as wicked and unjust.

But what is the significance of your anxiety, Roman pontiffs, in requiring each Emperor to confirm the *Donation of Constantine*, unless it be that you distrust its legality? But you are washing bricks [you labor in vain], as they say; for that *Donation* never existed, and since it does not exist it cannot be confirmed; and whatever the Caesars grant, their acts are due to deception as to the precedent of Constantine; and they cannot grant the Empire.

However, let us grant that Constantine made the *Donation* and that Sylvester was at one time in possession, but afterwards either he himself or another of the Popes lost possession. (I am speaking now of that of which the Pope is not in possession; later on I will speak of that of which he is in possession.) What more can I grant you than to concede the existence of that which never was and never could be? But even so, I say that you cannot effect a recovery either by divine or by human law. In the ancient law it was forbidden that a Hebrew be a Hebrew's slave more than six years, and every fiftieth year also everything reverted to the original owner. Shall a Christian, in the dispensation of grace, be oppressed in eternal slavery by the vicar of the Christ who redeemed us from our servitude? What do I say! Shall he be recalled to servitude after he has been set free and has long enjoyed his freedom?

How brutal, how violent, how barbarous the tyranny of priests often is, I do not say. If this was not known before, it has lately been learned

---

121. Gossip had it that Boniface VIII induced his predecessor to abdicate by angelic warnings, which he himself produced through improvised speaking tubes.

from that monster of depravity, John Vitelleschi, cardinal and patriarch, who wore out the sword of Peter, with which [the apostle] cut off the ear of Malchus, with the blood of Christians. By this sword he himself also perished.[122] But is it true that the people of Israel were permitted to revolt from the house of David and Solomon whom prophets sent by God had anointed, because their impositions were too heavy; and that God approved their act? May we not revolt on account of such great tyranny, particularly from those who are not kings, and cannot be; and who from being shepherds of the sheep, that is to say, of souls, have become thieves and brigands?

And to come to human law, who does not know that there is no right conferred by war, or if there is any, that it prevails just as long as you possess what you have gotten by war? For when you lose possession, you have lost the right. And so ordinarily, if captives have escaped, no one summons them into court; and so also with plunder if the former owners have recovered it. Bees and any other kind of winged creatures, if they have flown away far from my property and have settled on another's, cannot be reclaimed. And do you seek to reclaim men, who are not only free creatures, but masters of others, when they set themselves free by force of arms, [reclaim them] not by force of arms, but by law, as though you were a man, and they sheep?

Nor can you say, "The Romans were [considered] just in waging wars against the nations, and just in depriving them of liberty." Do not drag me into that discussion, lest I be forced to speak against my fellow Romans. However, no fault could be so serious that people should merit everlasting servitude therefor. And in this connection [one must remember also] that people often waged a war for which a prince or some important citizen in the Republic was to blame, and, being conquered, were undeservedly punished with servitude. There are everywhere abundant examples of this.

Nor in truth does the law of nature provide that one people should subjugate another people to itself. We can instruct others, we can urge them; we cannot rule them and do them violence, unless, leaving humanity aside, we wish to copy the more savage beasts which force their bloody rule upon the weaker, as the lion among quadrupeds, the eagle

---

122. The assassination of Vitelleschi, supposedly by order of the Pope, took place in March 1440, and is one of the means of dating Valla's treatise.

among birds, the dolphin among fish. Yet even these creatures do not vaunt authority over their own kind, but over an inferior. How much more ought we to act thus, and as men have due regard for men, since in the words of Marcus Fabius there is no beast upon the Earth so fierce that his own likeness is not sacred to him?

Now there are four reasons why wars are waged: either for avenging a wrong and defending friends; or for fear of incurring disaster later, if the strength of others is allowed to increase; or for hope of booty; or for desire of glory. Of these the first is rather honorable, the second less so, and the last two are far from honorable. And wars were indeed often waged against the Romans, but after they had defended themselves, they waged war against their assailants and against others. Nor is there any nation which yielded to their sway unless conquered in war and subdued; whether justly, or for what cause, they themselves could judge. I should be unwilling to condemn them as fighting unjustly or to acquit them as fighting in a just cause. I can only say that the Roman people waged wars against others for the same reason as other peoples and kings did, and that it was left open even to those who were attacked and conquered in war to revolt from the Romans just as they revolted from other masters; lest perchance (and none would agree to this) all authority should be imputed to the oldest people who were first masters; that is, to those who were the first to take possession of what belonged to others.

And yet the Roman people had a better right over nations conquered in war than had the Caesars in their overthrow of the Republic. Wherefore, if it was right for the nations to revolt from Constantine, and, what is far more, from the Roman people, surely it will be right to revolt from him to whom Constantine gave his authority. And to put the matter more boldly, if the Roman people were free either to drive Constantine out, as they did Tarquinius, or to slay him, as they did Julius Caesar, much more will the Romans or the provinces be free to slay him, who at any time has succeeded Constantine. But though this is true, yet it is beyond the scope of my argument, and so I want to restrain myself and not press anything I have said further than this, that it is folly to adduce any verbal right, where the right of arms prevails, because that which is acquired by arms, is likewise lost by arms.

This, indeed, the more, that other new peoples as we have heard in the case of the Goths, who were never subject to Roman rule, after putting to flight the earlier inhabitants, seized upon Italy and many provinces. What justice, pray, is there in restoring these to a servitude which they have never experienced; especially as they are the conquering peoples; and to servitude perchance under the conquered peoples? And if at this time any cities and nations, deserted by the Emperor at the arrival of the barbarians, as we know to have been the case, had been compelled to elect a king under whose leadership they then won victory, is there any reason why they should later depose this ruler? Or should they bid his sons, popular it may be for their father's praise, it may be for their own valor, become private citizens, that they might again become subjects of a Roman prince, even though they were greatly in need of their assistance and hoped for no aid elsewhere? If the Caesar himself, or Constantine, returned to life, or even the Senate and Roman people should call them before a general court such as the Amphictyony was in Greece, [the plaintiff] would at once be ruled out at his first plea because he was reclaiming to bondage and slavery those who once had been abandoned by him, their guardian, those who for a long time had been living under another ruler, those who had never been subject to a foreign-born king, men, in conclusion, who were freeborn and proclaimed free by their vigor of mind and body. How clear it should be, that if the Caesar, if the Roman people, is thus debarred from recovering control, much more decidedly is the Pope! And if the other nations which have been subject to Rome are free either to appoint a king for themselves or to maintain a republic, far more are the Roman people themselves free to do this, especially against the innovation of papal tyranny.

Estopped from defending the *Donation*, since it never existed and, if it had existed, it would now have expired from lapse of time, our adversaries take refuge in another kind of defense; figuratively speaking, the city being given up for lost, they betake themselves to their citadel – which forthwith they are constrained by lack of provisions to surrender. "The Roman church," they say, "is entitled by prescription to what it possesses." Why then does it lay claim to that, the greater part, to which it has no title by prescription, and to which others are entitled by prescription; unless others cannot act toward it as it can act toward them?

The Roman church has title by prescription! Why then does it so often take care to have the Emperors confirm its right? Why does it vaunt the *Donation*, and its confirmation by the Caesars? If this alone is sufficient, you seriously weaken it by not at the same time keeping silent about the other title [by prescription]. Why don't you keep silent about that other? Obviously because this is not sufficient.

The Roman church has prescribed! And how can it have entered a prescription where no title is established but only possession through bad faith? Or if you deny that the possession was a case of bad faith, at least you cannot deny that the faith [in the *Donation*] was stupid. Or, in a matter of such importance and notoriety, ought ignorance of fact and of law to be excused? Of fact, because Constantine did not make a grant of Rome and the provinces; a fact of which a man of the common people might well be ignorant, but not the supreme pontiff. Of law, because they could not be granted; which any Christian ought to know. And so, will stupid credulity give you a right to that which, had you been more conscientious, would never have been yours? Well! Now, at least, after I have shown that you held possession through ignorance and stupidity, do you not lose that right, if it was such? and what ignorance unhappily brought you, does not knowledge happily take away again? and does not the property revert from the illegal to the legal master, perchance even with interest? But if you continue to keep possession in the future, your ignorance is henceforth changed into malice aforethought and into deceit, and you become a fraudulent holder.

The Roman church has entered a prescription! O simpletons, O ignoramuses in divine law! No length of years whatever can destroy a true title. Or indeed, if I were captured by barbarians and supposed to have perished, and should return again home after a hundred years of captivity, as a claimant of my paternal inheritance, should I be excluded? What could be more inhuman! And, to give another example, did Jephthah, the leader of Israel, when the Ammonites, demanded back the land from "the borders of Arnon even unto Jabbok and unto Jordan," reply, "Israel has prescribed this now through three hundred years' occupation"? Or did he not show that the land which they demanded as theirs, had never been theirs, but had been the Amorites'? And the proof that it did not belong to the Ammonites was that they had never in the course of so many years claimed it.[123]

---

123. *Judges* xi, 12-28.

ECCLESIASTICAL MEGALOMANIA

The Roman church has prescribed! Keep still, impious tongue! You transfer "prescription," which is used of inanimate, senseless objects, to man; and holding man in servitude is the more detestable, the longer it lasts. Birds and wild animals do not let themselves be "prescribed," but however long the time of captivity, when they please and occasion is offered, they escape. And may not man, held captive by man, escape?

Let me tell why the Roman pontiffs show fraud and craft rather than ignorance in using war instead of law as their arbiter — and I believe that the first pontiffs to occupy the city [of Rome] and the other towns did about the same. Shortly before I was born, Rome was led by an incredible sort of fraud, I call those then present there to witness, to accept papal government or rather usurpation, after it had long been free.[124] The Pope was Boniface IX, fellow of Boniface VIII in fraud as in name — if they are to be called Boniface (benefactor) at all, who are the worst malefactors. And when the Romans, after the treachery had been detected, stirred up trouble, the good Pope, after the manner of Tarquinius, struck off all the tallest poppies with his stick.[125] When his successor, Innocent [VII], afterwards tried to imitate this procedure he was driven out of the city. I will not speak of other Popes; they have always held Rome down by force of arms. Suffice it to say that as often as it could, it has rebelled; as for instance, six years ago,[126] when it could not obtain peace from Eugenius, and it was not equal to the enemies which were besieging it, it besieged the Pope within his house, and would not permit him to go out before he either made peace with the enemy or turned over the administration of the city to the citizens. But he preferred to leave the city in disguise, with a single companion in flight, rather than to gratify the citizens in their just and fair demands. If you give them the choice, who does not know that they would choose liberty rather than slavery?

We may suspect the same of the other cities, which are kept in servitude by the supreme pontiff, though they ought rather to be liberated by him from servitude. It would take too long to enumerate how many cities taken from their enemies the Roman people once set

---

124. For these episodes, cf. Creighton, *History of the Papacy, etc.*, vol. I, *passim*.

125. Tarquinius, by striking down the tallest poppies with his cane, gave the hint that the leaders of the opposition should be executed; *cf.* Livy, I, 54.

126. The ensuing episode occurred in 1434 and thus fixes the date of the writing of this passage as 1439 or 1440. *Cf.* Mancini, *Vita di Lorenzo Valla*, p. 163.

free; it went so far that Titus Flaminius [Flamininus] set free the whole of Greece, which had been under Antiochus,[127] and directed that it enjoy its own laws. But the Pope, as may be seen, lies in wait assiduously against the liberty of countries; and therefore one after another, they daily, as opportunity affords, rebel. (Look at Bologna just now.) And if at any time they have voluntarily accepted papal rule, as may happen when another danger threatens them from elsewhere, it must not be supposed that they have accepted it in order to enslave themselves, so that they could never withdraw their necks from the yoke, so that neither themselves nor those born afterwards should have control of their own affairs; for this would be utterly iniquitous.

"Of our own will we came to you, supreme pontiff, that you might govern us; of our own will we now leave you again, that you may govern us no more. If you have any claim against us, let the balance of debit and credit be determined. But you want to govern us against our will, as though we were wards of yours, we who perhaps could govern you more wisely than you do yourself! Add to this the wrongs all the time being committed against this state either by you or by your magistrates. We call God to witness that our wrong drives us to revolt, as once Israel did from Rehoboam. And what great wrong did they have? What [a small] part of our calamity is the [mere] payment of heavier taxes! What then if you impoverish the Republic? You have impoverished it. What if you despoil our temples? You *have* despoiled them. What if you outrage maidens and matrons? You *have* outraged them. What if you drench the city with the blood of its citizens? You have drenched it. Must we endure all this? Nay, rather, since you have ceased to be a father to us, shall we not likewise forget to be sons? This people summoned you, supreme pontiff, to be a father or if it better eases you, to be their lord, not to be an enemy and a hangman; you do not choose to act the father or the lord, but the enemy and the hangman. But, since we are Christians, we will not imitate your ferocity and your impiety, even though by the law of reprisal we might do so, nor will we bare the avenging sword above your head; but first your abdication and removal, and then we will adopt another father or lord. Sons may flee from vicious parents who brought them into the world; may we not flee

---

127. Flamininus had defeated Philip V of Macedonia, and it was from Philip, not Antiochus, that he "freed" Greece.

from you, not our real father but an adopted one who treats us in the worst way possible? But do you attend to your priestly functions; and don't take your stand in the north, and thundering there hurl your lightning and thunderbolts against this people and others."

But why need I say more in this case, absolutely self-evident as it is? I contend that not only did Constantine not grant such great possessions, not only could the Roman pontiff not hold them by prescription, but that even if either were a fact, nevertheless either right would have been extinguished by the crimes of the possessors, for we know that the slaughter and devastation of all Italy and of many of the provinces has flowed from this single source. If the source is bitter, so is the stream; if the root is unclean, so are the branches; if the first fruit is unholy, so is the lump.[128] And *vice versa,* if the stream is bitter, the source must be stopped up; if the branches are unclean, the fault comes from the root; if the lump is unholy, the first fruit must also be accursed. Can we justify the principle of papal power when we perceive it to be the cause of such great crimes and of such great and varied evils?

Wherefore I declare, and cry aloud, nor, trusting God, will I fear men, that in my time no one in the supreme pontificate has been either a faithful or a prudent steward, but they have gone so far from giving food to the household of God that they have devoured it as food and a mere morsel of bread! And the Pope himself makes war on peaceable people, and sows discord among states and princes. The Pope both thirsts for the goods of others and drinks up his own: he is what Achilles calls Agamemnon, Δημβόρος βασιλεύς, "a people-devouring king." The Pope not only enriches himself at the expense of the republic, as neither Verres nor Catiline nor any other embezzler dared to do, but he enriches himself at the expense of even the church and the Holy Spirit as old Simon Magus himself would abhor doing. And when he is reminded of this and is reproved by good people occasionally, he does not deny it, but openly admits it, and boasts that he is free to wrest from its occupants by any means whatever the patrimony given the church by Constantine; as though when it was recovered Christianity would be in an ideal state – and not rather the more oppressed by all kinds of crimes, extravagances and lusts; if indeed it can be oppressed more, and if there is any crime yet uncommitted!

128. *A reminiscence of Rom.* xi, 16.

And so, that he may recover the other parts of the *Donation*, money wickedly stolen from good people he spends more wickedly, and he supports armed forces, mounted and foot, with which all places are plagued, while Christ is dying of hunger and nakedness in so many thousands of paupers. Nor does he know, the unworthy reprobate, that while he works to deprive secular powers of what belongs to them, they in turn are either led by his bad example, or driven by necessity (granting that it may not be a real necessity) to make off with what belongs to the officers of the church. And so there is no religion anywhere, no sanctity, no fear of God; and, what I shudder to mention, impious men pretend to find in the Pope an excuse for all their crimes. For he and his followers furnish an example of every kind of crime, and with Isaiah and Paul, we can say against the Pope and those about him: "The name of God is blasphemed among the Gentiles through you, you who teach others, but do not teach yourselves; who preach against stealing and yourselves are robbers; who abhor idols, and commit sacrilege; who make your boast of the law and the pontificate, and through breaking the law dishonor God, the true pontiff."[129]

But if the Roman people through excess of wealth lost the well-known quality of true Romans; if Solomon likewise fell into idolatry through the love of women; should we not recognize that the same thing happens in the case of a supreme pontiff and the other clergy? And should we then think that God would have permitted Sylvester to accept an occasion of sin? I will not suffer this injustice to be done that most holy man, I will not allow this affront to be offered that most excellent pontiff, that he should be said to have accepted empires, kingdoms, provinces, things which those who wish to enter the clergy are wont, indeed, to renounce. Little did Sylvester possess, little also the other holy pontiffs, those men whose presence was inviolable even among enemies, as Leo's presence overawed and broke down the wild soul of the barbarian king, which the strength of Rome had not availed to break down nor overawe.[130] But recent supreme pontiffs, that is, those having riches and pleasures in abundance, seem to work hard to make themselves just as impious and foolish as those early pontiffs were

---

129. Free quotations from *Rom.* ii, 21-24.
130. A reference to the well-known interview in which Leo I persuaded Attila to desist from his invasion of Italy.

wise and holy, and to extinguish the lofty praises of those men by every possible infamy. Who that calls himself a Christian can calmly bear this?

However, in this my first discourse I do not wish to urge princes and peoples to restrain the Pope in his unbridled course as he roams about, and compel him to stay within bounds, but only to warn him, and perhaps he has already learned the truth, to betake himself from others' houses to his own, and to put to port before the raging billows and savage tempests. But if he refuses, then I will have recourse to another discourse far bolder than this.[131] If only I may sometime see, and indeed I can scarcely wait to see it, especially if it is brought about by my counsel, if only I may see the time when the Pope is the vicar of Christ alone, and not of Caesar also! If only there would no longer be heard the fearful cry, "Partisans for the Church," "Partisans against the Church," "The Church against the Perugians," "against the Bolognese"! It is not the church, but the Pope, that fights against Christians; the church fights against "spiritual wickedness in high places."[132] Then the Pope will be the Holy Father in fact as well as in name, Father of all, Father of the church; nor will he stir up wars among Christians, but those stirred up by others he, through his apostolic judgment and papal prerogative, will stop.[133]

---

131. This other discourse did not appear.
132. *Eph.* vi, 12.
133. The *MS, Cod. Vat. Lat.* 5314, on which this translation is based, was finished December 7, 1451.

Appendix B

The Vatican Decree of 1870

IN HIS 1867 essay, "The Next General Council," published three years before the Council convened in 1870, Lord Acton commented:

> It is more profitable to study the consequences than to estimate the chances of success [of a Council's issuing a decree of papal infallibility]. A decree proclaiming the Pope infallible would be a confession that the authority of General Councils has been an illusion and a virtual usurpation from the first; so that having come to the knowledge of their own superfluousness, and having directed the Church into the way she ought always to have followed, they could only abolish themselves for the future by an act of suicide. It would invest, by its retrospective action, not the Pope and his successors only, but all his legitimate predecessors, with the same immunity. The objects of faith would be so vastly increased by the incorporation of the Bullarium, that the limits would become indistinct by distance. The responsibility for the acts of the buried and repented past would come back at once and forever, with a crushing weight on the Church. Specters it has taken ages of sorrowful effort to lay would come forth once more. The Bulls which imposed a belief in the deposing power, the Bulls which prescribed the tortures and kindled the flames of the Inquisition, the Bulls which erected witchcraft into a system and made the extermination of witches a frightful reality, would become as venerable as the decrees of Nicaea, as incontrovertible as the writings of S. Luke. The decision of every tribunal (by the decretal *Novit*) would be made subject to the revision of the Pope, and the sentences of every Protestant judge (by the Bull *Cum ex apostolatus officio*) would be invalid. The priesthood would be, by Divine right, exempt from all secular allegiance; and the supreme authority over all States would revert to the Holy See – for thus it stands in the Bull *Unam Sanctam*, repeated by Leo X in the Fifth Council of Lateran. Catholics would be bound, by order of Innocent III, to obey all the laws of Deuteronomy.

A successor of Alexander VI might distribute the New World over again; and the right by which Adrian disposed of Ireland would enable another Pope to barter it for a Concordat with America, or to exchange Great Britain for a French garrison. The assurance by which the Church has obtained her freedom would be revoked; and the survivor of the Irish bishops who signed the Declaration of 1826 would discover that he had deceived his country by false representations. The Church would take the place of a moon, reflecting passively the light which the Pope receives directly from Heaven, but liable to be left in total darkness, sometimes for three years together, during the vacancy of the Holy See, and during much longer periods of schism, when she knows not her rightful head. And as the Pope's decisions would be, not a testimony of the existing faith of the Church, but a result of his own enlightenment by the Holy Ghost, his interpretation and application of Scripture would be also infallible, the dogma could not be separated from the proofs, and the arguments of the mediaeval Bulls would become a norm for theology.... Rome has before now insisted on opinions which set a barrier to conversions and supplied a motive for persecution. The preservation of authority is a higher object than the propagation of faith. The advocates of Roman views are more used to controversy with their fellow Catholics than with Protestants. Their first aspiration is to suppress divisions of opinions within the Church; and this object could not be achieved more effectually than by converting the Vatican into a sort of Catholic Delphi.[1]

In a letter to the Archbishop of Munich, the foremost Roman Catholic historian in Germany, Ignaz von Döllinger, denounced the Vatican Decrees:

[The Pope's] authority is unlimited, incalculable; it can strike, as Innocent III says, wherever sin is; it can punish every one; it allows no appeal and is itself Sovereign Caprice; for the Pope carries, according to the expression of Boniface VIII, all rights in the Shrine of his breast. As he has now become infallible, he can by the use of the little word, "orbi," (which means that he turns himself round to the whole Church) make every rule, every doctrine, every demand, into a certain and incontestable article of Faith. No right can stand against him, no personal or corporate liberty; or as the Canonists put it – "The tribunal of God and of the pope is one and the same." This system bears its Roman origin on

---

1. "The Next General Council," *Chronicle,* July 13, 1867, 369-370; as quoted in MacDougall, *The Acton-Newman Relations.* New York: Fordham University Press, 1962.

its brow, and will never be able to force its way in German lands. As a Christian, as a Theologian, as a Reader of history, as a Citizen, I cannot accept this doctrine; for it is irreconcilable with the spirit of the Gospel, and with the clear declaration of Christ and the Apostles; it wishes directly to set up the kingdom of this world which Christ declined; it covets the Lordship over the Churches which Peter forbade to all and to himself. Not as a Theologian; for the whole, genuine tradition of the Church stands in irreconcilable opposition to it. Not as a Reader of history can I accept it; for as such, I know that the persistent striving to realize this theory of world domination, has cost Europe rivers of blood, has distracted and desolated whole countries, has torn to pieces the beautiful, organic constitution of the ancient Church, and had engendered, nourished, and maintained the worst ecclesiastical abuses. Finally, as a Citizen, I must beckon it away from me; because by its claims to the prostration of States and Monarchs and the whole political order of things under the authority of the Pope, and by the privileged position which it demands for the Clergy, it lays the foundation for an endless and destructive schism between Church and State, between Cleric and Layman. For I cannot conceal from myself, that this Dogma, among the consequences of which, the old German empire was destroyed, would, were it to become dominant in the Catholic section of the German nation, immediately also plant, in the new Empire, which has just been established, the germ of an incurable disorder.[2]

2. Ignaz von Döllinger, *A Letter Addressed to the Archbishop of Munich*. London, 1871; as quoted in MacDougall, *The Acton-Newman Relations*, Fordham University Press, 119-120.

Bibliography

Abbott, Leonard Dalton, editor. *Masterworks of Economics – Digests of 10 Great Classics.* Doubleday, 1946.

Abell, Aaron I. *American Catholicism and Social Action: A Search for Social Justice, 1865-1950.* University of Notre Dame Press, 1963.

Abell, Aaron I. "The Reception of Leo XIII's Labor Encyclical in America, 1891-1919," *The Review of Politics,* October 1945.

Acton, Lord. *Essays on Church and State.* Douglas Woodruff, editor. The Viking Press, 1953.

Andelson, Robert V. and James M. Dawsey. *From Wasteland to Promised Land: Liberation Theology for a Post-Marxist World.* Orbis Books, 1992.

Aretin, Karl Otmar von. *The Papacy and the Modern World.* Roland Hill, translator. McGraw-Hill, 1970.

Augustina (Ray), Sister Mary. *American Opinion of Roman Catholicism in the Eighteenth Century.* Octagon Books [1936] 1974.

Bauer, P. T. *Dissent on Development.* Revised edition. Harvard University Press, 1979.

Bauer, P. T. "Ecclesiastical Economics Is Envy Exalted," *This World,* Winter-Spring 1982, 56- 69.

Bauer, P. T. *Equality, the Third World, and Economic Delusion.* Harvard University Press, 1981.

Bauer, P. T. *Reality and Rhetoric – Studies in the Economics of Development.* Harvard University Press, 1984.

Belli, Humberto and Ronald Nash. *Beyond Liberation Theology.* Baker Book House, 1992.

Bendix, Reinhard and Guenther Roth. *Scholarship and Partisanship: Essays on Max Weber.* University of California Press, 1971.

Binchy, D. A. *Church and State in Fascist Italy.* Oxford University Press [1941] 1970.

Blakeney, R. P. *Manual of Romish Controversy, Being a Refutation of the Creed of Pope Pius IV.* The Hope Trust, 1851.

Blakeney, R. P. *Popery in Its Social Aspect, Being a Complete Exposure of the Immorality and Intolerance of Romanism*. George M'Gibbon, 1854.
Blanshard, Paul. *Communism, Democracy and Catholic Power*. Beacon Press, 1951.
Blanshard, Paul. *Freedom and Catholic Power in Spain and Portugal: An American Interpretation*. Beacon Press, 1962.
Block, Walter, Geoffrey Brennan, and Kenneth Elzinga, editors. *Morality of the Market: Religious and Economic Perspectives*. The Fraser Institute, 1985.
Block, Walter and Irving Hexham, editors. *Religion, Economics and Social Thought*. The Fraser Institute, 1986.
Boettner, Loraine. *Roman Catholicism*. Presbyterian and Reformed Publishing Company, 1962.
Bokenkotter, Thomas. *Church and Revolution: Catholics in the Struggle for Democracy and Social Justice*. Doubleday/Image, 1998.
Broderick, Francis L. *Right Reverend New Dealer*. Macmillan, 1963.
Brodrick, James. *The Economic Morals of the Jesuits: An Answer to Dr. H. M. Robertson*. 1934.
Brown, Robert McAfee. *Gustavo Gutierrez: An Introduction to Liberation Theology*. Orbis Books, 1990.
Bury, J. B. *History of the Papacy in the Nineteenth Century: Liberty and Authority in the Roman Catholic Church*. R. H. Murray, editor. Schocken Books [1930] 1964.
Calvez, Jean-Yves, S. J. *The Social Thought of John XXIII*. George J. M. McKenzie, translator. Greenwood Press [1965] 1977.
Cameron, Rondo, *A Concise Economic History of the World, from Paleolithic Times to the Present*. Second edition. Oxford University Press, 1993.
Canterbery, E. Ray. *The Literate Economist: A Brief History of Economics*. Harper Collins, 1995.
Catechism of the Catholic Church. Liguori Publications, 1994.
Chafuen, Alejandro Antonio. *Christians for Freedom: Late-Scholastic Economics*. Ignatius Press, 1986.
Charles, Rodger, S.J. *The Social Teaching of Vatican II: Its Origin and Development*. Ignatius Press, 1982.
Christiansen, Drew, S. J. and Walter Grazer, editors. *And God Saw That It Was Good. Catholic Theology and the Environment*. United States Catholic Conference, 1996.

Christman, Henry M., editor. *Communism in Action: A Documentary History.* Bantam Books, 1969.
Coleman, John and Gregory Baum. *Rerum Novarum: One Hundred Years of Catholic Social Teaching.* SCM Press, 1991.
Congregation for the Doctrine of the Faith (Franjo Cardinal Seper, prefect). *In Defense of the Catholic Doctrine on the Church (Mysterium Ecclesiae).* N. C. News Service translation. St. Paul Books and Media. June 24, 1973.
Congregation for the Doctrine of the Faith (Joseph Cardinal Ratzinger, prefect). *Instruction on Christian Freedom and Liberation.* Reprinted with permission from *L'Osservatore Romano.* Daughters of St. Paul. March 22, 1986.
Congregation for the Doctrine of the Faith (Joseph Cardinal Ratzinger, prefect). *Letter to Bishops of the Catholic Church on the Pastoral Care of Homosexual Persons.* Authorized Vatican translation. Ignatius Press, 1987 [October 1, 1986].
Coriden, James, Thomas J. Green, and Donald E. Heintschel, editors. *The Code of Canon Law: A Text and Commentary.* Paulist Press, 1985.
Cort, John C. *Christian Socialism.* Orbis Books, 1988.
Coulton, G. C. *Inquisition and Liberty.* Peter Smith [1938] 1969.
Dawson, Christopher. *Religion and the Modern State,* 1936.
Delpech, Jacques. *The Oppression of Protestants in Spain.* Beacon Press, 1955.
Dipboye, Carolyn Cook. "The Roman Catholic Church and the Political Struggle for Human Rights in Latin America, 1968-1980," *Journal of Church and State,* Volume 24, Autumn 1982, 497-524.
Dollene, Charles J., James K. McGowan, and James J. McGivern, editors. *The Catholic Tradition.* Fourteen volumes. McGrath Publishing Company, 1979.
Döllinger, J. H. Ignaz von. *The Pope and the Council.* London, 1869.
Dorrien, Gary J. *Reconstructing the Common Good: Theology and the Social Order.* Orbis Books, 1990.
Eire, Carlos M. N. *War Against the Idols: The Reformation of Worship from Erasmus to Calvin.* Cambridge University Press, 1986.
Eisenstadt, S. N. *The Protestant Ethic and Modernization: A Comparative View.* Basic Books, 1968.
Empie, Paul C. and T. Austin Murphy. *Papal Primacy and the Universal Church.* Augsburg Publishing House, 1974.

BIBLIOGRAPHY

Evangelauf, Jean. "Catholic U. Professor, Barred from Teaching Theology, Vows to Fight," *The Chronicle of Higher Education*, September 3, 1986, 44-47.

Fanfani, Amintore. *Catholicism, Protestantism and Capitalism*. University of Notre Dame Press [1934] 1984.

Flood, Charles Bracelen. *Hitler: The Path to Power*. Houghton Mifflin Company, 1989.

Fuellenbach, John. *Ecclesiastical Office and the Primacy of Rome*. The Catholic University of America Press, 1980.

Gardiner, Harold C., S. J. *Catholic Viewpoint on Censorship*. Revised edition. Image Books, 1961.

Genovese, Eugene D. "Secularism in the General Crisis of Capitalism," *The American Journal of Jurisprudence*, Notre Dame Law School, Natural Law Institute, Volume 42, 1997, 195-210.

Gierke, Otto von. *Political Theories of the Middle Age*. Translated by F. W. Maitland. Beacon Press [1900] 1959.

Goldhagen, Daniel Jonah. *Hitler's Willing Executioners: Ordinary Germans and the Holocaust*. Alfred A. Knopf, 1996.

Green, Robert W. editor. *Protestantism, Capitalism, and Social Science: The Weber Thesis Controversy*. Second edition. D. C. Heath, 1973.

Groethuysen, Bernard. *The Bourgeois: Catholicism vs. Capitalism in Eighteenth-Century France*. Mary Ilford, translator. Holt, Rinehart and Winston [1927] 1968.

Gutierrez, Gustavo. *The Truth Shall Make You Free*. Orbis Books [1986] 1991.

Hanson, Eric O. *The Catholic Church in World Politics*. Princeton University Press [1987] 1990.

Hayek, Friedrich A., editor. *Capitalism and the Historians*. University of Chicago Press, 1964.

Hayek, Friedrich A. *Law, Legislation and Liberty*. Three volumes. University of Chicago Press, 1976.

Hengel, Martin. *Property and Riches in the Early Church: Aspects of a Social History of Early Christianity*. Fortress Press [1973] 1974.

Hennesey, James. *American Catholics: A History of the Roman Catholic Community in the United States*. Oxford University Press, 1981.

Himmelfarb, Gertrude. *Lord Acton: A Study in Conscience and Politics*. University of Chicago Press [1952] 1962.

Hollis, Christopher, editor. *The Papacy: An Illustrated History from St. Peter to Paul VI.* Macmillan, 1964.
Hudson, Henry T. *Papal Power: Its Origins and Development.* Evangelical Press, 1981.
Hunt, Dave. *A Woman Rides the Beast.* Harvest House Publishers, 1994.
Hunt, E. K. *History of Economic Thought.* Second edition. Harper Collins, 1992.
Hutchison, Robert. *Their Kingdom Come: Inside the Secret World of Opus Dei.* St. Martin's Press, 1997.
Hunt, E. K. *Property and Prophets: The Evolution of Economic Institutions and Ideologies.* Harper Collins, 1995.
John XXIII. *On Christianity and Social Progress (Mater et Magistra).* NWCW translation. Daughters of St. Paul. May 15, 1961.
John XXIII. *Peace on Earth (Pacem in Terris).* NCWC translation. Daughters of St. Paul. April 11, 1963.
John Paul II. *The Ecological Crisis: A Common Responsibility.* January 1, 1990 [December 8, 1989]. United States Catholic Conference.
John Paul II. *The Encyclicals of John Paul II.* J. Michael Miller, editor. Our Sunday Visitor, 1996.
John Paul II. *On Human Work (Laborem Exercens).* Vatican translation. Daughters of St. Paul. September 14, 1981.
John Paul II. *On Social Concern (Sollicitudo Rei Socialis).* Vatican translation. Daughters of St. Paul. December 30, 1987.
John Paul II and Joseph Cardinal Ratzinger. *Catechism of the Catholic Church.* Libreria Editrice Vaticana. Liguori Publications, 1994.
Johnson, Paul. *Modern Times: The World from the Twenties to the Eighties.* Harper and Row, 1983.
Joseph de Arriaga, Pablo. *The Extirpation of Idolatry in Peru.* L. Clark Keating, translator. University of Kentucky Press, 1968.
Kelly, J. N. D. *The Oxford Dictionary of Popes.* Oxford University Press [1986] 1996.
Kent, Peter C. *The Pope and the Duce: The International Impact of the Lateran Agreements.* St. Martin's Press, 1981.
Kerr, William Shaw. *A Handbook on the Papacy.* Marshall, Morgan and Scott, 1950.
Krieger, David J. *The New Universalism: Foundations for a Global Theology.* Orbis Books, 1991.
Laquer, Walter. *Fascism: Past, Present, Future.* Oxford University Press, 1996.

BIBLIOGRAPHY

Lea, Henry Charles. *A History of the Inquisition of Spain*. Four volumes. AMS Press [1905] 1966.

Lee, Martin A. "Who Are the Knights of Malta?" *National Catholic Reporter*, October 4, 1983, 1, 5-8, 24.

Leo XIII. *On the Condition of the Working Classes (Rerum Novarum)*. NCWC translation. Daughters of St. Paul. May 15, 1891.

Leo XIII. *On the Restoration of Christian Philosophy (Aeterna Patris)*. Catholic World translation. Daughters of St Paul. August 4, 1879.

Lewy, Guenther. *The Catholic Church and Nazi Germany*. McGraw Hill, 1964.

Llorente, Juan Antonio. *A Critical History of the Inquisition of Spain*. John Lilburne Company [1826] 1966.

Lo Bello, Nino. *The Vatican Empire*. Simon and Shuster, 1969.

Lo Bello, Nino. *The Vatican Papers*. New English Library, 1981.

Lo Bello, Nino. *Vatican, U.S.A.* Trident Press, 1972.

MacDougall, Hugh. *The Acton-Newman Relations: The Dilemma of Christian Liberalism*. Fordham University Press, 1962.

MacGregor, Geddes. *The Vatican Revolution*. Macmillan, 1958.

Manchester, William. *A World Lit Only by Fire: The Medieval Mind and the Renaissance: Portrait of an Age*. Little, Brown, and Company, 1993.

Manhattan, Avro. *The Vatican's Holocaust*. Ozark Books, 1986.

Mantoux, Paul. *The Industrial Revolution in the Eighteenth Century*. Revised edition. Harper and Row, 1961.

Maritain, Jacques. *St. Thomas Aquinas*. Meridian Books [1931] 1958.

Marshall, Charles. "An Open Letter to the Honorable Alfred E. Smith, a Question That Needs an Answer." *Atlantic Monthly*, April 1927.

Marshall, Gordon. *In Search of the Spirit of Capitalism. An Essay on Max Weber's Protestant Ethic Thesis*. Columbia University Press, 1982.

Martin, David. *Tongues of Fire: The Explosion of Protestantism in Latin America*. Basil Blackwell, 1990.

Martin, Malachi. *The Decline and Fall of the Roman Church*. G. P. Putnam's Sons, 1981.

Martin, Malachi. *The Jesuits: The Society of Jesus and the Betrayal of the Roman Catholic Church*. Simon and Shuster, 1987.

Martin, Malachi. *Rich Church, Poor Church*. G. P. Putnam's Sons, 1984.

Marx, Karl and Friedrich Engels. *The Communist Manifesto*. Washington Square Press [1848] 1964.

Maryknoll. April 1987.

Maxwell, John Francis. *Slavery and the Catholic Church: The History of Catholic Teaching Concerning the Moral Legitimacy of the Institution of Slavery.* Barry Rose Publishers, 1975.

McCarthy, George E. and Royal W. Rhodes. *Eclipse of Justice: Ethics, Economics, and the Lost Traditions of American Catholicism.* Orbis Books, 1992.

Mecham, J. Lloyd. *Church and State in Latin America: A History of Politico-Ecclesiastical Relations.* University of North Carolina Press, 1934.

Minerbi, Sergio. *The Vatican and Zionism: Conflict in the Holy Land, 1895-1925.* Oxford University Press, 1990.

Mises, Ludwig von. *The Anti-Capitalistic Mentality.* D.Van Nostrand, 1956.

Mises, Ludwig von. *Human Action: A Treatise on Economics.* Third edition. Henry Regnery, 1966.

Mises, Ludwig von. *Socialism: An Economic and Sociological Analysis.* Liberty Fund [1922] 1981.

Monroe, Arthur Eli, editor. *Early Economic Thought: Selections from Economic Literature Prior to Adam Smith.* Harvard University Press [1924] 1930.

Moore, Edmund A. *A Catholic Runs for President: the Campaign of 1928.* Ronald Press Company, 1956.

Morris, Charles R. *American Catholics: The Saints and Sinners Who Built America's Most Powerful Church.* Random House/Vintage [1997] 1998.

Nash, Ronald, editor. *Liberation Theology.* Mott Media, 1984.

National Conference of Catholic Bishops. *Contemporary Catholic Social Teaching,* 1991.

National Conference of Catholic Bishops. *Economic Justice for All, Pastoral Letter on Catholic Social Teaching and the U.S. Economy,* 1986.

National Conference of Catholic Bishops, Ad Hoc Committee on Biblical Fundamentalism. *A Pastoral Statement for Catholics on Biblical Fundamentalism.* March 26, 1987.

Nichols, Peter. *The Pope's Divisions: The Roman Catholic Church Today.* Holt, Rinehart and Winston, 1981.

Norman, E. R. *Anti-Catholicism in Victorian England.* Barnes and Noble, 1968.

North, Douglass C. and Robert Paul Thomas. *The Rise of the Western World: A New Economic History.* Cambridge University Press, 1973.

Novak, Michael, editor. *Capitalism and Socialism: A Theological Inquiry.* American Enterprise Institute, 1979.

Novak, Michael. *The Catholic Ethic and the Spirit of Capitalism.* The Free Press, 1993.
Novak, Michael. editor. *The Denigration of Capitalism: Six Points of View.* American Enterprise Institute, 1979.
Novak, Michael. *Will It Liberate? Questions About Liberation Theology.* Paulist Press, 1986.
O'Brien, David J. *Public Catholicism.* Second edition, Orbis Books, 1996.
Oldenbourg, Zoe. *Massacre at Montségur: A History of the Albigensian Crusade.* Orion House [1961] 1998.
Ostling, Richard N. *Secrecy in the Church: A Reporter's Case for the Christian's Right to Know.* Harper and Row, 1974.
Paul VI. *The Coming Eightieth (Octogesima Adveniens).* Vatican translation. Daughters of St Paul. May 14, 1971.
Paul VI. *Declaration on Religious Freedom (Dignitatis Humanae)* NCWC translation. Daughters of St. Paul. December 7, 1965.
Paul VI. *On the Development of Peoples (Populorum Progressio).* NCWC translation. Daughters of St. Paul. March 26, 1967.
Paul VI. *Of Human Life (Humanae Vitae).* NC News Service translation. Daughters of St. Paul. July 25, 1968.
Phillipps, Ernest. *Papal Merchandise.* Charles J. Thynne.
Pichon, Charles. *The Vatican and Its Role in World Affairs.* Greenwood Press [1950] 1969.
Pius XI. *On Atheistic Communism.* Official Vatican text. Daughters of St. Paul. March 19, 1937.
Pius XI. *On Social Reconstruction (Quadragesimo Anno).* Official Vatican text. Daughters of St. Paul. May 15, 1931.
Pius XII. *Concerning Some False Opinions which Threaten to Undermine the Foundations of Catholic Doctrine (Humani Generis).* NCWC translation. Daughters of St. Paul. August 12, 1950.
Pius XII. *On the Function of the State in the Modern World.* Official Vatican text. Daughters of St. Paul. October 20, 1939.
Pontifical Biblical Commission. *The Interpretation of the Bible in the Church.* Libreria Editrice Vaticana text. Preface by Joseph Cardinal Ratzinger. United States Catholic Conference. January 1996 [1993].
Pontifical Commission Justice and Peace. Commentary on *Justice in the World*, by Philip Land (*An Overview*); Pedro Arrupe (*Witnessing to Justice*); Juan Alfaro (*Theology of Justice in the World);* Mary Linscott (*Educa-*

tion and Justice); Barbara Ward (*A New Creation? Reflections on the Environmental Issue*).Vatican City, 1971.

Pope Speaks, The: The Church Documents Bimonthly. Our Sunday Visitor Publishing.

Pullan, Brian. *The Jews of Europe and the Inquisition of Venice, 1550-1670.* Barnes and Noble, 1983.

Rand, Ayn. *Capitalism: The Unknown Ideal.* Signet, 1967.

Rand, Ayn. *Ayn Rand's Marginalia*. Robert Mayhew, editor. Second Renaissance Books, 1995.

Rauschenbusch, Walter. *The Righteousness of the Kingdom*. Max L. Stackhouse, editor. Abingdon Press, 1968.

Reese, Thomas J. *Inside the Vatican: The Politics and Organization of the Catholic Church*. Harvard University Press, 1996.

Rhodes, Anthony. *The Power of Rome in the Twentieth Century*. Franklin Watts, 1983.

Rhodes, Anthony. *The Vatican in the Age of the Dictators, 1922-1945.* Hodder and Stoughton, 1973.

Ridley, Francis A. *The Papacy and Fascism: The Crisis of the Twentieth Century*. Martin, Secker, Warburg [1937] 1973.

Robbins, John, editor. *Against the World: The Trinity Review 1978-1988.* The Trinity Foundation, 1996.

Robbins, John. *Without a Prayer: Ayn Rand and the Close of Her System.* The Trinity Foundation, 1997.

Rommen, Heinrich A. *The State in Catholic Thought*. Greenwood Press [1945] 1969.

Rosenberg, Nathan and L. E. Birdzell, Jr. *How the West Grew Rich: The Economic Transformation of the Industrial World*. Basic Books, 1986.

Rottenberg, Simon, editor. *The Economics of Legal Minimum Wages.* American Enterprise Institute, 1981.

Rummel, R. J. *Death by Government*. Transaction Publishers, 1995.

Ryan, John A. *Questions of the Day*. Books for Libraries Press [1931] 1967.

Sacred Congregation for the Doctrine of the Faith, Joseph Cardinal Ratzinger, Prefect. *Instruction on Certain Aspects of the "Theology of Liberation."* Vatican translation. Daughters of St. Paul, 1984.

Samuelsson, Kurt. *Religion and Economic Action: A Critique of Max Weber.* E. Geoffrey French, translator. Harper Torchbooks [1957] 1961.

Sandoz, Ellis. Editor. *Political Sermons of the American Founding Era, 1730-1805*. Liberty Fund, 1991.

Schaeffer, Franky, editor. *Is Capitalism Christian?* Crossway Books, 1985.

Schuettinger, Robert L. and Eamonn F. Butler. *Forty Centuries of Wage and Price Controls.* The Heritage Foundation, 1979.

Schumpeter, Joseph A. *History of Economic Analysis*. Elizabeth Boody Schumpeter, editor. Oxford University Press, 1954.

Schumpeter, Joseph A. *Ten Great Economists – From Marx to Keynes.* Oxford University Press [1951] 1969.

Second General Assembly of the Synod of Bishops. *Synodal Document on Justice in the World*. Approved by the Holy See. Daughters of St. Paul. November 30, 1971.

Second Vatican Council. *The Conciliar and Post Conciliar Documents. Volume 1*. Austin Flannery, editor. Revised edition. Costello Publishing Company and Dominican Publications [1975] 1996.

Second Vatican Council, with Pope Paul VI. *Constitution on the Church (Lumen Gentium)*. November 21, 1964.

Second Vatican Council, with Pope Paul VI. *Pastoral Constitution on the Church in the Modern World (Gaudium et Spes)*. December 7, 1965. United States Catholic Conference, 1996.

Segundo, Juan Luis, S. J. *The Liberation of Dogma: Faith, Revelation and Dogmatic Teaching Authority*. Orbis Books [1989] 1992.

Segundo, Juan Luis. *Signs of the Times: Theological Reflections*. Orbis Books, 1993.

Sellar, Robert. *The Tragedy of Quebec: The Expulsion of Its Protestant Farmers*. Third edition. Books for Libraries Press [1907] 1972.

Sigmund, Paul. *Liberation Theology at the Crossroads*. Oxford University Press, 1989.

Sirico, Robert A. "Catholicism's Developing Social Teaching," *The Freeman*, December 1991, 462-474.

Smith, Adam. *An Inquiry into the Nature and Causes of the Wealth of Nations*. The Modern Library, 1937.

Spiegel, Henry William. *The Growth of Economic Thought*. Revised edition. Duke University Press, 1983.

Stelzle, Charles, Jane Addams, Charles P. Neill, Graham Taylor, and George P. Eckman. *The Social Application of Religion*. Jennings and Graham, 1908.

Strayer, Joseph R. *The Albigensian Crusades.* The University of Michigan Press [1971] 1992.
Thomas Aquinas. *Aquinas: Selected Political Writings.* A. P. D'Entrèves, editor. Basil Blackwell [1959] 1970.
Thomas Aquinas. *Basic Writings of Thomas Aquinas.* Anton C. Pegis, editor. Random House, 1945.
Thomas Aquinas. *The Political Ideas of St. Thomas Aquinas.* Dino Bigongiari, editor. Hafner Publishing Company, 1953.
Thomas Aquinas. *St. Thomas Aquinas on Politics and Ethics.* Paul Sigmund, editor. W. W. Norton and Company, 1988.
Thompson, R. W. *The Footprints of the Jesuits.* New York, 1894.
Tierney, Brian. *The Crisis of Church and State, 1050-1300.* Prentice-Hall, 1964.
Tonsor, Stephen J. "The View from London Bridge," *New Individualist Review,* Summer 1965.
Trevor-Roper, H. R. *The European Witch-Craze of the Sixteenth and Seventeenth Centuries and Other Essays.* Harper and Row, 1969.
Troeltsch, Ernst. *Protestantism and Progress: A Historical Study of the Relation of Protestantism to the Modern World.* W. Montgomery, translator. Beacon Press [1912] 1958.
Troeltsch, Ernst. *The Social Teaching of the Christian Churches (Die sozialen Lehren der christlichen Kirchen und Gruppen).* Olive Wyon, translator. Two volumes. G. Allen and Unwin and Macmillan [1931] 1949.
Ullmann, Walter. *A Short History of the Papacy in the Middle Ages.* Methuen and Company, 1972.
United States Catholic Conference. *A Framework for Comprehensive Health Care Reform: Protecting Human Life, Promoting Human Dignity, Pursuing the Common Good.* United States Catholic Conference, June 18, 1993.
United States Catholic Conference. *Principles for Educational Reform in the United States,* 1995.
United States Catholic Conference. *Renewing the Earth: An Invitation to Reflection and Action on Environment in Light of Catholic Social Teaching,* 1992.
United States Catholic Conference. *U. S. Bishops' Statement on Capital Punishment.* November 1980.
Valla, Lorenzo. *The Treatise of Lorenzo Valla and the Donation of Constantine.* Christopher B. Coleman, translator. Russell and Russell [1922] 1971.

Valladares, Armando. *Against All Hope: The Prison Memoirs of Armando Valladares.* Alfred A. Knopf, 1987.

Van Dyke, Joseph S. *Popery the Foe of the Church and of the Republic.* Second edition. I. K. Funk and Company, 1871.

Viner, Jacob. *Religious Thought and Economic Society.* Jacques Melitz and Donald Wick, editors. Duke University Press, 1978.

Webber, Carolyn and Aaron Wildavsky. *A History of Taxation and Expenditure in the Western World.* Simon and Shuster, 1986.

Weber, Max. *The Protestant Ethic and the Spirit of Capitalism* (*Die protestantische Ethik und der Geist des Kapitalismus*). Charles Scribner's Sons [1905] 1958. The essay originally appeared in *Archiv für Sozialwissenschaft und Sozialpolitik,* volumes XX and XXI.

Webster, William. *The Church of Rome at the Bar of History.* The Banner of Truth Trust, 1995.

Yates, Gerard F. editor. *Papal Thought on the State: Excerpts from Encyclicals and Other Writings of Recent Popes.* Appleton-Century Crofts, 1958.

Zacchello, Joseph. *Secrets of Romanism.* Loizeaux Brothers, 1948.

Zahn, Gordon C. *German Catholics and Hitler's Wars.* University of Notre Dame Press [1962] 1989.

Index

Aaron 228, 250, 258
Abbott, Lyman 81
Abel 136
Abell, Aaron I. 44, 47, 81-84, 103, 164; Works: *American Catholicism and Social Action: A Search for Social Justice, 1865-1950* 64, 81, 83, 84, 103, 164; "The Reception of Leo XIII's Labor Encyclical in America, 1891-1919" 44, 47, 82, 84, 103
Abiram 250
Abraham 19, 256
Academe 10
accuracy of the Bible 158
Accursius 264
Achilles 282
acquisition 50
activism 19
Acton Institute 95, 149
Acton, Lord (John Emerich Edward Dalberg) 102, 111-113, 116, 117, 166, 172, 181, 195, 285; Works: *History of Freedom* 102; "The Next General Council" 285-286
Acton-Newman Relations, The (MacDougall) 102, 113, 286-287
Acts of Sylvester 271
Adrian 286
Aeneid (Virgil) 241, 243
Aeterna Patris, On the Restoration of Christian Philosophy (Leo XIII) 126-127

Africa 30, 211, 247
Against All Hope: The Prison Memoirs of Armando Valladares 177
Against the World: The Trinity Review 1978-1988 (Robbins) 128
Agamemnon 282
aggiornamento 77
aggression 134, 174
Ahasuerus 219
Albigenses 134
Albigensian Crusades, The (Strayer) 134
Alexander 218, 259, 268
Alexander III 134, 137
Alexander VI 286
Alexandria 211, 245
Alexius of Constantinople 120
Almagest (Ptolemy) 123
Ambrose 33
American Catholicism and Social Action: A Search for Social Justice, 1865-1950 (Abell) 64, 81, 83, 84, 103, 164
American Economic Association 83
American Journal of Jurisprudence, The 43
Americans with Disabilities Act 89
Ammonites 279
Amphictyony 278
anathema 214
Andreski, Stanislav 12-13, 16, 17, 73
Angleton, James Jesus 190
animals 139
Anschluss 162, 165

INDEX

Anselm 204
anthropology 128
anti-capitalism 30, 197
anti-communism 197
anti-Judaism 197
anti-Semitism 67, 174, 197
Antichrist 115-116
Antioch 211, 245
Antiochus 281
Apocrypha 220, 268
Apollinaris 268
apologetics 127
Apology (Tertullian) 242
apostates 133
apostles 117
Apostolic Letter on the Coming Eightieth; see *Octogesima Adveniens*
Aretin, Karl Otmar von 102, 164, 184; Works: *The Papacy and the Modern World* 103, 164, 184
Argentina 161
aristocracy 44, 50
Aristophanes 33; Works: *Ecclesiazusae* 33
Aristotle 29-30, 52, 53, 127, 129, 139, 160; Works: *Politics* 52, 139
Arriaga, Pablo Joseph de 56; Works: *The Extirpation of Idolatry in Peru* 56
Ars Poetica (Horace) 253
asceticism 115
Asia 211, 247
assassination 113
AT&T 9
Atheistic Communism, On; see *Divini Redemptoris*
Attila 283
Augustine 130
Augustus 114, 266
Austria 162

avarice 216
Azariah 264

Bachem, Karl 163
Balkans 173
Banco dello Spirito Santo 21
banks 83
baptism 20
Barry, C. J. 121, 125; Works: *Readings in Church History* 121, 125
basic communities 79
Basic Writings of Thomas Aquinas 131, 133
Basil 33
Bauer, Peter T. 62, 98; Works: "Ecclesiastical Economics: Envy Legitimized" 63; "Ecclesiastical Economics Is Envy Exalted" 98; *Reality and Rhetoric: Studies in the Economics of Development* 63
Baum, Gregory 172; Works: *Rerum Novarum: One Hundred Years of Catholic Social Teaching* 172
Bavaria 163
Beecher, Henry Ward 81
beggarie 22
Bel and the Dragon 220, 268
Beliefs of Catholics (Knox) 184
Bellarmine 114
Benedict 275
Benedict XIV 137
Benedict XV 189
Berman, Harold 20, 23; Works: *The Interaction of Law and Religion* 20, 23
Bernard of Clairvaux 118-119
Berning 165
Bible 11, 17-18, 74, 129, 178, 182, 266; accuracy of 158; inerrancy 157-158; *see also* Scripture

301

Bigongiari, Dino 129; *Works: The Political Ideas of St. Thomas Aquinas* 129
Bill of Rights 14, 49
Binchy, D. A. 168; *Works: Church and State in Fascist Italy* 168
biology 128
bishops 16, 18, 160
Bishops' Program of Social Reconstruction 84, 103
Bismarck 163
Blanshard, Paul 175, 184; *Works: Freedom and Catholic Power in Spain and Portugal* 175, 184
blasphemy 112
Bohemia 134
Bolivia 56
Bolshevism 165
Boniface IX 280
Boniface VIII 124, 125, 275, 280, 286; *Works: Unam Sanctam* 124-125, 131, 285
Bonneau, Alcide 207
bourgeoisie 44-45, 51, 104
Bourgeoisie: Catholicism vs. Capitalism in Eighteenth-Century France, The (Groethuysen) 73
Brazil 12, 35, 51, 56
Brazilian Episcopal Conference 36
brigandage 53
British Broadcasting Company 170
Broderick, Francis L. 84; *Works: Right Reverend New Dealer* 84
brotherhood of man 69
Brunner 208, 257
Buchanan, Pat 46
Bullarium 285
Bush, George 47
business 51
businessmen 64, 66
Byzantia 213

Byzantium 205, 245

Caesar 117, 219, 224, 228, 231, 234, 250, 252, 253, 256, 263, 267, 274, 277, 284
Cajetan, Tommaso 36; *Works: Summa Theologica cum commentariis Thomae de Vio Cajetan* 37
calling 13, 16, 19, 22
Calvin, John 13, 21-22, 51, 67, 75, 97
Calvinism 22, 51, 75, 175
Canaan 248
Canaanites 248, 258
Canada 192
Canon Law 10, 93, 131-132, 138, 139, 147-148, 179, 182, 204
Canterbury, E. Ray 67; *Works: The Literate Economist* 67
capital 21
capitalism 12, 13, 29, 41, 43, 45, 46, 48, 49, 50, 52, 55, 56, 57, 58, 60, 61, 64, 66, 67, 72, 81, 83, 88, 91, 92, 95, 97, 98, 99, 101, 105, 106, 107, 142, 158, 172
Capitalism: The Unknown Ideal (Rand) 62, 70, 92, 195
Carter, Jimmy 46
Cassidy, Edward Idris 196-197
Castanho, Amaury 36
Castro, Fidel 175-177
casuistry 112
Catechism of the Catholic Church 131, 151, 153-156, 160, 188
Catholic Action 169, 190
Catholic Church and Nazi Germany, The (Lewy) 163, 165
Catholic Ethic and the Spirit of Capitalism, The (Novak) 49, 73, 95-96, 104
"Catholic U. Professor, Barred from Teaching Theology, Vows to Fight" (Evangelauf) 148

Catholic University of America 82, 148
Catholic Worker 82
Catholicae Ecclesiae (Leo XIII) 138
Catholicism, Protestantism, and Capitalism (Fanfani) 44, 72, 74-76
"Catholicism's Developing Social Teaching" (Sirico) 73, 82-83, 95-97, 101, 103-104, 149
"Catholics and Marxists" (Deas) 192
Catiline 282
Cato 243, 267
Cavalli 185
CELAM 78, 192
Celestine I 215, 275
celibacy 139
censorship 138, 174, 179, 182
Centesimus Annus (John Paul II) 95, 98-107
Central Intelligence Agency 189-190
Central Verein 84
centralization 152
Chaldeans 234
charity 20-21, 38, 63, 82, 104, 151, 193
Charlemagne 121-122
Chetnik 173
child labor 84
child labor law 103
children 84
Chile 12, 56
China 47, 173
Christian Century 64
Christian Constitution of States, The; see *Immortale Dei*
Christian Democratic Party 72, 184
Christian Democrats 190
Christian Education of Youth, On (Pius XI) 92
Christian Register 82
Christian Socialism (Cort) 64

Christian Union 81
Christian View of Men and Things, A (Clark) 160
Christianity 74, 81, 135, 175, 196, 204-205, 282
Christianity and Social Progress, On; see *Mater et Magistra*
Christman, Henry M. 156; Works: *Communism in Action: A Documentary History* 156
Chronicle 286
church and state 177, 191, 195, 287
Church and State in Latin America: A History of Politico-Ecclesiastical Relations (Mecham) 48, 92
Church History (Eusebius) 236
"Church's Flight into the Wilderness, The" (Sherwood) 136
Cicero 33, 242, 251
civil rights 14, 22
civilization 144
Clark, Gordon 128, 160; Works: *A Christian View of Men and Things* 160
class structure 101
class struggle 56, 101
class warfare 48
"Classical Social Doctrine in the Roman Catholic Church" (Sadowsky) 54
Claudius 224
Clement 275
clergy 212, 238, 249, 253-254, 256, 283, 287
Clinton, Bill 47
Code of Canon Law, A Text and Commentary, The (Coriden) 132
Codex Parisiensis Lat. 208
Codex Vaticanus 207
coercion 180-181
Coleman, Christopher B. 203-204, 220, 237, 241, 246, 267, 271-272;

303

Works: The Treatise of Lorenzo Valla on the Donation of Constantine 203-284
Coleman, John 172; *Works: Rerum Novarum: One Hundred Years of Catholic Social Teaching* 172
collectivism 96
Commentaries on the Laws of the Ancient Hebrews (Wines) 154
"Commentary on 'Ad Tuendam Fidem' " (Ratzinger) 148
Commission for Religious Relations with Jews 196
Committees for the Defense of the Revolution 176
Commodus 266
common good 42, 45, 58, 63-65, 69, 70, 74, 78, 80, 81, 90, 97, 151, 167, 187-188, 192-194, 198
common use of goods 41, 57, 89; *see also* community of goods, universal destination of goods
communications 87
Communism 10, 31, 38, 57, 61, 64, 83, 142, 157, 160, 164-165, 171, 174-177, 198
Communism and the Conscience of the West (Sheen) 57
Communism in Action: A Documentary History (Chistman) 156
Communist China 173
Communist Manifesto, The (Marx and Engels) 44, 45, 104
Communist Party 47, 190
community of goods 31, 35, 40
competition 54, 61, 66, 69, 74, 91, 193
compulsory arbitration 84
concentration of power 54
concentration of wealth 53, 66, 71
Concordat of 1929 165

concordats 165
Concordantia Catholica, De (Cusanus) 206
Condition of the Working Classes, On the; see *Rerum Novarum*
conditions of freedom 159
confession, auricular 17
confiscation 135
conflict 101
Congregation for Extraordinary Ecclesiastical Affairs 184
congregationalism 23
conscience 22, 145, 156
consent of the governed 23
Constantine 114-115, 117, 122-123, 208, 210, 216-217, 219-221, 225, 231-237, 240-248, 250-267, 271-275, 274-275, 277-279, 282
Constantine the Great and Christianity (Coleman) 204, 207, 208, 220, 237, 241, 246, 267, 271-272
Constantinople 117, 203, 209, 211, 245-246
Constantius 236
Constitution on Divine Revelation 158
constitutional capitalism 23-25
constitutional republicanism 183
constitutionalism 14, 75
contract 20, 22, 49, 193
Coriden, James 132; *Works: The Code of Canon Law* 132
Cornelius 270
corporate state 164
corporations 54
corporativism 72-76, 162
Corpus Iuris Canonici 207
Cort, John C. 64; *Works: Christian Socialism* 64
Coughlin, Charles 83
Council of Basle 235
Council of Pavia 139

INDEX

Council of the Seventy Bishops 238
Council of Toledo 139
Council of Trent 126, 131
councils 18, 30, 143, 285
Coundenhove-Kalergi, Count 175;
   Works: Crusade for Pan Europe 175
courage 215
Cowderoy, Cyril 136
creativity 20, 96
credit 67
credulity 279
Creighton, Mandell 111, 280; *Works:*
   History of the Papacy 280
crime 32, 36, 70, 111, 250, 283
criminal law 112
criminals 49
Crisis of Church and State, 1050-1300,
   The (Tierney) 117-120, 122-127
Croatia 30, 161-162, 169-170
crop rotation 75
Crusade for Pan Europe
   (Coundenhove-Kalergi) 175
Crusades 134
Cuba 175-176
"Culture Change and the Rise of
   Protestantism in Brazil and
   Chile" (Willems) 13
Cum ex apostolatus officio 285
Curley machine 46
Curran, Charles 148
curse of Cham 138
Curtius 269
Cusanus, Nicholas 206; *Works: De*
   Concordantia Catholica 206
Cyrus 219, 259

Dachau 171
Daley machine 46
Daniel 267-268
Dante 113; *Works: De Monarchia* 113;
   The Divine Comedy 113

Darius 240, 253
Dathan 250
David 255, 260-261, 276
Dawson, Christopher 161; *Works:*
   Religion and the Modern State 161
Day, Dorothy 82
deacons 18
Death by Government (Rummell) 173
debts 198
Decalogue 115, 240
deceptions 199
Declaration of 1826 286
Declaration on Religious Freedom
   (Paul VI) 180
Decretales (Innocent IV) 123
Decretales Pseudo-Isidorianae et
   Capitula Angiliamni (ed.
   Hinschius) 207
Decretals 118
Decretum (Gratian) 204, 207, 209-210,
   217, 241
Delpech, Jacques 178, 185; *Works:*
   The Oppression of Protestants in
   Spain 178, 185
Delphi 286
Delphic Oracle 15
democracy 103, 131, 163, 175, 183
demons 254, 258, 268-269
deport 172
Deusdedit 204
devil 213
diadem 212, 249, 250, 256
Dickens, Charles 12, 52
dictatorship 61, 66, 183
Dictatus Papae (Gregory VII) 119
Dionysius 124
Diotrephes 114-116
directives 88, 186
Discourse on the Forgery of the Alleged
   Donation of Constantine
   (*Declamatio de falso credita et*

305

ementita donatione Constantini) (Valla) 206, 214-284
distributive justice 93
District of Columbia 190
Diuturnum Illud, Of Civil Government (Leo XIII) 142
Divine Comedy, The (Dante) 113
divine law 31, 141
divine right of kings 32, 133
Divini Redemptoris, On Atheistic Communism (Pius XI) 63-64, 74, 77, 87, 157
division of labor 34
Doctoris Angelici (Pius X) 128
Dollfuss, Engelbert 161-162
Döllinger, Ignaz von 102, 114, 116, 134-135, 181, 208, 259, 286-287; Works: *Papstfabeln des Mittelalters* 208, 259; *The Pope and the Council* 116, 134-135, 181; *A Letter Addressed to the Archbishop of Munich* 286-287
dominion 126, 218-219, 229
Domitian 136
Donation of Constantine, The 112, 115-118, 138, 203-284
Donation of Pippin 262
Dotti, Orlando 36
Dragons 267
Dred Scott case 141
Duchesne 208, 262
Duties of the Christian Citizen (Leo XIII) 147

"Early Attitudes Towards Trade and the Merchant" (Viner) 53
Early Economic Thought: Selections from Economic Literature Prior to Adam Smith (Monroe) 53
Eastern Christianity 19
Ecclesiastica Potestate, De (Giles of Rome) 125

"Ecclesiastical Economics Is Envy Exalted" (Bauer) 98
"Ecclesiastical Economics: Envy Legitimized" (Bauer) 63
Ecclesiazusae (Aristophanes) 33
Ecological Crisis: A Common Responsibility, The (John Paul II) 39, 193
economic development 62, 158, 194
economic dictatorship 66-67, 193
economic freedom 64
Economics 29
Economics of Legal Minimum Wages, The (Rottenberg) 83
Ecuador 56
education 13, 20, 49, 79, 87, 92-93, 127-128, 157
efficiency 106
Eger Cui Levia (Innocent IV) 122
egoism 70
Egypt 248, 258
Eire, Carlos M. N. 15, 74; Works: *War Against the Idols* 15, 74
Eisenstadt, S. N. 12-13, 19, 22, 56, 73, 75; Works: *The Protestant Ethic and Modernization* 12-13, 19, 22, 56, 73, 75
Eizenstadt, Stuart 162
Eleazar 228
Eliogabalus 136
Elisha 220, 226
Ely, Richard 83
Emerton, E. 273; Works: *Medieval Europe* 273
Emperors 210, 235
employers 54
encyclicals 98, 149
Encyclicals of John Paul II, The (Miller) 148-149
Engels, Friedrich 44-45, 104; Works: *The Communist Manifesto* 44-45, 104

INDEX

Ennius 259
entrepreneurs 96-98
environment 192
Epistle to the Galatians (Luther's commentary on) 22
Epistles of Erasmus 206
equal rights 73
equality 40, 134
equality before the law 146
equivocation 156
Erasmus 206
1 Esdras 240
espionage 174, 189
Essays on the Intellectual History of Economics (Irwin) 53
eternal law 30
"Ethical Kinship between Protestant Radicalism and Catholic Conservatism, The" 82
ethics 42, 127
Ethiopia 169
Ethiopian Coptic Church 169
Ethiopian Empire 169
Eugenius 274, 280
Eugenius IV 206
Eusebius of Caesarea 236, 267, 268
Eusebius of Nicomedia 236
Eutropius 234
Evangelauf, Jean 148; *Works:* "Catholic University Professor" 148
Evangelicals 157
exchange 52
excommunication 131, 135, 167, 214
exploitation 60
expropriation 35
Extirpation of Idolatry in Peru, The (Joseph) 56

Fabianism 69
fables 269
Factorum et Dictorum Memorabilium (Valerius) 270
faith 20, 22
Fall 34
family 45
family allowance 88
family wage 87-88
Fanfani, Amintore 44, 72-73, 75-76; *Works: Catholicism, Protestantism, and Capitalism* 44, 72-76
fascism 30, 35, 38, 39, 57, 58, 91, 102, 161-173, 175
Fascism: Past, Present, Future (Laquer) 167-170
fascists 66, 154, 198
fatherhood of God 69
fear of God 17
federal system 154
Federalist, The 159
Festgabe für Rudolf von Gneist (Zeumer) 207, 257
feudalism 30, 38, 53, 55, 65, 72-76, 142
Fifth Council of Lateran 285
Filipovic, Miroslav 170-171
finances 162
First Amendment 14, 156
Fischoff, Ephraim 73; *Works:* "The Protestant Ethic and the Spirit of Capitalism: The History of a Controversy" 73
Flavius Constantine 213
Footprints of the Jesuits, The (Thompson) 58, 146, 148
force 101, 133, 143, 198, 218; *see also* coercion
Fordham University 54
foreign aid 63
forgery 199, 203-204, 208, 237, 243, 252-253, 272, 273
Fortune 270

Framework for Comprehensive Health Care Reform: Protecting Human Life, Promoting Human Dignity, Pursuing the Common Good (U.S. Catholic Conference) 94
Franciscans 47
Francisco de Mesquita 36
Franco, Francisco 161
Franks 203, 209
frauds 199; *see* forgery
Frederick II 122
free association 49; economy 95; exercise of religion 22; market 62, 65, 67, 106; trade 45, 193; will 50, 115
freedom 69, 79, 143; of assembly 157; of conscience 181; of press 157, 178, 180; of religion 156, 177, 180; of speech 22, 157, 182; of thought 180, 182; of worship 157, 182; of writing 182
Freedom and Catholic Power in Spain and Portugal (Blanshard) 175, 184
Freeman, The 73, 82-83, 95, 103-104
Fremantle, Anne 194; *Works:* "The Papacy and Social Reform: The Great Encyclicals" 194
French Revolution 80, 86
Friedberg, A. 207, 243, 256
Fuggers 21
Führerprinzip 18; *see also* leadership principle
Fulda Pastoral Letter 167
fundamentalism 157-158

Gaius 224
Galba 224
Galbraith, John Kenneth 69
Gallicanus 213, 264
gambling 16
Gathering Storm, The (Walker) 121

Gaudium et Spes, Pastoral Constitution on the Church in the Modern World (Vatican II) 39-40, 42, 86-87, 187-188, 189
Gauls 224
Gelasius 210, 239
general welfare 57
Genocide in Satellite Croatia, 1941-1945: A Record of Racial and Religious Persecutions and Massacres (Paris) 172
Genovese, Eugene D. 43; *Works:* "Secularism in the Great Crisis of Capitalism" 43
Gentiles 23, 116, 120, 133, 229
Georgics (Virgil) 34
German Catholics and Hitler's Wars (Zahn) 164, 166-167
Germany 30, 50, 51, 66, 142, 161-163
Geschichte Italiens im Mittelalter (Hartman) 209
Gibbons, Cardinal 82-83, 186
Giles of Rome 125; *Works: De Ecclesiastica Potestate* 125
Ginder, Richard 9
Gladstone, William 144; *Works: The Vatican Decrees and Their Bearing on Civil Allegiances after 1870* 144
God 18, 33, 36, 38-39, 43, 121, 124, 164, 178, 212-213, 215, 219-221, 225-226, 231, 240-246, 255-256, 258, 260-262, 265, 269, 271, 282-283
Godfray, Thomas 207
Goebbels, Paul Joseph 166
Golden Legend (Voragine) 239
good works 15-16, 22, 180
Gospel 16-17, 20, 24, 78, 196-197, 287
Goths 277
government 23-24, 47
grace 15-17

INDEX

grants to mothers 88
Gratian 134, 204, 207, 209-210, 217, 237, 241, 245; *Works: Decretum* 237
Great Commission 24
Great Depression 84
Greece 211, 247
greed 49, 54, 67, 83
Greeks 19
Green, Thomas J. 132; *Works: The Code of Canon Law* 132
Gregory 237, 243
Gregory (I) the Great 137, 233
Gregory VII 119
Gregory IX 122, 137
Gregory XIII 169
Gregory XVI 137, 145, 177, 181
Gregory Nazianzen 34
Grizogono, Privislav 171
Groethuysen, Bernard 73; *Works: The Bourgeoisie: Catholicism vs. Capitalism in Eighteenth Century France* 73
Groos, Felix 163
Growth of Economic Thought, The (Spiegel) 29
guild socialism 30, 38, 53-55, 72-74, 142
Gutierrez, Gustavo 78; *Works: Theology of Liberation* 78
gypsies 170, 172, 173

Hadrian I 137
Hampden, John 22
Hartmann, Ludo Moritz 209; *Works: Geschichte Italiens im Mittelalter* 209
Hartz 165
Havana Cordon 176
health 24
health care 94
health insurance 49, 102
health services 79

Heaven 15, 17, 179-180, 230
Hebrews 129, 133, 220, 234
Hegel, G. W. F. 131
Heintschel, Donald E. 132; *Works: The Code of Common Law* 132
Hell 213, 230, 262
Henderson, E. F. 207, 241; *Works: Select Historical Documents of the Middle Ages* 207, 241
Hengel, Martin 33-34, 34; *Works: Property and Riches in the Early Church* 33-34
heretics 133-135
Hezekiah 260
hierarchy 161
hierocracy 17
Hildebrand 119
Himmelfarb, Gertrude 111-113, 116; *Works: Lord Acton: A Study in Conscience and Politics* 111-113, 116
Hinschius 207, 256; *Works: Decretales* 207, 256
Hirohito 70
historical criticism 205-206
history 42, 55, 102, 128
History of Economic Analysis (Schumpeter) 29
History of England (Macaulay) 51
History of Freedom (Acton) 102
History of Sylvester; see *Life of Sylvester.*
History of the Papacy (Creighton) 280
Hitler, Adolph 70, 141, 161-167, 173, 175
Holland 51
Hollywood 10
Holocaust 162, 196, 198
Holy Ghost 149, 286; *see also* God, Holy Spirit
Holy Roman Empire 122

Holy Spirit 149, 264, 269, 282; *see also* God
Homer 251, 259
Hoover, Herbert 83
Horace 253; *Works: Ars Poetica* 253
Hostiensis 123
housing 79, 84, 87, 103
Hudson, Henry 144; *Works: Papal Power: Its Origin and Development* 144
Hughes, John 159
Human Action: A Treatise on Economics (Mises) 59
Human Labor, On; see *Laborem Exercens*
human rights 79, 86
humanists 197
hunger 40
Hunt, Dave 164; *Works: A Woman Rides the Beast* 164
Hussites 134
Hutten, Ulrich von 206, 271

idleness 51
idolatry 16, 270, 283
ignorance 216
Ilford, Mary 73
immiseration of the proletariat 71
Immortale Dei, On the Christian Constitution of States (Leo XIII) 82, 144-145, 165, 177, 179-180, 185
imputed righteousness of Christ 16
inalienable rights 155, 195
Inca 56
Independent Catholic State of Croatia 170
Index of Prohibited Books 138, 179
indifferentism 143
individual initiative 91
individual responsibility 14, 19, 160

individualism 18-19, 45, 65, 73, 76, 80, 100, 104
indolence 13
indulgence 21, 138
industrialists 64
industrialization 61, 105
inequality 40, 59
inerrancy of the Bible 157-158
infallibility of the Bible 158
infallibility of the pope 102, 116, 118, 135, 147, 149, 150
inflation 21
Innocent III 119-121, 137, 144, 265, 285-286
Innocent IV 122, 123
Innocent VII 280
Inquisition 112, 116, 133-141, 198, 285
Inscrutabile (Leo XIII) 54
Inside the Vatican: The Politics and Organization of the Catholic Church (Reese) 10-11, 24
Instruction on Christian Freedom and Liberation (Ratzinger) 79-80
insurance 84, 157
intellect 13
intellectual honesty 21
Interaction of Law and Religion, The (Berman) 20, 23
interdependence 192
interest 21, 55, 67, 70
interference 46-47, 49, 83, 91
International Red Cross 171
Interpretation of the Bible in the Church, The (Pontifical Biblical Commission) 78, 158
interventionism 30, 35, 44, 81-94, 97, 99, 102-104, 152-153, 159
introspection 15
Ireland 51-52, 286

INDEX

irreformability of doctrine 138
Isaac 19
Isaiah 283
Isidorian Decretals 116
Israel 220, 229, 276, 279, 281
Italy 30, 47, 50, 66, 72, 161, 184, 211, 247-248

Jacob 19
James 120
James of Voragine 238
Janus (von Döllinger) 114
Jasenovac concentration camp 170
Jefferson, Thomas 155
Jehovah 271
Jephthah 279
Jeremiah 214
Jeroboam 220-221
Jerome 236, 266, 268
Jerusalem 211, 220, 245, 248, 260
Jesuits 52, 58, 92, 113, 169, 184
Jesus Christ 9, 11, 17, 19, 23-24, 29, 33, 115-116, 120, 122-123, 129-130, 132, 134, 139-140, 146, 148, 157, 166, 180, 182, 188, 196-197, 226, 228, 230, 245, 249-250, 255, 257, 265-266, 269, 271, 275, 283-284, 287; imputed righteousness of 16; *see also* God
Jews 67, 170, 172, 197, 220, 248, 266; *see also* Hebrews
Job 263
John 116-117, 136, 251
John Chrysostom 32
John Paul II 38-41, 60-62, 68-71, 79, 88-89, 91, 94, 95-96, 99-102, 105-106, 115, 144-145, 187, 192-193, 196-197
John the Baptist 257
John XXII 128

John XXIII 39, 45, 49, 54, 56, 87, 89-90, 93, 155, 186, 188, 192, 194-195
Johnson, Lyndon 35
Josephus 240
Joshua 136, 259
Josiah 260
Jotham 264
Jubal 240
Judah 220
Judas 227
Judas Maccabaeus 240
Judea 211, 247-248
Judgment 18
Julian 233-234
Julius Caesar 277
Juno Moneta 270
Jurichev, Dijonisije 173
jury 22
just wage 65, 87-88, 100, 193
Justice in the World (Synod of Bishops) 78, 80, 188, 193
justification by faith alone 16, 180
Juvenal 267

Kapital, Das (Marx) 43
"Kapitalismus und Kalvinismus" (Rachfahl) 13-14
Katholisches Gesangbuch 163
Keating, L. Clark 56
Kenrick, Francis Patrick 159
Kent, Peter C. 168-169; *Works: The Pope and the Duce* 168-169
KGB 189
kingdom of God 23, 228
kings 20, 111, 229
Klein, Joe 46-47
Knights of Malta 190
Knox, Ronald 184; *Works: Beliefs of Catholics* 184
Kremlin 191

311

Kulturkampf 163
Küng, Hans 182

La Civiltà Cattolica 185
labor 60, 99, 100; camps 141; law 49, 87; movement 64, 83, 103; theory of value 101; unions 69, 82
Laborem Exercens, On Human Labor (John Paul II) 39-41, 60-61, 68, 79, 88-89, 91, 94, 99, 101, 145
Lactantius 244, 251, 255
LaFarge, John 82
laissez-faire capitalism 23
Landless Rural Workers Movement 36
Laquer, Walter 167-170; *Works: Fascism: Past, Present, Future* 167-170
Lateran Agreements of 1929 168
Lateran Council of 1139 133-134
Lateran Palace 117, 205, 211, 237, 249-250
Latin America 30, 77, 192
law 20, 127; of nature 225, 276; of supply and demand 99
leadership principle 161, 174-175
Lebensraum 165
Lee, Martin A. 190; *Works:* "Who Are the Knights of Malta?" 190
legends 208, 270
Lehman, Stan 35-36
Lentulus 266
Leo I 283
Leo X 137, 285
Leo XIII 40, 45-46, 48-49, 53-58, 60, 71, 82-83, 98-101, 121, 126-127, 131, 137-138, 142, 144-146, 147-149, 165, 177-181, 183-186, 193
Letter Addressed to the Archbishop of Munich, A (von Döllinger) 287

Lewy, Guenther 163, 165; *Works: The Catholic Church and Nazi Germany* 163-165
L'Humanité 63
Liber Pontificalis 262
liberalism 41, 44-46, 61, 64, 69, 76, 92, 98, 101, 144, 161, 163, 165
liberation theology 30, 35, 38, 77-80, 101-102
Libertas Praestantissimum 121, 177-181, 183-184
liberty of conscience 178; of press 179; of speech 179; of teaching 180; of thinking 179; of worship 178
liberum arbitrium 50
Liechtenstein 190
Life of Constantine 236
Life of Sylvester 220, 241-242, 246, 267
Lilburne, John 22
Limbaugh, Rush 83
limited government 49, 142
Lingua Latina, De (Varro) 270
literacy 20
Literate Economist, The (Canterbery) 67
Living Wage: Its Ethical and Economic Aspects, A (Ryan) 83, 103
Livy 269-270, 280
Lo Bello, Nino 9, 162, 170, 171, 182, 190; *Works: Vatican, U.S.A.* 9; *The Vatican Papers* 162, 171, 182, 190
Lombards 203, 209
London Review of Books 192
London School of Economics 62
looting 35-36, 70
Louis the Pious 257, 272-274
Lucan 252, 259
Luctatius 270
Luke 285

INDEX

Lumen Gentium (Vatican II) 148, 150, 158
Lusk Committee 103
Luther, Martin 13-20, 22, 64, 97, 198, 205
Luthy, Herbert 20, 22, 75; *Works:* "Once Again: Calvinism and Capitalism" 22, 75

Macaulay, Thomas Babington 9-10, 12, 51; *Works: History of England* 51
MacDougall, Hugh 102, 113, 286-287; *Works: The Acton-Newman Relations* 102, 113, 286-287
MacGregor, Geddes 144; *Works: The Vatican Revolution* 144
Magisterium 24, 60, 79, 92, 98, 102, 147-150
Malchus 276
Manchester School 65
Mancini, Girolamo 206, 280; *Works: Vita di Lorenzo Valla* 206
Manhattan, Avro 170; *Works: The Vatican's Holocaust* 170
Manicheans 124
Manning, Henry Edward 82
Marcus Fabius 277
Marcus Genutius 270
Maritain, Jacques 127, 128; *Works: St. Thomas Aquinas* 127, 128
market 21, 97, 104
Martial 255
Martin, David 13; *Works: Tongues of Fire: The Explosion of Protestantism in Latin America* 13
Martin V 134
Marvels of Rome, The (Nichols) 271
Marx, Karl 41, 43-45, 55, 104; *Works: The Communist Manifesto* 41, 43-45, 55, 104

Marxism 34, 40, 43, 63, 175
Mary's house 15
Mass 167
Massachusetts 83
massacres 63, 134, 171
Mater et Magistra, On Christianity and Social Progress (John XXIII) 39, 45, 49, 54, 56, 90, 155, 188
materialism 24, 69
maternity leave 157
Matthew 251
Maxwell, John Francis 136-141; *Works: Slavery and the Catholic Church* 136-141
McSweeney, Edward 82
means of production 49, 61, 68
Mecham, J. Lloyd 48, 92; *Works: Church and State in Latin America* 48, 92
Medéllin 78
Medes 234
Medieval Europe 273
Melanchthon 34
Melchiades 236-237
Melchizedek 256
Memoirs (of von Papen) 164
Menaechmi 251
mendicancy 17
merchants 53, 70
"Method and Substantive Theory in Max Weber" (Andreski) 12-13, 17, 73
Metropolitan Conference of Bishops 178
Mette, Norbert 172; *Works:* "Socialism and Capitalism in Papal Social Teaching" 172
Mettius 270
Mexico 51
Middle Ages 15, 17, 21, 30, 44, 66, 74-75, 96, 119, 134, 143, 187

313

Mihailovic 173
Miller, J. Michael 149; *Works: The Encyclicals of John Paul II* 149
minimum wage laws 83, 88
Mirabilia urbis Romae 271
miracles 269
Mirari Vos (Gregory XVI) 145, 181
Mises, Ludwig von 44, 58-59, 70; Works: *Human Action* 59; *Socialism* 44, 70
Mitteilungen des Institus f. osterreichesche Geschichtsforschung 242
modernity 44, 142, 146
Mombritius 208
Monarchia, De (Dante) 113
monarchy 129, 133, 159, 183, 198
monasteries 163
money 22, 50, 52, 61, 67, 227
monks 22
monopolies 84, 103
Monroe, Arthur Eli 53; Works: *Early Economic Thought* 53
Moog 56
morality 14
Moses 115, 124, 240, 250, 258, 259
murder 133, 166, 171, 195, 216
music 240
Muslims 197
Mussolini, Benito 49, 66, 70, 161-162, 166-169, 168

Naaman 220, 226, 271
Naples 216
National Catholic Reporter 190
National Catholic War Council 84, 103
National Conference of Brazilian Bishops 36
National Conference of Catholic Bishops 84, 103
National Council of Churches 11

National Industrial Recovery Act 164
nationalization 47
NATO 162
natural law 30, 32, 38, 40, 42, 115, 141, 172, 186
natural right 32
naturalism 143
nature 20
Nazi Germany 163
Nazism 30, 35, 102, 161-173, 174-175, 198
Nebuchadnezzar 219
need 31-32, 35, 40, 69, 101, 106-107, 153-154
Negroes 140
Negus 169
Nero 136, 224, 271
Neubacher, Hermann 173
New Catholic Encyclopedia 191
New Deal 46-47, 66, 81, 83-84, 152, 164, 184
New Individualist Review 163
New Testament 34, 115-116, 197
New York Times, The 63
Newman, John Henry Cardinal 114
Newsweek 46
"Next General Council, The" (Acton) 285
Nicaea 285
Nicene and Post-Nicene Fathers (Schaff) 242
Nichols, F. M. 206, 271; Works: *Epistles of Erasmus* 206; *The Marvels of Rome* 271
Nigeria 63
Nihilism 142
North British Review 112
Notre Dame Law School 43
Novak, Michael 49, 73, 95-107; Works: *The Catholic Ethic and the Spirit of Capitalism* 49, 73, 95, 104

INDEX

nuns 22

O'Brien, David J. 47, 85, 152, 160, 164, 185; *Works: Public Catholicism* 47, 85, 152, 160, 164, 185
Octogesima Adveniens, Apostolic Letter on the Coming Eightieth (Paul VI) 69, 159, 188, 192-193
Office of Strategic Services 190
Old Testament 268
"On Kingship" (Thomas) 129
"Once Again: Calvinism and Capitalism" (Luthy) 22, 75
Oppression of Protestants in Spain, The (Delpech) 178, 185
oral tradition 18
Origen 268
Orthodox Church 170-171, 173
Orwell, George 156; *Works:* "Politics and the English Language" 156
Ostling, Richard N. 144; *Works: Secrecy in the Church* 144
Otho 224
Our Christian Heritage (Gibbons) 82
Our Country (Strong) 150
Outlook 81
ownership 39; *see also* property

Pacem in Terris, On Peace on Earth (John XXIII) 87, 89, 93-94, 186, 188, 192, 194-195
paganism 74, 260-261
Paine, Thomas 136
pantheism 143
papacy 47, 112-113, 114-116, 154-155, 162, 166, 169, 181, 203, 205, 210
"Papacy and Social Reform: The Great Encyclicals, The" (Fremantle) 194
Papacy and Fascism, The (Ridley) 114-115, 169, 174

Papacy and the Modern World, The (Aretin) 103, 164, 184
Papacy: An Illustrated History from St. Peter to Paul VI, The (Hollis) 194
papal infallibility 98, 113, 285
Papal Merchandise (Phillipps) 52
Papal Power: Its Origin and Development (Hudson) 144
Papal States 145
Papal Thought on the State: Excerpts from Encyclicals and Other Writings of Other Recent Popes (Yates) 142, 145
Papen, Fritz von 164
Papstfabeln des Mittelalters (von Döllinger) 208, 259
Paraguay 47, 58, 92
Paris, Edmond 172; *Works: Genocide in Satellite Croatia* 172
parks 24
Party line 174
Pascal, Blaise 184; *Works: Provincial Letters* 184
Paschal [I] 273
Pashur 214
Pastoral Constitution on the Church in the Modern World; see Gaudium et Spes
Pastoral Statement on Biblical Fundamentalism 157
Paul 16, 46, 117, 211, 213-215, 214-215, 226, 228-229, 246, 262-263, 266, 283
Paul I 203, 209-210, 244
Paul III 137, 140
Paul VI 38, 61, 69-71, 91-92, 159, 180, 187-188, 191-192
pauperism 21
Pavelic, Ante 161, 170
Peace on Earth, On; see Pacem in Terris

315

Pegis, Anton C. 131; *Works: Basic Writings of Thomas Aquinas* 131
penance 15, 17, 134
Penn, William 22
pensions 24, 89, 102
Perkins, William 22; *Works: The Works* 22
Peron, Juan 161
Perot, H. Ross 47
persecution 63, 113, 133-141, 142, 166, 195, 198, 286
Persians 234
Peru 51
Peter 114, 116-119, 120-125, 129, 131, 136, 148-149, 154, 157, 211-213, 215, 227, 229, 230, 235-237, 241, 244, 246, 249, 256-258, 262-263, 266, 272-273, 276, 287
Pharisees 250
Pharsalia 252
Philip V 281
Phillipps, Ernest 52; *Works: Papal Merchandise* 52
philosophy 127-128, 198
Phinehas 228
picketing 84
pilgrimages 15
Pippin 253
Pippin und die romische Kirche (Caspar) 209
piracy 53
Piso 270
Pius II 137
Pius VII 137
Pius IX 113, 138, 142-144, 174
Pius X 127-128, 189
Pius XI 41, 45-46, 48-49, 55, 58, 60, 61, 63-68, 72-74, 77, 87-88, 90, 92, 135, 147, 152, 157, 164, 166, 168-169, 189
Pius XII 39, 149, 162, 171-172, 194

planning 66, 91, 193
Plass, Ewald M. 18, 20; *Works: What Luther Says* 18, 20
Plato 160
Plautus 251
Pledger, John 136
pluralism 163
Poland 60
political correctness 10
Political Ideas of St. Thomas Aquinas, The (Bigongiari) 129-130
political science 128
Political Sermons of the American Founding Era, 1730-1805 (Sandoz) 136
politics 127, 149
Politics (Aristotle) 52, 139
"Politics and the English Language" (Orwell) 156
polytheism 24
Pontifical Biblical Commission 77-78
Pontius Pilate 242
poor 54
Pope and the Council, The (von Döllinger) 116, 135, 181
Pope and the Duce: The International Impact of the Lateran Agreements, The (Kent) 168-169
Pope Speaks: the Church Documents Bimonthly, The 148, 196-197
pope(s) 10, 16, 18, 24, 30, 38-39, 44, 63, 111, 130, 135, 139-140, 147, 197, 204-205, 216, 253-254, 256, 274, 282, 284
Popery the Foe of the Church and of the Republic (Van Dyke) 114
Populorum Progressio, On the Progress of Peoples (Paul VI) 38, 61, 62-63, 70, 91-92, 187, 191, 192-194
Portugal 30, 139, 161

positive law 30-31
poverty 22, 34, 53, 79, 176
power 121, 122, 132, 136, 143, 152, 187, 192, 218, 282
Power of Rome in the Twentieth Century, The (Rhodes) 43, 54, 144, 186
Praxagora 33
predestination 13
preferential option for the poor 101
prescription 279-280, 282
prices 21, 92
priesthood of all believers 17
priests 16, 22, 48
Principles of Educational Reform in the United States (U.S. Catholic Conference) 93
private judgment 145
Proculus 270
profit 50, 65, 70, 84, 90, 96, 99, 103, 106, 192
Progress of Peoples, On the; see *Populorum Progressio*
Progressive movement 47, 81, 103
proletariat 43, 54, 60, 69, 90
promises 10
property 20, 22, 34, 39, 49; private property 29-37, 38, 40, 64, 68, 80, 100, 104
Property and Riches in the Early Church: Aspects of a Social History of Early Christianity (Hengel) 33-34
Protestant Ethic and Modernization: A Comparative View, The (S. Eisenstadt) 12-13, 19, 22, 56, 73, 75
Protestant Ethic and the Spirit of Capitalism, The (Weber) 12, 50, 51
"The Protestant Ethic and the Spirit of Capitalism: The History of a Controversy" (Fischoff) 73

"Protestant Ethic Thesis in an Analytical and Comparative Framework" (Eisenstadt) 19, 56
"Protestant Worldview, A" (Clark) 128
Protestantism 12, 19, 24, 52, 73, 142-143, 158
Proudhon, Pierre Joseph 34
Provincial Letters (Pascal) 184
Pseudo-Clementines 32
pseudo-Isidore 114
Pseudo-Isidorian Decretals 204, 208, 241
Ptolemy 123; Works: *Almagest* 123
public authorities 35, 91, 155, 192
Public Catholicism (O'Brien) 47, 85, 152, 160, 164, 185
public health 87
public utility rates 84, 103
Purgatory 15
Puritanism 16, 22, 95

Quadragesimo Anno, On Social Reconstruction (Pius XI) 41, 45-46, 48, 55, 58, 64-68, 72-74, 88, 90, 135, 147, 152, 157, 164
Quaestiones Quodlibetales (Thomas) 130
Quanta Cura (Pius IX) 142

Rachfahl, Felix 13-14; Works: "Kapitalismus und Kalvinismus" 13-14
racism 166
Rand, Ayn 62, 70, 92, 95, 195; Works: *Capitalism: The Unknown Ideal* 62, 70, 92, 195
Ranke, Leopold von 22
rationalism 143
Ratzinger, Joseph Cardinal 79, 148; Works: *Instruction on Christian Freedom and Liberation* 79

Readings in Church History (Barry) 121, 125
Reagan, Ronald 189
Reality and Rhetoric: Studies in the Economics of Development (Bauer) 63
rebellions 142
"Reception of Leo XIII's Labor Encyclical in America, 1891-1919, The" (Abell) 44, 47, 82, 84, 103
recreation 49
redistribution of wealth 77, 187, 198
Reese, Thomas J. 10-11, 24, 191; *Works: Inside the Vatican* 10-11, 24, 191
Reformation 9, 11, 14-15, 19, 21-22, 29, 44, 51, 67, 74-75, 88, 98, 125, 142-143, 145, 183
Reformers 19, 180
regulation 35, 41-42, 47, 58, 107
Rehoboam 281
relations 198
"Relations Between the United States and the Holy See, 1797-1977" (Congressional Research Service) 191
relativism 24
relics 15
Religion and the Modern State (Dawson) 161
Religion, Economics and Social Thought (Block and Hexham) 54, 57
religious liberty 14, 121, 160; *see also* freedom, liberty
Religious Thought and Economic Society (Viner) 12
Renaissance 206
repentance 197-198
republics 183

"Requiem for Man" (Rand) 62, 70, 92, 195
Rerum Novarum, On the Condition of the Working Classes (Leo XIII) 40, 43-59, 60, 69, 79, 83, 87, 95-107, 137, 149, 193
Rerum Novarum: One Hundred Years of Catholic Social Teaching (Baum and Coleman) 172
Res Gestae Alexandri 253
resentment 44
Restoration of Christian Philosophy, On the; see Aeterna Patris.
revelation 18
Review of Politics, The 44, 47, 82, 103
revolution 69-70, 80
Rhodes, Anthony 43, 54, 144, 166, 186; *Works: The Power of Rome in the Twentieth Century* 43, 54, 144, 186; *The Vatican in the Age of Dictators* 166
Ridley, F.A. 114-115, 169, 174; *Works: The Papacy and Fascism* 114-115, 169, 174
Right Reverend New Dealer (Broderick) 84
right to assistance 69; to common use 41; to free enterprise 39; to life 39; to loot 36; to marriage 69; to ownership 41; to private property 39; to procure 40; to property 57; to publish 39; to rest and leisure 157; to speak 39; to strike 69; to teach 39; to think 39; to work 69, 156; to worship 39; to write 39
righteousness 23
rights 85, 89, 92, 143, 155
Rights of Man 80, 86
rites 17

roads 87
robbery 16
Robbins, John W. 128, 155; *Works: Against the World* 128; *Without a Prayer* 155
Roman Catholic Center Party 163
Roman Church-State: age of 9; assets of 9-10; power of 9; size of 9; wealth of 9; *passim*
Roman Emperors 120
Roman Empire 114, 117, 121-122, 168, 222, 224, 231, 233-234, 240, 248, 273-274
Romans 19
Roosevelt, Franklin 83-84, 103, 164
Rottenberg, Simon 83; *Works: The Economics of Legal Minimum Wages* 83
Rousseau, Jean-Jacques 34
Rufinus 236
rule of law 75
Rummell, R. J. 172-173; *Works: Death by Government* 173
Ryan, John A. 82-85, 103, 164, 184; *Works: A Living Wage* 103

sacraments 15, 17
Sacred Congregation for the Doctrine of the Faith 79-80
Sadowsky, James 54; *Works:* "Classical Social Doctrine in the Roman Catholic Church" 54
saints 270
Saints' Treasury of Merit 21
Salazar, Antonio 161
Sallust 243
salvation 15-17, 113, 115, 143, 158
Samuel 129
San Diego Union-Tribune, The 35
San Marino 190

Sanctuarium, sive Vitae collectae, ex codibus 208
Sandoz, Ellis 136; *Works: Political Sermons of the American Founding Era* 136
Saracens 139
Saul 261
Schaff, Philip 242; *Works: Nicene and Post-Nicene Fathers* 242
Schard, Simon 207
Scheffer-Boichorst, Paul 208, 242, 244, 257
schism 286
scholasticism 21, 23, 29, 96
Schriftprinzip 17-18; *see also* Scripture
Schumpeter, Joseph 29; *Works: History of Economic Analysis* 29
Schuschnigg, Kurt von 161-162
science 75, 90
Scipio 268
Scripture 18, 20, 98, 127, 138, 149, 244, 286; sufficiency of 158
Second Development Decade 193
Second General Assembly of the Synod of Bishops 188
Second Vatican Council 39, 42, 86-87, 148, 150, 158, 187, 189; *see also* Vatican II
secrecy 10
Secrecy in the Church: A Reporter's Case for the Christian's Right to Know (Ostling) 144
secret police 174
"Secularism in the General Crisis of Capitalism" (Genovese) 43
security 89
Select Historical Documents of the Middle Ages (Henderson) 207, 241
self-government 160
self-incrimination 22

self-interest 44, 51, 96, 97, 104, 106
Semi-Socialism 84
Senate Committee on Foreign Affairs 189-190
Seneca 34
separation of church and state 14
Serbs 170-173
Sermon on the Mount 23
sharing 90, 151, 193
Sheen, Fulton J. 56; *Works: Communism and the Conscience of the West* 57
Sherwood, Samuel 136; *Works:* "The Church's Flight into the Wilderness" 136
Sicily 216
Sicut Universitatis Conditor (Innocent III) 121
Sigismund 274
Simon Magus 282
sin 21, 36, 70, 112, 283
Sinon 241
sins 215
Sirico, Robert 73, 82-83, 95-107, 149; *Works:* "Catholicism's Developing Social Teaching" 73, 82-83, 95-107, 149
slave labor 176
slave trading 141
slaveholders 43
slavery 53-55, 94, 133-141, 275, 278
Slavery and the Catholic Church: The History of Catholic Teaching Concerning the Moral Legitimacy of the Institution of Slavery (Maxwell) 137
Social Concern, On; see *Sollicitudo Rei Socialis, On Social Concern*
social contract 23
Social Gospel 81, 83

social insurance 103
social justice 65, 77, 78, 81, 90, 97, 101, 151, 154, 193, 198
Social Justice 83
social mortgage 38, 68
Social Reconstruction, On; see *Quadragesimo Anno, On Social Reconstruction.*
social security 102
Social Teaching of the Christian Churches, The (Troeltsch) 19, 67
socialism 35, 55, 56, 58, 61, 64, 67-69, 83-84, 101-104, 102, 103, 105, 142, 161
"Socialism and Capitalism in Papal Social Teaching" (Mette) 172
Socialism: An Economic and Sociological Analysis (Mises) 44, 70
Socialist Party 163
sociology 48
Sodalitium pianum 189
sola Ecclesia 158
sola Scriptura 158
"Solemn Address to Christians and Patriots, A" (Wortman) 135-136
solidarity 45, 60, 63, 69, 80, 104, 151-160, 188, 192-194
Sollicitudo Rei Socialis, On Social Concern (John Paul II) 38, 68-71, 99, 187, 192
Solomon 23, 255, 260, 276, 283
soteriology 179
soul 18
Soviet Constitution of 1936 156
Soviet Union 47, 173
Spain 30, 139-140, 161, 178
Spann, Othmar 58
speculation 74
Spiegel, Henry William 29; *Works: The Growth of Economic Thought* 29

St. Bartholomew Massacre 112, 169, 198
Stalin, Joseph 156
Standard Oil 9
starvation 99
Statius 259
stealing 90
Stephen 272
Stephen II 203, 209
Stoicism 33
Strayer, Joseph R. 134; *Works: The Albigensian Crusades* 134
strikes 84
Strong, Josiah 150; *Works: Our Country* 150
subjectivism 16
submission of intellect and will 148, 150, 184
subsidiarity 80, 93, 151-160
Sullivan, Francis 149
Summa Theologiae (Thomas) 31-32, 52-53, 131, 133
superstition 74
supreme power 10
swastika 167
Switzerland 51
sword 118, 123-124
Syllabus of Errors (Pius IX) 55, 113, 142-144
Sylvester 117, 204-205, 208, 210-213, 216-217, 222, 225, 231-232, 240-242, 247, 249-252, 256-258, 263, 266-268, 271, 275, 283
syndicalism 65
Synod of Melfi 139
Synodal Document on the Justice in the World, The 71, 78
Syria 248

Taeschner, Franz 165

Tammany Hall 46
Taney, Roger 141
Tarquinius 277, 280
Tawney, R. H. 50-51
taxation 35, 47, 83-84, 103, 162, 185, 193-194
Te Deum 167
technology 75, 90
terror 134, 136
terrorism 170
Tertio Millennio Adveniente (John Paul II) 196
Tertullian 242; *Works: Apology* 242
theft 16, 32, 90
theocracy 120, 195
theology 127, 179, 198
Theology of Liberation (Gutierrez) 78
theory of value 55
Thomas Aquinas 29-32, 35-36, 52-53, 70, 77, 126, 127-132, 133, 139
Thomas, Cal 62
Thomism 128
Thompson, R. W. 58, 146, 148; *Works: The Footprints of the Jesuits* 58, 146, 148
thought control 134, 174
Thrace 211, 246-248
thrift 17
tiara 212, 251
Tiberius Caesar 224, 242
Tierney, Brian 117-120, 122-126, 127; *Works: The Crisis of Church and State, 1050-1300* 117-120, 122-126, 127
Tindal 136
Tito 173
Titus Livius 264, 266
toleration 178, 184-185
Tongues of Fire: The Explosion of Protestantism in Latin America (Martin) 13

Tonsor, Stephen J. 163, 165-166;
  Works: "The View from London
  Bridge" 163, 165-166
torture 135, 171-172, 285
totalitarianism 49, 133, 170, 174-182
trade 21, 55
tradition 21, 42, 77, 174, 269
transcendentalism 19
transportation 87
Trent; *see* Council of Trent
Trinity Review, The 128
Troeltsch, Ernst 19, 67, 73; *Works: The
  Social Teachings of the Christian
  Churches* 19, 67, 73
Trujillo, Monsenor Alfonso Lopez 192
truth 157
Twelve Tables 240
*Twentieth Century Encyclopedia of
  Catholicism* 123
tyranny 80

U.S. Steel 9
Udall, Walter 22
Ultramontanes 102, 113
Unam Sanctam (Boniface VIII) 124-
  125, 131, 285
unemployment 91, 99, 103, 156
unemployment insurance 84, 88
Union for Social Justice 83
United Nations 191, 194-195
United States 30, 51, 66, 192
United States Catholic Conference
  93-94
United States Constitution 154, 156
unity 112, 125, 129, 133, 178, 188
Universal Declaration of Human
  Rights 194
universal destination of goods 38-42,
  68, 78, 85, 89, 94, 100-101, 107,
  192, 198

universalism 180
University of Notre Dame 44, 103
unscrupulousness 50
Urban II 139
Urban VIII 137
use 39, 101
Ustasha 162, 170, 173
usury 54-55, 67

Valeriu, Julius 253
Valerius Martial 255
Valerius Maximus 269-270
Valla, Lorenzo 115, 203-209,
  215-216, 236, 241, 243-245,
  252, 255-257, 258, 267, 272, 276;
  *Works: The Discourse of Lorenzo
  Valla on the Forgery of the Alleged
  Donation of Constantine* 214-284
Valladares, Armando 175, 177; *Works:
  Against All Hope* 175-177
value 21
Van Dyke, Joseph S. 114; *Works:
  Popery the Foe of the Church and
  of the Republic* 114
Varro, Terrentius 266, 270
Vatican 44, 62, 162, 165, 167, 172,
  176, 189, 190, 196
Vatican City 24, 190-191
Vatican Council 113
*Vatican Decrees and Their Bearing on
  Civil Allegiance after 1870*
  (Gladstone) 144
Vatican I 132
Vatican II 38, 40, 56, 77-78, 158,
  180; *see also* Second Vatican
  Council
*Vatican in the Age of the Dictators,
  1922-1945, The* (Rhodes) 166
Vatican Papers, The (Lo Bello) 162,
  171, 182, 189-190

INDEX

Vatican Radio 190
Vatican Revolution, The (MacGregor) 144
Vatican, U.S.A. (Lo Bello) 9
Venerabilem Fratrem (Innocent III) 121
vengeance 60
Veritatis Splendor (John Paul II) 115
Verres 282
Vespasian 225, 266, 271
Vicar of Christ 123, 129-130, 132
Vietnam 63
"View from London Bridge, The" (Tonsor) 163, 166
Viner, Jacob 12, 53; *Works:* "Early Attitudes Towards Trade and the Merchant" 53; *Religious Thought and Economic Society* 12
violence 70, 78, 80, 198
Virgil 34, 222, 241, 243, 251, 259, 266; *Works: Aeneid* 243; *Georgics* 34
virtues 97, 106
Vita di Lorenzo Valla (Mancini) 206, 280
Vita Silvestri 271
Vitelleschi, John 275
Vitellius 225
Volney 136
Voltaire 136
Voragine 239
voucher programs 93

wage slavery 54-55
wages 21
Walker, C. S. M. 121; *Works: The Gathering Storm* 121
Wall Street Journal, The 62
war 53, 69-70, 133, 142, 187, 219, 223-224, 230, 233-235, 252, 276-277, 280

War Against the Idols: The Reformation of Worship from Erasmus to Calvin (Eire) 15, 74
war criminals 162, 196
water supply 87
Waterman, Anthony 57
"We Remember" 196-197
wealth 22, 50, 53
Weber, Max 12-13, 17, 22, 50-51, 75; *Works: The Protestant Ethic and the Spirit of Capitalism* 12-13, 50-51
Weimar Republic 163
welfare 88-89
What Luther Says (Plass) 18, 20
Whittier, Charles 191
"Who Are the Knights of Malta?" (Lee) 190
Willems, Emilio 12-13; *Works:* "Culture Change and the Rise of Protestantism in Brazil and Chile" 13
Wines, E. C. 154; *Works: Commentaries on the Laws of the Ancient Hebrews* 154
witchcraft 285
Without a Prayer: Ayn Rand and the Close of Her System (Robbins) 155
Woman Rides the Beast, A (Hunt) 164
woman's equal rights 69
women 84, 157
Word of God 11
work 16, 17, 60, 74, 80
work ethic 21, 97
workers 54
World Council of Churches 11
world domination 287
world government 135, 142, 152, 154, 180, 187-195
World War I 163

World War II 162, 173, 190
World's Parliament of Religions 82
worship 145, 247
Wortman, Tunis 135-136; *Works:* "A Solemn Address to Christians and Patriots" 136

Xenophon 259

Yates, Gerard F. 142, 145; *Works: Papal Thought on the State* 142, 145
Yugoslavia 170

Zacchi, Cesar 176

Zahn, Gordon 164, 166-167; *Works: German Catholics and Hitler's Wars* 164, 166-167
Zeumer, Karl 207, 209, 243, 255-256; *Works: Festgabe für Rudolf von Gneist* 207
Zwingli, Ulrich 34

Scripture Index

Acts
6:2 *228*
20:35 *226*

Apocalypse
see *Revelation*

Colossians
2 *19*

1 Corinthians
2:15 *124*
6:2-5 *229*
9:15 *226*

Deuteronomy *285*

Ephesians
6:12 *284*

Exodus
20 *19*

Galatians *16, 22*
1:19 *120*

Genesis
1:1 *125*
2 *19*
9:25-27 *138*

Jeremiah
1:10 *124*
48:10 *228*

Job *263*

John
5 *19*
8:31-32 *17*
12:47 *230*
18:11 *118*
18:36 *228*
19:2 *251*
21:15-17 *149, 228*

1 John
2:18 *115, 116*
2:22 *116*
4:3 *115, 116*

2 John
7 *116*

3 John
9-10 *116*

Judges
11:12-28 *279*

2 Kings
15:5 *264*

Luke
10:4 *227*
10:16 *149*
18:25 *227*
22:31-32 *149*
22:38 *118, 119*

Mark
10:25 *227*
11:17 *230*

Matthew
4:8-9 *230*
4:17 *228*
5:18 *261*
6 *23*
6:19 *227*
10:8 *226*
11:28-30 *231*
16 *130*
16:18 *230*
16:18-19 *149*
16:19 *120, 230*
17:25-26 *229*
19:17 *115*
19:24 *227*
20:25-26 *116*
20:25-28 *229*
22:21 *231*
26:52 *124, 230*
27:28 *251*

325

Nehemiah
4 *19*

Proverbs
22 *19*

Psalms
21:3 *257*
81:12 *250*
139:7 *214*

Revelation *261*
5:12 *244*
22:18-19 *261*

Romans *16*
1:28 *250*
11:13 *226*
11:16 *282*
13 *23, 46, 49*
13:1 *118, 124*

1 Samuel
8 *129*

2 Thessalonians
3 *19*

1 Timothy
4 *32*
5:20 *215*
6:7-11 *227*

2 Timothy
2:4 *228*

The Crisis of Our Time

Historians have christened the thirteenth century the Age of Faith and termed the eighteenth century the Age of Reason. The twentieth century has been called many things: the Atomic Age, the Age of Inflation, the Age of the Tyrant, the Age of Aquarius. But it deserves one name more than the others: the Age of Irrationalism. Contemporary secular intellectuals are anti-intellectual. Contemporary philosophers are anti-philosophy. Contemporary theologians are anti-theology.

In past centuries, secular philosophers have generally believed that knowledge is possible to man. Consequently they expended a great deal of thought and effort trying to justify knowledge. In the twentieth century, however, the optimism of the secular philosophers has all but disappeared. They despair of knowledge.

Like their secular counterparts, the great theologians and doctors of the church taught that knowledge is possible to man. Yet the theologians of the twentieth century have repudiated that belief. They also despair of knowledge. This radical skepticism has penetrated our entire culture, from television to music to literature. *The Christian at the end of the twentieth century is confronted with an overwhelming cultural consensus – sometimes stated explicitly but most often implicitly: Man does not and cannot know anything truly.*

What does this have to do with Christianity? Simply this: If man can know nothing truly, man can truly know nothing. We cannot know that the Bible is the Word of God, that Christ died for his people, or that Christ is alive today at the right hand of the Father. Unless knowledge is possible, Christianity is nonsensical, for it claims to be knowledge. What is at stake in the twentieth century is not simply a single doctrine, such as the virgin birth, or the existence of Hell, as important as those doctrines may be, but the whole of Christianity itself. If knowledge is not possible to man, it is worse than silly to argue points of doctrine – it is insane.

The irrationalism of the present age is so thoroughgoing and pervasive that even the Remnant – the segment of the professing church that remains faithful – has accepted much of it, frequently without even being aware of what it is accepting. In some circles this irrationalism has become synonymous with piety and humility, and those who oppose it are denounced as rationalists, as though to be logical were a sin. Our contemporary anti-theologians make a contradiction and call it a Mystery. The faithful ask for truth and are given Paradox. If any balk at swallowing the absurdities of the anti-theologians, they are frequently marked as heretics or schismatics who seek to act independently of God.

There is no greater threat facing the true church of Christ at this moment than the irrationalism that now controls our entire culture. Totalitarianism, guilty of tens of millions of murders – including those of millions of Christians – is to be feared, but not nearly so much as the idea that we do not and cannot know the truth. Hedonism, the popular philosophy of America, is not to be feared so much as the belief that logic – that "mere human logic," to use the religious irrationalists' own phrase – is futile. The attacks on truth, on revelation, on the intellect, and on logic are renewed daily. But note well: The misologists – the haters of logic – use logic to demonstrate the futility of using logic. The anti-intellectuals construct intricate intellectual arguments to prove the insufficiency of the intellect. The anti-theologians use the revealed Word of God to show that there can be no revealed Word of God – or that if there could, it would remain impenetrable darkness and Mystery to our finite minds.

Nonsense Has Come

Is it any wonder that the world is grasping at straws – the straws of experientialism, mysticism, and drugs? After all, if people are told that the Bible contains insoluble mysteries, then is not a flight into mysticism to be expected? On what grounds can it be condemned? Certainly not on logical grounds or Biblical grounds, if logic is futile and the Bible unintelligible. Moreover, if it cannot be condemned on logical or Biblical grounds, it cannot be condemned at all. If people are going to have a religion of the mysterious, they will not adopt Christianity: They will have a genuine mystery religion. "Those who call for Nonsense," C.S. Lewis once wrote, "will find that it comes." And that is precisely what has happened. The popularity of Eastern mysticism, of drugs, and of religious experience is the logical consequence of the irrationalism of the twentieth century. There can and will be no Christian reformation – and no reconstruction of society – unless and until the irrationalism of the age is totally repudiated by Christians.

The Church Defenseless

Yet how shall they do it? The spokesmen for Christianity have been fatally infected with irrationalism. The seminaries, which annually train thousands of men to teach millions of Christians, are the finishing schools of irrationalism, completing the job begun by the government schools and colleges. Some of the pulpits of the most conservative churches (we are not speaking of the apostate churches) are occupied by graduates of the anti-theological schools. These products of modern anti-theological education, when asked to give a reason for the hope that is in them, can generally respond with only the intellectual analogue of a shrug – a mumble about Mystery. They have not grasped – and therefore cannot teach those for whom they are responsible – the first truth: "And you shall know the truth." Many, in fact, explicitly deny it, saying that, at best, we possess only "pointers" to the truth, or something "similar" to the truth, a mere analogy. Is the impotence of the Christian church a puzzle? Is the fascination with pentecostalism and faith healing among members of conservative churches an enigma? Not when one understands the sort of studied nonsense that is purveyed in the name of God in the seminaries.

The Trinity Foundation

The creators of The Trinity Foundation firmly believe that theology is too important to be left to the licensed theologians – the graduates of the schools of theology. They have created The Trinity Foundation for the express purpose of teaching the faithful all that the Scriptures contain – not warmed over, baptized, secular philosophies. Each member of the board of directors of The Trinity Foundation has signed this oath: "I believe that the Bible alone and the Bible in its entirety is the Word of God and, therefore, inerrant in the autographs. I believe that the system of truth presented in the Bible is best summarized in the *Westminster Confession of Faith*. So help me God."

The ministry of The Trinity Foundation is the presentation of the system of truth taught in Scripture as clearly and as completely as possible. We do not regard obscurity as a virtue, nor confusion as a sign of spirituality. Confusion, like all error, is sin, and teaching that confusion is all that Christians can hope for is doubly sin.

The presentation of the truth of Scripture necessarily involves the rejection of error. The Foundation has exposed and will continue to expose the irrationalism of the twentieth century, whether its current spokesman be an existentialist philosopher or a professed Reformed theologian. We oppose anti-intellectualism, whether it be espoused by a neo-orthodox theologian or a fundamentalist evangelist. We reject misology, whether it be on the lips of a neo-evangelical or those of a Roman Catholic charismatic. To each error we bring the brilliant light of Scripture, proving all things, and holding fast to that which is true.

The Primacy of Theory

The ministry of The Trinity Foundation is not a "practical" ministry. If you are a pastor, we will not enlighten you on how to organize an ecumenical prayer meeting in your community or how to double church attendance in a year. If you are a homemaker, you will have to read elsewhere to find out how to become a total woman. If you are a businessman, we will not tell you how to develop a social conscience. The professing church is drowning in such "practical" advice.

The Trinity Foundation is unapologetically theoretical in its outlook, believing that theory without practice is dead, and that practice without theory is blind. The trouble with the professing church is not primarily in its practice, but in its theory. Christians do not know, and many do not even care to know, the doctrines of Scripture. Doctrine is intellectual, and Christians are generally anti-intellectual. Doctrine is ivory tower philosophy, and they scorn ivory towers. The ivory tower, however, is the control tower of a civilization. It is a fundamental, theoretical mistake of the practical men to think that they can be merely practical, for practice is always the practice of some theory. The relationship between theory and practice is the relationship between cause and effect. If a person believes correct theory, his practice will tend to be correct. The practice of contemporary Christians is immoral because it is the practice of false theories. It is a major theoretical mistake of the practical men to think that they can ignore the ivory towers of the philosophers and theologians as irrelevant to their lives. Every action that the "practical" men take is governed by the thinking that has occurred in some ivory tower – whether that tower be the British Museum; the Academy; a home in Basel, Switzerland; or a tent in Israel.

In Understanding Be Men

It is the first duty of the Christian to understand correct theory – correct doctrine – and thereby implement correct practice. This order – first theory, then practice – is both logical and Biblical. It is, for example, exhibited in Paul's epistle to the Romans, in which he spends the first eleven chapters expounding theory and the last five discussing practice. The contemporary teachers of Christians have not only reversed the order, they have inverted the Pauline emphasis on theory and practice. The virtually complete failure of the teachers of the professing church to instruct the faithful in correct doctrine is the cause of the misconduct and cultural impotence of Christians. The church's lack of power is the result of its lack of truth. The *Gospel* is the power of God, not religious experience or personal relationship. The church has no power because it has abandoned the Gospel, the good news, for a religion of experientialism. Twentieth-century American Christians are children carried about by every wind of doctrine, not knowing what they believe, or even if they believe anything for certain.

The chief purpose of The Trinity Foundation is to counteract the irrationalism of the age and to expose the errors of the teachers of the church. Our emphasis – on the Bible as the sole source of truth, on the primacy of the truth, on the supreme importance of correct doctrine, and on the necessity for systematic and logical thinking – is almost unique in Christendom. To the extent that the church survives – and she will survive and flourish – it will be because of her increasing acceptance of these basic ideas and their logical implications.

We believe that the Trinity Foundation is filling a vacuum in Christendom. We are saying that Christianity is intellectually defensible – that, in fact, it is the only intellectually defensible system of thought. We are saying that God has made the wisdom of this world – whether that wisdom be called science, religion, philosophy, or common sense –

foolishness. We are appealing to all Christians who have not conceded defeat in the intellectual battle with the world to join us in our efforts to raise a standard to which all men of sound mind can repair.

The love of truth, of God's Word, has all but disappeared in our time. We are committed to and pray for a great instauration. But though we may not see this reformation of Christendom in our lifetimes, we believe it is our duty to present the whole counsel of God because Christ has commanded it. The results of our teaching are in God's hands, not ours. Whatever those results, his Word is never taught in vain, but always accomplishes the result that he intended it to accomplish. Professor Gordon H. Clark has stated our view well:

> There have been times in the history of God's people, for example, in the days of Jeremiah, when refreshing grace and widespread revival were not to be expected: The time was one of chastisement. If this twentieth century is of a similar nature, individual Christians here and there can find comfort and strength in a study of God's Word. But if God has decreed happier days for us and if we may expect a world-shaking and genuine spiritual awakening, then it is the author's belief that a zeal for souls, however necessary, is not the sufficient condition. Have there not been devout saints in every age, numerous enough to carry on a revival? Twelve such persons are plenty. What distinguishes the arid ages from the period of the Reformation, when nations were moved as they had not been since Paul preached in Ephesus, Corinth, and Rome, is the latter's fullness of knowledge of God's Word. To echo an early Reformation thought, when the ploughman and the garage attendant know the Bible as well as the theologian does, and know it better than some contemporary theologians, then the desired awakening shall have already occurred.

In addition to publishing books, the Foundation publishes a monthly newsletter, *The Trinity Review*. Subscriptions to *The Review* are free to U.S. addresses; please write to the address on the book order form to become a subscriber. If you would like further information or would like to join us in our work, please let us know.

The Trinity Foundation is a non-profit foundation, tax exempt under section 501 (c)(3) of the Internal Revenue Code of 1954. You can help us disseminate the Word of God through your tax-deductible contributions to the Foundation.

JOHN W. ROBBINS

Intellectual Ammunition

The Trinity Foundation is committed to the reformation of philosophy and theology along Biblical lines. We regard God's command to bring all our thoughts into conformity with Christ very seriously, and the books listed below are designed to accomplish that goal. They are written with two subordinate purposes: (1) to demolish all secular claims to knowledge; and (2) to build a system of truth based upon the Bible alone.

PHILOSOPHY

Ancient Philosophy
Gordon H. Clark   trade paperback $24.95
This book covers the thousand years from the Pre-Socratics to Plotinus. It represents some of the early work of Dr. Clark – the work that made his academic reputation. It is an excellent college text.

Behaviorism and Christianity
Gordon H. Clark   trade paperback $6.95
Behaviorism is a critique of both secular and religious behaviorists. It includes chapters on John Watson, Edgar S. Singer, Jr., Gilbert Ryle, B. F. Skinner, and Donald MacKay. Clark's refutation of behaviorism and his argument for a Christian doctrine of man are unanswerable.

A Christian Philosophy of Education
Gordon H. Clark   trade paperback $8.95
The first edition of this book was published in 1946. It sparked the contemporary interest in Christian schools. In the 1970s, Dr. Clark thoroughly revised and updated it, and it is needed now more than ever. Its chapters include: The Need for a World-View,

The Christian World-View, The Alternative to Christian Theism, Neutrality, Ethics, The Christian Philosophy of Education, Academic Matters, and Kindergarten to University. Three appendices are included: The Relationship of Public Education to Christianity, A Protestant World-View, and Art and the Gospel.

A Christian View of Men and Things   hardback $29.95
Gordon H. Clark   trade paperback $14.95
No other book achieves what *A Christian View* does: the presentation of Christianity as it applies to history, politics, ethics, science, religion, and epistemology. Dr. Clark's command of both worldly philosophy and Scripture is evident on every page, and the result is a breathtaking and invigorating challenge to the wisdom of this world.

Clark Speaks from the Grave
Gordon H. Clark   trade paperback $3.95
Dr. Clark chides some of his critics for their failure to defend Christianity competently. *Clark Speaks* is a stimulating and illuminating discussion of the errors of contemporary apologists.

Ecclesiastical Megalomania:
The Economic and Political Thought
of the Roman Catholic Church   hardback $29.95
John W. Robbins   trade paperback $19.95
This detailed and thorough analysis and critique of the social teaching of the Roman Church-State is the only such book available by a Christian economist and political philosopher. The book's conclusions reveal the Roman Church-State to be an advocate of its own brand of global religious Fascism. *Ecclesiastical Megalomania* includes the complete text of the *Donation of Constantine* and Lorenzo Valla's exposé of the hoax.

Education, Christianity, and the State
J. Gresham Machen   trade paperback $9.95
Machen was one of the foremost educators, theologians, and defenders of Christianity in the twentieth century. The author of numerous scholarly books, Machen saw clearly that if Christian-

ity is to survive and flourish, a system of Christian schools must be established. This collection of essays and speeches captures his thoughts on education over nearly three decades.

Essays on Ethics and Politics
Gordon H. Clark					trade paperback $10.95
   Dr. Clark's essays, written over the course of five decades, are a major statement of Christian ethics.

Gordon H. Clark: Personal Recollections
John W. Robbins, editor				trade paperback $6.95
   Friends of Dr. Clark have written their recollections of the man. Contributors include family members, colleagues, students, and friends such as Harold Lindsell, Carl Henry, Ronald Nash, Dwight Zeller, and Anna Marie Hager. The book includes an extensive bibliography of Dr. Clark's work.

Historiography: Secular and Religious
Gordon H. Clark					trade paperback $13.95
   In this masterful work, Dr. Clark applies his philosophy to the writing of history, examining all the major schools of historiography.

An Introduction to Christian Philosophy
Gordon H. Clark					trade paperback $8.95
   In 1966 Dr. Clark delivered three lectures on philosophy at Wheaton College. In these lectures he criticizes secular philosophy and launches a philosophical revolution in the name of Christ.

Language and Theology
Gordon H. Clark					trade paperback $9.95
   There are two main currents in twentieth-century philosophy – language philosophy and existentialism. Both are hostile to Christianity. Dr. Clark disposes of language philosophy in this brilliant critique of Bertrand Russell, Ludwig Wittgenstein, Rudolf Carnap, A. J. Ayer, Langdon Gilkey, and many others.

Logic   hardback $16.95
Gordon H. Clark   trade paperback $10.95

Written as a textbook for Christian schools, *Logic* is another unique book from Dr. Clark's pen. His presentation of the laws of thought, which must be followed if Scripture is to be understood correctly, and which are found in Scripture itself, is both clear and thorough. *Logic* is an indispensable book for the thinking Christian.

Logic Workbook
Elihu Carranza   oversize paperback $11.95

Designed to be used in conjunction with Dr. Clark's textbook *Logic*, this *Workbook* contains hundreds of exercises and test questions on perforated pages for ease of use by students.

Lord God of Truth, Concerning the Teacher
Gordon H. Clark
and Aurelius Augustine   trade paperback $7.95

This essay by Dr. Clark summarizes many of the most telling arguments against empiricism and defends the Biblical teaching that we know God and truth immediately. The dialogue by Augustine is a refutation of empirical language philosophy.

The Philosophy of Science and Belief in God
Gordon H. Clark   trade paperback $8.95

In opposing the contemporary idolatry of science, Dr. Clark analyzes three major aspects of science: the problem of motion, Newtonian science, and modern theories of physics. His conclusion is that science, while it may be useful, is always false; and he demonstrates its falsity in numerous ways. Since science is always false, it can offer no objection to the Bible and Christianity.

Religion, Reason and Revelation
Gordon H. Clark   trade paperback $10.95

One of Dr. Clark's apologetical masterpieces, *Religion, Reason and Revelation* has been praised for the clarity of its thought and language. It includes these chapters: Is Christianity a Religion? Faith and Reason, Inspiration and Language, Revelation and Morality, and God and Evil. It is must reading for all serious Christians.

The Scripturalism of Gordon H. Clark
W. Gary Crampton   trade paperback $9.95
  Dr. Crampton has written an introduction to the philosophy of Gordon H. Clark that is helpful to both beginners and advanced students of theology. This book includes a bibliography of Dr. Clark's works.

Thales to Dewey: A History of Philosophy
Gordon H. Clark   trade paperback $24.95
  This is the best one-volume history of philosophy in English.

Three Types of Religious Philosophy
Gordon H. Clark   trade paperback $6.95
  In this book on apologetics, Dr. Clark examines empiricism, rationalism, dogmatism, and contemporary irrationalism, which does not rise to the level of philosophy. He offers an answer to the question, "How can Christianity be defended before the world?"

William James and John Dewey
Gordon H. Clark   trade paperback $8.95
  William James and John Dewey are two of the most influential philosophers America has produced. Their philosophies of instrumentalism and pragmatism are hostile to Christianity, and Dr. Clark demolishes their arguments.

Without a Prayer: Ayn Rand and the Close of Her System
John W. Robbins   hardback $27.95
  This is the only book-length critique of Rand's philosophy of Objectivism written by a Christian. Objectivism's epistemology, theology, ethics, and politics are discussed in detail. Appendixes include analyses of books by Leonard Peikoff and David Kelley, as well as several essays on Christianity and philosophy.

INTELLECTUAL AMMUNITION

THEOLOGY

Against the World: The Trinity Review 1978-1988
John W. Robbins, editor				oversize hardback $34.95
> This is a clothbound collection of the essays published in *The Trinity Review* from 1978 to 1988, 70 in all. It is a valuable source of information and arguments in defending Christianity.

The Atonement
Gordon H. Clark					trade paperback $8.95
> In *The Atonement,* Dr. Clark discusses the covenants, the virgin birth and incarnation, federal headship and representation, the relationship between God's sovereignty and justice, and much more. He analyzes traditional views of the atonement and criticizes them in the light of Scripture alone.

The Biblical Doctrine of Man
Gordon H. Clark					trade paperback $6.95
> Is man soul and body or soul, spirit, and body? What is the image of God? Is Adam's sin imputed to his children? Is evolution true? Are men totally depraved? What is the heart? These are some of the questions discussed and answered from Scripture in this book.

The Clark-Van Til Controversy
Herman Hoeksema					trade paperback $7.95
> This collection of essays by the founder of the Protestant Reformed Church – essays written at the time of the Clark-Van Til controversy – is one of the best commentaries on the events in print.

Cornelius Van Til: The Man and The Myth
John W. Robbins					trade paperback $2.45
> The actual teachings of this eminent Philadelphia theologian have been obscured by the myths that surround him. This book penetrates those myths and criticizes Van Til's surprisingly unorthodox views of God and the Bible.

The Everlasting Righteousness
Horatius Bonar   trade paperback $8.95
   Originally published in 1874, the language of Bonar's masterpiece on justification by faith alone has been updated and Americanized for easy reading and clear understanding. This is one of the best books ever written on justification.

Faith and Saving Faith
Gordon H. Clark   trade paperback $8.95
   The views of the Roman Catholic church, John Calvin, Thomas Manton, John Owen, Charles Hodge, and B. B. Warfield are discussed in this book. Is the object of faith a person or a proposition? Is faith more than belief? Is belief more than thinking with assent, as Augustine said? In a world chaotic with differing views of faith, Dr. Clark clearly explains the Biblical view of faith and saving faith.

God and Evil: The Problem Solved
Gordon H. Clark   trade paperback $4.95
   This volume is Chapter 5 of *Religion, Reason and Revelation,* in which Dr. Clark presents his solution to the problem of evil.

God's Hammer: The Bible and Its Critics
Gordon H. Clark   trade paperback $10.95
   The starting point of Christianity, the doctrine on which all other doctrines depend, is "The Bible alone, and the Bible in its entirety, is the Word of God written, and therefore inerrant in the autographs." Over the centuries the opponents of Christianity, with Satanic shrewdness, have concentrated their attacks on the truthfulness and completeness of the Bible. In the twentieth century the attack is not so much in the fields of history and archaeology as in philosophy. Dr. Clark's brilliant defense of the complete truthfulness of the Bible is captured in this collection of eleven major essays.

INTELLECTUAL AMMUNITION

The Holy Spirit
Gordon H. Clark   trade paperback $8.95
   This discussion of the third person of the Trinity is both concise
   and exact. Dr. Clark includes chapters on the work of the Spirit,
   sanctification, and Pentecostalism. This book is part of his multi-
   volume systematic theology that began appearing in print in 1985.

The Incarnation
Gordon H. Clark   trade paperback $8.95
   Who is Christ? The attack on the incarnation in the nineteenth
   and twentieth centuries has been vigorous, but the orthodox re-
   sponse has been lame. Dr. Clark reconstructs the doctrine of the
   incarnation, building and improving upon the Chalcedonian
   definition.

The Johannine Logos
Gordon H. Clark   trade paperback $5.95
   Dr. Clark analyzes the relationship between Christ, who is the
   truth, and the Bible. He explains why John used the same word to
   refer to both Christ and his teaching. Chapters deal with the
   Prologue to John's Gospel, *Logos* and *Rheemata,* Truth, and Saving
   Faith.

Justification by Faith Alone
Charles Hodge   trade paperback $10.95
   Charles Hodge of Princeton Seminary was the best American
   theologian of the nineteenth century. Here, for the first time, are
   his two major essays on justification in one volume. This book is
   essential in defending the faith.

Karl Barth's Theological Method
Gordon H. Clark   trade paperback $18.95
   Karl Barth's Theological Method is perhaps the best critique of the
   neo-orthodox theologian Karl Barth ever written. Dr. Clark discusses Barth's view of revelation, language, and Scripture, focus-
   ing on his method of writing theology, rather than presenting a
   comprehensive analysis of the details of Barth's theology.

Logical Criticisms of Textual Criticism
Gordon H. Clark trade paperback $3.25
> Dr. Clark's acute logic enables him to demonstrate the inconsistencies, assumptions, and flights of fancy that characterize the science of New Testament criticism.

Predestination
Gordon H. Clark trade paperback $10.95
> Dr. Clark thoroughly discusses one of the most controversial and pervasive doctrines of the Bible: that God is, quite literally, Almighty. Free will, the origin of evil, God's omniscience, creation, and the new birth are all presented within a Scriptural framework. The objections of those who do not believe in Almighty God are considered and refuted. This edition also contains the text of the booklet, *Predestination in the Old Testament*.

Sanctification
Gordon H. Clark trade paperback $8.95
> In this book, which is part of Dr. Clark's multi-volume systematic theology, he discusses historical theories of sanctification, the sacraments, and the Biblical doctrine of sanctification.

Study Guide to the Westminster Confession
W. Gary Crampton oversize paperback $10.95
> This *Study Guide* may be used by individuals or classes. It contains a paragraph by paragraph summary of the *Westminster Confession*, and questions for the student to answer. Space for answers is provided. The *Guide* will be most beneficial when used in conjunction with Dr. Clark's forthcoming *What Christians Believe?* and his *What Do Presbyterians Believe?*

The Trinity
Gordon H. Clark   trade paperback $8.95
   Apart from the doctrine of Scripture, no teaching of the Bible is more fundamental than the doctrine of God. Dr. Clark's defense of the orthodox doctrine of the Trinity is a principal portion of his systematic theology. There are chapters on the deity of Christ, Augustine, the incomprehensibility of God, Bavinck and Van Til, and the Holy Spirit, among others.

What Calvin Says
W. Gary Crampton   trade paperback $7.95
   This is a clear, readable, and thorough introduction to the theology of John Calvin.

What Do Presbyterians Believe?
Gordon H. Clark   trade paperback $10.95
   This classic is the best commentary on the *Westminster Confession of Faith* that has ever been written.

CLARK'S COMMENTARIES ON THE NEW TESTAMENT

Colossians	trade paperback $6.95
Ephesians	trade paperback $8.95
First Corinthians	trade paperback $10.95
First John	trade paperback $10.95
New Heavens, New Earth (*First* and *Second Peter*)	trade paperback $10.95
The Pastoral Epistles	hardback $29.95
(*1* and *2 Timothy* and *Titus*)	trade paperback $14.95
Philippians	trade paperback $9.95

   All of Clark's commentaries are expository, not technical, and are written for the Christian layman. His purpose is to explain the text clearly and accurately so that the Word of God will be thoroughly known by every Christian.

The Trinity Library

We will send you one copy of each of the 51 books listed above for $400 (retail value: $568.95), postpaid to any address in the U.S. You may also order the books you want individually on the order form on the next page. Because some of the books are in short supply, we must reserve the right to substitute others of equal or greater value in The Trinity Library. This special offer expires June 30, 2001.

Order Form

NAME _____

ADDRESS _____

_____

TELEPHONE AND E-MAIL _____

Please: ❑ add my name to the mailing list for *The Trinity Review*. I understand that there is no charge for *The Review* sent to a U.S. address.

❑ accept my tax deductible contribution of $ _____ .

❑ send me ___ copies of *Ecclesiastical Megalomania*. I enclose as payment $ _____.

❑ send me the Trinity Library of 51 books. I enclose US $400 as full payment.

❑ send me the following books. I enclose full payment in the amount of $ _____ for them.

The Trinity Foundation
Post Office Box 68, Unicoi, Tennessee 37692
Website: www.trinityfoundation.org
Email: jrob1517@aol.com
United States of America

Please add $5.00 for postage. For foreign orders, please enclose 20 percent of the total value of the books ordered.